D0721240

FIRESTORM

AP PHOTO / MARK LENNIHAN

STEPHEN PRINCE

FIRESTORM

AMERICAN FILM IN THE AGE OF TERRORISM

COLUMBIA UNIVERSITY PRESS
NEW YORK

COLUMBIA UNIVERSITY PRESS
Publishers Since 1893
New York   Chichester, West Sussex

Copyright © 2009 Columbia University Press
All rights reserved

Library of Congress Cataloging-in-Publication Data

Prince, Stephen, 1955–
Firestorm : American film in the age of terrorism / Stephen Prince.
p. cm.
Includes bibliographical references and index.
ISBN 978-0-231-14870-2 (cloth : alk. paper)—ISBN 978-0-231-14871-9 (pbk. : alk. paper)—ISBN 978-0-231-52008-9 (ebook)
1. Motion pictures—United States—History—21st century. 2. September 11 Terrorist Attacks, 2001—Influence. 3. Motion pictures—Political aspects—United States. 4. Terrorism in motion pictures. 5. Psychic trauma in motion pictures. 6. War in motion pictures. I. Title.

PN1993.5.U6P745 2009
791.43′6552—dc22

2009013483

Columbia University Press books are printed on permanent and durable acid-free paper.
This book is printed on paper with recycled content.
Printed in the United States of America

C 10 9 8 7 6 5 4 3 2
P 10 9 8 7 6 5 4 3 2

References to Internet Web sites (URLs) were accurate at the time of writing. Neither the author nor Columbia University Press is responsible for URLs that may have expired or changed since the manuscript was prepared.

COVER & INTERIOR DESIGN BY **MARTIN N. HINZE**

PN
1993.5
.U6
P745
2009

For my parents

CONTENTS

ACKNOWLEDGMENTS

ON A DELIGHTFUL evening in Lund, Erik Hedling spoke enthusiastically to me about Wolfgang Peterson's *Troy* and about how the film was not simply an epic about the ancient world but was a symbolic drama about current events. Erik's insight planted the seed that grew into this project. I thank him for that and for his gracious hospitality.

I worked out some of the ideas in the book by first presenting them in a Virginia Tech colloquium on film and terrorism sponsored by the Humanities Department. Neal King kindly invited me to participate in that event. I'd also like to thank the panelists and lively audience members at a session on terrorism and film at the 2008 SCMS conference in Philadelphia. The session showed how salient the events of 2001 yet remain.

It was a pleasure working with Columbia University Press. Special thanks go to Jennifer Crewe, Associate Director and Editorial Director, for her keen interest in the project, for green-lighting my various requests, and for seeing that the manuscript moved along during the review and production process in a speedy fashion. Senior Manuscript Editor Roy Thomas was a joy to work with. His careful work and input, and his suggestions about some new things to consider, have helped to make this a better book. Martin Hinze created a lively and eye-catching cover design, and Marisa Pagano created some spot-on catalog copy.

And a thank you also for the kind assistance from the representatives at AP Images and Kobal.

FIRESTORM

INTRODUCTION

WHEN THE WORLD TRADE CENTER ERUPTED in fireballs and came crashing down on 9/11, many people felt they were seeing a Hollywood movie come to life. And when American film was discussed in this context, many respondents ventured the opinion that Hollywood henceforth would have to change its ways. 9/11, it was said, made a certain kind of film obsolete. That was the action film bristling with explosions, mass death, and a wisecracking hero who was amused and unscathed by all the carnage. The industry did curtail the production of these movies for a little while, but the notion that American film would be changing in a post-9/11 world raised larger questions about the relationship between the September attacks and the content and form of American cinema. Some of these questions can be formulated as follows: Did 9/11 influence Hollywood film production? If so, in what ways? What kinds of movies were made in response to the attacks? How factual were the presentations? Alternatively, how much poetic or ideological license was exercised? How did filmmakers working inside a fictional framework respond in comparison with the responses by documentary filmmakers? Did films for the big screen differ in their presentations from those movies and television series made for the small screen? And in terms of the legacy of 9/11—the Iraq War, controversies over warrantless domestic surveillance, forcible rendition, Abu Ghraib and policies of torture—how did American film respond to and portray these issues?

After the attacks by al Qaeda, commentators predicted that Hollywood storytelling would have to find new formulas.[1] Certainly, Hollywood was fearful that the trauma of 9/11 would hurt the box office performance of the action films that had been such reliable sources of industry profit. Television critic Lisa Stasi no doubt voiced the sentiments of many when she wrote, "I lived through 9/11—I don't need to see the whole nightmare treated like some disaster movie by every media outlet on earth."[2] Certainly, the studios moved slowly to dramatize the events of 9/11, and the reasons why were clear. The attacks had left deep scars, and their visual record—the photographs, films, and videos taken on September 11—was profoundly emotional. University educators, for example, who were using film in the classroom to explore the meanings of 9/11 ran up against the same problems that Hollywood filmmakers were encountering.[3] They found their ventures to be fraught with difficulties. The material was red hot, and it triggered volatile emotional responses in viewers. For some students, the feelings generated by the disaster remained overwhelming. As one professor reported, "The iconic power of the images they 'witnessed,' for many in real time, still seemed inexplicable. It was almost as if meaning were suspended or overwhelmed by the spectacle that assaulted their imaginations."[4] Speaking from her own experience as a movie viewer, another educator said that every film she saw seemed somehow associated with 9/11. "The pressing nature of the event on my consciousness (as a former New Yorker and a critic of popular culture) meant that every film I saw related to 9/11. For example, while watching *Spiderman* (Sam Raimi, 2002), I was stunned by the destruction of the Roosevelt Island tram, which I took often as a teenager."[5] The feelings of being overwhelmed and stunned that 9/11 triggered proved to be both powerful and tenacious, and the Hollywood studios were understandably fearful about intruding into such emotion-laden territory, one where the recent imagery of 9/11 was so inherently upsetting. As E. Ann Kaplan noted, "this event seemed to feed trauma by being so highly visible in its happenings."[6]

But filmmakers did turn their cameras on the event, both as it was happening and also afterward in the form of dramatizations. And now, years after the attacks, there is perhaps enough perspective and distance on them, and on the filmmaking they elicited, to explore the role that American film has played in the age of terrorism. As I discuss in the first chapter, terrorism is not a new phenomenon, but I use this phrase—the age of terrorism—to refer to the distinctive features of our own period. Terrorism has furnished a defining experience for our time, encompassing policy, politics, emotion, perception, insurgent strategy, aesthetics, and violence in ways that seem insurmountable. Like the Cold War during its heyday, there seems no way out of, beyond, or past the psychological and political spaces that terrorism has established for the modern period. In part, this is because terrorism has challenged the thinking of the leaders of the Western democracies, who rightly fear the likelihood of new attacks and who find it difficult to defend against these without doing violence to parliamentary traditions and democratic institutions. It also has helped to engender a climate of fear as one of the conditions of modern life. Political violence is centuries old. What makes it deadlier today and more intimidating are new technologies of violence and mass communication. Osama bin Laden knew that the airplane attacks of September 11 would be photographed and videotaped and that these images would be broadcast around the world, making the event into a horrifying theater of mass destruction. This symbolic value, achieved by way of modern media and the manner in which they would inevitably collude to emphasize the theatricality of the attacks, was of tremendous importance to al Qaeda. It made bin Laden world famous and elevated the political cachet of al Qaeda in ways that a lesser and less photographed plot could not have achieved. But while bin Laden shrewdly counted on the role of electronic communication to broadcast the attacks around the world, al Qaeda used a rather old technology of violence—passenger airplanes—to kill thousands. The new technologies of violence—attempts on civilian lives using biological or nuclear weapons—are the primal fear of Western democracies as they envision how the attacks might come in the future.

For Americans, the fallout from 9/11 has included the emergence of a new culture of anxiety. The airplane passenger sitting next to you on the flight might try to light a fuse in his shoe—one cannot know for sure that something like this will not happen. This anxiety is masked by a curious sense of apathy induced by the passage of many years in which a second, massive attack inside the United States did not occur. But fear remains a continuing feature of American life in the new millennium, and it has set a difficult context for the Hollywood film studios. Denying fear or assuaging it with fantasy and pleasant comedy is a surer means toward profitability than is making risky films that remind people of the uncertain world in which they live or that portray very unpleasant events, like those of 9/11, that so many people witnessed firsthand or in real time via the electronic news media. The top five box office films of

2007 were all entertaining fantasies—*Spider-Man 3, Shrek the Third, Transformers, Pirates of the Caribbean: At World's End,* and *Harry Potter and the Order of the Phoenix*. The close of 2007 saw a flurry of films in release about the Iraq War, the CIA policy of forcible rendition, and other aspects of our post-9/11 world. Each of these films did quite poorly at the box office. Robert Redford's *Lions for Lambs,* for example, which starred Redford, Meryl Streep, and Tom Cruise, grossed $14 million domestically, a paltry sum. *Rendition,* starring Reese Witherspoon, and *A Mighty Heart,* starring Angelina Jolie, each grossed less than $10 million domestically. Brian De Palma's *Redacted* grossed $65,000. By contrast, *Spider-Man 3* took in $336 million domestically. The only year-end films dealing with terrorism that found a reasonably sized audience—*The Kingdom* ($47 million gross) and *Charlie Wilson's War* ($35 million gross)—were those that played up the comforts of familiar genre pleasures. *The Kingdom* was an action shoot-'em-up, and *Charlie Wilson's War* was a Tom Hanks comedy-drama. They were also about terrorist bombings in Saudi Arabia and the CIA's effort to arm the Islamist mujahideen in Afghanistan, but this political content was secondary to the genre packaging.

9/11 and its aftermath, then, have remained treacherous topics for filmmakers to explore. Despite this, in the years that have elapsed since the attacks, numerous films have tried to come to terms with the events of September 11 and their impact, and many of these films have been quite distinguished. In the chapters that follow, I explore the output of films made about September 11 and its aftermath and the terms by which they portray these events. By the aftermath of 9/11 I mean chiefly the responses of the administration of President George W. Bush in its efforts to fight what it referred to as a global war on terror. In this context, the wars in Afghanistan and Iraq are part of this aftermath, as are the controversies over the administration's policy of designating terrorist suspects as illegal enemy combatants and holding them beyond the reach of civil and military law. The administration's use of torture, forcible renditions, and secret prisons belongs to the legacy of 9/11, as does the expansion of domestic and foreign surveillance by the FBI, CIA, and NSA, often conducted without warrants. The Constitutional issues that arise from these novel policies are also part of the new climate of the post-9/11 world. The attacks plunged American society and its political institutions into a set of problems and challenges that they are still struggling to master. For filmmakers concerned about any aspect of 9/11 or its aftermath, the attacks and their legacy offer a tremendously rich and challenging body of material. The resulting films range from those that seek simply to exploit 9/11 for entertainment purposes to those that seek to understand, explain, and interpret this recent history.

As the title of the book indicates, I examine American film. This means that I do not cover some noted and at times notorious films made overseas about 9/11 and its legacy. These include Nick Broomfield's UK production, *Battle for Haditha* (2007), which portrays the 2004 killings by U.S. Marines of twenty-four Iraqi civilians, or the German-Swiss documentary directed by Heidi Specogna, *The Short Life of José Antonio Gutierrez* (2006), about the first U.S. soldier killed in Iraq.

One of the most controversial of the overseas productions, *11'09"1—September 11* (2002), is an anthology film featuring segments directed by eleven international filmmakers—Youssef Chahine, Amos Gitai, Alejandro González Iñárritu, Shohei Imamura, Claude Lelouch, Ken Loach, Samira Makhmalbaf, Mira Nair, Idrissa Ouedraogo, Sean Penn, and Danis Tanovic. The assembled perspectives on 9/11 issue from Egypt, Israel, Mexico, Japan, France, the UK, Iran, India, Burkina Faso, the U.S., and Bosnia-Herzegovina. The film's concept is designated by its title. Each filmmaker's segment runs 11 minutes, nine seconds, and one frame. Because the film includes a range of international perspectives on the attack, some are critical of U.S. foreign policy. The Ken Loach segment, for example, focuses on the other September 11, in 1973, when the Chilean military, backed by the Nixon administration, overthrew the democratically elected government of Salvador Allende. A character in the segment writes a letter of condolence to Americans, grieving that the "enemies of freedom" on 9/11 attacked the United States in such a deadly manner. But he also aims to hold the U.S. to account for its support of the military's September 11th attack on the Chilean people. In the Youssef Chahine segment, the ghost of an American Marine killed in the 1983 bombing of the Beirut Marine barracks visits a Palestinian family living under Israeli occupation and finds popular support for suicide bombers and a hatred for the U.S. because of its support for Israel. In its review of the film, *Variety* called it "stridently anti-American."

Mat Whitecross and Michael Winterbottom's *The Road to Guantánamo* (2006), produced in the United Kingdom, uses faux-documentary footage to tell the story of three British Muslim men—the Tipton Three—who were arrested by U.S. forces in Afghanistan and held at Guantánamo for two years. They were finally released without any charges being filed. The film's jittery, unstable compositions and fast, unmotivated camera movement, in today's cinema syntax, signal authenticity to a popular audience. The style is meant to look like documentary footage shot under fast-breaking and unpredictable circumstances. But it makes the film's narrative difficult to follow, and Whitecross and Winterbottom show little skepticism toward the claims of the three men that they were merely visiting in Afghanistan. While, as I discuss in a subsequent chapter, U.S. forces swept up in Afghanistan and Iraq and threw into area prisons many innocent people, the film would be stronger if the filmmakers had maintained a perspective that was separate from that of the Tipton Three and allowed a portrait of guilt or innocence to emerge more gradually through what is shown.

Another UK production, *Death of a President* (2006), uses documentary-style footage to tell a fictional story about a father, enraged by his son's death in the Iraq War, who plots and successfully carries out the assassination of President Bush. Critics received the film as a notorious and disreputable exploitation picture because of its chilling presentation of the assassination on-camera, using an actor who closely resembles the President. Many critics took the film as the utmost in bad taste. But, in fact, the movie visualizes the kind of Presidential assassination, carried out by a disturbed loner, that has been relatively frequent in U.S. history, and the movie offers a very positive, even glowing, portrait of President Bush as a strong, capable, and humane leader. Contrary to its reputation, it is not an anti-Bush film at all.

These and other overseas productions show that 9/11 has influenced filmmakers in many countries. In part, the attacks have provided an opportunity for some overseas filmmakers to address the U.S. on its foreign policies and standing in the world. Another book could be written about how international filmmakers have viewed these events, and many interesting contrasts could be drawn with the portraits offered by films produced in the United States. As *11'09"1 —September 11* demonstrates, the international views are diverse and, at times, are more skeptical and critical of U.S. foreign policy than what one finds in American movies. But the tradition of response in the American cinema is important to consider because, in its own way, it is diverse and also because it was being formed in the heat of the moment and under the pressure of immensely emotional and confusing circumstances. This gives it value as a series of historical and human documents and also as a set of voices from the society that al Qaeda had attacked.

Chapter 1—"Theater of Mass Destruction"—examines the depiction of terrorism in American film before 9/11. In contrast to European cinema, which had produced numerous classics about terrorism (*The Battle of Algiers* [1966], *State of Siege* [1972], *The Lost Honor of Katharina Blum* [1975]), Hollywood film had been indifferent to the subject as a basis for films for many decades. In *Sabotage* (1936), Alfred Hitchcock first visualized a terrorist bombing on camera, but at this time he was still working in the British cinema. What we would today call terrorist themes begin to emerge in Hollywood's disaster movies of the 1970s, although at the time nobody referred to these as being movies about terrorism. Hollywood took more explicit interest in terrorism during the 1980s in the wake of several high-profile and effective attacks on U.S. forces overseas. But the industry responded mainly in terms of action-adventure formulas, with terrorism furnishing an effective prop for the action. As fireballs became a reliable ticket-selling feature of action movies, terrorist characters were a fast, efficient way of motivating the explosions. Take one mad bomber, add one wise-cracking hero, mix with crowds of anonymous characters, let sit and . . . boom! You have a recipe for action movie mayhem. These were the kinds of films that made Hollywood look very bad in a post-9/11 world.

Chapter 2—"Shadows Once Removed"—examines the films made by Hollywood studios and by independent filmmakers that were clear responses to 9/11. These include such little-seen pictures as *The Guys* (2002) and *WTC View* (2005) alongside such widely discussed pictures as Oliver Stone's *World Trade Center* (2006) and Paul Greengrass' *United 93* (2006). But they also include Spike Lee's *25th Hour* (2002) and three films by Steven Spielberg that stand as a series of reflections on 9/11 and terrorism, *The Terminal* (2004), *War of the Worlds* (2005), and *Munich* (2005). The films examined in this chapter dramatize or allude to actual events, and therefore I compare the dramatizations found in the films with what is known of the events in question. The attacks of September 11 are among the most widely investigated and photographed events in U.S. history, and a considerable body of knowledge now exists about what happened on that day and why events unfolded as they did. I emphasize the importance of dramatic license and the differences between fiction and documentary, but I also view the films in terms of this record of knowledge and discuss where they follow it and where they diverge from it. Examining the omissions, distortions, and reinventions of the known record often provides great insight into the ways in which particular films are framing the various proposed meanings of 9/11, and I will say more about this approach in a moment.

Dramatizations of 9/11, such as *World Trade Center* and *United 93,* had great problems finding an audience. Many viewers had no desire to see a film about a terrible event that they felt they already knew only too well. Documentary films, in a sense, did not face this problem because viewers implicitly understood why these would be produced. 9/11 was an important event and therefore a fitting one for documentarians to explore. The reasons why a Hollywood filmmaker would offer a dramatization were less clear to audiences who had seen so much 9/11 imagery in the electronic news media during the weeks following the attacks. Compared with the relatively meager output of dramatizations by the film studios, documentary films about 9/11 were more plentiful and were also often more powerful and more deeply reflective and considered in their exploration of what happened and what it meant. Chapter 3—"Ground Zero in Focus"—examines these documentary portraits of 9/11. One hundred and two minutes elapsed between the time that American Airlines Flight 11 hit the North Tower and it collapsed (the South Tower fell first), providing New Yorkers and media news crews with ample time to film and photograph the crisis. The resulting, elaborate visual record facilitated the production of several outstanding documentaries that are comprised largely of photographs and videos made by witnesses. But while there is no dearth of usable images, documentary filmmakers had to struggle with the meanings to attach to the images. Thus, most of these films propose different kinds of narratives as a means for understanding 9/11, and the most common of these narratives involves the values of progress, heroism, and redemption, which are proposed as the deep-level meaning of the crisis. This use of narrative by many documentary filmmakers was a way of managing conceptual and emotional responses to an overwhelming and horrifying event.

Another and burgeoning group of documentaries are the conspiracy films. These films are typically distributed via the Internet and as DVDs, produced by groups that are convinced that 9/11 was an inside job orchestrated by the Bush administration. *Loose Change* (2007), *911: In Plane Sight* (2004), *911 Mysteries: Demolitions* (2006), and other conspiracy films postulate a variety of alternative explanations for what happened on September 11: the U.S. air defense system was ordered to stand down, United 93 never crashed in Pennsylvania, the Pentagon was hit by a missile, and the World Trade Center was brought down by explosives placed inside the towers before the planes hit. I examine these charges and profile some of the most popular of the conspiracy films. While the allegations made by the films are often wacky, the movies have a huge and devoted audience. And, indeed, 9/11 has grown to be like the assassination of President Kennedy in that it is surrounded now by myths and suspicions that have become ineradicable and that point to a widespread public feeling that the whole story remains unknown and that key facts have been suppressed.

Like 9/11, the Iraq War has stimulated a great deal of documentary filmmaking. Chapter 4—"Battleground Iraq"—examines the portraits of the war that documentary filmmakers have offered and the connections between the war and 9/11. Some of these films, such as *Occupation: Dreamland* (2005), *Gunner Palace* (2005), *Combat Diary* (2006), and *The War Tapes* (2006) provide a narrowly focused, soldier's-eye view of ground operations. The filmmaking approach is ethnographic and observational and in general is centered on the American presence. By contrast, *Inside Iraq: The Untold Stories* (2004), *Iraq in Fragments* (2006), *My Country, My Country* (2006), and other films emphasize Iraqi perspectives on the invasion and occupation of their country.

As noted, many of the Iraq War documentaries were filmed in the midst of crises and combat operations, and their perspective is thus a somewhat narrow one. *Off to War* (2006), by contrast, takes a larger view, studying the experiences of a group of Army National Guardsmen, plucked from the small town of Clarksville, Arkansas, and deployed for eighteen months. The film follows their experiences and shows the impact of the deployment on the town from the weeks before they leave to the weeks after they have returned. Other documentaries take a more historical view, such as *Why We Fight* (2005) and *No End in Sight* (2006), which attempt to explain the origins of the war. These films are very critical of the web of rationales cited by the administration for its necessity. A few documentaries—*WMD: Weapons of Mass Deception* (2004), *Buying the War* (2007)—take these rationales as their subject, parse them, and find them wanting. Critical views are also offered by films such as *The Ground Truth* (2006) and *Soldiers Pay* (2004). These documentaries examine the physical and psychological injuries sustained by many of those who served.

The Iraq War documentaries are a diverse group of films and yet collectively they offer a very pessimistic portrait of this war and its likely outcome. Their imagery of a devastated country and of Americans in a land and culture they poorly understand offered a powerful antithesis to the administration's claims that the war was going well.

The attacks of September 11 also influenced content on the small home screen of television, and chapter 5—"Terrorism on the Small Screen"—examines how movies and dramatic series produced for television have portrayed and been influenced by 9/11. Numerous dramatic series took terrorism as a theme. These included *The Agency, Threat Matrix, The Grid,* and *Sleeper Cell.* But the most famous and popular of these series was *24,* which each season portrayed a final day's countdown to a devastating terror strike against the U.S. Only the super agent Jack Bauer could save the day, which he reliably did season after season. The show was popular but offered a quasi-totalitarian vision of state and society. It also openly advocated torture as an effective method of eliciting information. Because of the show's fame, I take an extended look at its tropes and themes.

Made-for-television (MFT) movies often were more celebratory of the Bush administration and the Iraq War than were documentaries or Hollywood films. Three key television movies—*DC 9/11: Time of Crisis* (2003), *Saving Jessica Lynch* (2003), and *The Path to 9/11* (2006)—offered overtly positive views of the war and of the administration's handling of the attacks. *DC 9/11* and *The Path to 9/11,* in particular, are politically partisan in a way that differs from the war documentaries and Hollywood films. Hollywood's narratives about these events tend to hew to a middle-of-the-road course while the war documentaries, on the whole, tend to be liberal or left-wing. By contrast, *DC 9/11: Time of Crisis* and *The Path to 9/11* criticize the Clinton administration's efforts against bin Laden while portraying President Bush as a Lincolnesque figure capably guiding the nation through a terrible crisis. In fact, the real story is that each administration manifested a dismal record in dealing with al Qaeda, but the various right- and left-inflected media productions have tended to gloss this shared failing. By contrast, *Path to Paradise: The Untold Story of the World Trade Center Bombing* (1997) is a model of fine filmmaking for the small screen. Its portrait of the first bombing attempt against the Twin Towers, led by Ramzi Yousef, is a chillingly prophetic film when viewed in light of subsequent events.

It is common in many quarters today when discussing conflict with Islamist radicals to refer to a "clash of civilizations." This notion of an inherent and intractable struggle with Islam is deeply embedded in Western culture, at least since the time of the Crusades. And among policy wonks it has been reinforced in recent years by Samuel Huntington's influential article in *Foreign Affairs*, "The Clash of Civilizations?," in which he wrote that the fault lines of future global conflict would be drawn in terms of religion and the ancient schisms between the West and the Islamic world. While recent history gives us many instances of political violence rooted in hatred and religious intolerance, the attacks of 9/11 being a primary instance, I have resisted throughout this book the temptation to subscribe to the clash-of-civilizations view. History offers many instances of peaceful coexistence among peoples of the monotheistic religions. And in Hollywood's movies, there is such a manifest love for destruction and violent spectacle that it seemed far too easy to replicate this preference for violent conflict in the way that I write about recent events. Rigid, intolerant perspectives helped to produce 9/11, and a cultural commentator should be wary about adding to the abundance of such perspectives that now circulate as explanations of our current predicaments. Thus, when referring to bin Laden and al Qaeda, I frequently use the term *Islamist* to designate violent religious fundamentalism, as distinct from *Islamic* as a broader term designating the community of those who worship from the tradition established by Muhammad.

Writing about the films of 9/11 raises two kinds of issues that have been widely studied by scholars. These are issues of trauma and of cultural memory as encoded by film. "Trauma studies" is an academic discipline focusing on the responses by individuals and cultures to traumatic events. Often theoretical in orientation, it examines connections between individual trauma and collective or social trauma, conceptualized as a shared response by numerous individuals to a precipitating event, such as 9/11 or the Holocaust. The field also looks at the role of the media in disseminating images of traumatic events. E. Ann Kaplan's *Trauma Culture,* for example, examines the aesthetics of film as they relate to phenomena of individual and collective trauma, such as those posed by World War II or mass violence in Rwanda and Iraq. "Mediated trauma," for Kaplan, is an outcome of the way that mass media may frame, model, and disseminate traumatic events in the form of news coverage or docudramas. As she writes, "Most people encounter trauma through the media, which is why focusing on so-called mediated trauma is important."[7] Kaplan suggests that the media may induce states of "vicarious trauma" in viewers who see images of such things as famine, terrorist violence, and natural disasters. On the one hand, there is no question that some individuals who witnessed 9/11 by way of television news coverage found that the images were reawakening past personal traumas. Irene Kacandes has written a deeply moving account of the way in which the 9/11 tragedy revived her own tortured memories of the killing of two close friends, Susanne and Half Zantop.[8] The Zantops were professors at Dartmouth College who were senselessly murdered by two intruders. Kacandes writes that when she saw the images of a plane hitting the World Trade Center, she also saw "two adolescent boys stabbing my friends to death." Kaplan, too, notes that 9/11 evoked her own disturbing memories of being a child in London during World War II.

In these cases, the imagery of a public disaster has evoked details of an individual's past personal history, with past and present achieving even a kind of fusion. There is also no question that many of the images associated with 9/11 were terrifically disturbing, particularly within the immediate period of the attack and its aftermath. News media, for example, quickly moved to stop publishing or broadcasting pictures of people jumping from the burning buildings, and there were virtually no photographic or moving picture images of the mangled bodies on the pavement where they landed. The attacks were deeply disturbing to the national audience that watched them unfold, and there are reports that the number of prescriptions written for antidepressants and sleep aids rose in the following weeks. But despite all of this, I remain skeptical of claims that films about 9/11, or that contain 9/11 imagery, necessarily induce a vicarious collective trauma in their audiences.

It is not clear, for example, how one moves from the localized level of varied individual responses to 9/11, many of which are clearly traumatic, to propositions about a collective trauma induced or disseminated by film and media coverage. The 9/11 *event* was traumatic for individuals and for society. But now years after the event it is not clear that the visual images of it necessarily carry trauma. It is also not clear where the necessary threshold should be located for differentiating what is disturbing and upsetting from what is traumatic. Is a viewer who finds the portrait of the struggle between airline passengers and hijackers in *United 93* to be disturbing and upsetting experiencing a form of trauma? In her classic book, *Trauma and Recovery,* Judith Herman writes that "psychological trauma is an affliction of the powerless. At the moment of trauma, the victim is rendered helpless by overwhelming force," and she quotes from the *Comprehensive Textbook of Psychiatry* that "the common denominator of psychological trauma is a feeling of 'intense fear, helplessness, loss of control, and threat of annhiliation.'"[9] This is not the ordinary profile of emotional response that cinema elicits in its audiences. Susan J. Brison stresses that an individual's experience of helplessness is a key component of trauma-inducing events. She writes, "What survivors of trauma have in common . . . is the experience of utter helplessness in the face of overwhelming, life-threatening violence of human origin."[10] Movies do not induce such states of utter helplessness in their viewers, not at this self-shattering level of destructive intensity. Moreover, Herman describes some characteristics of traumatic memory that are uniquely different from the imagery contained in ordinary movies. She writes that the traumatic memories of an individual are images without context. "Traumatic memories lack verbal narrative and context; rather, they are encoded in the form of vivid sensations and images."[11] The fragmentary nature of the memory, its lack of context, gives it a heightened presence, and she speculates that there may be a biological basis for this. "These unusual features of traumatic memory may be based on alterations in the central nervous system. A wide array of animal experiments shows that when high levels of adrenaline and other stress hormones are circulating memory traces are deeply imprinted. The same traumatic engraving of memory may occur in human beings."[12]

In contrast to these features of an individual's traumatic memory, movies do feature verbal narrative and dramatic context, so that the structure of imagery, as found in cinema, differs from the visual structure of traumatic memory found in suffering individuals, as described by Herman. Moreover, movie narratives achieve closure; traumatic memories remain frozen, giving rise to what Herman calls the "dialectic of trauma," the competing imperatives for the individual to tell what happened and to deny that anything happened. Moreover, movies typically provide their audiences with pleasurable experiences, even when the narrative content may be about horrifying events. The box office success of a film such as *Schindler's List* would be inexplicable if the film were inducing vicarious states of trauma in its audiences. Instead, it allows viewers to bear witness to trauma, and this is a very important point—

as we will see, a prime function of the 9/11 documentaries is just this, bearing witness to atrocity. But this is quite distinct from visiting trauma upon viewers. The notion of collective trauma also fails to account for why large audiences of moviegoers turned out for a film such as *Cloverfield,* which recycled 9/11 imagery of Manhattan's destruction in the context of a monster movie.

In a critique of efforts to conjoin individual and social trauma as integrated domains of experience, Wulf Kansteiner writes that it is a misleading assumption "that representations of symptoms of trauma replicate such symptoms in the minds of the audience and produce a collective trauma which unites individuals who have never experienced or directly witnessed acts of extreme violence."[13] He notes that "the media cause trauma only rarely, although they represent an important source of social knowledge about trauma."[14]

I am suggesting, therefore, that one can write about the films of 9/11 without invoking notions that their public reception by audiences involves a condition of collective or social trauma. Films are not inducing this state in viewers, either directly or vicariously, unless individuals are predisposed to react thusly based on personal experiences, such as living in the area or knowing victims who perished. What films do provide, as Kansteiner notes, is a form of social knowledge about trauma or about events such as 9/11. They may even provide a kind of social memory about these events; by framing the events according to various narrative and emotional templates, films offer a means of explaining and understanding them and a form of closure on them. Indeed, numerous scholars have emphasized the ways in which films, photographs, and other kinds of media constitute versions of social memory. Referring to both photography and cinema, Marita Sturken writes that "the camera image constitutes a significant technology of memory in contemporary American culture."[15] Alison Landsberg writes that the social memories encoded in cinema are "prosthetic memories." These do not derive from a person's lived experience. "Prosthetic memories circulate publicly, and although they are not organically based, they are nevertheless experienced with a person's body as a result of an engagement with a wide range of cultural technologies. Prosthetic memories thus become part of one's personal archive of experience."[16] Sturken notes that forgetting is an essential part of the formation of social memories about events; some details are strategically forgotten or repressed while others are preserved. She claims that this type of memory is essentially a narrative process; it is dynamic rather than static. It is not a replica of what happened but a story about what it means.

Sturken's insight is instructive to a point. While there may well be a social memory component that attaches to cinema, movies are not simply an archival trove of collective memories. Films are designed and produced for many reasons, some of which have nothing to do with a collective process of remembering. Many movies, for example, are genre films, telling stories according to narrative formulas that prevail in the genre. In action movies, for example, the bad guys tend to be really bad shots with their automatic weapons, missing the hero consistently and at close range. Although such a thing is highly improbable, audiences accept it as "real" within that genre. Generic narrative formulas are extremely important, and they are very persistent and relatively unchanging over time. A filmmaker who strays too far outside their parameters risks rejection by viewers, who may feel that the movie is not a satisfying example of the genre. Moreover, many films are constructed on the basis of market research, with Hollywood tweaking storylines or endings based on guesstimates about what viewers will like most or what will translate into the best box office. Furthermore, many movies imitate other movies, especially ones that have been commercially or artistically successful. And viewers, for their part, remain critically aware that they are watching a movie and are unlikely to assent to all the details of a film's presentation of events present or past. Viewers know that many elements in a film are there *because* it is a movie. They understand the artifice involved, that they are experiencing a manufactured representation of the world. All of these factors should make us cautious about assuming that film content or style necessarily reflects a social consensus about the nature or meaning of events.

Sturken's emphasis on forgetting and on the dynamic processes of narrative memory leads her to claim that questions about the truthfulness of the memory are of little relevance. "We need to ask not whether a memory is true but rather what its telling reveals about how the past affects the present."[17] Film narratives perhaps are not true or false in a propositional way. In fact, it is debatable whether films make propositions about states of affairs at all. All the same, I am not convinced that evaluating the veracity of the manner in which a film constructs its account of the historical past is entirely beside the point. As noted earlier, the events of 9/11 have been studied extensively and a great deal of empirical information about them now exists. Many of these films—*World Trade Center* and *United 93* prominently among them—are proffered as docudramas, as filmic re-creations of actual events. It is, therefore, important to ask about the relationship between what is known historically about the 9/11 attacks and the manner in which films reconstruct and represent these events. This gap or interstice is one of the places where meaning arises. As Sturken notes, thinking about what is forgotten and omitted can be as instructive as looking at what has been selected for inclusion in the cinematic portrait. Therefore, in the pages that follow, I try to remain sensitive to the nuances and poetic domain of narrative and drama, and to the artifice of cinema, while also measuring these dramas with reference to our knowledge of the events. The latter task seems especially important in light of the degree to which the events of 9/11 have been overtaken by proliferating conspiracy theories and political agendas.

The films examined in the following chapters are responses to a historical period that engulfs all of us, that has not ended, and that shows no signs of ending any time soon. And yet the time period covered in this book coincides with a clear unit of history. The attacks of 9/11 occurred shortly after the inception of the Bush administration and the publication of this book follows upon the conclusion of that administration. The two-term Presidency of George W. Bush furnishes the historical period in which the bulk of the filmmaking that I examine takes place. Many of the films examined in these pages are reflections upon and examinations of the policies the administration enacted after September 11 as a means of countering further attacks. I therefore conclude the book with some reflections upon the strengths and weaknesses of the administration's response and the manner in which films have commented upon this. While we all remain imprisoned within the age of terrorism and while new developments and incidents will undoubtedly occur, the years that have elapsed since the attacks of September 11 are more than adequate for illuminating the key responses of American film in this period. In the final chapter I aim for summary and closure on the failures and triumphs of American film in relation to the age of terrorism. Because I am writing about circumstances that are in motion, the book, in a sense, will be dated by the time of its publication—other films will have been made, other terrorist incidents will have occurred. But the value of this inquiry should not be measured solely in terms of covering the most recent films. It should be measured in terms of illuminating the core responses by American cinema in the period. Hopefully, these pages go some way toward accomplishing that.

Since I have noted earlier the way that the boundaries between calamities at the collective and the individual level may overlap, I will end this introduction on a personal note of my own. I was viewing the documentaries about 9/11, which form the basis for chapter 3, in April 2007. That month a deranged student at Virginia Tech, where I work and teach, shot and killed thirty-two students and teachers. As I watched the documentary films showing the Twin Towers falling amidst those ghastly clouds of smoke, I was also engulfed by the horrifying developments at Virginia Tech. And so it seemed whether I looked out at the world at large or at my local community that violence and death were close at hand. Traumatic events were occurring where I live and work as I watched the film record of the disaster in Manhattan. Trauma was in both the near and the far environment, and I asked myself why I would do this, why write this book under those circumstances? I kept working for many reasons, among which was the feeling that there was some virtue to be found in not looking away from 9/11. And in that spirit I offer this accounting of the films.

1

CHAPTER ONE

THEATER OF MASS DESTRUCTION

FLYING AIRPLANES INTO BUILDINGS on a holy warrant from God is behavior that hungers for apocalypse. Indeed, many terrorists throughout history have shared a desire for apocalypse. The Irish terrorist O'Donovan Rossa, for example, dreamed of destroying a city and launched a "dynamite campaign" in the 1880s that aimed to reduce London to ashes.[1] Dynamite alone couldn't accomplish his epic goal, but more than a century later, expanding technologies of violence promised to give terrorists the means at last of fulfilling grand ambitions. The destruction of the World Trade Center promised terrible things to come—the potential scope and scale of future incidents was now off the charts.

In pursuing visions of epic destruction, filmmakers got there first, well before al Qaeda did. During the decade-and-a-half that preceded September 11, numerous films gave us stories in which terrorists launch grandiose plans for destruction, and many of these movies—*Nighthawks,*

Speed, Broken Arrow, Die Hard 2, Blown Away—picture voluptuous spectacles of fiery death. Others—*Die Hard, Executive Decision, True Lies, The Peacemaker, The Siege*—seem to anticipate in often eerie ways the events of September 11. In still others—*Independence Day, Godzilla, The Day After Tomorrow*—filmmakers blew up, burned down, and knocked over beloved public landmarks, including the Empire State Building, the World Trade Center, and the Statue of Liberty. As if it were an obsessive-compulsive disorder, moviemakers repeatedly reduced Manhattan to smoldering ruins. By the time the attacks did occur, they seemed disturbingly entangled with the movie fantasies that Hollywood had spun so regularly. Exclamations that the destruction of the Twin Towers seemed like something out of a movie were common. This helped to give the event what Claire Kahane called "an uncanny ambiguity."[2]

To understand where American film went after September 11, we need to see where it was before al Qaeda's attack, and this chapter surveys terrorism-themed films produced during the 1980s and 1990s, in a period when heightened awareness about terrorism overseas was coupled with an odd complacency about the probability of an attack on American soil. Terrorism seemed for many like something that happened elsewhere and not in the United States. This complacency helps to account for why Hollywood was so slow in making movies on the subject. Before getting to these films, a quick historical overview will show how wrong the idea itself was. One of the things commonly said after September 11 was that now everything had changed because the events of that day showed that America was not immune from terrorism. In fact, for a long time the U.S. had attracted theoreticians and advocates of terrorism and also suffered from terrorist violence. The assassination of President McKinley in 1901 was a local accompaniment of the wave of political violence—bombings and killings of public figures—that swept Europe in the late nineteenth century and that marked the onset in the West of terrorism as a political weapon. McKinley's killer was an anarchist inspired by the murder of King Leopold I of Italy.

European anarchists immigrated to America and found in the ongoing labor struggles a receptive climate for their advocacy of political violence. In the early 1880s, in the pages of his journal *Freiheit,* Johann Most published articles providing advice for terrorists and instruction manuals on how to prepare dynamite. "Rescue mankind through blood, iron, poison, and dynamite," he proclaimed.[3] *Freiheit* also published Karl Heinzen's terrorist manifesto, "Murder," in which he explains the imperative for carrying out acts of massive political violence and declares that, "The greatest benefactor of mankind will be he who makes it possible for a few men to wipe out thousands."[4]

Luigi Galleani was the most influential Italian anarchist operating in the United States at the beginning of the new century.[5] Convinced that capitalism was an oppressive system and needed to be destroyed, he preached the necessity of violent war against the government and its political institutions. A very gifted orator, his rhetoric inspired thousands of followers. Like Most, he published a bomb-making manual, and beginning in 1914 his followers launched an ambitious and extensive bombing campaign directed against financiers, politicians, judges, police officers, and such institutions as banks, courthouses, and churches. This campaign, which aimed to smash the institutions of capitalist power, bears striking similarities to the current threat posed by al Qaeda. Galleani's followers were secretive, living and operating underground, possessed of a messianic fervor and devoted to the cause of "propaganda by the deed" (i.e., political persuasion achieved through violence), implacably opposed to the capitalist West, and were mobile and capable of striking throughout the country. Their actions, in turn, elicited a government crackdown on civil liberties in an effort to smash the movement. Following Galleani's arrest in 1917, his followers mobilized for war against police, judges, politicians, and financiers. Bomb plots were carried out in numerous cities from New York to San Francisco.

Enraged by the government's efforts to deport their members, in April 1919 the Galleanists launched a new plot, sending nearly three dozen bombs through the mail to prominent financiers, mayors, government and city officials, and a Supreme Court justice. Most of these mail bombs were identified before they were delivered, so casualties were few. One month later Galleanists detonated eight bombs simultaneously in Boston, New York, Paterson, Philadelphia, Pittsburgh, Cleveland, and Washington, a feat that demonstrated their powers of organization. (Similarly, al Qaeda's simultaneous 1988 bombings of U.S. embassies in Kenya and Tanzania were intended to demonstrate its tactical skills.) One of these bombs mostly destroyed the house of Attorney General A. Mitchell Palmer when the bomber inadvertently blew himself up while placing the charge. Enraged, Palmer launched a crackdown marked by the arrest and deportation of aliens that became known as the Palmer Raids, targeting anarchists, socialists, and communists.

The most spectacular attack attributed to Galleanists was the September 16, 1920, bombing of Wall Street, which many in government believed was retribution for the arrest and prosecution of Sacco and Vanzetti, known Galleanists. The perpetrators were never identified, though a resourceful Galleanist named Mario ("Mike") Buda is believed to have driven the wagon. Shortly after noon, as workers poured into the intersection of Wall and Broad

Street on lunch break, Buda parked a horse-drawn wagon in front of the J. P. Morgan bank. The wagon carried 100 pounds of dynamite packed with iron slugs and wired to a timer. The iron was meant to shred and pulverize bystanders in the street, which it did. Forty people were killed, and the bank was damaged. As on 9/11, this attack targeted the symbols of American financial power, and as on 9/11 soldiers formed a protective ring around the financial district because further attacks were feared. Most importantly, this bombing was the kind of modern terrorism that we recognize. As Beverly Gage has written, "The blast on Wall Street . . . seemed to be purely symbolic, designed to kill as many innocent people as possible in an assault on American power."[6] In a lament whose terms are familiar to us today, the *St. Louis Post-Dispatch* wrote, "There was no objective except general terrorism. The bomb was not directed against any particular person or property. It was directed against a public, anyone who happened to be near or any property in the neighborhood."[7] Such wholesale targeting of civilians was unusual for the anarchists. As Walter Laqueur has pointed out, they typically targeted official figures—generals, police chiefs, politicians—and aimed to avoid killing women and children, unlike al Qaeda jihadists.[8] Galleani was deported in 1919 and by the time of his death in 1931 anarchist terrorism had been crushed in the United States.

In the modern period terrorists have been a familiar feature of American life. The eclipse of the global youth movement of the 1960s spawned several left-wing terrorist groups that plagued Western democracies. Italy saw the Red Brigades and Germany the Baader-Meinhof group and Red Army Faction. Their counterpart in the U.S. was the Weathermen, which went on a very prolific bombing campaign during the 1970s. Also known as the Weather Underground Organization, this group bombed police departments in Berkeley, San Francisco, and New York, a National Guard headquarters in Washington D.C., courthouses in Washington D.C., New York, and California, prison facilities in New York and California, the corporate offices of Gulf Oil, the Kennecott Corporation, and the Anaconda Corporation, the U.S. State Department, the U.S. Capitol, and the Pentagon.

This is an impressive list of targets, and yet the campaign has been largely forgotten today, perhaps because it was mainly directed at property rather than people. Also active in this period was the Black Liberation Army, which specialized in bombings and in gunning for police officers. FALN, an acronym designating the group of guerrillas fighting for the independence of Puerto Rico, set off numerous bombs in Manhattan in 1975, and the following year it bombed the New York office of Mobil Oil and threatened to bomb the World Trade Center. It continued its bombing campaign through the end of the decade. The Unabomber employed mail bombs to wage a Luddite vendetta against engineering and computer science professors, geneticists, and an array of other victims. The campaign lasted from 1978 to 1995. In the 1990s the Army of God launched a campaign of bombings directed at abortion clinics and shootings of abortion providers.

Clearly, then, neither Oklahoma City nor the events of September 11 marked the beginning of terrorism in the United States. The spillover of anarchist philosophy from Europe to America in the 19th century brought with it numerous advocates of political violence, and the 1970s had seen a wave of bombings. But Oklahoma City and September 11 did bring something relatively new, which was the wholesale targeting of people, something not witnessed in the U.S. since the 1920 Wall Street bombing. The Weathermen aimed to end the Vietnam War. The Black Liberation Army and the FALN saw themselves conducting a war for racial or national liberation, which was a predominant political framework in the period, in which the targets for violence were selectively chosen and in which the objective did not include killing people en mass. As Martin Miller has emphasized, the "limited terrorism" of earlier periods has been replaced by the "terrorism without boundaries of our time."[9] As Walter Laqueur has stressed, the old terrorism "was, by and large, discriminate, selecting its victims carefully." By contrast, "contemporary terrorism has increasingly become indiscriminate in the choice of its victims. Its aim is no longer to conduct propaganda but to effect maximum destruction."[10]

This shift was one of the most sinister things that September 11 represented. It compelled U.S. political culture and public life to assimilate the probability of future acts of mass murder. But if this eventuality seemed to become more real after September 11, in the realm of popular culture it already existed. Since the 1980s, movies about terrorism had been offering audiences the promise of mass destruction as a means of providing entertainment. But before the 1980s this was rare—until then few American films focused on terrorism. Indeed, in comparison with literature, where terrorism is a subject that has interested a great many writers, it occupied a small niche in American cinema until recent years. Surveying terrorism as a theme in the two mediums, Walter Laqueur concluded that film producers and directors seemed to feel it was of little audience interest.[11] Laqueur was writing in the mid-1980s, just before the big surge in film production on this subject. Nevertheless, the disparity between the wealth of literature that he analyzes and the relatively paltry number of films is striking. From the world's greatest authors—Dostoyevsky (*The Possessed*), Joseph Conrad (*The Secret Agent*), André Malraux (*The Human Condition*), Jean-Paul Sartre (*Dirty Hands*)—to the countless writers of popular fiction (Thomas Harris, Frederick Forsythe, Alistair MacLean), the topic has retained an enduring interest.

HOLLYWOOD'S INITIAL FLIRTATIONS WITH THE TOPIC

Hollywood had remained uninterested in terrorism, except for the odd production such as John Ford's *The Informer* (1935), based on a novel by Liam O'Flaherty, who had fought with the IRA. A number of films dealt with subjects that, with a nudge here or there, could have encompassed a terrorist theme. In *Suddenly* (1954), Frank Sinatra leads a determined group of men planning to ambush and assassinate the President of the United States. Elia Kazan's *Panic in the Streets* (1950) is a crime film about the threat of bubonic plague being spread in a city, except in this case it isn't deliberate. The killer on the loose doesn't know that he carries the disease. In *The Manchurian Candidate* (1962), agents of a foreign power (Red China) plot to assassinate a Presidential candidate using a "sleeper," a sniper whose subconscious mind has been programmed to carry out the plot, but the portrait carries no terrorist inflection. Nor do the portraits of crazed, lone snipers in *Targets* (1968) and *Two Minute Warning* (1976), even though in the latter film the killer sets up his gear in a football stadium during a big league game.

The Satan Bug (1965), directed by John Sturges from a novel by Alistair MacLean, got much closer to the mark in its story about the theft of a secret, government-manufactured super-toxin and the threat it poses if unleashed in American cities. In *Rollercoaster* (1977), a bomber extorts money from amusement parks by threatening to blow up their roller coasters. And in *Juggernaut* (1974), a bomber places seven explosive devices aboard a luxury ocean liner and threatens to detonate them unless he's paid a huge sum. Although this is an extortion plot more than a politically motivated act of terrorism, the template that it offered of a mad bomber or extortionist threatening massive violence proved to be very durable and influenced numerous films in the 1980s and 1990s.

In *The FBI Story* (1959) a killer blows up a passenger airliner carrying his mother because he wants her insurance money. It's an act of mass murder but not terrorism. Threats of violence against airplanes could be found in *Skyjacked* (1972) and in the popular hit, *Airport* (1970), wherein a madman played by Van Heflin detonates a bomb on board a Boeing 707. Were this movie made today, it would be inflected more strongly as a terrorist narrative, but in 1970 terrorism wasn't on Hollywood's radar. *Airport, Juggernaut, Rollercoaster,* and others were part of a genre in the period known as "disaster movies." The disaster film emphasized extraordinary physical calamity befalling a cross-section of characters, often played by aging Hollywood stars (Ava Gardner, Fred Astaire, Jennifer Jones) then in the twilight of their careers. In many instances, the disasters were natural calamities rather than ones that today look like terrorism. *Earthquake* depicts the destruction of Los Angeles. A tidal wave upends an ocean liner in *The Poseidon Adventure*. An out-of-control train carries plague in *The Cassandra Crossing*. A midair collision cripples a 747 in *Airport 1975*. A fire rages through a high-rise in *The Towering Inferno*.

The disaster movie was a prominent genre in the 1970s, and while it might be inflected to include bomb threats against public targets, these were not emphasized with the kind of self-consciousness that would be routine today. One simply doesn't find a terrorist focus very often in American cinema before the 1980s. In addition to some of the disaster movies, Hollywood's spy films occasionally seemed to broach the subject of terrorism, but always in an outlandish fashion. Some of the James Bond movies, for example, such as *You Only Live Twice* (1967), feature megalomaniac villains bent on either world domination or world destruction, and they aim to achieve their goals by threatening massive violence. And spy movies inspired by Bond's popularity, such as *Our Man Flint* (1966), which features a cabal of eco-terrorists bent on world domination, did the same. On occasion, Hollywood's international coproductions took up the subject of terrorism. *Hennessy* (1975), for example, produced by American International Pictures, starred Rod Steiger as an IRA bomber who journeys to London intending to blow up Parliament. In the climax, he wears a suicide vest laced with explosives, much like a modern jihadist might do.

Ironically, one of Hollywood's best-known directors—Alfred Hitchcock—provided the most indelible, powerful, and literal image of terrorist violence in early cinema, and yet this was before he joined the American film industry. In *Sabotage* (1936), made during his British period, young Steve (Desmond Tester), son of the film's heroine (Sylvia Sidney), unwittingly carries a bomb to Piccadilly Circus. Verloc (Oscar Holmolka), the anarchist agent who gave him the bomb, insists that the package must be delivered before 1:30 that afternoon, but, alas, poor Steve is delayed by a passing parade which he pauses to watch and is also corralled by a street peddler selling toothpaste and hair tonic. When Steve does get free of the peddler and the parade, he boards a double-decker bus, which becomes bogged down in heavy traffic. And time grows late, too late. At 1:45, the bomb explodes, killing Steve and the other passengers on the bus.

Hitchcock later said that he felt it was a mistake to have killed the boy because audiences hated that turn of events. He told interviewer François

Truffaut that "when the bomb exploded and he was killed, the public was resentful."[12] All the delays in the sequence—the peddler, the parade, the heavy traffic—enabled Hitchcock to generate considerable tension and anxiety, and he felt, having done this, having worked viewers up, that it was too cruel for the bomb actually to explode on screen. But this very cruelty is the essence of terrorism when it targets innocent people instead of property, as in the 1920 Wall Street bombing. It is Hitchcock's evocation of this quality, against his own inclinations, that makes this such a signal sequence—it points toward our world today. The shock of the sequence is sharpened by Hitchcock's emphasis on the humanity of those on the bus who are about to die. (This evocation is very similar to what Gillo Pontecorvo shows in *The Battle of Algiers* when he turns his camera on the faces of people who are about to be killed by bombs placed in a bar and a discotheque.) The conductor, at first, won't let Steve on because he's carrying flammable canisters of film which are forbidden from public transport. But when he sees that one of the films is "Bartholomew the Strangler," evidently a personal favorite, he relents, cracking a joke that as long as Steve isn't Bartholomew, he can come aboard. Steve sits next to an elderly lady holding a puppy, and he interacts with the dog, playing with it and petting it. Another woman sits across from Steve with a book on her lap. All these people, whose humanity Hitchcock has carefully evoked, will die, and this turn of events is not typical of Hitchcock's moral universe. Despite his frequent depiction of murderers, spies, and sabotage, Hitchcock's moral sensibility is worlds away from the indiscriminate violence of modern terrorism. Violence in Hitchcock's films usually occurs on a smaller scale. He enjoyed, on occasion, terrifying his audience, but terrorism itself was not a type of violence that he comfortably explored. He much preferred the pathology of elegant killers like Uncle Charlie (in *Shadow of a Doubt* [1943]) to the cold and depersonalized calculus of the political terrorist.

Sabotage was based on Joseph Conrad's novel, *The Secret Agent*, in which Conrad views the political world and its agents of anarchist subversion, in the words of Irving Howe, "from a great and chilling distance."[13] Whereas Hitchcock shows the bombing in a straightforward, linear fashion, Conrad embeds its portrait in different chapters across the novel, and he goes much farther in portraying the physical toll the violence exacts. The body lies in a morgue, "a heap of rags, scorched and bloodstained, half concealing what might have been an accumulation of raw material for a cannibal feast." The investigating officer says the victim was "blown to small bits: limbs, gravel, clothing, bones, splinters—all mixed up together. I tell you they had to fetch a shovel to gather him up with." Hitchcock doesn't show these details; he couldn't, in this period of cinema, even if he had wanted to. And this reticence about the effects of bombs on the human body would continue to inform the visual design of terrorist films into the 1980s and 1990s and beyond.

Sabotage isn't about terrorist acts carried out on American soil. But with the bus bombing in Piccadilly Circus, Hitchcock had vividly delineated a type of violence that Hollywood filmmakers of subsequent generations would study more closely. As we have seen, they initially broached it in terms of the disaster film, and in 1977 that genre morphed in a way that gave us the first prominent disaster spectacle that was also explicitly and emphatically about terrorism. Jack G. Shaheen has described *Black Sunday* (1977) as "the first feature film to display Palestinian terrorists on American soil."[14] Directed by John Frankenheimer from a novel by Thomas Harris (in his pre–Hannibal Lecter days), the film portrays a group of Black September terrorists that hatches a plot to detonate the Goodyear Blimp over the Orange Bowl, hurling thousands of steel rifle darts into the crowd in the stands. To accomplish this, Black September member Dahlia Iyad (Marthe Keller) seduces and manipulates a disaffected Vietnam veteran, Michael Lander (Bruce Dern), into prepping the blimp with the bomb and darts and piloting it into the stadium.

Dern made a career specialty of playing psychos, and his volatile character here is in line with a widespread tendency in seventies cinema to scapegoat Vietnam veterans as crazed and villainous characters. Dahlia works for Mohammad Fasil (Bekim Fehmiu), who, in the narrative, is said to have masterminded the assault on the Israeli athletes at the 1972 Munich Olympics. This was one of the period's most notorious real-life acts of terror, which led to the death of all the kidnapped Israelis when German authorities launched an ill-considered and bungled rescue attempt. The origins and affiliations of Black September remain murky; some scholars view the group as a vehicle for parent organizations (the PLO's Fatah, for example) to carry out terrorist acts which would be too risky to pursue openly.[15] The Munich events, along with the group's acts of sabotage in West Germany and the Netherlands, its hijacking of a Belgian airliner, and its attack on the Saudi embassy in Khartoum in 1973 gave Black September sufficient cachet for popular culture to invoke its name as a means of motivating the action in *Black Sunday.* Two U.S. officials were killed in the Khartoum attack, but Black September had never launched any actions inside the United States. Nevertheless, the film proposes that Black September is engineering the attack at the Orange Bowl as a means of revenge on the United States for its support of Israel. Dahlia tapes a message to be used after the attack in which she says, "The American people have remained deaf to all the cries of the Palestinian nation." Therefore, she concludes, Americans now will be made to suffer "as we have suffered."

Dahlia and Fasil are portrayed as stone killers, in contrast to the Israeli agent who is hunting them, David Kabakov (Robert Shaw). Kabakov has gained a reputation as a ferocious assassin who targets Israel's enemies, but now he has grown tired of killing and has come to feel that the world is no better now than when he started. "Doubt has entered in," he tells his assistant, Robert Moshevsky. In the film's opening act, a raid on Fasil's Beirut headquarters, Kabakov had cornered Dahlia but spared her life. When she subsequently murders Moshevsky, Kabakov realizes that his moral qualms need to be put aside. The film thus pits a group of cold killers plotting mass murder against a hero who has a conscience and is troubled by violence. The film briefly raises a more complex moral perspective on Kabakov when an FBI agent (Fritz Weaver) lectures him about not pursuing his assassin's game inside the U.S. "Whatever you think of our methods, you'll play by our rules or leave," he tells Kabakov. But this critique of Kabakov's extra-legal methods is quickly abandoned. It is trumped by the spectacular nature of the violence that Dahlia and Lander are planning. The large scale of the attack situates the film inside the era's cycle of disaster movies, and at the same time, because the attack is premeditated political violence that targets ordinary people for slaughter, it takes the action from disaster to terrorism proper.

The climax has Kabakov in a helicopter, chasing the blimp, now commandeered by Lander and Dahlia. This time he doesn't hesitate—Kabakov machine-guns Dahlia, and he uses the helicopter to tow the blimp offshore where the explosion occurs without loss of life. On one level, the climax seems very far-fetched, like something out of a James Bond film, with Kabakov performing outlandish heroics as he tries to seize control of the blimp, and with

FIGURE 1.1 Pursuing the blimp in a helicopter, Kabakov (Robert Shaw) machine-guns the terrorists before they can destroy the Super Bowl stadium in *Black Sunday*. (Frame enlargement)

the terrorists' rather surreal conception of the blimp as an attack weapon. But what in 1977 seemed like outlandish fantasy has been overtaken by events. Today one can't watch the climax without feeling uneasy. What seemed improbable then no longer is. *Black Sunday*'s climax is no more garish and startling than the effort on 9/11 to hijack four airplanes and crash them into U.S. landmarks. But *Black Sunday* was a fantasy—it offered its audience a reassuring message about heroic action preventing mass murder, unlike what happened on 9/11. The palliative effect of this kind of reassuring narrative closure became a persistent feature of Hollywood's films about terrorism, which, as a group, seek to reassure their audiences that government authorities are taking all necessary measures to protect them.

However, unlike many subsequent films, *Black Sunday* proposes a blowback theory of terrorist violence. "Blowback" is a CIA term designating the unintended consequences of foreign policy. The idea pictures "chickens coming home to roost." Although the film's Dahlia and Fasil are caricatures, the story motivates their action as a response to U.S. policy in the Middle East. Dahlia explains that she is acting because of U.S. anti-Palestinian policies. Chalmers Johnson, a policy analyst who has written extensively about blowback, notes

> *The United States has obviously not proved immune to terrorist attacks—witness the 1993 bombing of the World Trade Center in New York, the blowing up of the Murrah federal office building in Oklahoma City in 1995, and the assaults on New York and Washington of September 2001. In one way or another—one of the Murrah terrorists was a Gulf War veteran—these incidents all suggest blowback from U.S. government activities in foreign countries.*[16]

Osama bin Laden always has explained his motives in these terms. In a 2004 videotape, he pointed to U.S. support for Israel's 1982 invasion of Lebanon as a chief example. "They started bombing, killing, and wounding many, while others fled in terror. I still remember those distressing scenes: blood, torn limbs, women and children massacred. All over the place, houses were being destroyed and tower blocks were collapsing, crushing their residents.... As I looked at those destroyed towers in Lebanon, it occurred to me to punish the oppressor in kind by destroying towers in America, so that it would have a taste of its own medicine."[17]

In a 2002 letter addressed to the people of America, he set out to answer the question, "Why are we fighting and opposing you?" Among the reasons he enumerated were these: "You attacked us in Palestine.... You attacked us in

Somalia; you supported the Russian atrocities against us in Chechnya, the Indian oppression against us in Kashmir, and the Jewish aggression against us in Lebanon." He wrote, "Your forces occupy our countries, you spread your military bases throughout them; you corrupt our lands."[18] All this made it necessary to "punish the oppressor in kind."

Black Sunday's invocation of blowback in explaining the motives of Dahlia and Fasil gives the film a contemporary resonance. But in this respect the film is relatively singular among Hollywood movies about terrorism. Hollywood's productions rarely give blowback due consideration as a motivation underlying terrorist actions because American political culture as a whole does not invite this kind of inquiry. It often is seen as being unpatriotic or as not a responsible line of inquiry. But acknowledging that blowback can occur does not necessarily mean validating an adversary's cause or motives. Understanding those motives provides a way of knowing one's enemy, and knowing one's enemy provides a good strategy for understanding how to defeat that enemy or neutralize his appeal. Hollywood terrorists tend to have minimal motives for acting or stereotypical ones—bin Laden, by contrast, has clearly articulated his reasons for waging jihad. He is a wily, intelligent, dedicated, and deadly adversary of the United States. Hollywood's terrorists, in contrast, have tended toward caricature, especially when the Middle East is involved, and they are rarely given motivations that have much political specificity.

At the same time, *Black Sunday*'s portrait of the Palestinian terrorists points to a major difference between the terrorism of this earlier period and our own. Neither Dahlia nor Fasil is an Islamist, a religious fundamentalist. Their politics are those of national liberation, and, in this, they mirror the secular, Marxist-Leninist orientation of the PLO's two main groups in that era, Fatah and the Popular Front for the Liberation of Palestine (PFLP). This focus also informs the depiction of Palestinian terrorism in *The Little Drummer Girl* (1984), whose story involves the efforts of an Israeli intelligence unit to use an American actress, Charlie (Diane Keaton), to infiltrate a terror cell led by Kalil (Sami Frey). The climax involves Kalil's attempt to bomb an Israeli advocate for peace, but it isn't the kind of suicide bombing that targets civilians and that is now so closely identified with Islamist terror. And Kalil is not portrayed as a fanatic but as a quiet, reflective guerilla commander who has a sense of irony and humor. While the film sides primarily with the Israelis, it does show a measured regard for the Palestinians, and it evokes the grievances on each side. This gave the film a degree of controversy in its day.

Islamist terror has its roots in the 1930s and Egypt's Muslim Brotherhood, an organization formed in 1928 in opposition to the British military occupation of Egypt, but by the 1970s it was a growing force in several of the region's repressive states (Egypt as well as Saudi Arabia and Pakistan). It began to focus its animus on America in the wake of the Soviet defeat in Afghanistan, and in 1996 and again in 1998 Osama bin Laden declared jihad on the United States because of its military presence in Saudi Arabia, which is home to Mecca and Medina, the two holiest cities in Islam.[19] He considered the U.S. military presence an affront to Islam. Before Islamist terror ripened into its present international scope, however, it was not religion but anticolonialism and armed struggle for national liberation that furnished the motivation for terror groups. Italy's Red Brigades, Germany's Red Army Faction, Peru's Shining Path, Fatah and the PFLP saw themselves as fighting for national liberation or against Western imperialism, and in this regard, the success of Algeria's National Liberation Front (FLN) in its use of terror against French colonialism was an inspiration. This sense of a shared struggle encouraged cooperation among some of these groups. In 1972, for example, the Japanese Red Army launched an attack on Israel's Lod Airport on behalf of the PFLP. In 1976 the PFLP hijacked an Air France plane to Entebbe, Uganda, and demanded the release of several of Germany's imprisoned Red Army Faction members. The following year, the PFLP hijacked a Lufthansa flight and demanded that Germany release the captured members of the Red Army Faction who the year before had kidnapped the German industrialist Hanns-Martin Schleyer. Thus in this period there emerged a kind of "international brigade," composed of German, Japanese, Arab, and Latin American commandos (one of the hijackers in a 1970 PFLP plot was Nicaraguan).[20]

This internationalizing of a cadre of violent political radicals provides the context for the portrait of the terrorist Wulfgar (Rutger Hauer) in *Nighthawks* (1981), which was marketed as an action vehicle for Sylvester Stallone. Wulfgar is a lone contractor who works for several groups. He is probably modeled on Ilich Ramirez Sánchez, aka "Carlos the Jackal," who gained prominence following his 1975 attack on OPEC headquarters in Vienna. Wulfgar is German, and he has an Irish contact in London, a Moroccan assistant, and a Middle Eastern employer, a profile that evokes a combination of the IRA, the Red Army Faction, and the PLO/PFLP. As the film begins, he bombs a London department store and telephones a newspaper to announce that "the Wulfgar command has just struck a blow against British colonialism." Thus our character is firmly positioned within the international brigade of secular, left-wing terrorists that had dominated world attention throughout the 1970s.

Intent on spreading mayhem, Wulfgar travels to New York City, pursued by an Interpol agent, Peter Hartman (Nigel Davenport). Hartman says, with unfortunate prescience relative to 9/11, that Wulfgar has come to Manhattan because if you want worldwide coverage of a terrorist incident, this is where you stage it. The bulk of the film is a cat-and-mouse game between Wulfgar and the Manhattan cop tracking him. The cop, Deke DaSilva (Sylvester Stallone), is recruited by Hartman to join an elite squad—Anti-Terrorism Attack Command (ATAC)—formed as an alliance between Interpol, U.S. federal and state authorities, and the NYPD with the purpose of hitting back hard at terrorists. DaSilva is troubled by the tactics Hartman is advocating, and the conflict between these two characters enables the film to pose questions about the response of democracies to terrorist attack.

Hartman believes that, until now, the police have not been ruthless enough in responding to terrorism, and he intends to teach methods that will enable the ATAC recruits to "meet your terrorist adversary on equal terms." He tells the ATAC squad that human rights, civil liberties, and a proportional use of force have all hindered police efforts to fight terrorists. DaSilva objects that Hartman is training them to be nothing but assassins, and Hartman explodes, "Oh, for Christ's sake, man, to combat violence you need greater violence. To defeat a violent people you have to be trained to react in a given situation with ruthless, cold-blooded violence as well."

Hartman personifies the deep-level threat posed by terrorism to democratic states, namely, the erosion of civil liberties by political authority, a process justified by leaders as a necessary way of coping with violence against the state. The 1970s had provided several object lessons in this regard, and these motivate the film's delineation of Hartman. Responding to the Red Army Faction, West Germany greatly expanded its internal security apparatus as the political Right gained strength. Released from prison after sixteen years, a former Red Army Faction member bitterly remarked that the RAF's tactics had seemed only to succeed at strengthening the authoritarianism of the state and at being used by right-wing politicians to pursue their agenda. "West German terrorism had . . . this unbelievable effect because it allowed itself from the very beginning to be used by interested parties. We thought with our political actions to overcome the exploitation and domination and, in reality, were only used to make the conditions that we wanted to change uglier yet."[21] Left-wing violence in Argentina during the 1970s produced a more extreme response from the government, which abducted and "disappeared" upwards of 9,000 Argentines after the 1976 military coup, in comparison to 700 victims of violence by leftist guerrillas.[22]

The authoritarian responses by the state in West Germany and, in more extreme form, in Argentina loom behind the strategic debates over antiterrorist policy in *Nighthawks*. Furthermore, in a post-9/11 world that has seen the administration of President George W. Bush greatly expand warrantless surveillance of the American public by the CIA, the FBI, and even the Pentagon,[23] and declare that the President has supreme powers to imprison anyone without warrant, trial, or judicial review, the debate within the film has proven to foreshadow the dialogue that is now ongoing within America. Despite this relevance for today, *Nighthawks* in its period was mainly intended as a cop action film; as a result, the debate between DaSilva and Hartman does not go very far. In the storyline, the two men eventually become friends, and subsequent scenes fail to extend the issues. Certainly *Nighthawks* is no *Battle of Algiers* (1966), Gillo Pontecorvo's classic depiction of the Algerian FLN's fight against the French and the French counterstrategy carried out by the OAS, including the military occupation of Algiers and the torture of Muslims by the Tenth Paratroop Division. Nevertheless, in its halting way, *Nighthawks* envisions that a time will come when the United States will be tempted to revise its own Constitutional system in the interest of formulating an appropriately ruthless response to terrorist violence. This gives the film its chief claim on our attention today. Wulfgar, of course, is subdued and defeated by DaSilva, who guns him down in a manner that invokes the assassination policy that he had earlier objected to. And this denouement enables *Nighthawks* to provide the same kind of therapeutic reassurance to the audience that *Black Sunday* had provided. It offers a vision of the nation's security forces rising to the occasion and stopping a deadly terrorist. As we will see, until 9/11 this was a basic formula of Hollywood's terrorist thrillers. If *Nighthawks* has a troubled conscience, it lies in its awareness of how fragile democracy is—but its conception of terrorism in terms of the lone operator, Wulfgar, ultimately means that the threat isn't too severe and therefore the state's own corruption isn't truly imminent.

HOLLYWOOD MARKETS TERRORISM AS ACTION-ADVENTURE

With its terrorist focus, *Nighthawks* was a bit of an outlier in 1981. The subject was not yet a familiar trope for American cinema, but this changed in just a few years. By the mid-1980s, a cinematic focus on terrorism began to take shape across a large cycle of films, many of them cheapie exploitation pictures. Chuck Norris was an action star in the period, and in *Invasion USA* (1985), which he cowrote, a hodge-podge band of terrorists—Latin, Asian, Black, Arabic—invade America at Christmas and begin blowing up shopping malls, churches, and families at home celebrating the holidays. A renegade

Soviet officer leads the team, and only Chuck Norris as America's hero can save the day. The cartoonish nature of the film set a tone that other pictures emulated. In *Terminal Entry* (1986), Muslim assassination squads plot to kill U.S. politicians and military figures. In *Wanted: Dead or Alive* (1987), Arab terrorists go on a killing spree in the United States and threaten to release poison gas. Rutger Hauer, now a hero and reformed from his *Nighthawks* villainy, aims to stop them. *Terror Squad* (1987) gives us Libyans threatening Indiana, and in *Terror in Beverly Hills* (1991) the title tells all. While these films pictured a terrorist threat on U.S. soil, other films had U.S. forces project their muscle overseas to attack and defeat terror threats in the Middle East. These pictures included *The Delta Force* (1986), *Death Before Dishonor* (1987), *Iron Eagle II* (1988), and *Navy Seals* (1990).

Why was there a sudden upsurge in terror-themed films? A likely answer is that by the mid-1980s, American targets of political violence from groups in the Middle East seemed more common than a decade earlier. Throughout the 1970s, the PFLP put airline hijacking on the map as a favored terrorist stratagem, but the targeted nations were typically Israel and on a few occasions Germany in order to free captive Red Army Faction members. Abu Nidal struck in Germany and Belgium, and Fatah in France. One of the most sustained terrorist campaigns in the period didn't involve the Middle East at all. The IRA waged a very aggressive bombing campaign against England, frequently striking in London (at tube stations, Hyde Park, Regents Park, the Houses of Parliament, Westminster Palace, and other locales). In the United States, the Unabomber struck periodically since 1978, but these incidents were not as theatrical and attention-grabbing as an airline hijacking or airport bombing. And they were not the work of a foreign power.

Things began changing in 1983. A suicide truck bomber hit the U.S. Marine Barracks in Beirut, killing more than 200 Marines. Also in Beirut that year, the U.S. Embassy was bombed, killing more than 60. The group responsible remains unknown, although Hezbollah, a radical Islamist group known to employ suicide attacks, seems the likeliest candidate. In 1985, two members of Hezbollah hijacked TWA Flight 847 and beat and killed a U.S. Navy diver on board. Also that year, Palestinian terrorists hijacked the *Achille Lauro* cruise ship and singled out a Jewish man from New York, Leon Klinghoffer, and executed him despite the fact that he was confined to a wheelchair. In 1986, Libyan agents bombed a discotheque in Berlin where U.S. soldiers were known to congregate, and in 1988 Libya again struck against the U.S. by bombing Pan Am Flight 103 over Lockerbie, Scotland, killing 270 people. This was also a fateful year in that the Soviet Union began to withdraw its forces from Afghanistan, and the following year the Islamist mujahideen, who had been financed by the CIA, Saudi Arabia, and Pakistan, took control of the country. Believing that their jihad had vanquished one superpower, they began to refocus Islamist rage on the United States, the world's remaining superpower, because of its military presence in Islamic lands.

This string of attacks on the U.S. from the Middle East seemed to crystallize the topic of terrorism for Hollywood. Jack G. Shaheen has suggested that there was a political motive behind many of the anti-Palestinian films of that period. A number of these (e.g., *The Delta Force, Invasion USA, Bloodsport* [1988]) were made in Israel and by Cannon Films, owned by Israeli producers Menahem Golan and Yoram Globus.[24] But the effusion of terrorism into American film in this period is broader and more extensive than the anti-Palestinian films alone. In the second half of the 1980s, terrorism crossed over from exploitation pictures of the Golan-Globus variety and became an item in numerous big-budget, high-profile Hollywood movies. Many of these blockbusters did not deal with Middle Eastern terrorism at all. Recent events established a kind of cognitive priming for the culture, establishing "terrorism" as a label and a prism through which to view not just modern political violence but crime itself. Thus, some films, like *True Lies* (1994) or *Executive Decision* (1995), might portray Arab terrorists while many others avoided the Middle East entirely and used terrorism as a convenient generic prop for mounting high-octane action thrillers that had plenty of explosions. *Die Hard*, for example, which was one of the highest-grossing films of 1988 and launched the film career of Bruce Willis, is actually a heist film in which the bad guys are attempting to steal millions of dollars in negotiable bearer bonds from a high-rise office building. But everybody in the movie behaves as if they are in a film about terrorists.

A gang of high-tech thieves led by Hans Gruber (Alan Rickman) takes over the Nakatomi Building and holds the company's employees hostage along with their chief executive, Joseph Takagi (James Shigeta). Gruber interrogates Takagi and tries to intimidate him into divulging the access code to the company's vault where the bonds are stored. Gruber tells Takagi the truth, saying that he wants the bearer bonds. Takagi is astonished. "You want money?" he exclaims. "What kind of terrorists are you?" Gruber replies, "Who said we were terrorists?"

Indeed, the gang has made no political demands or speeches of any kind. And yet many of the film's characters reflexively apply the concept of terrorism in order to explain what is happening. It's a default cognitive response, which makes sense in terms of the string of high-profile bombings and killings of U.S. targets in the Middle East that had begun a few years previously.

Thus, during one of his early skirmishes with the gang, our cop hero, John McClane (Bruce Willis), gets the drop on one of Gruber's men and kills him. Until now McClane has been running about shoeless. So now he takes the dead man's shoes and remarks, "Nine million terrorists in the world, I gotta kill one with feet smaller than my sister." It never occurs to McClane that the gang might be something other than terrorists. When word of the building takeover leaks to the news media, a local reporter (William Atherton) does an on-camera report in which he editorializes about what he believes is happening. "This is Richard Thornburgh live from Century City. Tonight Los Angeles has joined the sad and worldwide fraternity of cities whose only membership requirement is to suffer the anguish of international terrorism." Much later in the film, when McClane's wife, Holly (Bonnie Bedelia), sees Gruber with the bearer bonds, she remarks with some disappointment that he is nothing but a common thief. She would, it seems, have preferred a terrorist. "I'm an exceptional thief," Gruber sniffs. For his part, he is willing to play to the general perception. In a bluff, he tells the police that his demands are freedom for his "revolutionary brothers" held prisoner in Northern Ireland, Canada, and Sri Lanka. In an aside to one of his men, Gruber says he has no idea who those people might be.

The disjunction between what is actually going on in the movie, and the interpretations placed on events by characters, is fascinating and suggests that by the late 1980s "terrorism" had emerged as a potent political label and a conceptual template for understanding and perceiving acts of violence in the world. *Die Hard* shows that the label doesn't need actually to connect with the phenomena it is invoked to describe—the invocation itself is sufficient to orient characters to their environment and to provide a sense of the meaning of events. As employed in the film, "terrorism" is not an empirical term because none of the violence is politically motivated or is intended to terrorize a public larger than the hostages Gruber holds and who are his principal targets. It is a rhetorical term that creates its own kind of theater and makes the characters feel that they are caught up in events that are more significant than they actually are. Being held hostage by an international terrorist is more exciting than being held by a common thief, and the police that surround the building expend more energy on a perceived terrorist than they may have otherwise. *Die Hard,* then, is a film that points to an ongoing investment by characters in finding terrorism wherever they look and to the emotional gratifications that this search for theater-in-real-life provides them. The film, though, doesn't do much with this disjunction between rhetoric and actuality, beyond noting it, and for the film's popular audience, it was the explosions that provided much of the emotional gratification.

HOMEGROWN ENEMIES PROLIFERATE

Die Hard grossed nearly $140 million worldwide on a production budget of $28 million. Terrorism, even of the pseudo variety found in this film, could be a major box office attraction because it provided a vehicle for action, violence, and explosions. *Die Hard* and its sequels (1990, 1995, 2007) were successful blockbusters that offered audiences the high-octane violence that action films in the period were establishing as their norm. *Die Hard's* commercial success meant that there would be the inevitable sequels. The third film, *Die Hard: With a Vengeance*, is, like the first picture, a heist film in which Hans's brother, Simon (Jeremy Irons), plots to rob the Federal Reserve Bank in New York. Its terrorist element lies in the bombing threats that Simon phones in to the police to disguise his true plans. The second film, *Die Hard 2: Die Harder*, introduces a plot device that numerous terrorist films of the period utilized—this time around, the chief bad guy terrorist is one of "us." There were two categories of homegrown enemies in the pre-9/11 films. One category, examined in this section, was composed of renegade figures from the security services—police officers, military officers, covert operations specialists—that had turned against Americans or their government.

Discussing the many action films that feature a homegrown enemy, Eric Lichtenfeld writes, "This is an ideal Hollywood villain for a post–Cold War America, in which the climate of political correctness made foreign villains seem anachronistic at best and downright racist at worst."[25] In *Die Hard 2*, a U.S. Army Colonel named Stuart (William Sadler) leads a band of mercenaries who take control of Washington D.C.'s Dulles airport and commandeer a runway so that a fugitive Latin American general, Ramon Esperanza (Franco Nero), can land and, with the mercenaries' help, escape extradition by U.S. drug authorities. Esperanza is a notorious, high-level drug-dealer, and while it is never very clear why Stuart and his men are determined to help Esperanza, their threats to blow up airplanes and destroy innocent lives carry more of the blowback implication that we saw operating in *Black Sunday*, namely that unsavory aspects of U.S. foreign policy have the potential to cause trouble at home. The Esperanza-Stuart relationship seems to have been modeled on the Manuel Noriega–CIA relationship, which eventually soured, producing an invasion of Panama by the U.S. amid accusations that Noriega was running drugs. There are also echoes in the film's premise of the durable but unsubstantiated charges that the CIA used drug shipments in the 1980s to help fund the Nicaraguan "Contras" in their effort to overthrow the elected government of Nicaragua. In that era, the United States used Honduras as a military base to support the Contras and intimidate the Nicaraguan government. In the film, the first mercenary that hero John McClane kills is revealed to have been an American adviser in Honduras.

So the film connects Stuart's terrorism to the U.S. military role in Latin America, although this connection is definitely a subsidiary aspect of the story. The main business involves Stuart's threats to exercise extraordinary violence against airplane passengers, and, in a sequence that possibly took its cue from Hitchcock in *Sabotage*, Stuart's men sabotage the electronic ground-level information that the airport sends to planes coming in, causing them to think the ground is 200 feet lower than it actually is. One flight inbound from London carries 230 people on board. It's low on fuel and needs to land, and, as Hitchcock did with the bus passengers in *Sabotage*, director Renny Harlin portrays the people on the plane who are about to die, humanizing them, and then brutally extinguishes their lives as the pilots unwittingly fly the aircraft into the ground. The explosion that results is one of the film's key moments, one of its "money shots," the kind of expensive image of something big blowing up that audiences had come to see.

In *Chill Factor* (1999), an embittered Army officer aims to steal a deadly chemical weapon and sell it to the highest international bidder. In *Broken Arrow* (1996) a rogue officer in the Air Force steals two nuclear missiles and intends to extort $250 million from the government in exchange for not detonating the bombs. Major Deak Deakins (John Travolta) is a stealth bomber pilot who is embittered because he's been passed over for promotion, so, rather like Colonel Stuart, he recruits a band of military commandos to assist with his extortion plans and help him transport the bombs to their destination. In *Die Hard 2*, once Stuart has taken over the airport, an Army Special Forces unit arrives to try and stop him, but the members of this unit turn out to be in league with him, thereby broadening the web of the conspiracy. In *Broken Arrow*, by contrast, Deakins' treachery is offset and counterbalanced by the heroic actions of his copilot, Captain Riley Hale (Christian Slater), who risks his life to find the bombs and stop Deakins. If, then, *Die Hard 2* suggests that terrorism can begin at home, *Broken Arrow* is more ambivalent about the extent to which the institutions of government or the military may help to inculcate a terrorist response. By contrast, *Under Siege* (1992) is far less ambivalent. Its villain, William Stranix (Tommy Lee Jones), is a rogue CIA officer who has become psychotic and uses his agency-trained skills at violence to hijack a battleship and seize its nuclear-tipped cruise missiles, which he hopes to sell on the black market. He is assisted by the battleship's executive officer, Commander Krill (Gary Busey).

As *Die Hard 2*, *Broken Arrow*, and *Under Siege* suggest, fears that rogue or disaffected elements in the American military or intelligence community might turn to terrorism furnished a durable template for thriller narratives in this period. But the template offered a crude conception of terrorism—the villains here are mentally unbalanced or criminal or are angry because the government isn't treating them or their friends well. In contrast, Timothy McVeigh, who is the clearest real-life analogue of the homegrown military movie terrorists, destroyed the Alfred P. Murrah Federal Building in Oklahoma City in what he considered to be a political action. Whereas movies like *Broken Arrow* and *Under Siege* give us villains who are raving, out-of-control narcissists, McVeigh explained his actions in composed and clear terms, without the kind of ranting that movie villains display. He said that he attacked the government (personified for him in the Murrah building) because of its violent assaults on the Branch Davidian headquarters at Waco, Texas, and on Randy Weaver and his family at Ruby Ridge in Idaho (both events were seen by McVeigh as examples of excessive federal government power and its abuse of liberty). During the FBI raid on the Weaver property in 1992, federal agents and a sniper wounded Weaver and killed his son and his wife. At Waco in 1993, the Treasury Department's Bureau of Alcohol, Tobacco, and Firearms (ATF) raided the Davidian ranch, precipitating a gunfight in which six Davidians and four ATF agents died. The FBI then laid siege to the ranch for fifty-one days, playing blaring music and amplified animal screams as part of a psychological warfare strategy. The FBI fired tear gas into the building, and a devastating fire broke out. Seventy-six Davidians died, twenty-one of them children. McVeigh had gone to Waco to witness the siege.

He had been a decorated soldier in the Gulf War, honored with the Bronze Star, an award for bravery and meritorious service. But he was disturbed by the violence directed against Iraqis in the war, and his experiences there helped to turn him against the American government. Waco and Ruby Ridge solidified this alienation. In a letter to writer Gore Vidal, he explained why he blew up the Murrah building, where the ATF and FBI had regional offices. "Foremost, the bombing was a retaliatory strike: a counter-attack, for the cumulative raids (and subsequent violence and damage) that federal agents had participated in over the preceding years (including but not limited to Waco)."[26] He continued, "I decided to send a message to a government that was becoming increasingly hostile, by bombing a government building and the government employees within that building who represent that government. Bombing the Murrah Federal Building was morally and strategically equivalent to the U.S. hitting a government building in Serbia, Iraq, or other nations." He concluded, "From this perspective what occurred in Oklahoma City was no different than what Americans rain on the heads of others all the time."

McVeigh's example informs *The Rock* (1996), a big-budget Don Simpson–Jerry Bruckheimer action extravaganza. Angry because the U.S. government abandoned his special operations group in the Gulf War, Marine Corp. Brigadier General Frank Hummel (Ed Harris), gathers a group of mercenaries and steals fifteen VX poison gas rockets. Hummel's group positions these rockets on Alcatraz Island, aims them at San Francisco, and threatens to release the gas on the city unless its demands are met. Like McVeigh, the Gulf War has turned Hummel against his government. The film begins with imagery of Hummel reverently donning his uniform and visiting his wife's grave. He kisses the headstone, lays his medal atop it, tells her that he misses her, and asks, for what he is about to do, that she not think less of him. The opening presents Hummel as an honorable and decent officer who takes extreme action only as a last resort and after deep reflection. These are also the terms by which McVeigh viewed himself and his actions.

Once they have set up the missiles at Alcatraz, Hummel gives his men a pep talk, telling them that, for what they are about to do, they will be branded as traitors, just as George Washington and Thomas Jefferson were branded as traitors by the British government when, in fact, they were acting as the greatest of patriots. McVeigh, too, felt that he was expressing a higher form of patriotism by attacking a government that, in his view, had become tyrannical and oppressive. In McVeigh's and Hummel's logic, the U.S. government is an unjust regime which true patriots are duty bound to resist. But whereas McVeigh believed that he was counterattacking the government using its own methods,

FIGURE 1.2 In *The Rock,* Frank Hummel (Ed Harris) prepares to launch poison gas rockets into the heart of San Francisco. The figure of Timothy McVeigh stands behind this homegrown terrorist. (Frame enlargement)

Hummel's plan is an extortion scheme. He tells the men that his group, Marine Force Recon, carried out illegal operations throughout the world, about which the government maintained a policy of official denial. Eighty-three of his men were killed in China, Laos, Iraq, and other places. The families of these men were denied benefits and told lies about how the men died. Hummel says he's choked on these lies all of his career and now they must stop, and his action with the VX missiles is designed to expose the government's duplicity. One of his demands will be for money to pay reparations to the families.

The Rock has worked so hard to endorse Hummel's sense of moral outrage that it seems not to notice his unsavory background. What sort of illegal operations did Hummel and his group carry out? The movie doesn't say, but it seems reasonable to assume that these included assassinations, sabotage, bombings, and other acts of violence against regimes that the U.S. was not at war with. To people on the receiving end, these might be viewed as acts of terrorism. What Hummel wants, therefore, is not for the government to renounce these acts of violent subversion but to carry them out openly, although being honest about such policies would instantly make the United States into a renegade and rogue nation. Hummel's policy would brand the U.S. as a nation openly sponsoring terrorism and turn it into an international outlaw. But the film seems unaware of this eventuality.

The Rock offers some counterarguments to Hummel's position. One of the heroes, John Mason (Sean Connery), tells Hummel, "I don't quite see how you cherish the memory of the dead by killing another million, and this is not combat. It's an act of lunacy." A Navy Seal commander (Michael Biehn), sent to retake Alcatraz, tells Hummel that his duty is to defend the country against enemies external and internal, but then he admits that he agrees with Hummel's political position. Counterarguments are not given much weight in the film, and in the climax Hummel reveals that it was all a bluff, that he never intended to fire the missiles, as if that excuses his previous actions. Inevitably, the story's conflicts are resolved with numerous fireballs, gunfights, and explosions.

Marketing terrorism for entertainment, as all the films examined in this chapter do, seems to entail that audiences and filmmakers share a tacit acceptance, within the realm of imaginary fiction, that death on a massive scale is necessary, even if it is not overtly and openly desirable according to the moral terms proposed by the narratives. Its necessity is not moral but rather is a matter of narrative need and aesthetic appeal. The narrative basis lies in the manner in which massive death and destruction furnish the premise and motor of the story, and its aesthetic basis lies in the manner in which filmmakers treat violent slaughter in a voluptuous and sensual way. The attention lavished on explosions and fireballs, for example, is close and loving. In the imaginary realm, then, most of these films propose that terrorism is a desirable act; within the realm of fiction, terrorist violence provides the transaction between filmmaker and audience with its reason for being. It may be startling to contemplate this fact, and certainly the stories in the films overtly disavow any affiliation with terrorist violence and often portray terrorists as nasty villains. And viewers who enjoy the big bangs are not thereby assenting to real-world violence. Nevertheless, these films need their terrorists as a way of motivating the explosions that provide the appeals of visual spectacle.

This goes some way toward accounting for the moral confusion that sometimes creeps into these movies, the way in which characters such as Frank Hummel are portrayed as hero and villain or in which a Deke Deakins in *Broken Arrow,* whom Travolta plays with boyish charm and enthusiasm, is proffered as a companionable guide to mayhem. They do objectionable things, but the movies often find these characters to be charismatic and appealing. A case in point is the freelance arms merchant, Gabriel Shear, whom Travolta plays with rakish charm in *Swordfish,* a film that was released in June 2001, just before the al Qaeda airplane attacks. Shear is another of the "one of us" villains. He's a kind of special operations commando in league with Senator James Reisman (Sam Shepard), who is chairman of a joint subcommittee on crime. Together, they plan for Shear to rob a bank that contains billions in stored DEA money, and the film begins in medias res, with Shear at the bank holding hostages while police and FBI agents encircle the building. Shear has rigged the hostages with C4 explosive and packets of ball bearings. When one of the hostages explodes, the ball bearings devastate the surrounding property and, of course, shred the hostage and a few police officers. Shear's ruthless and deadly nature is thus established.

But the film wants to have things two ways, giving us Shear as a cold-blooded terrorist and as a hero defending America. When Shear reveals his reasons for stealing the money, it turns out that he plans to launch a war on overseas terrorists, and the money will fund it. He belongs to an ultra-secret, elite group called Black Cell, which, according to the film, J. Edgar Hoover founded in the 1950s to protect American freedoms at all costs. "That's my job," Shear tells Stanley Jobson (Hugh Jackman), a computer hacker Shear is coercing to help in the bank job. Americans take their freedoms for granted, Shear says, and have no idea what it really takes to protect those freedoms. As in *The Rock,* the charismatic terrorist whom the film offers as a figure to admire honors a conception of freedom that would make the U.S. a rogue, outlaw nation. Shear tells Stanley that America is at war with terrorist states. "Someone must bring their war to them. They bomb a church, we bomb ten. They hijack a plane, we take out an airport. They execute American tourists; we tactically nuke an entire city. Our job is to make terrorism so horrific that it becomes unthinkable to attack Americans." Shear admits to being a murderer but one with ethics and rules. His ethic is rooted in a concept of the greatest good—people will have to die so that American citizens may continue with their lives unmolested.

Shear's willingness to kill innocent people leads Stanley to say that he's no different from the terrorists he's after. It's a valid point but one that the film insists on fudging. The story concludes by endorsing Shear's mission. He gets away with the DEA money, eludes the FBI, and embarks on his program of vengeance against overseas terrorists. At the end we see Shear and his girlfriend in Monte Carlo. Shear pilots a boat out to sea as a jaunty musical theme kicks in, and a newscaster in voice-over on the soundtrack announces that a notorious Middle Eastern terrorist suspected of bombing the U.S. embassy in Istanbul was killed in an explosion aboard a yacht in the Mediterranean, the third such killing of a terrorist in as many weeks. The film ends here, switching gears to make Shear a hero, and giving us a glimpse of Shear on his mission, portrayed as an exciting and glamorous adventure.

Of course, it helps that he isn't blowing up a church or nuking an entire city as he had threatened to do. Who could object in the imaginary world of a movie to the targeted assassination of a terrorist, especially when his crime resonates with real headlines? The fictional bombing of the Istanbul embassy evokes one of al Qaeda's opening acts of aggression against the United States, the August 1998 bombings of the U.S. embassies in Nairobi (Kenya) and Dar es Salaam (Tanzania). The bombings killed nearly 300 people and wounded more than 5,000. In this respect, Shear provides an imaginary solution to real events, representing a wish-fulfilling response to circumstances that in the real world proved more complicated and intractable. In 1996, for example, the CIA's Counterterrorist Center established a special office whose purpose was to track Osama bin Laden's activities, and the following year the CIA began formulating plans to abduct bin Laden and bring him to trial for funding terrorist activities from his base in Afghanistan. These efforts accelerated following the 1998 embassy bombings. But, according to Steve Coll, in his history of the CIA in Afghanistan, taking the next step, toward an official policy of trying to kill bin Laden, proved to be very difficult for the CIA because of the Presidential ban on assassinations signed by Gerald Ford and renewed by President Reagan. Coll describes a lengthy series of debates in 1997 and 1998 by agency officials and White House lawyers over the legality of undertaking a program to hit bin Laden amid fear that such a program could tarnish the CIA. "They spent long hours on subtle legal issues that arose in America's lethal covert action programs: When is a targeted killing not an assassination?

When is it permissible to shoot a suspect overseas in the course of an attempted arrest?"[27] Moreover, in 1998 the Lewinsky scandal had weakened Clinton's Presidency and undermined his abilities to launch covert actions that might be both risky and controversial. As Coll points out, Clinton could have authorized the CIA to use deadly force against bin Laden. "The assassination ban did not apply to attacks carried out in preemptive self-defense where it seemed likely that the target was planning to strike the United States."[28] But Clinton did not take this step. Instead, he signed a series of top-secret Memorandums of Notification (MON) that seemed to lean in all directions, authorizing the CIA to arrest bin Laden, to shoot down his helicopter, and to kill him. As Coll writes, "The exact language Clinton sent to [CIA headquarters] in his bin Laden–related MONS zigzagged on the issue of lethal force."[29] CIA head George Tenet, as well, canceled several operations at the last moment. As Tim Weiner writes in his history of the CIA, "Commanders in the Pentagon and civilian leaders in the White House continually backed down from the political gamble of a military mission against bin Laden."[30] This hesitation angered some members of the CIA's bin Laden unit, who felt that there had been several good opportunities to kill him.

In contrast, then, to the gratifications offered by a fantasy figure like Gabriel Shear, who, in pursuit of terrorists, acts above the law with impunity and ruthlessness, the actual events surrounding U.S. efforts to go after Osama bin Laden were far more halting, hesitant, conflicted, and ambivalent. While some CIA field agents lobbied for bin Laden's assassination, President Clinton instead opted to fire cruise missiles into Afghanistan at locations that intelligence suggested bin Laden might be found. But he wasn't there, and the outcome on 9/11 of these failed policies was evident.

This gap between the fantasy solutions proposed by *Swordfish* and the complexities and hesitancies that characterized actions in the real world is a striking one. At a time when the United States was tripping over its own feet in an effort to get bin Laden, the film proffers the charismatic and ruthless Shear as the answer for dealing with terrorist enemies. Moreover, the terms of the movie's fantasy suggest a collective yearning to dispense with the legal rules of nation-to-nation conduct in the interests of dispensing vigilante justice. Like *Nighthawks,* the film also suggests that America's democratic foundation might be a very fragile thing and that the government might move quickly to sacrifice it, although in some ways the movie seems to view this as a good thing. But these reflections are neither deep nor substantive. Until 9/11, most films in Hollywood's cycle of terrorism-as-entertainment go out of their way to avoid evoking real-world complexities or to overly complicate their storylines with irony or competing moral perspectives. In fact, some of the most reliable story props ensured the least irony. "Mad bomber" characters, for example, provided effective hooks for action and an abstract way of motivating it that might avoid real-world complexities. Why is he planting bombs? Because he's crazy. In the stripped-down, straight-ahead plotting of an action-adventure movie, no further motivation is needed, but this level of abstraction also shows how disconnected from the actual world many of these movies had become.

Mad bomber stories, which go back at least to Richard Lester's *Juggernaut*, proved to be a trusty standby in the period. The Wesley Snipes action film, *Passenger 57* (1992), pits Snipes as hero John Cutter against a psychotic aristocrat with a penchant for blowing up airplanes. Charles Rane (Bruce Payne) thrives on chaos and violence and has already bombed four airplanes when he and his men hijack a plane carrying Cutter to the West Coast. Cutter fights back aboard the aircraft and eventually defeats Rane. The film's terrorist-as-psycho premise makes for efficient action storytelling because motivations never need be explored. Rane has no political demands and is a figure of simple, stark anarchy. The terrorist-as-psycho also makes an appearance in the form of the mad bomber played by Dennis Hopper in *Speed* (1994). Howard Payne (Hopper) is an embittered, retired ex-bomb-squad officer who bombs buildings and busses as a means of extorting money. The film makes a flip gesture toward the political world of terrorism only to mock it. Aboard a bomb-rigged bus, Annie Porter (Sandra Bullock) asks the film's hero, Jack Traven (Keanu Reeves), "Why is all this happening? I mean, what'd we do? Bomb the guy's country or something?" Traven replies, "No, it's just a guy who wants money."

Another mad bomber creates havoc in *Blown Away* (1994) but, again, not for political reasons. Ryan Gaerity, a psychopathic IRA member, escapes from a prison in Northern Ireland and comes to Boston where he learns that another ex-IRA member, James Dove (Jeff Bridges), now works for the Boston Bomb Squad. Gaerity hates Dove for purely personal reasons that date to their days in the IRA, and he launches a bombing campaign designed to kill everyone in Dove's squad. As Gaerity tells him, "I've come here to create a new country for you called chaos and a new government called anarchy." Chaos and anarchy substitute in the film for anything approaching a political motivation. The IRA also figures in *The Devil's Own* (1997). On the run from the police, IRA member Rory Devane (Brad Pitt) hides out in America, living with a solid New York family headed by cop Tom O'Meara (Harrison Ford). In contrast to the mad bomber plot of *Blown Away*, however, *The Devil's Own* spends little screen time depicting terrorist acts, focusing instead on the friendship that develops between Devane and O'Meara. The film is a psychological drama, not an action thriller like the other pictures in this film cycle.

Another prominent terrorist-themed film of the period was *Air Force One* (1997), a preposterous fantasy about a group of Russian terrorists who seize the President's plane in order to blackmail the U.S. and Soviet governments into releasing a right-wing, nationalist Russian general from prison. Harrison Ford, as the President, goes mano a mano with the terrorists and, of course, wins the day. In the film's prologue, President Marshall (Ford) is in Moscow, where he announces that the U.S. will no longer tolerate state-sponsored terrorism. About states that support terror, he declares that it's their turn to be afraid and says that the new policy of the U.S. will be to strike militarily at any government that supports or sponsors terrorism. Immediately, in the storyline, Saddam Hussein moves two Republican Guard brigades to Iraq's northern border. This plot device demonstrates that, following Desert Storm, Saddam and Iraq were still handy villains for Hollywood storytelling, but, more importantly, the prologue and Marshall's announcement reflect the prevailing view of U.S. terrorist policy in that period, which regarded threats as mainly coming from other states, such as Iran or Libya, which funded such groups as Hezbollah and organized bomb plots such as the one that brought down Pan Am Flight 103. In 1996, when this film was made, the international Islamist threat, which was stateless and globally dispersed, and had gained strength during the previous decade in Afghanistan, largely was off the government's radar. In this regard, the perspective on terrorism in *Air Force One* has an archaic quality about it, at least in terms of where the most potent threat was now originating. Once the hijacking gets under way, the film becomes increasingly far-fetched and disconnected from any actual world in which terrorism might really occur. *Air Force One*, then, opens with a prologue that situates the action within the perceived threat coordinates of the period only to rather quickly abandon these in the interests of far-out action-adventure.

CASUALTIES OF THE POST-9/11 LANDSCAPE

The events of 9/11 made the prevailing fantasy world of movie terrorism look unacceptably irresponsible and disconnected, at least for a little while. Two prominent films—*Collateral Damage* and *The Sum of All Fears*—in production before September 11 and released after the attacks, seemed instantly anachronistic and irrelevant because 9/11 had obliterated Hollywood's terrorist-thriller conventions. Released on February 4, 2002, *Collateral Damage* was an Arnold Schwarzenegger action thriller. Arnold plays a fireman, Gordy Brewer, whose wife and son are blown up in a bombing of Colombia's embassy in Los Angeles. They are having a snack at a sidewalk café next door when the notorious and elusive Colombian terrorist El Lobo (Cliff Curtis) arrives disguised as an L.A. cop and detonates the bomb. The film's director, Andrew Davis, stated that the bombing was filmed before 9/11 and that his main point of visual reference was Pontecorvo's *The Battle of Algiers*, which contains several bombing scenes in which Pontecorvo's camera surveys the damage to people and property.[31]

Pontecorvo's film, however, is much more vivid in dramatizing the dazed, stunned, and pained reactions of the survivors, and he also spent more screen time humanizing those who were about to die. Davis gives the camera to Gordy's wife and son before the blast, but the other victims remain anonymous, helping to make the violence relatively sanitized. Pontecorvo showed bodies being extracted from the rubble and burned survivors staggering out of it, but there are almost no bodies visible in the aftermath of the explosion in *Collateral Damage*. Following the explosion, the narrative jumps forward to the FBI investigators on scene, and all the bodies have been removed save for a few that are tastefully draped with sheets. There are no screams of pain and confusion, howls of rage or despair, except briefly from Gordy as he witnesses the bombing from across the street. The sequence is emotionally flat, expressionless, save for the special-effects pyrotechnics on hand in the fireballs that erupt from the buildings. The scene, in other words, largely erases the human cost of the explosion, except as a means for motivating the film's revenge plot, which has Gordy improbably traveling to Colombia to hunt and execute El Lobo.

The scene's lack of human feeling provides a reliable measure of how terrorism was functioning in the world of action-adventure. It served to motivate the hero's righteous vengeance and carried little emotional valence beyond that function. Thus we accept that Gordy's wife and kid need to die—if they don't, we don't have a story, and we won't get to see Arnold in action. In the world of action-adventure, people are expendable because they are plot devices, a characteristic of the form that shows yet another point of affinity with the acts of terrorism that are being depicted. Upon the film's release, the bombing scene was criticized as being in bad taste; the slaughter on September 11 had made it so. But it wasn't merely the film's sanitizing of bomb violence and its reduction of human tragedy to a plot device that made *Collateral Damage* so out-of-synch with the period in which it was released. It was the way the film so completely falsified the political world of contemporary terrorism.

The film's portrait is anachronistic. It looks backward in time, as if it were still part of the Cold War landscape, specifically, the United States' covert war during the 1980s against indigenous guerrilla movements in Latin and South America which the U.S. perceived as Soviet proxies.[32] The guerrilla groups, active in Nicaragua, El Salvador, Guatemala, and Colombia, were manifestations of the global rise of anticolonial liberation movements in the post–World War II period. A coalition of groups in Colombia challenged its government and military—the Revolutionary Armed Forces of Colombia, the 19th of April Movement, the National Liberation Army, and the Popular Liberation Army. As in El Salvador and Guatemala, the challenge by leftist guerrillas elicited a program of state-supported terrorism from the ruling authorities in the form of violence by paramilitary groups and death squads.[33] Despite the egregious human rights record of these countries, the United States provided massive military assistance to the Colombian government, as it did for El Salvador and Guatemala.

The fanciful spin given to these events by *Collateral Damage* is the invention of the rogue terrorist El Lobo, who has decided to strike back at the U.S. for what he sees as interference in Colombia. "As long as America continues its aggression in Colombia, we will bring the war home to you, and you will not feel safe in your own beds. Colombia is not your country. Get out now." This rhetoric and tactic of launching wholesale violence against Americans in their own country had no basis in the left-wing guerrilla struggles of the period, but it did characterize Osama bin Laden's declaration of war against Americans, which he launched from Afghanistan in 1998. In his manifesto for the International Islamic Front for Jihad Against Jews and Crusaders, he declared, "The judgment to kill and fight Americans and their allies, whether civilians or military, is an obligation for every Muslim who is able to do so in any country."[34] Thus, El Lobo's particular brand of terrorism is more al Qaeda than *revolucionario guerrillera*. Nevertheless, the film spins contemporary terrorism in terms of 1980s politics, as when offering a spokesman for the fictitious Latin American Solidarity Committee, based in Los Angeles, who defends El Lobo's terrorism. The scene seems meant as a slam of such prominent 1980s groups as the Committee in Solidarity with the People of El Salvador, sympathetic to the Salvadoran guerrillas.

The film's climax, in which El Lobo tries to bomb the State Department Annex in Washington D.C., recycles the 1993 bombing of the World Trade Center. An associate of El Lobo drives a white van containing the bomb into the underground parking garage of the Annex, and El Lobo plans to detonate it by remote control. In 1993 Ramzi Yousef drove a yellow Ford Econoline van into the underground parking garage of the World Trade Center, between the Vista Hotel and the North Tower, and detonated the equivalent of 1,500 pounds of dynamite, killing six people and wounding more than 1,000. But the fantasy offered by the movie gives us a hero who thwarts the bombing and kills El Lobo and his associate. As we have seen, a principal comfort offered by Hollywood's action thrillers is the continuing reassurance that government authorities and security officials are acting aggressively to keep ahead of terrorist plots. In Hollywood's version of terrorism, American officials are quick and efficient in their responses. They see the terrorist plots coming. They often engage in physical combat with the terrorists and generally thwart them when the bombs are seconds away from detonation. This, for example, is the scenario of *Black Sunday*. In *Collateral Damage*, El Lobo sets up a decoy bombing of Union Station, but the FBI, CIA, and D.C. police all mobilize quickly and efficiently to track the threat. In *The Peacemaker* (1997), the FBI, FEMA, the National Guard, and the NYPD act in concert and move preemptively to thwart a nuclear bombing of New York City. And on the television show *24*, counterterrorism officials remain aggressively abreast of ever-unfolding attacks.

Reality, thus far, is much less encouraging. American intelligence did not foresee the attacks against the World Trade Center, the embassies in Kenya and Tanzania, and the USS *Cole*. In the years before 9/11, the CIA was on hyper-alert because director George Tenet and the agency's Counterterrorist Center felt very strongly that a massive attack from al Qaeda was imminent. Despite this, Mohammed Atta and his conspirators were able to enter the country and hijack the planes. Moreover, institutional rivalries between the FBI and CIA, and laws governing their investigatory jurisdictions, hindered intelligence analysis before 9/11.[35] On that day the institutionalized tensions between New York City's police and fire departments harmed the abilities of these first responders to communicate with one another about the crisis at the World Trade Center.[36] Each department, for example, operated on a different radio frequency. This disparity between the recent history of terrorism and Hollywood's version of it suggests that a chief function of these films is to first evoke and then to allay public anxieties by portraying, much as did the 1950s science fiction films about giant monsters threatening cities, coolly successful responses by military and security forces to threats against the state.

If the response comes too late, as it does in *The Sum of All Fears*, Hollywood fantasy narratives still work hard to provide reassurance. Released on May 29, 2002, the film gave audiences a younger version of Jack Ryan (Ben Affleck), the hero of Tom Clancy novels who previously had been seen on screen as an older character in *The Hunt for Red October* (1990), *Patriot Games* (1992), and *Clear and Present Danger* (1994). In *The Sum of All Fears*, terrorists detonate a nuclear bomb and destroy Baltimore. Ryan and the intelligence community are aware of the unfolding plot but cannot stop it in time. U.S. President Robert Fowler (James Cromwell) and his entourage are in Baltimore at the stadium watching a football game, and Ryan barely has time to warn the group that the bomb is going to detonate in the stadium. Moments before it goes off, the Secret Service evacuates the President. The film's depiction of the explosion may be symptomatic of the newly sensitive context for such depictions that followed 9/11. Whereas terrorist thrillers before 9/11 positively luxuriated in fireballs and thunderous audio effects, *The Sum of All Fears* portrays the explosion in an oblique and indirect manner. As the President is being evacuated, the action cuts to a downtown hospital where Ryan's lover, Dr. Cathy Muller (Bridget Moynahan), works. Electronic noise suddenly replaces the live feed on a television set behind Muller, and a split second later a shock wave blows out the large window facing her, knocking Muller and her colleagues backwards and out of the frame. The scene then cuts to the President's convoy, heading out of town. The spreading shock wave engulfs the cars and knocks them around like toys. Ryan is in a helicopter nearby, and the shock wave throws it out of the sky. The sequence has shown no fireball, no roiling clouds of flame, no multiple explosions, no imagery of mighty buildings crashing to the ground. The visual lexicon of terrorist thrillers, as it has existed for more than a decade, is largely abandoned.

The film spends rather more time on the aftermath of the explosion, unusual in this genre, but even this attention is sanitized because most of it is concentrated on a rescue mission outside the city for the President. When Ryan does drive into the devastation downtown, the film gives us a few quick shots of burning rubble but no long shots that show the scale of the destruction. Baltimore itself, as a major urban center, remains largely off-camera, as do people. Just as the film hides the scale of property destruction, it avoids a portrait of the massive death and suffering that must have accompanied the blast. There are no burn victims, no dismembered corpses, no dead children, and there is no radiation. Ryan is hit by the explosive shock wave, and he drives through ground zero shortly after the blast. He experiences no radiation poisoning, and apparently neither does anyone else. Cathy Muller survives with barely a scratch, despite all that flying glass, and in the film's final scene, the two of them relax on the grass near the White House, and they joke about getting married. Baltimore may be rubble, but its fate certainly hasn't interfered with the love life of our hero and his girlfriend. The epic slaughter that climaxes the film has left no lingering scars of any kind, neither physical nor psychological.

This portrait of the nuking of Baltimore offers audiences a most perfect expression of their anxieties about weapons of mass destruction. The film evokes these fears and then allays them by suggesting that, should the worst occur, it really won't be so bad. It certainly won't interfere with our hero's wedding plans, and the filmmakers won't do anything as crass as showing thousands of dead bodies. This duplicity at the climax of *The Sum of All Fears* is the most egregious to be found in the cycle of terrorist-thriller films. Moreover, in the Tom Clancy novel that was the source for the film, the villains were a hodge-podge that included German communists, an American Indian, and Palestinians. While the film was in preproduction, the Council on American-Islamic Relations (CAIR) persuaded the filmmakers that they ought not to depict Middle Eastern characters as terrorists. CAIR, the Arab-American Anti-Discrimination Committee, and other groups had been very critical of such depictions in past films including *The Siege, True Lies,* and *Executive Decision.* The film's director, Phil Alden Robinson, agreed with CAIR's recommendation and wrote the organization, "I hope that you will be reassured that I have no intention of promoting negative images of Muslims or Arabs, and I wish you the best in your continuing efforts to combat discrimination."[37] The events of 9/11 rendered this decision controversial, with numerous commentators charging that it represented a form of capitulation that served to disavow the Islamist threat to America.

9/11 also made CAIR newly controversial. Formed in 1994, the group was dedicated to promoting an understanding of Islam amongst non-Islamic publics and to safeguarding the civil rights of American Muslims. After 9/11, critics charged that the organization had financial and personnel ties to terrorist groups, which CAIR has denied. CAIR has been active in many arenas, which includes the media, where it has regularly scrutinized depictions of Arabic and Muslim characters in film and television programming.

The changes recommended by CAIR, and which the filmmakers accepted on *The Sum of All Fears,* helped to make the film especially disconnected from the new context that 9/11 had established. The film proffered an international cabal of neo-Nazis as the villains, a group led by Dressler (Alan Bates), an aristocrat with ambitions for world domination. As Jonah Goldberg observed, "Whereas in real life most neo-Nazis smash cans of beer against their heads while dancing in the woods, in Hollywood's vision they wear perfectly tailored suits and plot world domination from the highest corridors of power."[38] In the film's nonsensical storyline, Dressler explains his objectives. He says that it is wrong to think that, in the struggle between communism and capitalism, fascism was "just a hiccup." The followers of Hitler thrive, he claims, and his goal is to provoke a nuclear war between Russia and the U.S. in which they will destroy each other, after which his Nazis can take over the world. He neglects to mention that the world might be a tad radioactive. While the preproduction plot revisions, therefore, were well intentioned, the resulting storyline seemed especially irrelevant after 9/11. As numerous commentators pointed out, neo-Nazis were the one group that nobody would object to as villains, but they lacked resonance when pitched as terrorists in the contemporary world.

While these attributes of the film—its villains and its envisioning of terrorist violence—work to disconnect it from its contemporary context, one of the narrative events in the depicted Baltimore bombing does resonate unpleasantly with reported events just before 9/11. In the film, President Fowler and his officials evacuate the stadium, but the public is not informed about the threat. The rationale in the story is that there simply is no time to issue a warning, and Fowler says, from the back of his limousine as it rushes away, "Get those people out of the stadium." But, receiving no warning, the fans in the stadium are vaporized. One of the most contentious issues that has surrounded the events of 9/11 is what the government knew or didn't know, and conspiracy theories postulate that the Bush administration had full knowledge of the coming attacks.[39] Unusual items reported in the news have helped fuel these suspicions. CBS News, for example, reported on July 26, 2001, that Attorney General John Ashcroft had stopped flying commercial airlines following an FBI threat assessment.[40] Following 9/11, CBS News anchor Dan Rather is reported to have said that the Ashcroft warnings indicated a high level of concern and asked, "Why wasn't it shared with the public at large?"[41] *Newsweek* reported that a group of Pentagon officials had canceled flights just before 9/11. "*Newsweek* has learned that while U.S. intelligence received no specific warning, the state of alert had been high during the past two weeks, and a particularly urgent warning may have been received the night before the attacks, causing some top Pentagon brass to cancel a trip. Why that same information was not available to the 266 people who died aboard the four hijacked commercial aircraft may become a hot topic on the Hill."[42] In this context, the film's depiction of government officials evacuating from the stadium, while the public is left in the dark about a looming threat, is the single detail in the film that connects most directly with the events of 9/11, as reported, suspected, or theorized. Otherwise, *The Sum of All Fears* locates terrorism in a mostly imaginary landscape.

ISLAMIST TERROR ON FILM

While movie terrorists before 9/11 were a mostly daft lot—loonies, crackpots, and embittered ex-police or military officers—Islamist characters emerged as villains in only a few major productions. The films were heavily criticized by CAIR, and Hollywood thereafter seemed to back away from further depictions of Islamist jihadists. The films were *True Lies* (1994), *Executive Decision*

(1995), and *The Siege* (1998). Of the three, *True Lies* is the most simple-minded, offering cartoonish villains in a plot that is a knowing riff on James Bond adventures. A radical Palestinian group, Crimson Jihad, aims to detonate a nuclear bomb in an American city, and it's up to Arnold Schwarzenegger to stop it. The preposterous nature of the film's fantasy is evident in the casual way that the nuclear explosion is portrayed. After Arnold has beaten the bad guys, the bomb explodes out at sea, away from the Florida Keys, and the mushroom cloud furnishes the romantic backdrop for a kiss between hero Harry Tasker (Arnold) and his wife (Jamie Lee Curtis). The portrayal of Islamist terrorists in *Executive Decision* and *The Siege* is more serious. In *Executive Decision*, terrorists hijack an airplane and plan to use it as a bomb, while in *The Siege* a sustained bombing campaign in New York City leads the government to impose martial law, imperiling American democracy. In each case, the storyline resonates in clear and compelling ways with 9/11 and the events that followed. The films, therefore, merit close attention because of their claim to a degree of predictive insight.

As noted earlier, bombings and hijackings overseas against American targets helped to trigger the onset in the 1980s of Hollywood's terrorist thrillers. The subsequent emergence of Islamist movie terrorists in the 1990s seems also to have been connected to key events. As Jack Shaheen has shown, Arabic and Palestinian villains have a long history in Hollywood. But in earlier pictures, such as *Black Sunday* or *Wanted: Dead or Alive*, their grievances and motivations tended to be political (when they were given motivations at all). By contrast, the terrorists in *Executive Decision* and *The Siege* are motivated at least as powerfully by religion, and this was a new element in Hollywood's action thrillers. The timing was significant. The 1993 bombing of the World Trade Center had exposed the workings of a radical Islamist group based in New Jersey, which also had plans to destroy other area landmarks. *Executive Decision* was released just as the FBI and CIA were identifying in secret and classified bulletins an emerging new threat in the form of radical Islam. The FBI's 1995 report was entitled "Ramzi Ahmed Yousef: A New Generation of Sunni Islamic Terrorists." Yousef was the ringleader of the New Jersey bombers. The report stated that "a new generation of terrorists has appeared on the world stage over the past few years."[43] Rather than being a state-sponsored group, "Islamic extremists are working together to further their cause," and the groups are "autonomous and indigenous."

The trigger for the reports was the Yousef bombing. It was engineered by a group of radicals in the New York–New Jersey area that had coalesced around the figure of the blind sheikh Omar Abdel Rahman. Rahman's group also planned to bomb a host of area landmarks—the United Nations, the Lincoln and Holland Tunnels, the George Washington Bridge, the PATH train line, and FBI headquarters. In a classic example of blowback, Yousef had learned to make bombs in Afghanistan using materials and resources supplied by the CIA and its Pakistani counterpart, the ISI (Directorate for Inter-Services Intelligence). Yousef, and his uncle Khalid Sheikh Mohammed, had also targeted airplanes. In 1995 Philippine police found their computer files, which described plots to bomb a dozen American airplanes and to hijack a plane and fly it into the Pentagon.[44] The year after Yousef's failed attempt to topple the World Trade Center, Mohammed determined to try again and visited bin Laden in Afghanistan, where he pitched the idea of training pilots to fly airplanes into buildings.[45]

Other incidents in these years included the 1994 hijacking of Air France Flight 8969 by the Armed Islamic Group (GIA), which had formed in opposition to the Algerian government. During a standoff with the French police, the GIA demanded that the plane be fully stocked with fuel, a demand that elicited speculation that the group might attempt to fly it into a landmark building like the Eiffel Tower. The various plots in these years involving airlines and public landmarks led the CIA, in its secret 1995 report, to write about a "new terrorist phenomenon" involving a loose coalition of groups operating independently and transnationally to target the United States. Specifically, the agency warned, "Several targets are especially at risk: national symbols such as the White House and the Capitol, and symbols of U.S. capitalism such as Wall Street. . . . We assess that civil aviation will figure prominently among possible terrorist targets in the United States."[46] This was six years before the attacks of September 11.

The storyline of *Executive Decision* is rooted in this context of plots surfacing in 1994 and 1995 involving airline strikes on public buildings by radical Islamic groups. The film extrapolates from these a scenario in which an Islamist leader, Nagi Hassan (David Suchet), and a team of eight hijackers seize a passenger jet traveling from Athens to Dulles Airport in Washington D.C. As on 9/11, the hijackers terrorize the plane's passengers and intimidate them into submission. As on 9/11, the hijackers burst into the pilot's cabin. And, just as Mohamed Atta announced on American 11, one of the planes that would hit the World Trade Center, Hassan tells the passengers that if they remain calm, no harm will come to them. In his official demands to the U.S. government, Hassan says that he wants to exchange the plane and its passengers for money and the safe release of his boss, the international terrorist El Sayed Jaffa (Andreas Katasulas), who is now in U.S. custody. But this is just a ploy to get the aircraft inside U.S. airspace and over Washington D.C., where he plans to detonate a canister of stolen Soviet nerve toxin, DZ-5, which will kill thousands in the area. It is, thus, a suicide mission, and, in another of the film's details that presage the 9/11 hijackings, Hassan has not informed all of his cohorts about this. Some of them do not know that they are on a suicide mission.

When, after Jaffa is released by the U.S., one of them challenges Hassan and asks whether their mission is now over, Hassan replies, "Allah has chosen for us a task far greater than Jaffa's freedom. We are the true soldiers of Islam. Our destiny is to deliver the vengeance of Allah into the belly of the infidel." It is, thus, a suicide mission to be carried out in the name of Islam rather than for any specific political reasons. When his challenger tells Hassan, "This has nothing to do with Islam. This is not Allah's will. You're blinded by hatred," Hassan kills the man. Although this moment of dissent supplies a point of view that honors Islam and counters the Islamist fundamentalism of Hassan, it carries less weight in the film because the character is incidental to the plot, compared with Hassan's motives which are central to the story. And it was this identification of Islamist fundamentalism with terrorism that worried CAIR and led it to request that Warner Bros. edit offending material out of the film, which the studio declined to do.[47]

While Arabic characters traditionally have furnished convenient villains for Hollywood, as have many non-White ethnic, racial, or religious groups, and while *Executive Decision* is hardly an example of literate, nuanced filmmaking, peopled as it is by stock character types, it is also true that the film was drawing on contemporary events and sensing where a new generation of terrorists was likely to be found. In this regard, writing in *Middle East Quarterly*, Daniel Mandel points out that these portraits correspond to real phenomena familiar to the moviegoing audience and that CAIR's critique amounts to a position that films simply should not portray Islamist terrorism. He writes,

> *Verisimilitude is the all-important consideration and by that standard Hollywood can be vindicated. Accordingly, objections to the effect that Hollywood could not get away with substituting blacks or Jews in these movies' hateful roles miss the point. There are simply no Jewish versions of Usama bin Ladin or black versions of Sheikh Omar Abdul Rahman. Should there ever be, we are likely to see their fictionalized counterparts in Hollywood movies.*[48]

Hassan's suicide mission, for example, has numerous precedents, as does a scene that occurs near the beginning of the film in which one of Hassan's

FIGURE 1.3 An Islamist suicide bomber seconds before he destroys a Marriott Hotel in London, as portrayed in *Executive Decision*. (Frame enlargement)

followers walks into a Marriott hotel in London and detonates a dynamite vest attached to his chest. It shows the type of suicide bombing that came to the fore in the Middle East during the 1990s when Hamas used the tactic with devastating results against Israel. The imagery in the film has a haunting and iconic power because it connects with such brutal directness to the suicide bombers who were even then blowing up buses, pizzerias, and markets in Israel. And yet this kind of imagery—a suicide bombing against a civilian establishment—had not appeared before this in Hollywood's terrorist action films. This is the only such scene in the cycle of pictures released before 9/11. Several scenes in *The Siege* approximate this one, but none show a suicide bombing with such on-camera exactitude. And after 9/11 such scenes have been very rare.

The Tamil Tigers in Sri Lanka, fighting for Hindu Tamil secession from the ruling Sinhalese Buddhist majority, regularly employed suicide bombings (some say the Tigers invented this tactic) and used a female bomber to assassinate the former Indian Prime Minister Rajiv Gandhi in 1991. But the Tigers are not primarily a religious group and, therefore, do not have to wrestle with the issues that suicide poses within a religious tradition. Islamist terrorists do—there is a strong prohibition on suicide in the Qur'an. Thus when Middle Eastern terrorists took up suicide as a weapon—in the 1983 truck bombing of the Marine Barracks in Lebanon and in Hamas' attacks on Israel—self-annihilation had to be reconceptualized as martyrdom, which is an honorable course of action. This kind of revisionist thinking is controversial, as witnessed by the refusal of many Afghani jihadists to undertake the suicide missions against the Soviets advocated by their brethren from Saudi

Arabia, Jordan, and Algeria.[49] Thus, in the film, Hassan's challenger might also have responded that suicide is un-Islamic—except that, for Hassan, as for bin Laden and his associate Ayman al-Zawahiri, martyrdom in God's name is a calling. For Zawahiri, suicide bombers represent "a generation of mujahideen that has decided to sacrifice itself and its prosperity in the cause of God. That is because the way of death and martyrdom is a weapon that tyrants and their helpers, who worship their salaries instead of God, do not have."[50]

Thus the film's villain, Nagi Hassan, personifies these trends and embodies what Malise Ruthven has termed "a fury for God."[51] Ruthven notes, "Religious violence differs from violence in the 'secular' world by shifting the plane of action from what is mundane, and hence negotiable, to the arena of cosmic struggle, beyond the political realm."[52] Hassan's irresolute and unshakable demeanor suggests his belief that he is enacting a higher logic; he describes himself as "the sword of Allah." Such rhetoric is very like bin Laden's own:

> *Concerning the Muslims, I tell them to trust in the victory of God, and to answer the call of God, and the order of His Prophet, with jihad against world unbelief. And I swear by God, happy are those who are martyred today, happy are those who are honored to stand under the banner of Muhammad, under the banner of Islam, to fight the world Crusade. So let every person amongst them come forward to fight those Jews and Americans, the killing of whom is among the most important duties and most pressing things.*[53]

The tone and content of Hassan's remarks also are similar to the notes left behind by Sayyid Nosair, one of Yousef's collaborators in the 1993 World Trade Center bombing. In his journal, Nosair wrote that bringing down the Trade Center would be a means to "break and destroy the enemies of Allah."[54] Thus, when the film's hero, David Grant (Kurt Russell), and a team of commandos succeed in retaking the plane and disarming the bomb, rather than accept defeat and live to fight again another day, Hassan machine-guns the cockpit, killing the pilots and sending the aircraft into a death dive. He will not countenance the loss of his prospect for martyrdom, nor did the hijackers at the controls of United Flight 93, who in their last moments, as the passengers beat on the cockpit door, talked about flying the plane into the ground. Seconds later it did crash, either because of a struggle in the cockpit with the passengers or as an intentional act of suicidal martyrdom by the hijacker pilots.

But *Executive Decision*, which otherwise evokes numerous resonances with the events of 9/11, evades this outcome. David Grant is an amateur pilot, and he improbably gains control of the aircraft and lands it not safely but successfully. Like the other films in Hollywood's terrorist action cycle, *Executive Decision* evokes anxieties in order to allay them. The security forces that David represents carry the day with minimal loss of life except for the terrorists. And, like *Air Force One* and *Passenger 57*, but unlike the events on 9/11, the film offers the comforting vision of heroic combat on board the hijacked aircraft, with our heroes stealthily maneuvering their way through backdoor and below-floor compartments and passageways in order to get the drop on the terrorists and take them out.

Executive Decision was one of three films in this period that seemed especially prescient in envisioning events such as those that culminated on 9/11. The others are *The Siege* and *Fight Club* (though *Fight Club* is otherwise dissimilar in that it does not depict Islamist terrorism). *The Siege* lacks the reassuring emphasis on military derring-do that pervades *Executive Decision* and many other terrorist action films. Indeed, it aims to warn its viewers about several dangers to the republic, only one of which is terrorism. The other danger is the erosion of civil liberties that a war on terror can easily produce. Like many films of the 1990s, *The Siege* builds its storyline from a network of references to contemporary events, and, because this is a more self-conscious film than the others, its orientating references also include classic works of political cinema. Shots of the U.S. Army marching up a street in Brooklyn recall the imagery from Pontecorvo's *The Battle of Algiers* in which the French paratroopers march through Algiers. The title of the film recalls the title of Costa-Gavras' film about the Tupamaros guerrillas in Uruguay, *State of Siege* (1972), and a plot detail—the detention and torture of prisoners held in a sports stadium—recalls a similar practice of the Pinochet dictatorship in Chile as portrayed in Costa-Gavras' *Missing* (1982).

The film's self-awareness may result in part from Lawrence Wright's participation as one of the screenwriters. A journalist and scholar, Wright today is best known for his book, *The Looming Tower: Al-Qaeda and the Road to 9/11* (2007), which won the Pulitzer Prize and the National Book Award. After the book was published, Wright recalled his work on the film. He said that *The Siege*

> *anticipated, in certain eerie ways, the attacks on America by Islamist terrorists and the damage that these attacks would cause to our country and our civil liberties. While researching the film, I had the opportunity to speak to agents in the New York office of the FBI and hear their anxieties about possible strikes against the American homeland. "The Siege" reflects those concerns, which turned out to be so shockingly premonitory. When I watched the*

attacks on America that Tuesday morning in September, I thought, "This looks like a movie." Then I had the sickening realization, "This looks like my movie."[55]

The Siege constructs its storyline from the history of U.S. involvement in Iraq and Afghanistan. It invents a radical Iraqi sheikh, Ahmed bin Talal, who is wanted by the U.S. for launching terrorist attacks on U.S. facilities overseas. These include an actual bombing, the 1996 attack on Khobar Towers, a military complex in Dhahran, Saudi Arabia, housing American soldiers enforcing the no-fly zone in Iraq. News footage of the bombing opens the film, followed by footage of President Clinton responding to the Khobar attack. Clinton says, "The explosion appears to be the work of terrorists, and if that is the case, like all Americans I am outraged by it. . . . Those who did it will not go unpunished." Although this bombing is considered to have been the work of Hezbollah operating with Iranian support, in the film's fictional world it was engineered by bin Talal. In response to the attack and operating outside the law, a prestigious but maverick general, Devereaux (Bruce Willis), engineers the ambush and kidnapping of bin Talal, who is then held in a secret location that is not divulged even to senators and other high-ranking government officials.

It should by now be clear that the model for bin Talal is Osama bin Laden, whom the CIA aimed for years to kidnap from Afghanistan. Here the film grossly simplifies its sources. Bin Talal improbably travels unescorted in a single limousine, making the snatch an easy operation. By contrast, bin Laden never traveled alone, moved frequently, operated within an impenetrable ring of security, and was protected by the Taliban government. Reliable information about his location was rarely available; thus, the CIA could not launch snatch operations without relying on a certain amount of guesswork, and President Clinton settled for firing cruise missiles at targets where he potentially might have been. The film simplifies these realities in order to launch its premise—that the kidnapping of bin Talal triggers a series of terror attacks in Manhattan by jihadists motivated by rage over the kidnapping and by hatred for America.

As a result, three armed men with explosives strapped to their bodies hijack a Brooklyn bus, but make no political demands. When the media cameras arrive, they blow up the bus, killing everyone aboard. The FBI learns that one of the men, Ali Waziri, came to the U.S. from Frankfurt on a student visa and got into the country despite being on a terrorist watch list. These story events are modeled on actual incidents. Omar Abdel Rahman, a ringleader of the 1993 World Trade Center bombing, had been on a terrorist watch list, but the State Department and the CIA nevertheless allowed him to immigrate to the United States in 1990. The ringleader of the 9/11 hijackers, Mohammed Atta, was based in Germany—Hamburg, not Frankfurt—and applied for a student visa in the U.S. Moreover, the CIA knew that two al Qaeda operatives were inside the U.S. in the period just before September 11, but did not report this to the FBI, and these men subsequently participated in the plot.

Covering the bus bombing, a newscaster announces, "Beirut comes to Brooklyn," but, as the film shows, a more accurate description would invoke Afghanistan rather than Beirut. *The Siege* dramatizes the unintended consequences of CIA support for the anti-Soviet mujahideen in Afghanistan, and this focus makes it one of the rare Hollywood films to take the concept of blowback seriously. Late in the film, CIA agent Sharon Bridger (Annette Bening) tells FBI agent Hubbard (Denzel Washington) the truth about a suspected terrorist, Samir Nazhde (Sami Bouajila). Nazhde was on the CIA payroll in Iraq, helping bin Talal to overthrow Saddam Hussein. The Agency was financing bin Talal, but then a policy shift occurred and the Agency pulled out its support. Hussein's forces massacred the rebels. Hubbard presses Bridger about what the CIA had Nazhde doing, and then he guesses the truth—the CIA taught them how to make bombs. "Now they're here doing what you taught them to do," he tells her. These events in the backstory of the film blend the history of U.S. involvement in Iraq and Afghanistan. The CIA had encouraged the Kurds in Iraq to rise up following the Gulf War, and, absent the U.S. support that had been promised to them, they were killed by Saddam's army. The more salient details in the backstory, however, give us the origins of bin Laden and his fatwa against America. The CIA and the ISI poured huge monies into Afghanistan in the 1980s, along with military resources, which helped fuel the rise of a fundamentalist Islamist army and regime, the Taliban. When the Soviets left Afghanistan, so, too, did many jihadists in order to continue their struggle elsewhere. One godless superpower had just been defeated, and now it was the turn of the United States. As the bin Laden figure, bin Talal evokes this history.

In production during 1997, the film sees very clearly the implications of the pro-mujahideen policy in Afghanistan, and it predicts that the fallout from this policy would lead to fundamentalist religious terror on American soil. In response to the kidnapping of bin Talal, suicide bombers blow up the bus and its passengers in Brooklyn and then bomb a crowded Broadway theater. This latter sequence is more horrific than the bombing scenes in Hollywood thrillers have been, which sanitize the violence by avoiding portraits of the aftermath. When Hubbard and Bridger arrive, they see dazed, burned, and bloodied people screaming on the sidewalk. One woman in an elegant evening gown descends a remaining staircase in the ruined building. She looks dazed and then turns to the side, revealing that she is missing an arm. In these respects, the film is more honest about the effects of the bombings that are otherwise so routinely portrayed in Hollywood's action thrillers. The Broadway bombing is followed by a cataclysmic event, which, given the film's general prescience, one might expect to involve the World Trade Center. Instead, One Federal Plaza, housing the FBI and other government offices, is obliterated by a truck bomb. (The model here seems to have been the bombing of the Murrah Federal Building in Oklahoma City.) Six hundred people die, and the bombing campaign creates not only fear and panic but also a political demand that something be done.

And herein lies the second danger that the movie wishes to portray and to warn against. It is an attack on civil liberties, employed as a political response to terrorism and in ways that endanger the democratic principles of the nation. In the film, the FBI's failure to stop the bombings produces a growing conviction amongst the public and in Congress that conventional law enforcement is not enough, that a military solution is necessary. The President declares martial law in New York City, and Devereaux leads a force of 10,000 soldiers to occupy Manhattan, seal off Brooklyn, and conduct house-to-house roundups of Arabic men, who are then detained in a floodlit sports stadium. What follows in the latter third of the movie is a conflict between two different approaches to terrorism—personified by Hubbard and by Devereaux—in which the problem is viewed as either one of law enforcement or as a war amenable to a military solution. One sequence that skillfully poses the difference in diametric terms shows Hubbard and his men visiting a garage where they arrest Tariq Husseini (Amro Salama), one of the conspirators. Hubbard successfully makes the arrest only to have Devereaux show up with his military force and provoke a firefight in which the army demolishes the garage. In this case, the civil procedures of law enforcement had accomplished the goal quite nicely, without the violence and destruction unleashed by Devereaux.

In contrast to the civil procedures that Hubbard advocates, Devereaux practices torture on his captives. Following the assault on the garage, Devereaux takes Husseini to the stadium, where he is tied naked to a chair in a bathroom in imagery that now evokes the abuse photos from Abu Ghraib prison in Iraq. As Hubbard watches uneasily, Devereaux and his men discuss which method of torture would produce the quickest results—shaking, electric shock, water, or cutting. Hubbard explodes, "Are you people insane? What if what they [the terrorists] really want is to force us to herd children into stadiums like we're doing, and put soldiers on the street, and have Americans looking over their shoulders, bend the law, shred the Constitution just a little bit? Because if we torture him, general, we do that and everything that we have bled and fought and died for is over, and they've won." Devereaux has Hubbard escorted from the room; outside, we hear Husseini screaming. Shortly afterward, Bridger comes out, saying sadly that the man knew nothing. A gunshot then issues from the room. The implications are clear—Devereaux's men have tortured Husseini until they realize he is useless to them, and then they execute him with a gunshot to the head.

Devereaux believes he is acting in the best interests of the country, and he has a measure of political support for his actions. But the film also implies that he is a potential dictator waiting in the wings to seize power. It turns out that Devereaux may have abducted bin Talal to provoke just the kind of crisis that would enable him to use military force against an American city, and from that base to potentially expand his appeal as the country's solution in its period of crisis. As one senator says during the debate over whether to recommend that the President invoke martial law, "You don't fight a junkyard dog with ASPCA rules. What you do is take the leash off your own bigger, meaner dog." Indeed, as Walter Laqueur has pointed out, modern states are always more powerful than terrorists. The question is, to what ends they will resort in self-defense? The most extreme end was represented by the military dictatorship in Argentina, which used terror in the 1970s to combat a guerrilla army seeking its overthrow. The military government detained, tortured, and "disappeared" thousands of Argentine citizens.

In respect of an outcome like this, *The Siege* is heavy-handed and clumsy in its depictions of the threat of military rule in America. The events of 9/11 show how clumsy. The Bush administration did not declare martial law, but it did move aggressively to expand Presidential power and to order warrantless surveillance of American citizens, which, however objectionable, is a more benign response than what *The Siege* shows. And the administration was cleverer than the scenario that the film offers. Instead of rounding up citizens and immigrants and holding them in a public stadium, those detained were declared "enemy combatants" and held offshore and in secret, beyond the reach of courts of law. MSNBC commentator Erik Lundegaard put it well when he observed that the filmmakers "assumed the terrorists would think small (buses, schools) and our reaction would be loud (martial law, herding Arab-Americans into stadiums). Instead the terrorists thought big . . . and our reaction, at least in rounding up suspects, has been relatively quiet and secretive. Put it this way: We're not doing it in a stadium with the lights on."[56]

While the film may veer too far toward melodrama in its depiction of Devereaux and the occupation of Brooklyn, it was shrewdly perceptive in noting that torture would be included in the package of counterterror responses and also in warning that such an outcome would irreparably damage the standing of the United States. One of the reasons for housing "enemy combatants" beyond the reach of the law at Abu Ghraib and other secret prisons evidently was so that they might be tortured or, to put it more euphemistically, be subjected to aggressive interrogation. David Cole and James X. Dempsey write,

> *If there was ever any doubt, it became clear in June 2004 that the torture at Abu Ghraib could not be dismissed as the responsibility of a few bad actors. Two leaked memos, one dated August 2002 to White House Counsel Alberto Gonzales from the head of the Justice Department's Office of Legal Counsel, and the other dated March 2003 to Defense Secretary Rumsfeld from a "Working Group on Detainee Interrogations in the Global War on Terrorism," made crystal clear that the Bush administration consciously sought out every loophole it could construct in order to justify inflicting physical and psychological pain on captives for intelligence purposes.*[57]

The international uproar that followed the release of the Abu Ghraib photographs provides a self-evident illustration of Hubbard's warning to Devereaux. It's very clear how *The Siege* evaluates the question of whether terrorism is best countered through war or through law enforcement. It advocates the latter course of action. Hubbard brings down the last of the terrorists and then obtains a writ from District Court for Devereaux's arrest on charges of the kidnapping and murder of an American citizen (Husseini). Devereaux is led away in handcuffs, and, in the last image, military vehicles leave Brooklyn amid the cheers of a diverse crowd of mixed races, ethnicities, and religions that is meant to personify the best attributes of civic cooperation and mutual respect in American society. Of course, this ending is improbable, offering an unconvincing resolution of a question that is rather more complex than the film acknowledges, namely, how to distinguish the conditions under which law enforcement or military force provides the best response to terrorism.

Despite the clarity of the film's allegiance to civil liberties, an ambivalence about how to cope with terrorism creeps into the movie. When the bus is hijacked, Bridger tells Hubbard to use his snipers and kill the hijackers because they're on a suicide mission and have no intention of negotiating. But Hubbard believes in negotiation, and he tries to talk with the hijackers, hoping to explore with them a way out of the crisis. As Bridger predicted, they blow up the bus. Hubbard is stunned, and during a subsequent hostage crisis—a suicide bomber holds a classroom of schoolchildren captive—Hubbard forgoes dialogue, bursts into the room, and shoots the man dead. Later in the film, when the FBI locates a three-man terrorist cell, Hubbard waits for a warrant before arresting them. Again Bridger warns him he's making a

FIGURE 1.4 After the bus bombing, agent Hubbard (Denzel Washington) reviews the intelligence dossier on one of the bombers, Ali Waziri, a character whose background prefigures that of 9/11 hijack ringleader Mohammed Atta. (Frame enlargement)

mistake. You're not Sir Thomas Moore, she says, and they have a warrant from God. They're ready to die. The timely arrival of the warrant closes the debate, but in this scene, and the others just mentioned, *The Siege* acknowledges that an effective response to terror may be hampered by legal procedures. The film, though, doesn't venture very sympathetically into this territory, apart from the threads in these scenes. It intends to warn its audience that Islamist terrorism is a new danger to America and that authoritarian political responses, fed by panic and opportunism, may prove equally destructive to the country.

In doing so, the film attempts to reproduce a range of voices and points of view about the nature of religion, Islam, and terrorism. It shows the bombings eliciting a rise in hate crimes and racism directed at New York's Muslim population, and it condemns the blunt racial profiling carried out by Devereaux's troops, who round up all Arabic men of a certain age. It also suggests that religion is used as a tool of manipulation by those who recruit the suicide bombers. In a poignant monologue, Samir recalls how his brother, who loved movies and was not especially religious but lived amid despair in the Palestinian camps, was approached by a sheikh who convinced him that dying for Allah was a great calling and that the martyr would live forever in paradise. His brother subsequently strapped dynamite to his chest and bombed a movie theater. Given the skepticism that Samir shows in this scene toward the political machinations that produce suicide bombers, it makes little sense when he is revealed at the film's climax to be a suicide bomber himself. Although this plot twist diminishes the anguish that he has expressed over the death of his brother, the earlier scene nevertheless remains notable as the only such occasion when Hollywood film of this period attempted a portrait of the material conditions that can produce suicidal violence. At the same time, this portrait fails to account for the prevalence of a bourgeois, professional and technocratic background among many radical jihadists. The four suicide pilots on 9/11, for example, all had pursued higher education at universities. As Malise Ruthven notes, "the overwhelming majority of the leaders of Islamist movements have scientific educational backgrounds and qualifications."[58] She speculates that this technical training contributes to feelings of alienation from Islam and the West that can result in a renewed sense of religious radicalism.

On the other hand, consistent with many other Hollywood films, in *The Siege* the specifics of organizational identities remain vague. Are Samir and his brother Hamas, Fatah, Islamic Jihad, or Popular Front for the Liberation of Palestine? As Jordan Wagge has observed, "most Middle Eastern terrorists in movies are never even assigned organizations, as if just being Middle Eastern or of Middle Eastern descent is enough to make a terrorist."[59]

Finally, through the character of a Lebanese FBI agent, Frank Haddad (Tony Shalhoub), the film attempts to balance out its portraits of the Islamist bombers. Haddad is a patriotic American and a government agent devoted to his job. CAIR and other groups, however, protested that Haddad was in the "one good Indian" tradition of Hollywood stereotyping and that, overall, *The Siege* equated Islam with terrorism. Like *Executive Decision, The Siege* generated controversy of a sort that the film industry thereafter wished to avoid, and one result was the changes in *The Sum of All Fears* that made the villains a group of neo-Nazis. Thus, ironically, as Osama bin Laden and company brought an Islamist attack to America, Hollywood film had begun to reject Islamist villains from the screenplays of movies about terrorism. Within the context of Arabic stereotyping that has pervaded Hollywood film for many decades, *Executive Decision* and *The Siege* may well have seemed like more of the same at the time they were released. But now, with Islamist terror having emerged as a very real phenomenon, these films seem prescient in a way they could not have appeared when released. They are pulp melodramas, but the scenarios they evoke have achieved some validation from history. *The Siege* does not equate Islam with terrorism, but it does portray Islamist terrorism, and in this respect it's a film that seemed to see what was coming.

After 9/11, Islamist terrorists largely disappeared from studio films. *Iron Man* (2008), for example, features a sequence set in Afghanistan where hero Tony Stark, a wealthy American weapons manufacturer, is kidnapped by a terrorist group that wants him to make weapons for them. But they are generic bad guys, nonspecific, not identifiable as Islamists. In respect of Hollywood's turn away from Islamist terrorists as movie villains, Ross Douthat notes that "an air of omission, even denial" hangs over recent American film. "Terrorist baddies turn out to be Eurotrash arms dealers (2006's *Casino Royale*), disgruntled hackers (2007's *Live Free or Die Hard*), a sinister air marshall (2005's *Flightplan*), or the handsome white guy sitting next to you in the airport lounge (2005's *Red Eye*). Anyone and anybody, in other words, except the sort of people who actually attacked the United States on 9/11."[60]

THE REJECTION OF MODERNITY

During the years that Hollywood was producing its cycle of terrorist thrillers, the only major act of terrorist violence that occurred on American soil was the April 19, 1995, Oklahoma City bombing of the Alfred P. Murrah Federal Building, carried out by Americans who were disaffected and alienated with their government. It capped a series of violent clashes between the FBI and militia, splinter or segregationist groups in the mid-West—the 1992 assault on white separatist Randy Weaver's cabin at Ruby Ridge in Idaho and the 1993 assault on the Branch Davidian headquarters in Waco, Texas. The government killings of members of the Weaver family and the Davidians spurred the growth of right-wing militia groups in the mid-West that were antigovernment and radical proponents of gun rights, fearful that the government would try to confiscate firearms that were in the possession of ordinary Americans. Timothy McVeigh claimed that the attack on the Murrah building was meant in part as payback to the government for the Waco assault, and he also cited the need to protect the right to bear arms. "It was at this time, after waiting for non-violent checks and balances to correct ongoing federal abuses and, seeing no such results, that the assault weapons ban passed and rumours surfaced of nationwide, Waco-style raids scheduled for spring 1995, to confiscate firearms."[61] As a result, he said he made a decision to "go on the offensive."

The radical right-wing militia movement is the other category of homegrown enemy identified in Hollywood movies of the pre-9/11 era. Militia groups were not involved in the Oklahoma bombing, but McVeigh is a figure who straddles both categories of homegrown enemy as depicted in Hollywood movies. He was a disgruntled former soldier, and he frequented gun shows, which were a gathering place for militia members, and was motivated by some of their issues, such as the fear of a government conspiracy to seize firearms. McVeigh thus connects the two categories of threat that Hollywood was depicting. Costa-Gavras' *Betrayed* (1988) dramatizes the racial prejudice that animates much of the militia movement but does so in a heavy-handed, almost caricatured manner. *Arlington Road* (1999) weaves a fictionalized version of the Ruby Ridge assault into a story about right-wing militias operating like sleeper cells and infiltrating urban areas, where they wait to unleash spectacular acts of bombing. Michael Faraday (Jeff Bridges) teaches college courses on terrorism; he had been married to an FBI agent killed during the film's version of the Ruby Ridge assault. His grief makes him an easy target for manipulation by Oliver and Cheryl Lang (Tim Robbins, Joan Cusack), a model suburban couple who live across the street, seemingly ordinary people but who are secretly plotting to blow up the J. Edgar Hoover building in Washington D.C. They set Jeff up as a fall guy for the bombing, and when Oliver's mask of suburban gentility is removed, he is revealed to be a ruthless, antigovernment crusader on a religious mission. "Are you happy in your godless suburban life?" he asks Michael, as the film suggests that the bombers are motivated partly by religious fundamentalism. Unlike the terrorist action thrillers in which a hero prevails, *Arlington Road* concludes on notes of maximum paranoia. Racing to the Hoover building to warn the FBI that the Lang group is plotting an attack, Michael realizes too late that the bomb has been stashed in *his* car; he has delivered it. It explodes, destroying the building, and newscasts of the destruction deliberately evoke the imagery of Oklahoma City. The news media report that a federal investigation has concluded that Michael was the bomber and that he was motivated by guilt and rage against the government over the death of his wife. Through this denouement, the film evokes the rich tradition in American history and culture of paranoia and conspiracy. By casting doubt on the conclusion of the federal investigation, the film acknowledges the lingering questions that have surrounded other epochal acts of violence, such as the assassination of President Kennedy, the Murrah bombing, and, by implication for it was two years away, the events of September 11.

The terrorists of *Fight Club* (1999) are not right-wing militia types, but like Osama bin Laden, and the Langs of *Arlington Road,* they are motivated by animosity for the perceived moral bankruptcy of American society and by hostility toward modernity. In this respect, they share the radical Islamist hatred for the materialism of a society of abundance. The protagonist of *Fight Club* is an unnamed narrator (Edward Norton) who is consumed by anguish and despair over the banality and emptiness of his corporate life. He obsesses about filling his apartment with catalog items from Ikea. "I'd flip through catalogs and wonder what kind of dining set defines me as a person," he tells us in sardonic voice-over. He eventually experiences a psychotic break with reality and conjures up a fantasy companion, Tyler Durden (Brad Pitt), through whom he can vent his anger at corporate America and plot revenge.

Durden, as the narrator's alter ego, describes the psychological emptiness that modern America creates in its citizens by making them into consumers. "Murder, crime, poverty—these things don't concern me. What concerns me are celebrity magazines, television with 500 channels, some guy's name in my underwear." The things that you own, he says, end up owning you, and he imagines a looming apocalypse. "Martha [Stewart] is polishing the brass on the *Titanic*, and it's all going down."

Durden and the narrator assemble "fight clubs" across the country. These are bands of hostile, angry, disaffected men who feel oppressed in their lives, and Durden offers them a war against America that he defines as a spiritual and righteous action, essentially a jihad. He tells the members of one club, "Advertising has us chasing cars and clothes, working jobs we hate so we can buy shit we don't need. We're the middle children of history, no purpose or place. We have no great war, no Great Depression. Our great war is a spiritual war. Our Great Depression is our lives."

So the fight clubs launch Project Mayhem, an escalating series of terrorist actions directed at corporate property, climaxed by a plot to turn several city blocks into smoldering rubble, what the narrator calls a great "theater of mass destruction." They plant explosives in a dozen financial buildings, to bring about what Durden calls "the collapse of financial history." With this ambition, he reenacts the Galleanists' dreams of destroying Wall Street from the previous century. The film's penultimate imagery shows the demolition and collapse of a group of World Trade Center–like high-rise office buildings, an apocalypse of destruction that is impossible to watch after 9/11 without an almost unbearable sense of foreboding. The destruction that Durden and the narrator unleash, the effort to destroy "financial history" is an effort, like al Qaeda's, to turn back the clock to a precapitalist, premodern era that the terrorists imagine to be more benign and less corrupt. In this respect, what *Fight Club* expresses are the psychological rage and alienation that help to spawn terrorism. If Hollywood's action films, which are fixated on the visual spectacle of outlandish fireballs, give us the externals of terrorism, *Fight Club* maps its interior coordinates.

Its characters are motivated by an alienation from modernity that is similar to the Islamists. Osama bin Laden and other radical fundamentalists are putting into practice the ideas expressed in tracts by Hasan al-Banna and Sayyid Qutb, Egyptian writers who became the intellectual fathers of the radical Islamist insurgency. Both decried the godless modernism of American society and advocated a program of jihad to restore the caliphate, a pure Muslim state. As if furnishing a model for Tyler Durden, al-Banna described how materialism had poisoned Western culture, like "a viper's venom [creeping] insidiously into their affairs, poisoning their blood and sullying the purity of their well-being."[62] And, like Tyler Durden, al-Banna believed the end was coming. The West "is now bankrupt and in decline. Its foundations are crumbling and its institutions and guiding principles are falling apart. . . . The millions of its wretched and hungry offer their testimony against it."[63]

Al-Banna founded the Muslim Brotherhood in 1928, an insurgent, jihad-oriented group that Qutb subsequently joined, following a visit to America in 1949—New York, Washington, D.C., San Francisco, and Greeley, Colorado—which confirmed his antipathy for the unholy, capitalist country. Malise Ruthven notes, "Qutb's visit to the United States deserves to rank as the defining moment or watershed from which the 'Islamist war against America' would flow."[64] Qutb wrote that in America "new gods are worshipped, which are thought to be the aim of human existence—the god of property, the god of pleasure, the god of fame, the god of productivity."[65] But in fact a bitter emptiness pursues people there "like a fearsome ghost."[66] Tyler Durden in *Fight Club* is such a ghost, who chases the narrator, in flight from his true inner nature.

The rejection of modernity in *Fight Club* links the film's characters with the Islamist terrorists who would find a way to act on Durden's dream of destroying financial history. But this theme, of hostility toward historical notions of progress, is also one of the founding principles of terrorism in the Western tradition. The rejection of modernity, so profoundly manifest in Islamist radicalism, has been also a motivating force behind terrorist violence in the West. Martin Miller writes that Western terrorists reject "the moral and legal foundations of the modern state . . . [and aim] to annihilate the implicit social contract that had traditionally defined and bound together Western societies."[67] He continues, "Terrorists are the expression of that part of Western culture that has moved beyond the paradigm of progress that has dominated our thinking since the eighteenth-century Enlightenment . . . they believe that secular evil can be overcome by destroying the value system of progress itself."[68] From this standpoint, bin Laden and his ilk demonstrate the same impulse that has been manifest in Western terrorism, namely, an attack on liberalism and modernity, and Paul Berman has argued that the antiliberal totalitarianism of radical Islam, in fact, has its roots in the totalitarian movements of Western culture.[69]

The efforts of al Qaeda and of *Fight Club*'s Project Mayhem to turn back the clock of history share this originating impulse, this antipathy for the materialism of the West and the liberal democracy that proved to be such an engine for industrial development. It is this commonality of intent that helps to make the ending of *Fight Club* so extraordinarily eerie and chilling. The

FIGURE 1.5 At the end of *Fight Club,* the narrator (Edward Norton) and his girlfriend relax as happy spectators enjoying the spectacle of mass destruction, watching as World Trade Center–like buildings crash down. (Frame enlargement)

narrator and his girlfriend stand before the window in a high-rise office building. "Trust me, everything's going to be fine," the narrator says as the explosions go off. They join hands and watch as the skyscrapers across from them collapse and fall, gutted by the explosives of Project Mayhem. The last pair of buildings to fall is a replica of the World Trade Center, not as tall relative to surrounding buildings, but sporting the WTC's bland, monolithic exterior and sheared-off, flat top. One tower begins to topple into the other, as if fulfilling Ramzi Yousef's dream, but then they fall straight down as they did on September 11. The imagery so literally maps onto the sight of the World Trade Center's collapse as to become deracinating. It warps the ending of the film. *Fight Club* throughout has been a manifesto for terrorists, but now, at the end, the indulgences that fiction claims for itself mock the physical and emotional realities of a context in which buildings really did fall.

This uncomfortable intersection of fiction and fact, whereby *Fight Club* becomes the harbinger of events that it is ill-equipped morally and politically to handle, furnishes an appropriately telling riposte to Hollywood's cycle of terrorist thrillers. 9/11 killed this cycle of films—its ideological limitations were inadequate responses to the events of that day. This was because the films offered mainly an aesthetic response to terrorism, one grounded not in politics or issues of morality but in cinematic spectacle. Terrorism for Hollywood before 9/11 provided a vehicle for stories in which filmmakers could stage huge explosions, and the viewing position allocated for the spectator was exactly that of the narrator and his girlfriend at the end of *Fight Club,* holding hands pleasurably, secure in the knowledge that they will be fine. "We have front-row seats for this theater of mass destruction," the narrator tells us, implicating the film's viewers in the voyeuristic terms of terrorism Hollywood-style. It's a largely guilt-free viewing zone, from which epic fireballs or the destruction of an urban skyline can be enjoyed for the scale and power of the devastation, and this is why the violence is nearly always sanitized by avoiding the details of human suffering or body mutilations that would accompany such events. As Murray Pomerance wrote, "the image of disaster permits us to stand back from it and gasp, a reaction of such complete uninvolvement, even superiority, that we stun ourselves into guilt by experiencing it as beautiful."[70] And as Susan Sontag pointed out in her classic discussion of 1950s science fiction films, images of disaster in the movies tend to emphasize damage to *things* rather than to people. This emphasis invites "a dispassionate, aesthetic view of destruction and violence—a *technological* view. Things, objects, machinery play a major role in these films. A greater range of ethical values is embodied in the décor of these films than in the people."[71]

Terrorists, too, take a very detached, distanced view of the people they plan to kill. Moreover, taken in historical terms, terrorism has often pursued violence as theater, with its attendant emotional gratifications. An anarchist in the 1880s waxed lovingly over his weapon of choice:

> *Dynamite! Of all the good stuff, this is the stuff. Stuff several pounds of this sublime stuff into an inch pipe (gas or water-pipe), plug up both ends, insert a cap with a fuse attached, place this in the immediate neighborhood of a lot of rich loafers who live by the sweat of other people's brows, and light the fuse. A most cheerful and gratifying result will follow.*[72]

The attacks of September 11 were a political and military action, but they were also, in their audaciously visual staging, an act of theater. Responding in an injudiciously literal way to this conception, the composer Karlheinz Stockhausen called the attacks a "work of art," a phrase that elicited outrage. Terror as theater, though, could have a natural affinity with Hollywood film, and for a decade and a half the industry built ever bigger fireballs to give its audience audacious violence with a rush and minimized the ethical values inherent in so much carnage. As Eric Lichtenfeld wrote, action filmmakers showed "reverence for destruction."[73] The explosions that result when a bus collides with an airplane in *Speed* look apocalyptic, as does the detonation of an abandoned ship in *Blown Away*. *Broken Arrow* aimed for quantity as well as quality of destruction. It offered viewers four helicopter explosions, one nuclear explosion, one stealth bomber explosion, and one train explosion, all with appropriately lengthy fireballs. During the helicopter explosion, the same footage is replayed twice, captured by multiple cameras, so that the chopper explodes several times. Once simply is not enough when it comes to the voluptuous pleasure of big things going bang. Travolta as the villain watches the explosions and shouts enthusiastically, “God damn! What a rush!,” an outburst meant to personify the joy that the movie’s audience was intended to take at the fireballs. Novelist James Hall suggested that, in fact, Hollywood had a formula for the preferred number of fireballs in an action movie. “Just before Sept. 11 changed storytelling in America forever, my Hollywood agent explained that my new novel was doomed in movieland because it lacked sufficient ‘explosive moments.’ It was exactly nine fireballs short of the prevailing formula.”[74]

9/11 rang down the curtain on Hollywood’s theater of mass destruction, at least for a little while. Hall was wrong. It didn’t change storytelling in America forever. But now filmmakers had a real event, at home, to which they could respond if they so chose. The World Trade Center had collapsed. A section of the Pentagon was incinerated. A plane full of passengers had smashed into a field in Pennsylvania before it could strike its target. Death and destruction at home were no longer a popcorn dream. The next chapter shows how Hollywood responded and adapted to these events.

CHAPTER TWO

SHADOWS ONCE REMOVED

SHORTLY AFTER THE ATTACKS ON 9/11, director Robert Altman issued a jeremiad blaming Hollywood for what had happened. He targeted the studios' action films, rife with images of big things blowing up. "The movies set the pattern, and these people have copied the movies. Nobody would have thought to commit an atrocity like that unless they'd seen it in a movie. How dare we continue to show this kind of mass destruction in movies? I just believe we created this atmosphere and taught them how to do it."[1] Although this idea is provocative, the assertion cannot be proven. But we do know that the 9/11 hijackers were watching Hollywood action films to pass time while they waited to carry out their plans. Lawrence Wright reports that favorite films included movies about skyjacking and Arnold Schwarzenegger action epics.[2] Certainly, Schwarzenegger films such as *True Lies* and other Hollywood pictures had been envisioning the kind of large-scale destruction that al Qaeda was plotting. Hollywood had previewed the destruction to come, although no one suspected these films were trailers for actual coming attractions. At the beginning of *Armageddon* (1998), for example, a meteor shower strikes New York City, destroying many of its landmark buildings, which erupt into fireballs and crash to the ground. A shot of the skyline shows the twin towers of the World Trade Center heavily damaged and smoking. It could be an image from 9/11 except that the shot shows much of the Manhattan skyline in ruins. Another meteor crashes into Earth in *Deep Impact* (1998), creating a tidal wave that engulfs Manhattan and topples the World Trade Center, which is last seen lying on its side and partially submerged beneath the waves. The destruction of public landmarks, in fact, was an obsession for the makers of disaster movies.[3]

But these filmmakers were working within a long-standing tradition. A practice in fiction and the visual arts of envisioning the destruction of New York is centuries old, as Max Page has shown in his study of apocalyptic fantasies about Manhattan in literature, film, and the graphic arts. For two centuries, Manhattan has been subjected to these fantasies. "America's writers and imagemakers have pictured New York's annihilation in a stunning range of ways. Earthquake, fire, flood. Meteor, comet, Martian. Glacier, ghosts, atom bomb. Class war, terrorism, invasion."[4] He points out that while many such fantasies have spared the Empire State Building ("there has been a curious delicacy about depicting harm to the building"),[5] the World Trade Center has not been so lucky and has often been shown in ruins, toppled, in flames, or engulfed by flood.

As soon as the structure was completed, the World Trade Center began to attract the apocalyptic imaginations of filmmakers. The building was dedicated in 1973 and by 1976, in a Dino de Laurentiis remake of a movie classic, King Kong was climbing to its top where he defiantly made his stand against military aircraft firing automatic weapons at the building. Even if the ensuing twenty-five years of movie destruction centered on Manhattan didn't give al Qaeda the inspiration for its plot, moviemakers seized their opportunity and began designing grand images of tall buildings crashing down or destroyed in other ways. Yet it wasn't just filmmakers who were thinking in these terms. Lawrence Wien, the owner of the Empire State Building, feared that the novel construction techniques used in erecting the World Trade Center left it weakened and unsafe compared with hardened buildings such as his own. He warned in 1964 that the World Trade Center was structurally vulnerable and was "unsafe in an explosion or if hit by an airplane."[6] In 1968 Wien ran an ad in the *New York Times* that pictured a commercial airliner flying into the building. The context for the action depicted in the ad is not terrorism but a scenario in which a plane might inadvertently veer off-course. One of the bragging points about the World Trade Center, cited by developers and administrators, was that it could survive a collision with a 707, at that time the largest commercial airliner. In 1981 a Boeing 707 nearly did hit the towers, coming within 90 seconds of impact. An airplane had hit the Empire State Building in 1945, a 12-ton U.S. Army Air Corps B-25 that flew straight into the 79th floor in heavy fog. The plane's 8,000 gallons of jet fuel ignited, and, as at the World Trade Center in 2001, some of it flowed down elevator shafts and started fires in the lobby.

Historical precedent, then, clearly existed for ideas about airplane strikes on tall buildings in New York City or for other kinds of disasters such as fires. The World Trade Center, in fact, had been a target for arson on several occasions. In 1975 a custodian at the Trade Center set a fire on the eleventh floor that quickly spread up to the seventeenth and down to the ninth

FIGURE 2.1 As landmark buildings, the Empire State Building and the World Trade Center held an enduring attraction for Hollywood filmmakers crafting fantasies of epic destruction. Both buildings suffered collisions with airplanes. On 9/11 the Trade Center's destruction was real. (AP Photo/Marty Lederhandler)

floors.[7] Numerous building violations of the fire safety code helped to make the fire worse than it would have been otherwise. Three months later, the arsonist struck again, setting seven fires in the South Tower. Perhaps some filmmakers were aware of these precedents; many were simply invested in spectacle as a box office asset. Either way, Hollywood moviemakers were drawn to scenarios of mass destruction. However improbable the ideas cooked up in the movie scripts may have been, their target was an inviting one. From an architectural standpoint, for example, the design of the World Trade Center looked arrogant and aggressive. It towered above Manhattan and was visually disconnected from the surrounding skyline; critics of the structure complained that the design was so large as to be inhuman. Not only did it command attention but it was also a symbol of world financial power. This symbolism provided Osama bin Laden with his rationale for the attacks: "As for the World Trade Center, the ones who were attacked and who died in it were part of a financial power. It wasn't a children's school! Neither was it a residence."[8] Thus it was an obvious target, first in the imaginations of filmmakers and subsequently for real. Hollywood didn't have to provide an inspiration to al Qaeda about a strike against the World Trade Center. Filmmakers and terrorists could operate on fully parallel tracks, responding independently, but with a common logic, to the visual provocation offered by the structure.

ASSAULTING THE WORLD TRADE CENTER

Before turning to the main subject of this chapter—Hollywood's responses to 9/11—it is worth briefly examining the prehistory of Hollywood's imagined assaults on the World Trade Center. In the most striking instance, the building complex was depicted through a surrogate and was subjected to a devastating fire. This film was one of its era's most prominent disaster movies, *The Towering Inferno* (1977). It portrayed the outbreak of deadly fires in a majestic glass tower in Los Angeles. At 135 floors, the building in the movie was the world's largest skyscraper. In 1976–77, when the film was in production and release, the World Trade Center was the world's tallest building, making it the real-life counterpart of the film's glass tower. Moreover, each building boasted an elegant restaurant at the very top. The Promenade Room in *The Towering Inferno* was the counterpart of the Trade Center's Windows on the World, and in the movie, as in life, people are trapped in the restaurant when fire breaks out, unable to use stairs or elevators to descend to safety.

The film prefigures the events of 9/11 in numerous ways. First is its depiction of how inadequate safety features imperil the lives of people trapped on the highest floors as a fire rages out of control below them. The tragedy in the movie begins when an overloaded conduit box sparks a fire in a local storage room, and the building's ducts and air vents quickly channel the blaze to multiple floors. The building's architect, Doug Roberts (Paul Newman), had set technical specifications for the building that exceeded code. "The code's not enough for that building, and you know it. That's why I asked for insulations that were way, way above code." But the tower's developer, James Duncan (William Holden), cut corners to save money, and Roberts finds wiring carrying too heavy a load, corridors without fire doors, duct holes that are not firestopped, and numerous other safety violations. As a result, once the fire breaks out on the upper floors, it is virtually unstoppable, and the film shows the impossible task that firemen confront in battling a blaze in a skyscraper. At the end, Fire Chief O'Hallorhan (Steve McQueen) says they were lucky, that the body count is below 200, but he predicts that someday 10,000 people will die in one of these firetraps unless developers start asking firemen how to build them. In this respect, the film is a plea to prioritize policies of fire safety in tall buildings, and the warning was especially relevant to the World Trade Center.

The Trade Center was constructed during an interval in which New York City had revised its building codes in ways that favored developers.[9] The mandated number of exit stairwells was reduced by half, the stairwells were clustered together to maximize rentable office space, a firetower (a reinforced stairwell with a ventable air system to keep smoke out) was not required or built, and the structural steel in the building was fireproofed in a novel and untested manner. Earlier high-rise buildings, like the Empire State Building, were heavily fortified with concrete and masonry encasing the structural steel, but the developers planning the World Trade Center argued that these older skyscrapers were "overbuilt," that such elaborate fireproofing was not necessary. By dispensing with masonry as an insulating material, the World Trade Center could be built taller and lighter, thereby maximizing the amount of revenue-generating office space. Glass and drywall were used instead of masonry, and fireproofing for the steel was simply sprayed on as an asbestos layer one-half inch thick, a specification that had no basis in science or engineering and had never been subject to a laboratory test to determine its effectiveness.[10] When the planes hit the building, virtually no one above the impact area survived because the stairwells, centered in the core of the building, were nearly all damaged. The reason that older building codes specified that stairwells be spread out was so that no single event could render them unusable. The flimsy drywall encasing the stairwells at the World Trade Center collapsed and blocked them, and they quickly filled with smoke. The impact of the planes knocked the thin fireproofing off the structural steel, and temperatures soared to a point where it began to weaken.

And, in a building without many internal columns, the fires raged through the open spaces, facilitated by extensive ductwork and drywall paneling. As fire safety experts point out, "New insulating materials do not tend to absorb heat, as masonry and concrete do, *but tend to reflect the fire's heat*. . . . Multiple openings penetrate floors and walls for duct work, power and communications systems, thereby creating air spaces which can sustain and feed fires and allow it [*sic*] to spread throughout a building, rapidly, and sometimes tragically [italics in original]."[11] The result on the high floors of the World Trade Center was what *The Towering Inferno* had dramatized, a conflagration that cannot be stopped. And that film's warning about the failure of building code specifications to address safety needs in super-tall buildings was unfortunately all too prescient.

The skyscraper in *The Towering Inferno* does not fall like the World Trade Center did, but the film's imagery in other respects anticipates some of the horror that unfolded in the Twin Towers. The fire in the film engulfs the elevator shafts, incinerating people in the elevators who are trying to escape, as it did on 9/11. Sections of the collapsed building block the exit stairwell, and there are an insufficient number of escape routes. Only one elevator and one stairwell connect the Promenade Room with the lower floors. Thus those at the top of the building are cut off from rescue. An effort to mount a rooftop helicopter rescue founders when the chopper crashes in high winds. At the World Trade Center, billowing smoke and high winds precluded the NYPD from landing any craft on the roof. A wrenching sequence in the film shows one of the building's executives, Dan Bigelow (Robert Wagner), and his lover trapped in their office. As did many Trade Center victims, they jam a towel underneath the door and try to use the phone, but there is no hope. The fire's advance is relentless. Bigelow is burned alive, and his lover breaks a window to escape the smoke and then leaps to her death from the upper floor. Imagery of the tower's exterior shows fires raging on multiple floors and smoke billowing from the upper reaches of the building. With all these evocative details, the one attribute that the film minimizes is smoke, which should be far more terrible than what is depicted.

Among the most wrenching images of 9/11 were the photographs of people falling or jumping from the upper floors of the Twin Towers, and the film contains numerous instances of such horror. Several victims are shown falling from the building. This imagery from 1974 is now fused with the context of 9/11. In other words, it is impossible now to watch these scenes in the film without thinking of the World Trade Center. But the imagery is also informed by the tragic history of fires in tall buildings. In 1911, the 10-story factory building of New York's Triangle Waist Company burned, the fire escape collapsed, and the exit doors on upper floors were locked. One hundred forty people died, with many victims leaping to their deaths from the top floors. Like the violent war waged by Galleanists against the U.S. government, the Triangle fire gives us another instance of history repeating itself. Like the designers of the World Trade Center, the Triangle Company (which manufactured women's blouses, known as shirtwaists) had used innovative construction methods—turning the cutting tables into giant bins for discarded fabric—that made the fire more deadly. And like the Trade Center, the shirtwaist building had not used safety measures, such as sprinklers and shielded fire doors and walls, that were available at the time.

When the fire broke out, company employees were trapped on the upper floors because escape routes were either locked, were too narrow, or had collapsed. As the fire moved implacably toward them, many began to jump from the upper floors, to the horror of onlookers who had gathered below. This history is so like 9/11 that it bears going into some detail. People jumped individually and in pairs, holding hands, and to witnesses they were visibly alive to the very end. By one count, fifty-four victims leaped to their deaths. "One girl tried to keep her body upright. Until the very instant she touched the sidewalk, she was trying to balance herself," one witness wrote.[12] There were so many bodies in the air that, as at the World Trade Center, police prevented people in the building lobby from leaving by usual routes lest they be struck and killed. And as at the Trade Center, the noises of impact were horrifying. A witness recalled, "I learned a new sound, a more horrible sound than description can picture. It was the thud of a speeding, living body on a stone sidewalk."[13] As on 9/11, it was a beautiful, clear day, and the weather both enticed and mocked the jumpers as they stood at the windows high above the ground, a searing fire behind, a clear, inviting vista in front. David Von Drehle's description of what the Triangle jumpers faced before making their leap serves, too, as an evocation of what the 9/11 victims saw. "The view from the windows was a vicious, almost mocking, juxtaposition of life and death, of the temperate and the hellish. . . . This, then, was their universe: panic and fire behind them, horror and helplessness on the faces far, far below—and something cool, something beautiful, *just out of reach* beyond the heat waves and the blinding smoke."[14]

After the Triangle fire, the city's building inspector warned, "The *Titanic* was unsinkable—yet she went down; our skyscrapers are unburnable—yet we shall have a skyscraper disaster which will stagger humanity." *The Towering Inferno*'s Chief O'Hallorhan echoed this warning, and what that film imagined and dramatized became reality once again at the World Trade Center. The connection was not lost on witnesses to the Trade Center disaster. French filmmaker Gédéon Naudet was in the streets of Manhattan that day, filming the reactions of pedestrians after the two planes had struck. His footage appears in the documentary *9/11* (2002), discussed in the next chapter. Gazing with horror at the fires, one man filmed by Naudet exclaims, "It's like something out of *The Towering Inferno,* like a movie!"

If *The Towering Inferno* has a direct and almost literal relevance to the World Trade Center fires of 9/11, imagery from other films in the years before 2001 connects in more oblique and metaphorical ways. As I have already said, violence against large buildings is very pervasive in Hollywood's action films, such as *Independence Day,* which shows the White House blowing up, and disaster movies such as *Armageddon* and *Deep Impact.* In the climax of *True Lies,* the hero, Harry Tasker (Arnold Schwarzenegger), uses a Harrier jet to go after the villain, Salim Aziz (Art Malik), and in the process destroys a tall office building. A group of Aziz's men are on the top floor of a glass-walled high-rise, and Tasker uses the Harrier's powerful machine guns to decimate the entire floor. Then, with Aziz improbably perched atop the Harrier, Tasker loses control of the jet, and it slams into another high-rise office building, destroying an entire upper floor. Tasker then fires a rocket through the gaping hole in the first building to blow up a helicopter carrying the terrorist gang. Tasker destroys two skyscrapers in a climax built to maximize the visual fascination of the spectacle. It is the same fascination that is at work in *Die Hard,* where the Nakatomi skyscraper is progressively destroyed over the course of the film, most elaborately when John McClane (Bruce Willis) sets off an explosive charge in an elevator shaft, blowing out an entire floor with a fireball that explodes out the windows in a manner now fused with the imagery of jet fuel erupting from the Twin Towers.

Other films contain moments that seem almost like premonitions, not in sequences showing destruction, but at points where terrorism is linked, sometimes suggestively, sometimes explicitly, with the World Trade Center. In the climax of *The Peacemaker,* a Serbian terrorist, Dusan Gavrich (Marcel Lures), flies to Manhattan to detonate a nuclear bomb, and one of the film's heroes, Julia Kelly (Nicole Kidman), urgently telephones Washington D.C. to announce that terrorists are bringing a weapon of mass destruction into the country. The action cuts to a shot of Dusan on a plane, high above Manhattan. He gazes out the window at the skyline below. It's the financial district with the World Trade Center visible. Paranoid conspiracy theorists may regard this kind of imagery as an example of "synchronicity," a secret message embedded in films by Hollywood to subliminally prepare audiences for a planned future event. In *The*

Peacemaker, for example, as Thomas Devoe (George Clooney) searches for a terrorist at New York's JFK airport, a series of odd-numbered desks are visible behind him, with one shot framing his head between desks 9 and 11. On the Internet, the Illuminati Conspiracy Archive identifies this image as an example of 9/11 synchronicities and adds several other examples from films including *Gremlins* (1984), where a car radio dial sits between 9 and 11, and *Traffic* (2000), where boxes of drugs have 911 stamped on them.[15] The authors of the Web site view these details as subliminal messages planted in films by Hollywood, examples of "predictive programming," working in concert with the government in order to gradually adjust the public to planned future events.

HOLLYWOOD REACTS TO THE ATTACKS

Such paranoia which sees arcane numerological signs in pre-9/11 Hollywood film, foretelling the future, is an extremist reading of popular cinema. But outside of this paranoid domain, the Hollywood industry began to scrutinize its own films for "signs" that before 9/11 had been innocuous and were now ominous. The World Trade Center became a synchronicity that the industry deleted from its films. Images of the Twin Towers were removed from numerous movies that were released in the months after the attacks. *Zoolander, Serendipity, Spider-Man, Men in Black II,* and *People I Know* were all in production before September 11 and included scenes that incorporated the Twin Towers as part of the urban background. The films were all slotted for release after 9/11, and imagery of the World Trade Center became taboo. Hollywood studios felt these shots would offend viewers or would pull them out of the imaginary world of the story with a visual reminder of unpleasant reality. So the Twin Towers disappeared from these movies, just as they had from the landscape of Manhattan. Writing in *Variety,* Todd McCarthy objected, "Deletion of the towers from the picture is infinitely more disruptive, not to mention insulting, than leaving them in."[16]

Perhaps the film studios acted precipitously in removing these images. On the other hand, a case can be made that films post-9/11 ought to picture Manhattan's skyline with the same fidelity as those made before 9/11 when the World Trade Center routinely appeared in such movies as Francis Ford Coppola's *The Godfather Part III* and Peter Bogdanovich's *They All Laughed*. Sydney Pollack's *Three Days of the Condor* (1975) features extensive footage of the Trade Center, and Pollack filmed scenes inside the towers, showing the elevators, hallways, the ground-floor lobby, and the second-floor mezzanine lobby. Viewed today, these scenes furnish a kind of memoriam for the Trade Center, and its presence in the film is startling because of the intimate access Pollack had to the building. The Trade Center's presence also haunts *Man on Wire* (2008), a documentary about Philippe Petit, who, in an audacious stunt, walked between the buildings on a wire in 1974. The film does not reference 9/11. It doesn't have to; footage of the newly constructed building speaks eloquently of this disaster-yet-to-come. While digitally erasing the landscape from films may seem a little Orwellian, the omission of the Twin Towers from films released just after the attacks does definitively place them in the world they had come to inhabit. A viewer watching the films ten years from now will understand, on the basis of the skyline, the period of time that the imagery marks.

Soon after 9/11, the White House sought to enlist the film and television industry in shaping images of America and of terrorism in ways that would assist and promote U.S. foreign policy. As Sharon Waxman reported, one month following the attacks, "Chris Henick, deputy assistant to the president, and Adam Goldman, an administration liaison to the entertainment industry, met in Beverly Hills on Wednesday with about 30 television power brokers, including CBS President Leslie Moonves, HBO Film President Colin Callender, Showtime President Jerry Offsay, and Warner Brothers Television President Peter Roth."[17] Waxman reported that Frank Capra's name was used at the meeting to describe the kind of patriotic, pro-America film and television production desired by the White House. Capra was the great Hollywood director of *Mr. Smith Goes to Washington* (1939) and, during World War II, the *Why We Fight* series of documentary productions that explained to audiences the rationale for waging war against the Axis powers. According to Waxman, participants at the meeting said that few specific ideas were discussed. But the subsequent work of producer-director Lionel Chetwynd, one of the participants at the meeting, certainly exemplifies the kind of productions that the White House seemed to want. Chetwynd wrote and produced *DC 9/11: Time of Crisis* (2003), a TV movie starring Timothy Bottoms as a heroic, gutsy President Bush responding with decisive leadership to the attacks, and *Celsius 41.11: The Temperature at which the Brain . . . Begins to Die* (2004), a documentary intended to expose the "lies" of Michael Moore's *Fahrenheit 9/11*. (I examine these films in subsequent chapters.)

Compared with Chetwynd's movies, Hollywood productions were less ideologically overt in their responses to 9/11. The industry viewed 9/11 as a kind of box office poison, as a topic that audiences would prefer not to see depicted on movie screens, and so the studios were loathe to green-light productions that took the attacks as their subject. Spike Lee was the first major filmmaker to reference 9/11, although the film in question is not principally about

9/11. It was appropriate that Lee be the first major director to mark the loss of the Twin Towers because he is a New Yorker. He said, "I felt compelled to do it because I'm a New Yorker; I'm an American; I'm a world citizen. I live here. I grew up here. So this is my home. It's always going to be my home. I felt that it would be a missed opportunity if we did not somehow reflect how the world has changed. That's what we wanted to do."[18]

25th Hour (2002) is a psychological drama about a Manhattan drug dealer, Monty Brogan (Edward Norton), who reflects on his life and personal relationships during the final twenty-four hours of his freedom before reporting to prison to begin a seven-year sentence. The film's tone is very mournful as it points toward what might have been in Brogan's life, had he lived it differently. The poignant final act is comprised of a fantasy, narrated by Brogan's father (Brian Cox), that portrays Brogan growing old, in freedom, surrounded by his family, wife, and children. This is the life that he did not live, the path he did not claim. The film sets Brogan's personal tragedy—a life essentially wasted—against a larger tragedy, the attacks on Manhattan and the lives lost on 9/11. Thus the film portrays, on these two levels of the personal and the collective, lives whose trajectories did not follow their full and expected arc. In this way, the film uses 9/11 as a means of creating an emotional framework to surround Brogan's story.

25th Hour announces itself as a post-9/11 film by opening with imagery of the great loss. The credit sequence shows graphical renditions of Manhattan skyscrapers with twin beams of blue light shining upward to mark the loss of the Twin Towers. From mid-March to mid-April 2002, twin skylights in Manhattan were beamed toward the heavens to make a memorial for the World Trade Center, and the film's credit sequence incorporates these beams of light as a motif identifying the film as a work made after the attacks. The opening image of the credit sequence shows an airplane streaking toward a building, and elsewhere in the film Lee points to the events of that day. A "Wanted: Dead or Alive" poster bearing Osama bin Laden's picture appears on the office door of the stockbroker headquarters where Frank (Barry Pepper), one of Brogan's close friends, works. When Brogan shares a meal with his father in an Irish pub, Lee shows photographs on the wall of New York firemen who were killed on 9/11. The most extended reference occurs in a scene where Frank and another of Brogan's friends, Jacob (Philip Seymour Hoffman), talk about whether they will ever see Brogan again after he's gone to prison. As they converse in Frank's apartment, the camera moves to the window and reveals that it overlooks Ground Zero. Just outside is the yawning hole left by the removal of the debris from the collapsed towers, and Lee films his characters for the remainder of the scene against the backdrop of the site and the recovery effort. The imagery is not a special effect; the apartment is real, and its proximity to the location is real. Lee knew that this scene would be controversial and that the film's distributor, Disney, would not care for this use of the location. "We knew going in that there would be people who'd dislike dealing with something like the reference to Ground Zero. But that's no reason not to do it." He added, "If we wanted to stay in that comfort zone, we wouldn't have included the 9/11 references at all because Disney did not want us to do any of that stuff. That's in line with all the thinking at Sony with *Spider-Man* and all these other films that chose to stick their heads in the sand by removing the World Trade Center buildings. Studios say that they're doing it out of respect for the audience, but I find that hard to believe. I just think they're steering clear of anything that might even remotely impact on the bottom line."[19]

As Frank and Jacob look at the devastation, they grow reflective. Jacob says that, according to the *New York Times*, the air down there is bad, and Frank replies that he reads the *Post* and the EPA says the air is fine. Jacob retorts, "Somebody's lying." In this exchange, Lee points to one of the biggest controversies that engulfed the reclamation effort at Ground Zero, namely, whether the EPA acted in haste in announcing that no serious toxins were in the environment as a result of the towers' collapse. As things turned out, Jacob was right. By 2007, more than 2,000 firefighters who worked at Ground Zero and 70 percent of nearly 10,000 recovery workers had difficulty breathing or had developed other serious respiratory problems.[20] The film's reference to this controversy evokes the history of that period, with the fictional characters of the narrative juxtaposed against it. In this history, thousands of lives had vanished at this site. In the fictional narrative, Jacob and Frank talk about one person who is about to vanish forever from their lives. Lee uses the reality of the disaster to anchor the story and to give it an emotional weight that harmonizes with the film's themes. As the scene ends, Lee offers a montage showing the excavation work at Ground Zero and a close shot of a group of workers screening the dirt for human remains. The montage is set to music that Lee intended to sound warlike, with Arabic and Irish elements in contention, the latter as a means to reference a community heavily represented in the Fire Department and which bore major losses that day.

A melancholy film, *25th Hour* situates Brogan's story within the larger frame of New York City's loss. Lee shows the aftermath of 9/11, and its effects on Manhattan in ways that are sometimes direct and sometimes oblique and poetic. Lee has made many documentaries; *25th Hour* is a fiction film, yet Lee incorporates the references to 9/11 as elements of the real placed within the fictional story, as markers describing coordinates in time and the emotional resonances attaching to them. These emotions are given their most candid expression when Brogan launches into a rant about everything in the city and everyone he hates. The list includes bin Laden for whom Brogan has this wish: "On the names of innocent thousands murdered, I pray you spend the rest of eternity with your seventy-two whores roasting in a jet-fueled fire in hell."

STEVEN SPIELBERG AND 9/11

While Lee moved rapidly to incorporate 9/11 into *25th Hour*, another prominent Hollywood filmmaker known for his fast production schedules spent time deliberating on the attacks before he was able to explore them in a substantive way on screen. When he did, the events of 9/11 proved to exert a sustained influence over Steven Spielberg's films. In *The Terminal* (2004), *War of the Worlds* (2005), and *Munich* (2005), Spielberg reflected at length upon the attacks and their impact on America. He was the only front-rank American filmmaker to inquire into the meaning of 9/11 at such length, although, in two of these films, he approaches the topic through the conventions of popular entertainment and thus remains at some distance from the subject. *Munich*, by contrast, is a more direct portrait of terrorist violence and the problems and challenges that arise in crafting a response to it. The previous two films offer more indirect portraits.

Just prior to 9/11, Spielberg embarked on *Minority Report*, adapted from a short story by Philip K. Dick, who specialized in using science fiction to portray future worlds where political repression is conjoined with an abundance of consumer goods. Although *Minority Report* was in production before the attacks of 9/11 occurred, when it was released in June 2002 it seemed remarkably in synch with the new political context in which the Bush administration had launched extensive programs of domestic surveillance. The FBI and CIA were conducting warrantless wiretaps of American citizens' telephone and electronic communications. These were extensive, and many were in violation of the FBI and Justice Department's own regulations.[21] In 2005, the year the story broke, according to the *Washington Post*, the FBI issued 19,000 "national security letters," which, by authority of the Patriot Act, compel the release of private information without the authorization of a judge or grand jury. This batch of letters contained "47,000 separate requests for information." After the *Post* had revealed the extent of the surveillance, FBI director Robert Mueller admitted that the Bureau had abused the authority given it under the USA Patriot Act.[22] *Minority Report* portrays a future world in which widespread crime has led to the formation of the Department of PreCrime, which uses a team of "precogs" to visualize crimes that are about to be committed. Alerted by the visions of the precogs, SWAT teams then swoop in to arrest the individual who has not yet committed a crime but who has *intended* to do so. A "war on crime" motivates the extensive police and government surveillance that the film portrays, just as a "war on terror" motivated the Bush administration's assumption of new and extensive powers to monitor and survey.

In both cases—the fictional and the real—the government manifests an interest in tracking evidence of intent or pre-crime. In some recent real cases, "pre-crime" was enough to get people arrested. The New York City Police Department conducted extensive surveillance of political protestors before the 2004 Republican National Convention, held in Manhattan. The NYPD traveled throughout the U.S., Canada, and Europe to follow political activists, and during the convention it conducted a large number of preemptive arrests.[23] According to the *New York Times,* for example, the pacifist group, the War Resisters League, "announced plans for a 'die-in' at Madison Square Garden. They were arrested two minutes after they began a silent march from the World Trade Center site. The charges were dismissed."[24] The NYPD had construed the group's intent to conduct a peaceful protest as a pre-crime. Thus, although *Minority Report* cannot be said to be a film about 9/11, the futuristic society that it portrays mirrors the domestic political context that had begun to emerge following the attacks, in which thought itself came to bear the shadow of crime. In numerous instances after 9/11 when people were arrested on charges of terrorism, hard evidence was often minimal; it was the alleged intent to act that mobilized authorities. In this regard, terrorism poses a real challenge to existing criminal law under which people are prosecuted for their actions. No responsible law enforcement authority will wait for a terrorist to act before making an arrest. Thus the intent to act becomes the critical measure by which an alleged terrorist might be apprehended. *Minority Report* maps this new standard onto the contours of its futurist world—its ability to do so provides a striking instance of synchronicity between a film and its historical moment.

Spielberg's subsequent films were produced after the attacks and are unquestionably influenced by them. *The Terminal* is a whimsical and gentle comedy about Victor Navorski (Tom Hanks), who visits America and finds himself caught in a Kafkaesque bureaucratic limbo, confined by the U.S. Department of Homeland Security in the international lounge of JFK Airport, where he is essentially a prisoner. While Navorski was en route to America, a military coup overthrew the government of his country, Krakozhia, and because the United States does not recognize the new regime, Navorksi temporarily becomes a man without a country and thus cannot enter the U.S. He becomes a long-term "resident" of the airport.

This premise enables Spielberg to explore the idea that "America is closed," as one of the Homeland Security officials explains to Navorski. "America closed," Navorski repeats. The only element in the film that explicitly alludes to post-9/11 America is the emblem of the Department of Homeland Security, which abruptly looms into the frame in close-up. The chief of Homeland Security at the airport, Frank Dixon (Stanley Tucci), denies Victor the privilege to enter America. Dixon sentences him, instead, to the limbo of the international lounge. Dixon is the villain of the film, an insensitive and rigid man who comes to feel spite for Navorski, and he thus personifies in negative terms this policy of "America closed" and the film's critique of the politics of post-9/11 national security. Although the film does not explicitly evoke 9/11—apart from the Homeland Security emblem—it suggests that America has walled itself into a posture of international isolation through an excessively bureaucratic response to the problems of the day. As Lester Friedman writes, the film "comments on repressive governmental actions, in this case the restrictive practices and pervasive xenophobia sanctioned under the Department of Homeland Security and ostensibly meant to protect American citizens."[25] And for Victor, America cannot be found. It lies tantalizingly beyond the doors of the lounge that he has been forbidden to use, the doors that open onto the streets of New York. The cutting irony is that Victor is a lovely and gentle man, as are the other Americans whom he meets as workers in the airport shops. And when, at the end, Victor does get out of the airport and into New York, America dazzles him with its beauty and cultural energy. All the greater shame, then, to keep it locked up, walled off, through a rigidly inflexible set of bureaucratic rules and policies that deny all the best values that America represents.

The Terminal is foremost a comedy linked with romance that sees Victor falling in love with a flight attendant played by Catherine Zeta-Jones. Questions about what heavy-handed Homeland Security policies aimed at keeping foreigners out of the country might do to the values of America remain a subordinate element in the film, although they furnish the narrative with one of its premises. In Spielberg's next two films, however, the linkages with 9/11 become more explicit. *War of the Worlds* is a reimagining of the 1898 H. G. Wells novel and also a remake of the 1953 film directed by Byron Haskin. Unlike Spielberg's earlier science fiction classics—*E.T.: The Extra-Terrestrial* (1982) and *Close Encounters of the Third Kind* (1977)—which are optimistic depictions of encounters with alien beings, *War of the Worlds* is a grim, dark, violent portrait of an alien invasion that lays waste to America.

In these terms, it is an imaginative reworking of the events of 9/11, albeit on a larger and more apocalyptic scale. Spielberg has acknowledged that the film speaks to the anxieties roused by al Qaeda's attacks on Manhattan and Washington D.C., and in this regard the film adapts the topical anxieties of the 1950s science fiction films to the contemporary period. Speaking about films such as *Invaders from Mars* (1953) and *Earth vs. the Flying Saucers* (1956), Spielberg said, "I always was very interested in the fact that these films came out in response to our fears about the Soviet Union and a possible nuclear war someday between America and the Soviets, and those films were analogous and very metaphorical and preyed on our fears of being attacked from another country or from being attacked from the sky. Now in the shadow of 9/11, it felt that *War of the Worlds* had a special significance."[26] Like contemporary action thrillers, *Earth vs. the Flying Saucers* has imagery of alien spaceships smashing and toppling famous Washington D.C. landmarks.

The metaphors in *War of the Worlds* are more powerful and pointed in their significance than what Spielberg had countenanced in *The Terminal*. The story begins in Manhattan and its surrounding boroughs. Ray Ferrier (Tom Cruise) works in the shipyard and is a selfish and irresponsible parent, but finds, once the aliens begin their attack, that the impulse to protect his children becomes overpowering. The movie follows his efforts to take his son and daughter to safety away from the zones of devastation. Screenwriter David Koepp wanted to avoid imagery showing landmark buildings being destroyed, understanding that such images had become clichés of disaster

FIGURE 2.2 9/11 news imagery of crowds in Manhattan fleeing the collapsing Trade Center towers influenced Spielberg's depiction of crowds fleeing the aliens in *War of the Worlds*. (Frame enlargement)

movies and also feeling that it would be inappropriate since New York had experienced such events for real. Thus most of the action occurs outside the city, on highways and in rural countryside, creating some conceptual distance from the indelibly urban imagery of the 9/11 attacks.

But in other ways Spielberg evokes that day in clear terms. The horrific imagery of New Yorkers fleeing through the streets as the trade towers fell provides the film with its basic narrative premise—run from the invaders—and the visual design of its action scenes. As Ray wanders through one scene of devastation, a blizzard of detritus—clothing, papers, and pieces of hundreds of victims who have been vaporized by the aliens—floats down from the sky. The imagery is modeled on the iconic storm of papers and other bits of the Twin Towers that rained down on Manhattan after the planes struck and again after the buildings fell. An airplane crash in the film causes great devastation. A passenger jet hits a suburban home, and the grotesque imagery of the destroyed airplane amid suburbia conveys a surreal jolt like that of the planes striking the Twin Towers. Ray also sees murals posted on walls, composed of photographs of missing loved ones and notes asking for information about their whereabouts. Hundreds of these photos and notes appeared throughout Manhattan following the loss of the Twin Towers, and they became one of the icons of that event. As Warren Buckland summarizes these connections, "The first attack scene borrows from the iconography of the World Trade Center attacks: the destruction of an American city street; large numbers of people fleeing the scene of an attack, some covered in ash and dust; boards full of notes to and photos of missing people; a downed jumbo jet wreaking havoc."[27]

Like the 9/11 hijackers and Omar Abdel Rahman's circle of conspirators, the aliens in the film are sleeper cells lying undetected in America until they launch their attack. Huge war machines lie below the surface of the Earth, which the aliens activate by riding bolts of lightening into the machinery. The war machines then erupt to the surface and begin incinerating people and buildings. When the attack begins and Ray flees with his children, they each ask about the destruction, "Is it terrorists?" While this dialogue is part of the film's metaphoric discourse, it nevertheless seems out of place in the fictional fantasy because it is too literal and too unconnected to any social realities that have been established in the story. By contrast, the imagery that Spielberg creates works much better because it isn't literal and because it is rooted in the story context.

War of the Worlds is a blunt and one-dimensional film, showing an extreme situation eliciting a narrow range of emotional responses by the characters, mainly terror and blind panic. People spend a lot of time screaming at one another and fighting with each other. In this respect, it fails to get one of the most memorable things about 9/11, which was the impressive spirit of cooperation that prevailed at the World Trade Center amongst office workers and the first responders as the buildings were being evacuated. People were not trampling one another in a blind rush for the stairs. They moved in an orderly and organized way and helped those who were hurt or whose personal infirmities handicapped their abilities to exit the building. Spielberg seems not to have aimed to capture this spirit of cooperation. He shows instead panic, disorder, anger, and antisocial violence, as people turn on one another in a fight for scarce resources. Oddly enough, given what the film shows, he said about disasters, "We really do come together to help each other survive, especially when we have a common enemy." Not only does the film not show this spirit of cooperation, the idea itself—as stated—is irrelevant to what transpired on 9/11. The spirit of cooperation at the Twin Towers didn't result because there was a perceived common enemy (unless the fire is construed as the enemy; Spielberg, though, was talking about a political enemy). It resulted through people responding at their best because they were in the worst of circumstances, a quality of human behavior that eludes the film. The perception that al Qaeda had attacked America came later, and, when it did, it fostered a tremendous spirit of unity in the country. This unity is what Spielberg seems to have been referring to, whereas the responses of people in duress and under the immediate trauma of an unfolding calamity are depicted rather unflatteringly in the film, as compared with the noble and uplifting behavior evident in the midst of the real attacks. Moreover, the scale of the destruction depicted in the film—the aliens launch a massive attack on numerous cities using advanced, very deadly weaponry—contains an irony. As Lester Friedman has pointed out, the highly mechanized destruction we witness in the film is much closer to the devastation the U.S. inflicted on Iraq than to 9/11.[28] Indeed, screenwriter Koepp said, "I view [the film] as an antiwar film, especially an anti–Iraq War film."[29]

Spielberg also said that "this film touches mostly on how this much catastrophe can bring about that much healing." While many who lost friends and relatives on 9/11 have moved on with their lives, it seems inappropriate to frame 9/11 in positive terms as an event that produced healing. And certainly the film shows little of this beyond the rehabilitation of Ray Ferrier into a more effective parent. The balm that Spielberg offers viewers at the end is the abrupt destruction of the aliens by common bacteria (a plot twist in the Wells novel) and the survival of the Ferrier family, which improbably includes Ray's son who was last seen rushing into the fireball of combat between the U.S. military and the aliens. But this is where popular entertainment has always pulled back. If the apocalypse does come and we lose our major cities, it won't be so bad—our films have been making this promise throughout the age of terrorism. We may lose Baltimore in *The Sum of All Fears*, but our hero and heroine will muddle through and then joke about getting engaged. In Spielberg's variation, the hero's family must survive. Ray's death, or more especially, the death of one or both of his children, is utterly unthinkable. An alien invasion might incinerate New York and other major cities, but children must not perish. Thus, at the end, Ray and his kids join his ex-wife and her parents in a Boston home that has remained untouched by the destruction. Perhaps a warm turkey dinner awaits them in the dining room.

War of the Worlds is a simplistic and not very ambitious film; it stays within the comfortable boundaries of popular entertainment, evoking topical anxieties and countering these with warm sentiment. Judging from his next film, Spielberg evidently felt that 9/11 required a response that was less arch than what he offered in *War of the Worlds* and that was more sophisticated and nuanced. With *Munich*, therefore, Spielberg embraced a style less adorned by cinematic flourishes than *The Terminal* and *War of the Worlds* because it was not conceived as an entertainment film. The influence of 9/11 is felt more profoundly here than in his two previous pictures, partly because this one deals with real terrorism and actual history rather than the domains of whimsy and fantasy. Although *Munich* portrays events that occurred more than a quarter century ago, Spielberg and screenwriter Tony Kushner clearly saw the narrative as a contemporary one, and they draw connections with 9/11 at numerous places in the film. The movie portrays the terrorism at the Munich Olympics and its aftermath as the 9/11 of that era.

On September 5, 1972, eight Black September terrorists stormed the Munich apartment of the Israeli Olympic weightlifting team, killed two members of the team, and held the remaining nine as hostages. The kidnappers demanded that two hundred Palestinian prisoners held in Israeli jails be freed, along with the two founding members of Germany's Baader-Meinhof gang, Andreas Baader and Ulrike Meinhof. After hours of fruitless efforts by Munich authorities to negotiate with the terrorists, the kidnappers demanded transportation to Cairo and were taken by helicopter to Furstenfeldbruck, a military airport where the German authorities planned an ambush. But the ambush was horribly botched in a series of amateurish mistakes, such as the failure to station enough snipers to take out the terrorists, the failure to equip the snipers with walkie-talkies so that they could coordinate their attack, and the failure to adequately light the airfield so that the snipers could find their targets. In the ensuing firefight, Black September slaughtered all the hostages and blew up one of the helicopters.

In his history of this affair, Simon Reeve wrote that "the events in Munich were the beginning of the modern era of international terrorism. The Munich attack was the 9/11 of the 1970s. Millions of Germans, and hundreds of millions of other viewers around the world, watched transfixed as hooded gunmen stepped onto the global stage and orchestrated a theatrical and bloody day-long siege that ended in a massacre."[30] Several factors make it reasonable to view these events in the terms that Reeve describes and that Spielberg proposes in the film, namely, as an analogue of September 11. The first is the overly theatrical nature of the terrorist act. The Olympics are an international competition and ceremony whose keynote is peace among nations, and the sporting events are a constructive way of sublimating national conflicts. The violence that Black September brought to the Olympic village at Munich was improbable in that context, and therefore terrifically shocking, as were the acts of flying airplanes into buildings on a beautiful fall day in New York. In both cases, horrific cruelty suddenly erupted by careful design in a context whose serene tone seemingly excluded it. Secondly, the event unfolded on television where it was watched by a global audience, most of whom were horror-struck. Shortly after the athletes were seized, network news covered the crisis and the shootout at Furstenfeldbruck. The news coverage produced images that became iconic, like the smoke from the Twin Towers. Chief among these was the picture of a terrorist with his head encased in a stocking mask, pacing on the balcony outside the apartment. The image looked frightening, alien, irrational, a constellation of perceptions that would be evoked years later by the imagery of United 175 hitting the South Tower. In both cases, the images showed a ruthless violence directed against civilians whose perpetrators had conceived it as flamboyant political theater. Thirdly, the attack was experienced in Israel in profound psychological and emotional terms. Here were Jews being killed in Germany once again. Munich shocked, terrified, and angered the Israeli public on a level that Americans would come to understand on September 11. In each case, the slaughter of civilians said to the respective nations, in effect, "you have no right to exist."

Looking backwards at 1972 from our present vantage point, then, the shadow of 9/11 falls upon Black September's attack on the Munich Olympics, and Spielberg and Kushner have designed the film so that the events of 1972 speak to the events of 2001. In this respect, *Munich* can be understood as Spielberg's effort to understand the al Qaeda attacks with reference to the past. Spielberg has always been our most American of contemporary filmmakers. He resembles John Ford and Frank Capra in that he is interested in the meaning and the mythology of America as a nation, a culture, an idea, and a people. *Amistad* (1997), *Saving Private Ryan* (1998), and *The Terminal* are reflections on American history, culture, and character. Given this orientation in his work, it was natural that he would respond to the events of 9/11 and natural, too, that they would compel him to explore his own heritage in *Munich* as a Jewish filmmaker, a path that simultaneously enabled him to traverse the meanings of September 11. By delving into Munich, Black September, and its execution of the Israeli athletes, Spielberg delves into his own Jewish and American heritage because the problems of terrorism that he evokes in the film are to be understood as dilemmas that have not been resolved and that continue to plague our world. In fact, it can be argued that Munich led to September 11. As Reeve writes of Munich, "the political issues raised by the slaughter went unresolved, and without a peaceful settlement in the Middle East the mantle of terrorism passed from one generation to the next, and evolved from the weapon of secular militants into the apocalyptic game of fanatics who glory in death."[31]

Thus, Spielberg gives us a film about an iconic act of terrorism and about the political and moral issues that arise in crafting a response to such terrorism. Most of the film deals with the covert operation launched by Mossad against Palestinian leaders that it held responsible for planning and organizing the attack. Implementing a campaign of targeted assassinations, Israel launched several teams, working undercover to track and kill the designated targets. Spielberg's film portrays one such team, led by Avner (Eric Bana), a former bodyguard of Golda Meir. The other members are Steve (Daniel Craig), the getaway driver, Carl (Ciarán Hinds), responsible for cleanup and disinformation, Robert (Mathiew Kassovitz), the bombmaker, and Hans (Hans Zischler), the document handler and forger.

Connections with 9/11 are skillfully established. In a scene where Golda Meir (Lynn Cohen) meets with her cabinet and deliberates over whether to green-light the covert operation, she reflects about the violence at Munich and the rage that lies behind it. "These people—they've sworn to destroy us," she says. The line is motivated by the immediate dramatic context, but it is also salient in reference to al Qaeda's campaign against the U.S. When bin Laden presented his manifesto against America in 1998, he stated it was the duty of Muslims to kill Americans wherever they were found. When Avner is recruited for the task and meets with Meir and her generals, one of them stresses that the Munich events are epochal and cannot be ignored by Israel. "This is something new—what happened in Munich changes everything." The single most common remark heard about 9/11 in the months that followed was that everything had changed. In both cases, the film is saying, the traumas were transforming events for the respective countries.

And in both cases, the traumas produced behaviors in conflict with basic principles. As the Golda Meir character says, "Every civilization finds it necessary to negotiate compromises with its own values." In showing these compromises, *Munich* rises to a level of moral complexity rarely seen in Hollywood films. The movie does not question the need for Israel to respond with violence, but it shows what that response costs those who are its instruments and shows that a cycle of violence and vengeance, once transacted among political antagonists, may be unstoppable. And, the film suggests, it may also be ineffective. Israel's policy of targeted killings, which it has continued in the years since the Munich retaliations, has not deterred acts of terrorism. It actually may have helped to motivate some as acts of revenge. Avner's team is good at its job, and Avner comes to feel that his humanity is being diminished with each kill. By the end, he turns on his Mossad boss, Ephraim (Geoffrey Rush), and asks whether they have accomplished anything at all. "Every man we killed has been replaced by worse." He argues that they should have arrested many of these people rather than kill them. It is the civil law argument for handling terrorism, one that, in our own context, was de-emphasized by President Bush and his administration in favor of a war response, which is epitomized in the film by Ephraim. When Ephraim assures Avner that there is compelling evidence against all those they killed, Avner protests, "Evidence that nobody has seen." Indeed, Avner's team was given only photographs and names of targets but not the evidence linking them to crimes. The resonance of this dialogue for our own era of extraordinary renditions, indefinite detentions, and secret military tribunals is powerful. Ephraim tells Avner that he killed the men for Munich, for peace, and for the future, but Avner replies, "There's no peace at the end of this, no matter what you believe. You know this is true." The film arrives at a dark place, finally. It finds a moral necessity for violent retribution but finds as well that there can be no escape from the cycle of violence unleashed by retribution.

This truth is dramatized through the extraordinary empathy that Spielberg builds into the film. He details the depth of the outrage experienced by Israelis in connection with Munich, but he also shows the humanity of the Palestinians targeted by Avner's team. In some cases, they are figures of culture and learning and occupy positions of professional respect within Western Europe. Wael Zwaiter (Makram Khoury), for example, is a professor who has spent years translating the *Arabian Nights* into Italian, and when we meet him he is giving a reading of his translation to an audience in Rome at a sidewalk café. Before he is murdered by Avner, he stops in a delicatessen and shares kind words with its manager, whom he calls by name, clearly a friend in the local neighborhood. When Avner throws down on him in an apartment corridor and asks if Zwaiter knows why he has come, the old man meekly raises his hand and tries to move Avner's gun away from his chest. The gunshots supplied by sound designer Ben Burtt are intentionally harsh and loud,

FIGURE 2.3 Robert (Mathieu Kassovitz) and Avner (Eric Bana) draw down on Zwaiter, their first targeted assassination. (Frame enlargement)

and the bullets burst a bottle of milk that Zwaiter has been clutching to his chest. He falls amidst the milk, an action that replicates the assassination of Sen. Thomas Jordan (John McGiver), a very sympathetic character, by the brainwashed Raymond Shaw (Laurence Harvey) in *The Manchurian Candidate* (1962). By humanizing Zwaiter in compelling terms (and for film buffs by referencing *The Manchurian Candidate*), Spielberg complicates the viewer's response to this assassination.

Dr. Mahmoud Hamshari (Igal Naor), another victim, is a well-to-do PLO official with a wife and little girl. "We are for twenty-four years the world's largest refugee population, our homes taken from us, living in camps, no future, no food, nothing decent for our children," he says to Robert (who is posing as a reporter) in a very reasonable tone. When Robert asks if this justifies the attack in Munich, Hamshari's response provides an illustration of the cyclic nature of vengeance killings. Hamshari says, evasively, that the PLO condemns attacks on civilians even though for twenty-four years "our civilians have been attacked by the Israelis." Hamshari's wife asks, rhetorically, after all this bloodshed who mourns for the Palestinians? And Hamshari adds that Israel has just bombed two refugee camps in Syria and Lebanon, killing two hundred people. "Right after Munich they did this." Then his wife asks the question at the core of the film, "And where does it end? How will it ever end?" Following this conversation, and taking care not to kill the little girl, Avner's team blows up Hamshari with a telephone bomb. Ephraim has instructed Avner to use bombs whenever possible because they are more terrorizing than bullets and will spread alarm among the Palestinians. Is such a strategy not terrorism?

Before bombing the hotel room of another target, Avner shares an awkward moment with the man he is about to kill on adjoining hotel balconies in

Cyprus. Avner is posing as a tourist, and, as with Zwaiter and Hamshari, this victim's humanity is emphasized in unambiguous terms. The last we see of him is after the bombing. One of his arms hangs from a ceiling fan.

The most substantive encounter between Avner and his adversaries comes when Avner's team inadvertently shares a hotel room with a group of Palestinian fedayeen. Avner, posing as a member of Germany's Red Army Faction, speaks with one of the Palestinians, Ali (Omar Metwally), who talks passionately about the Palestinian need for a home. Unlike Zwaiter and Hamshari, who were actual targets of the Mossad operation, Ali is a fictional character invented in order to highlight the ironic similarity between the Israelis and the Palestinians, namely, the desire of each people for a home and land to call their own. "We want to be a nation," Ali says. He predicts that the Arab world will rise against Israel and wipe it out because Arabs dislike Jews even more than Palestinians. Avner tells him this is a delusion, that Palestinians have nothing to bargain with and that every time they kill Jews, the world thinks them animals. "Yes, but then the world will see how [Israelis] have made us into animals. They will start to ask questions about the conditions in our cages." Avner asks Ali if he truly misses his father's olive trees; does he really think he must get back that chalky soil for his children? Is that truly what he wants? Ali says it absolutely is. "Home is everything." This very idea is voiced later by Avner's mother, who tells him that everything he did was justified because it protects Israel. Speaking of the land, she says, "A place on earth, at last, we have a place on earth."

These common aspirations, cloaked in violence, locked in political antagonism, are the darkest ironies shown by the film and provide, simultaneously, the reasons why peace ought to be possible and why it has never been achieved. As a moral document, *Munich* affirms the need to respond with principled violence to terrorism that targets civilians but shows that doing so can compromise a democratic society's core values. In the case of Israel, what is sacrificed is a commitment to the rule of law and the belief in Jewish righteousness, that Jews do not wantonly and coldly kill others. In the case of the United States, the values are those enshrined in the Bill of Rights, which have come under pressure from the government with its claim that special war powers are needed to combat terrorism, and in the prohibition against torture contained in the Geneva Conventions. The film's honesty in showing the intractable nature of the Israeli-Palestinian conflict brings it to a very dark and cheerless conclusion. In the final moments, the film counterpoints Avner's anguished moral doubt about the rightness of the policy of targeted assassinations with Ephraim's cold-blooded *realpolitik*. Avner asks whether their targets were really terrorists or whether Israel was, in fact, targeting the entire Palestinian leadership, and he says that new terrorists continue to appear. Ephraim replies, "I shouldn't cut my nails because they grow back?" Their rift cannot be healed, and as they walk off separately, the camera pans to follow Avner and settles on the film's final composition. It is a long shot of Manhattan with the World Trade Center looming in the distance. The emblematic image of the Twin Towers, which is a digital effect because they can no longer be photographed, provides a haunting and explicit connection between the terrorism of this period and of our own and emphasizes that the moral paradoxes and challenges of responding to such terror confront us today. Al Qaeda's hatred for America and the West is a religiously motivated rage stirred up by its perceptions of American foreign policy; the Palestinian struggle against Israel in the 1970s was not. The terrorism practiced by Palestinian fedayeen was political, not sacred. And yet the era that Munich helped to usher in, with slaughter conceived in terms of its impact as a mass media image, remains one in which we are caught and in which we are beset by the problems that the film has so acutely portrayed. And thus far, as Spielberg shows, there is no way out.

THE RESPONSE BY INDEPENDENT FILMMAKERS

To date, *Munich* remains the most sophisticated moral examination of terrorism and the response of a democratic society to it that Hollywood has produced. But like Spielberg's other films in this period, and like Spike Lee's *25th Hour,* it is not a film directly about 9/11. It gets to that topic obliquely, just as *25th Hour* had done. A direct engagement from Hollywood with the events of September 11 was not forthcoming until 2006, when *World Trade Center* and *United 93* were released. *World Trade Center* depicts the attacks on Manhattan, and *United 93* depicts the hijacking of the titular flight and the aggressive response by passengers when they learn that the other airline hijackings that day have been suicide missions. I will discuss these films momentarily. First, though, it is important to point out that, while Hollywood moved slowly to mount portraits of 9/11, independent film was more nimble in coming to terms with the attacks. In fact, several independent films play like dispatches from the front, composed under fire, as it were. *WTC View* (2005) is based on a play conceived and written less than a year after the attacks and which the playwright, Brian Sloan, intended to function as a portrait of the strange days that immediately followed the destruction of the towers. Although the film was not released until 2005, its source material was written and produced on the stage immediately after the attacks. The play focused on a New York photographer who struggles with feelings of depression and confusion in the weeks following 9/11. Adapting his play to the screen, Sloan retained the original cast of actors, who give wonderful performances as ordinary New Yorkers caught inside a terrible moment of history. Sloan uses humor to probe the emotional effects of the attacks upon his characters, and this is a very unusual gambit for films about 9/11, which tend to be somber and serious, as if humor necessarily would be disrespectful. In a plot situation based on Sloan's own experience, the photographer, Eric (Michael Urie, in a terrific performance), places an ad for a new roommate on September 10. His phone starts ringing on the 11th with calls from people answering the ad, a development that he finds surreal under the circumstances. The action of the film is confined to Eric's apartment and follows his interactions with a series of men who come to look the place over. Inexorably, Eric and his visitors find themselves compelled to talk about where they were on the day of the tragedy.

Eric's window provided a view of the World Trade Center. Now it's gone, and people visiting the apartment stand before the window gazing at the smoke in the distance. In the film, these views are always off-camera. Nothing is shown of the city as viewed from the window, and this gambit furnishes an excellent metaphor for representing that which is now absent. One prospective roommate stands in a foreground close-up, framed by a wide angle lens. Looking at the window off-camera, he asks about the towers with wonderment, "Could you see them from here?" At the end of the film, Eric gazes at the view off-camera and murmurs that the smoke is "kind of white today, wispy almost." The towers had been part of his emotional landscape for the ten years he was in the apartment, and now their loss defines a different configuration of his emotional world. *WTC View* is about Eric's effort to regain his moorings, a struggle that the film suggests was shared by many New Yorkers.

Written so soon after the tragedy, the play eloquently captured numerous details of the period's zeitgeist. These are carried over into the film so that watching it is to experience a kind of poetic sociology of the period. Eric's friend Josie tells him how disorienting it is to attend a dinner party where everyone is *so nice* to one another. "Everyone was being so sincere and thoughtful and interested in what you had to say. It was kind of freaking me out." She also reacts to all the flags that appeared in New York and to all the lovemaking that is said to have followed the collapse of the towers. "I don't want to have some tacky, patriotic 9/11 baby along with the rest of the city," she declares. "I love my country and everything but this flag stuff . . . it's like living in Texas!" These are riffs created within the slice of time to which they refer.

WTV View was screened at the New York Lesbian and Gay Film Festival and is distributed mainly on DVD. It's a sensitive, well written, at times funny, and finely acted dramatization of the aftermath of the attacks, a personal interpretation by Sloan and his actors of a moment in time that is now gone but for which the film provides an enduring portrait.

It places the epic scale of 9/11 into small, human terms, as does *The Guys* (2002), which also is an adaptation of material originally performed on the stage. In the dark days after 9/11, New York's Flea Theater commissioned a play that could be performed as a response to the attacks. The idea was to use art as a means of intervening in a desperate situation. Anne Nelson's play opened on December 4 and provided a cathartic experience for audiences who were still reeling from the loss and destruction. The play, like the film, focuses on two main characters—Joan, an Upper West Side writer and mother, who agrees to help Nick, an FDNY captain who lost nine men in the towers and who must now deliver eulogies for them. Joan's tools are words, and she writes the eulogies based on what Nick tells her about the men. The play and film focus on their dialogue about the first four men Nick has to eulogize and the emotional connection that Joan and Nick reach with one another through their collaboration.

Nelson wrote the screenplay for the film, with Sigourney Weaver and Anthony LaPaglia as Joan and Nick. Like the play, the film was timely in relation to what it showed. It was released in December 2002, a mere fifteen months after the attacks. As with *WTC View*, this timeliness gives the film its power. What it may lose over the longer view, it gains in vividness and immediacy as the portrait of a crisis created from within the eye of the storm. One of Joan's monologues, for example, addresses the meaning of the question, "Are you okay?," which, she says, people were asking one another all the rest of September, in situations of varying proximity to the disaster. Most immediately, "Were you at Ground Zero and wounded, suffocated, or covered in white ash? No? I guess you're okay." More distantly, "If someone died in the towers you had dinner with once and thought was a really nice person, are you okay?," or "If you look at a flier of a missing person in the subway and you start to lose it, are you okay?" Is anyone okay? she asks finally.

The film's opening is tremendously poetic. Video footage with a time counter from a camera mounted on the door of a fire station shows a solitary firefighter looking down the street at 8:38 A.M. on September 11. He is joined by another firefighter, as hell is about to arrive, initially in the form of a solitary piece of paper that floats ominously down from the now wounded North Tower. The video footage is accompanied by the traditional Irish song, "The Dawn of the Day," with new lyrics beautifully written by singer Mary Fahl

FIGURE 2.4 Nick (Anthony LaPaglia), an FDNY captain, braces himself before delivering a eulogy for one of his fallen firefighters in *The Guys*. (Frame enlargement)

that provide a lament for the loss of life on 9/11. In the next moments, these men take their truck out of the station, heading for the towers. They vanish in the collapse, no trace of them found. Joan and Nick must verbalize the enduring value of their lives so that this gift, the eulogy, can be offered to their families, friends, and colleagues. Like *WTC View*, *The Guys* scales the magnitude of citywide trauma to an intimate level and illuminates the emotional landscape of loss in honest and nonmelodramatic terms.

In the years that followed, independent film continued to address 9/11. *Day Night Day Night* (2006) is a minimalist portrait of a female suicide bomber's preparations for death in a planned bombing of Times Square. The film strips all political, personal, and biographical detail from the story, creating an abstract, purely formal portrait of a suicide bomber.

The War Within (2005) chronicles the destructive interaction of a radicalized Pakistani, Hassan (Ayad Akhtar), and a prosperous, Westernized Muslim family living in Jersey City. As the film opens, Hassan is an innocent man who is the victim of an extraordinary rendition. CIA agents kidnap him on the streets of Paris and send him back to Pakistan, where he is beaten and tortured. In prison there, he meets a member of the Muslim Brotherhood and becomes radicalized. Hassan's political transformation is the narrative premise of the film. Released from prison three years later, he travels to Jersey City and rooms with the family of his childhood friend, Sayeed. Unknown to them, Hassan belongs to an Islamist cell plotting to bomb Grand Central Station.

The film counterpoints Hassan's brand of violent Islam with the practices of the Jersey community in which he finds himself. Sayeed is a doctor. His family is prosperous, and the Muslim community of which they are part has assimilated to American society. As Sayeed tells Hassan over a meal, "Look at this restaurant here. There are Jews, Christians, Muslims, everyone sitting here eating comfortably, safely, peacefully, going to school together, business together. What's wrong with that?" The leader of a local mosque tells his congregants that jihad is the struggle of everyday life, the challenge of being good in response to the ordinary uncertainties of daily living. But Hassan cannot reconcile these views with the violent fundamentalism that he has adopted, and the irony is that his brand of Islam, which is secretive and deceptive in its relations with Sayeed and the family, cuts him off from the mainstream Islamic community in Jersey City. Hassan remains isolated and angry, and when he succeeds in a suicide bombing of Grand Central Station, he also destroys the family that had adopted him. The FBI arrest Sayeed, and Duri, Sayeed's sister, is killed in the blast. The film's title evokes the multilayered conflict that the story dramatizes, a war within America, within Islam, and within the minds and hearts of those individuals who are affected.

This Revolution (2005) is an homage to Haskell Wexler's *Medium Cool* (1969), substituting the Iraq War for Vietnam and the 2004 Republican National Convention in New York for Chicago's Democratic National Convention of 1968. As in *Medium Cool*, a television cameraman, with the filmic name Jake Cassavetes (Nathan Crooker), becomes involved with street protests against the war. He also learns that his television network has turned over his footage of the protesters to the Department of Homeland Security (a plot point that derives from the Wexler film). The station's broadcast operations manager says that when the Pentagon or Homeland Security asks for our material, we're only too happy to give it to them. *This Revolution* is not as politically shrewd as *Medium Cool*, but it does contain exceptionally vivid footage of the real protests that surrounded the convention, including footage of actress Rosario Dawson being arrested for real by the NYPD, who assumed they were detaining a real rabble-rouser and not an actress working on a film. The movie also is a rarity, a genuinely left-wing narrative feature that enables its characters to voice ideas seldom broached in mainstream commercial film. Tina Santiago (Dawson), for example, tells Jake that wars are fought all the time by the rich for land or oil or a cheap labor pool, the working class does the dying, and if the media had pushed this idea as much as they pushed the Iraq War on the public, there'd be an uprising in the streets.

OLIVER STONE'S WORLD TRADE CENTER

The major Hollywood films about 9/11—*World Trade Center* and *United 93*—differ from these independent productions in drawing a broader, more ambitious, and epically scaled portrait. *World Trade Center* generated controversy as soon as the project was announced because Oliver Stone was set to direct. Remarks made by Stone after 9/11 at a public forum, about the attacks being the result of American foreign policy, incensed many people. As reported in the *New York Observer,* Stone had said "The Arabs have a point, whether they did it right or not," and he referred to "the revolt of September 11."[32] Stone subsequently clarified his intended meaning this way: "I said that 9/11 was a rebellion against what Arabs considered an oppressive system of capitalism and military troops in the Middle East. I got killed for that."[33] Many commentators and viewers also felt that he was an inappropriate choice for the film because of his previous work—*Platoon* (1986), *Wall Street* (1987), *JFK* (1991)—which critiqued U.S. domestic and foreign policy. *JFK,* in particular, earned Stone his reputation as a conspiracy theorist because of its portrait of a vast right-wing cabal plotting the assassination. But Stone surprised everyone by making a film that emphasized heroism and moral uplift and did not include a social or political perspective on the attacks. This was a different kind of film than the more political work he had intended to make before the storm of criticism his remarks elicited descended upon him. As he told blogger Stephen Applebaum, "Suffice it to say that after the criticism I got I kind of shied away [from a political film]. I didn't want to be the bad guy again."[34]

This gambit worked to the financial benefit of the film. Not only did it ensure that the finished product avoided the expected controversy, but it enabled conservative pundits to embrace the movie. Numerous commentators on the political right, who ordinarily regarded Stone with antagonism, lauded the film and praised his work as director. Cal Thomas, for example, wrote that the film is "one of the greatest pro-American, pro-family, pro-faith, pro-male, flag-waving, God Bless America films you will ever see. What? Oliver Stone, who hangs out with and praises Fidel Castro? Oliver Stone, who indulges in conspiracy theories and is a dues-paying member of the Hollywood left? Yes, THAT Oliver Stone."[35] Aware of Stone's reputation among political conservatives, Paramount Pictures, the film's distributor, hired a conservative public relations firm, Creative Response Concepts, to push the film favorably among its constituency. The firm's client base included the Republican National Committee, the Christian Coalition, and Regnery Publishing, the house that issued *Unfit for Command,* the Swift Boat Veterans' attack on John Kerry's military record. If politics makes strange bedfellows, Hollywood marketing is an orgy of spouse swapping. Certainly, this combination of Oliver Stone and the coalition of interests represented by Creative Response was a startling turn of events and a savvy move on the part of Paramount Pictures. Courting the opinion leaders on the political right helped to defang Stone's reputation and helped the film avoid becoming the incendiary provocation that many feared it might be.

But Stone also cooperated in this makeover. The storm of criticism had humbled him. Moreover, his previous film, *Alexander* (2004), a deeply personal project, had been released to critical scorn and became a box office failure in the U.S. Budgeted at $155 million, it grossed only $34 million domestically. *Alexander* was the kind of colossal failure—a genuinely bad movie that struck out with critics and the public—that can set back a filmmaker's career, especially when he has been a kind of rebel against the system, as Stone has been. He needed, therefore, a box office success, and he had also come to feel worn down by the ideological struggles that many of his films had elicited. His documentary on Castro, *Commandante* (2003), had not been released in the U.S. for political and commercial reasons. Thus, when the script for *World Trade Center* was being shopped for directors, Stone was not on the A list of first choices. Paramount Pictures, however, was willing to take a chance with him because the script emphasized human drama, not politics, and also because Stone promised to deliver a film that faithfully reflected the script. In his audio commentary, which appears on the DVD release of the film, Stone admits that, while the script moved him deeply, it wasn't the kind of depiction of September 11 that he typically would have created. He called it a microcosmic portrait, one that concentrated on the lives of five people, sacrificing a more expansive point of view for a perspective constrained by what these individuals saw on that day.

The five characters are two real Port Authority policemen who were trapped alive in the rubble of the collapsed South Tower, their wives, and a former Marine, who was living in Connecticut and who traveled to Manhattan to help in the emergency and found the trapped men. PA officers John McLoughlin (Nicolas Cage) and Will Jimeno (Michael Peña) were among the first responders on the scene. McLoughlin was leading Jimeno and three other officers, bearing rescue equipment through the shopping concourse beneath the Trade Center plaza, when the South Tower came down, crushing the concourse and trapping them in the rubble. Along with McLoughlin and Jimeno, Dominick Pezzulo (Jay Hernandez) survived, but he was subsequently killed by debris dislodged in their underground prison when the North Tower fell. The bulk of the film, then, focuses on McLoughlin and Jimeno's ordeal, cutting between their efforts to stay alive amid the debris and the anxious efforts of their wives, surrounded at home by family members, to find out whether their men are alive. While the McLoughlin-Jimeno narrative is a remarkable one, more so is the story of David Karnes (Michael Shannon). A former Marine, he left his job in Connecticut, told his pastor to ask God to guide him to victims in need of rescue, drove down to Manhattan, walked out onto the rubble pile at Ground Zero, and found McLoughlin and Jimeno. He then reenlisted and spent two tours of duty in Iraq.

The narrative of these events is extraordinarily compelling, and Stone felt a deep sense of obligation to portray the events correctly and to honor the men involved and their families. Thus the film aims to tell a factually oriented story at all times, and most of what we see on screen is based on the recollections of participants in the events, with John and Donna McLoughlin and Will and Allison Jimeno sharing screenplay credit with writer Andrea Berloff and providing the firsthand information that formed the core of the script. Jimeno's recollections of Pezzulo's death in the rubble, for example, enabled Stone to portray the officer's last moments. The portrait emphasizes Pezzulo's efforts to save his comrades and how, at the moment of his death, he fired his pistol in a final effort to send a signal to anyone above that his comrades were alive. The events depicted in the film are so extreme, and the behavior that victims and rescuers exhibit is so noble, that it is difficult not to be tremendously moved while watching the film.

At the same time, the consequence of the film's restricted point of view is to minimize the scale of the disaster to the extent that it becomes an offscreen

FIGURE 2.5 John McLoughlin (Nicolas Cage) pauses in the shopping concourse beneath the Trade Center plaza moments before the South Tower collapses. (Frame enlargement)

event. The film does not show the airplanes striking the Twin Towers. The impact is portrayed impressionistically because neither McLoughlin nor Jimeno witnessed it. As an on-duty Jimeno talks with pedestrians on the street, a passing shadow darkens their faces, and the shadow of an airplane briefly appears on the face of a nearby building. Then Stone cuts inside the Port Authority, where officials hear a muffled but powerful boom. Only a few shots in the film show the smoking Trade Center towers—these are digitally animated re-creations—and one shot shows a jumper falling from the North Tower, another digitally animated effect. We are eight-and-a-half minutes into the film when Jimeno sees the passing shadow on the building face, and at twenty-four-and-a-half minutes the South Tower falls, trapping McLoughlin and Jimeno. The remaining 104 minutes of the film are spent either in the darkness beneath Ground Zero or well away from it, inside the homes of the McLoughlin and Jimeno families. Thus the amount of screen time devoted to the disaster as it unfolds is minimal. In real time, 102 minutes elapsed between the first strike on the North Tower and that tower's collapse. This interval, filled with a tremendous amount of activity as the thousands of people in the two towers reacted with alarm and confusion and then evacuated or were trapped by the fires, and as police and firefighters raced into the buildings, occupies only sixteen minutes of screen time. Even this abbreviated interval, however, is obliquely portrayed. Much of the time is spent traveling with McLoughlin and other officers as they drive from the Port Authority office to the financial district and then spent underground in the shopping concourse as McLoughlin and his men assemble their equipment. By confining the film's focus to what the principal characters experienced, Stone is unable to capture the enormity of the event. It is portrayed indirectly and rapidly and in miniature, with the film's focus restricted to the eye-witness perspectives of McLoughlin and Jimeno.

In other films, Stone has powerfully integrated the psychological dimension of his characters with larger social and historical contexts. In *Platoon,* his focus alternates between capturing the physical experience of combat in a jungle environment and a moral commentary on the war as symbolized in the competing loyalties that the protagonist, Taylor (Charlie Sheen), feels for the two sergeants, Elias (Willem Dafoe) and Barnes (Tom Berenger). In *Born on the Fourth of July* (1989), the ruined body of Ron Kovic (Tom Cruise) emblemizes the destructive effects of the Vietnam War on American society. The lure of capitalism and its excesses are seductively embodied by Gordon Gekko (Michael Douglas) in *Wall Street.* The densely structured montages of *JFK* comment on how impermeable to investigation the factual core of the assassination has become. Of course, Stone's interpretations of history are controversial—

everyone does not agree with his points of view. But his aggressive views are one of the factors that have made him a singular and important filmmaker. In light of his abilities to synthesize psychologically powerful portraits of men operating under duress with provocative portraits of the larger social forces that are acting upon them, his choice not to do this in *World Trade Center* reduces the range of experience the film can capture and works to simplify its overall point of view. This makes it a startling film for a director as feisty as Stone normally is. (His next film, *W* (2008), was a return to form, offering a critical but empathetic portrait of President Bush's rise to power from a debauched and unfocused period early in his adulthood.)

It also gives rise to ironies that Stone is unable to control without expanding the complexity of the discourse in the film. Without going outside, and beyond, the points of view of the main characters, without taking the larger view, by staying inside his microcosmic framework he cannot create a dialogue among the perspectives raised by the events that the film portrays. Jimeno, for example, reported that he had a vision of Christ during a particularly terrible period when he was trapped in the rubble. Seeing Jesus, he said, brought him back from the point of death. Stone faithfully incorporates this vision into the film. Several shots during the sequences depicting Jimeno's ordeal show a spectral Christ, surrounded by white light and holding a water bottle. David Karnes, who is a devout Christian, is shown speaking with his pastor and gazing at the cross in his church before journeying to Manhattan. When he arrives at Ground Zero amid the dust cloud left by the collapse of the towers, he tells a fireman, "It looks like God made a curtain with the smoke, shielding us from what we're not yet ready to see." With these portraits, Stone is being faithful to the experiences and outlook of his sources and is honoring their point of view and motivations. He is portraying them with the integrity and respect that they deserve.

On the other hand, Stone's unwillingness to shift gears and levels of presentation, to take a larger view that goes beyond the experiences of these participants, raises issues in the narrative that go unexamined. Faith in God helped to sustain the rescue workers who spent weeks combing through the rubble. Prayer stations and makeshift chapels sprung up near Ground Zero to provide rescuers with spiritual consolation amid all the horror. Religion aided immeasurably in the recovery efforts. At the same time, the September 11 attacks were acts of religious violence, carried out in the name of God. The transcript of United 93's cockpit voice recorder, for example, released in April 2006, revealed numerous invocations of God—"Allah the most merciful," "Allah is the greatest"—by the hijackers. The failed effort in 1993 to destroy the Twin Towers was also motivated by a religiously inspired rage against the

West. One of the plotters, Sayyid Nosair, wrote about the need for destroying the skyscrapers of "the enemies of God," and Sheikh Omar Abdel Rahman, a ringleader of the plot, wrote of the necessity of striking terror into the enemies of God. This idea of a jihad for God was popularized in the writings of Sayyid Qutb, whose influence on a generation of Islamist fundamentalists helped make him one of the ideological founders of such religiously motivated violence. His most influential book, *Milestones,* was completed in 1964 while Qutb was imprisoned for suspicion of participating in an assassination plot against Egypt's leader, Gamal Abdel Nasser. Qutb wrote that jihad in God's name was a Muslim duty and that secular and non-Islamic societies were "enemies of mankind," cesspools of depravity that belonged in hell.[36] He wrote of the animalistic desires that motivate people in the West, wallowing in sex and sin and materialism, and of the West as a giant rubbish heap. Through the influence of his writings, Qutb bequeathed this rage against modernity and desire for moral purity to generations of subsequent jihadists, who included Nosair, Abdel Rahman, Mohammed Atta, and Osama bin Laden.

One of the issues arising, then, from the narrowed focus of *World Trade Center* is that its emphasis on the moral force of Christianity can operate to place the events of September 11 within a religious war or clash-of-civilizations perspective. In an influential essay written a decade before the attacks, Samuel Huntington proposed that "the fault lines between civilizations will be the battle lines of the future" and that centuries-old religious traditions would form one of the matrixes in which conflict between the West and the non-Western world would unfold.[37] Since 9/11 this idea that a clash of civilizations and contest of religions is under way has gained considerable currency in today's debates about Islam and the West. It provides one of bin Laden's most powerful motivations. Bin Laden has often spoken of a crusade and has called for the Islamic cavalry to mount up. Bin Laden was amused when President Bush injudiciously used the term "crusade" in describing the war on terror. "The odd thing is," bin Laden said, "that he [Bush] has taken the words right out of our mouth."[38] When an interviewer asked him if a clash of civilizations was inevitable, he responded, "I say there is no doubt about this. This clash of civilizations] is a very clear matter, proven in the Qur'an and the traditions of the Prophet."[39]

But as I noted in the introduction, this perspective tends to minimize the historical periods of peaceful coexistence between Christianity, Islam, and Judaism and the openness to modernity that had been part of the Islamic experience.[40] The rise of religious fundamentalism as a political force in the last third of the twentieth century has been, in significant measure, a reaction to the failure of secular regimes that were oppressive, such as those imposed by the U.S. in Egypt and Iran. These failures of the secular state have helped motivate the rejection of modernity by many Islamists. In turn, this rejection by religious extremism turns easily to violence. The Islamist hijackers, for example, believed they were fulfilling God's will and that their violence against the West was righteous. The film's invocation of religion, therefore, creates ironies that are perhaps unintended by the filmmakers, especially when measured against the larger context of the day's attacks and their motivating forces. Perhaps *World Trade Center* is not proposing that there is an essential and inevitable conflict between Christianity and Islam, but the film's restricted narrative focus leaves it unable to do justice to the complex role that religion played in the events of that day.

The film's narrow focus creates another and greater limitation. By telling a story about life, the film fails to tell one about death. The scale of life lost at the World Trade Center gives that day one of its indelible meanings. Take that away, and one risks reducing the magnitude of the event. Studio marketing executives probably found a story centering on lives that were saved to be more positive and to carry less box office risk than a story that captured the scale of the loss. Stone's film is a fine and moving portrait, yet because it remains, to date, the only major Hollywood film to portray events at the Twin Towers, the skewing of its focus becomes more problematic than it would be if there were other films about the subject offering a variety of points of view. Writing in the *New York Post,* John Podhoretz praised the film as "undeniably powerful, an immensely affecting and well-meaning real-life tale of two Port Authority policemen trapped in the rubble underneath the collapsed concourse between the North and South Towers." But he went on to say that "because 'World Trade Center' tells a story of joyous survival rather than a story of death, it is a fundamental falsification of the meaning of 9/11—even though the story it tells is true."[41]

PAUL GREENGRASS' UNITED 93

The other major Hollywood film about the events of September 11, *United 93,* is more resolute in facing the terrible losses of that day. The director, Paul Greengrass, brought a powerful realist style to the story of the last flight to be hijacked in al Qaeda's attack on America. Greengrass had shown a shrewd and intelligent command of realist film style in *Bloody Sunday* (2002), his portrait of an Irish protest march in Derry and the violent response by British occupation authorities, filmed in a quasi–cinema vérité style. Like Oliver Stone, Greengrass wanted to honor the facts of what transpired on September 11, and, also like Stone, he wanted to honor the memories of those who participated in the events and of those who lost family members on that day. Both filmmakers, therefore, turned to strongly realist styles in designing their films. But whereas Stone aimed for realism through a drastic restriction of point of view and narrative focus—showing us only what the major participants saw and knew that day—Greengrass opted for a more expansive focus and for a more radical deployment of film style.

Unlike *World Trade Center,* which occludes from on-screen portrayal most of what happened on September 11, *United 93* provides a more comprehensive view. It portrays the efforts by air traffic controllers to respond to the alarming behavior of American Airlines Flight 11 and United Flight 175, which hit the Twin Towers, and American Flight 77, which hit the Pentagon, as well as the titular fight, one that ultimately crashed in a field in Pennsylvania. Unlike Stone's film, which does not show the strikes on the World Trade Center, Greengrass includes a dramatic and powerful re-creation of the second strike, on the South Tower, as viewed by air traffic control administrators in the Newark center. Moreover, Greengrass moves much farther from Hollywood style in his choices to avoid using recognizable actors and to rely on many nonprofessional performers, a group that included actual participants in the day's events. *World Trade Center* foregrounds the Hollywood star, Nicolas Cage, and prominent actors Maria Bello and Maggie Gyllenhaal, whereas *United 93* features a cast mixed between professional actors—but none who are familiar by name or face—and nonprofessionals. Greengrass wanted to emphasize that those who were caught up in the attacks were ordinary people, not celebrities from whom a viewer might expect extraordinary initiative or wild plot turns. There was no hero played by Kurt Russell or any group of infiltrated American commandoes on board United 93 that day, ready to perform the kind of Hollywood heroics that audiences had seen in films such as *Executive Decision.* Instead of the fantasy superheroes fighting terrorism that viewers had enjoyed in Hollywood movies for more than a decade, Greengrass shows average people caught in a situation that was unimaginable and unthinkable and in which they nevertheless had to act.

The style of the film is naturalistic, as Greengrass eschews overt pictorial embellishments by the camera or the editing. The visual design is faux cinema vérité, with camera setups that purposely occlude the viewer's line of sight in compositions where the main narrative focus is often off center or partially glimpsed. The opening of the film, for example, shows Ziad Jarrah, the hijacker who would pilot United 93, praying in the Days Inn motel on the morning of the assault. As soon as we see him in close-up, the back of another member of the hijack team abruptly intrudes into the camera's line of sight, blocking our view. This is an intentionally "bad" composition. The camerawork simulates footage that a documentary filmmaker might capture in an uncontrolled environment, where premeditated staging does not prevail. A similar strategy informs the sound design, which is rich with the ambient noises of airport lounges and multiple, overlapping conversations.

This camera style, of course, is manufactured in order to *simulate* actuality, and the fact that it is a style is emphasized by Greengrass' subsequent work. He pushed the jittery camerawork of *United 93* to distracting extremes in fictional entertainments such as *The Bourne Ultimatum* (2007). While the camera style is a manufactured one, in other respects the shooting style of *United 93* emphasized strict temporal realism. Scenes in the control centers and on the airplane were shot using multiple cameras, with staggered start and reload times. This permitted Greengrass to obtain takes of up to one hour and offered the performers the extraordinary advantage of performing in real time for extended intervals. The sense of authenticity conveyed in these scenes is undeniable. Real air traffic controllers, flight crew, and military personnel played their roles in the film in an uninterrupted span of time that broke down the artificiality of the filming process. By working in ways that emphasized realism and authenticity, Greengrass was aiming to evoke what he has called "a believable truth."[42]

The principal locations re-created in the story—the interior of United 93, Boston and New York Air Traffic Control Centers, the national Air Traffic Control System Command Center in Herndon, Virginia, and the office of NORAD's Northeast Air Defense Sector in Rome, New York—are populated by this mix of actors and real people. The airplane passengers are mostly actors, but the two pilots of United 93, Jason Dahl and Leroy Homer, are portrayed by professional pilots, and the stewardesses on the plane are professional stewardesses. The personnel who appear at the air traffic control centers are mostly real controllers, and the NORAD personnel are real military. The personnel at Newark air control who witness United 175 hitting the South Tower are people who were there that day. The most remarkable nonprofessional in the film is Ben Sliney, the Air Traffic Command Center's national operations manager and the man who gave the unprecedented order, after the Pentagon was hit, to ground all the nation's air traffic. He plays himself in the film, re-creating his reactions to the events of that morning.

His performance and those of the controllers and military officials are notable for being so candid about what happened. In re-creating their disbelieving reactions to the unfolding series of events, they show how the air traffic control system and the defense of U.S. airspace broke down that morning because the events were so unprecedented. It had been years since a plane had been hijacked inside the United States, and there had never been seizures of multiple planes. Hijackings had always ended with the airplane landing somewhere, followed by demands and negotiations. That a hijacked plane would be used as a guided missile was beyond what anyone in the air traffic control and defense sectors had been trained for or would easily imagine. One of the ironies that the film effectively shows is how the Cold War mindset of NORAD focused its attentions on a threat coming into U.S. airspace from overseas and not on a threat that was internal. Moreover, events unfolded that morning too rapidly for an effective response. In contrast to Hollywood's action thrillers, which tend to show the nation's security forces responding to terrorism efficiently and effectively, *United 93* shows the confusion, paralysis, and incomprehension that gripped the air control and defense systems. In doing so, the film does not cast blame; its purpose is to create a visual record through drama of what happened and why, and its point of view corresponds very closely with this judgment rendered by the 9/11 Commission:

> *The defense of U.S. airspace on 9/11 was not conducted in accord with preexisting training and protocols. It was improvised by civilians who had never handled a hijacked aircraft that attempted to disappear, and by a military unprepared for the transformation of commercial aircraft into weapons of mass destruction. . . . We do not believe that the true picture of that morning reflects discredit on the operational personnel at NEADS or FAA facilities. NEADS commanders and officers actively sought out information and made the best judgments they could on the basis of what they knew. [FAA personnel] thought outside the box in recommending a nationwide alert, in groundstopping local traffic, and, ultimately, in deciding to land all aircraft and executing that unprecedented order flawlessly.*[43]

Greengrass and his screenwriters consulted the 9/11 Commission's report and wove the information that it furnished into the narrative of the film. Much of what we see factually corresponds to the documented record of events. The cockpit voice recorder indicated that the hijackers seized a woman inside the cockpit, probably a stewardess, and silenced or killed her. This is portrayed, as are the documented cries of "Mayday" and "Hey, get out of here—get out of here" from the pilots. United 93 was delayed getting out of Newark, and once airborne, the hijackers were slow to move. The other teams seized aircraft within thirty minutes of takeoff, but the United 93 hijackers waited forty-six minutes. Greengrass shows this delay in a manner that builds excruciating suspense. The film documents the confusion over how many hijackers were on board—passengers described three, not four—and Greengrass follows the 9/11

Commission report in showing why. The report speculated that Ziad Jarrah, the hijacker who had trained as a pilot, remained seated and inconspicuous during the seizure and, after passengers had been herded to the back of the plane, only then entered the cockpit. This is what the film shows.

The Commission's report also speculates that Jarrah, once in command of the plane, could have learned that the other flights had hit the World Trade Center from cockpit messages that United was sending to its airborne flights. In line with this suggestion, the film shows Jarrah reacting jubilantly to the successful missions of "the other brothers." The film replicates numerous other data from the 9/11 report, but in some cases Greengrass has changed the order of events in order to enhance the drama. In the film, for example, Jarrah is shown making a cell phone call from the airport while waiting to board with the other passengers. He says "I love you." In fact, Jarrah's final call to his girlfriend, Aysel Senguen, was made from the hotel early on the morning of September 11.[44] But showing it occurring amidst the other passengers enhances the irony of Jarrah's claiming a privilege for himself that he will deny to the others, the ability to say goodbye to loved ones.

A more drastic alteration of the timeline concerns the analysis by Boston's air traffic center of a transmission from Mohammed Atta on American 11 in which he says "We have some planes." The transmission had been garbled, and Boston pulled the tapes and analyzed them. When the message was clarified, Boston alerted the Herndon Command Center about its content at 9:05, just after United 175 struck the South Tower. The film, however, shows this information reaching Herndon *before* either plane has hit the World Trade Center. In the film, when Herndon gets the information, United 93 has just taken off, and American 11 and United 175 are en route to Manhattan. Thus, as shown in the film the information on the tapes becomes more portentous. The film's timing of events creates a terrible sense of foreboding. "We have some planes" points toward a frightening set of events yet to unfold. In actuality, however, the information got to Herndon too late. The Trade Center was already hit, and the recording therefore merely confirmed what had already become quite evident by the time of the attack on the South Tower.

Other changes in the film appear to work for simplicity's sake. In actuality, the air traffic control center in Cleveland was tracking the flight of United 93 when it received the Mayday transmission from the cockpit along with sounds of a struggle, and Cleveland was also involved in tracking Delta 1989, a flight suspected of being another hijack. But the film omits Cleveland Center altogether in order to concentrate on traffic control in Boston and New York. The film also mutes details about one of the most intelligent moves by three out of the four hijack teams, which included those on board United 93. They turned off the transponders in the planes. These send information about the plane's identity and altitude and are used by controllers to track the flight. Turning off the transponder was an effort to hide and evade detection. When the transponders were turned off, the planes vanished from the controllers' screens. American 77, for example, which would hit the Pentagon, was being tracked by Indianapolis Center when it abruptly changed course and all of its data suddenly disappeared from the screen. Unaware of the hijacking, the controller thought the plane had crashed.[45] The plane then traveled undetected for more than thirty minutes toward Washington D.C.

The 9/11 Commission report emphasized that a sudden loss of the transponder signal along with radio communication would typically point toward a catastrophic loss of the plane. "The simultaneous loss of radio and transponder signal would be a rare and alarming occurrence, and would normally indicate a catastrophic system failure or an airplane crash."[46] Without the transponder signal, a controller could still track a plane using primary radar returns, but this entailed reconfiguring the tracking system because these returns aren't typically displayed—the transponder signal is the default display. The film glosses this development and its importance. Although characters in the control centers refer to a loss of transponder signal, the film does not show how deeply alarming this would have been for the controllers. Instead, the film emphasizes the loss of radio communication, the lack of reply from cockpits to controller queries, and portrays this as the main signal of deviant behavior by the planes. Data from the flights never disappear from the controller's scopes until the very last moment when American 11 and United 175 hit the World Trade Center, and the controllers experience no difficulty in tracking the flights. These omissions in the film work to downplay some of the most extraordinary developments of that morning.

In fairness to Greengrass and his screenwriters, they have done exceptionally well at transposing the complex events of that morning into the film. They are particularly adept at showing NORAD's difficulties in getting reliable information. After American 11 had crashed into the North Tower, for example, NORAD received a report from the FAA stating that American 11 was not a hijack and was still in the air, and this is portrayed in the film. When American 77 is finally detected approaching Washington and the FAA alerts NORAD, the on-site commander learns that the military fighters scrambled from Langley are following their Cold War protocols and heading out over the ocean. The film reproduces his exclamation about the need to get them turned around and over Washington—"I don't care how many windows you break!"

One challenge in basing the film on the factual record is that some things are not known and may never be clarified. Why did the hijackers wait much longer than the other teams to seize the plane? The film implies that Jarrah hesitates from a loss of nerve, and that, rather than waiting for his signal, the other members of his team take the initiative. A most important and difficult question involved the use of force by the hijackers and how much of this violence to show in the film. It is not known what happened to the pilots or how the hijackers gained entry to the cockpit or how they overpowered the crew. It is probable but not confirmed that the pilots were killed. Using cell phones and airphones, callers from the plane reported that a flight attendant and a passenger had been killed and that two bodies were on the floor by the cockpit. These were probably the pilot and copilot. Because they are dramatizing the hijacking, the filmmakers opt to be more definitive than the factual record allows. Thus, the film posits that the hijackers coerced a stewardess to knock on the cabin door, prompting the pilots to open it, at which point they were attacked with knives. The killing of the pilots and the stewardess is shown very obliquely. While there is no ambiguity about what is happening, the camera setups tend to be off-angle, with unclear and often blocked sight-lines on the violence, and the editing imposes a choppy, staccato rhythm that serves to occlude details about the killings as they are happening. The filmmakers' were trying to protect the feelings of the families of United 93's passengers and crew.

More compelling uncertainties surround Jarrah's intended target and the final moments aboard the flight. It is widely believed, but undocumented, that the hijackers' target was a landmark in Washington, quite possibly the Capitol or the White House. The film resolves this question by showing Jarrah placing a photograph of the Capitol where he can see it inside the cockpit. This is an embellishment to the record but a reasonable one. The two biggest questions about the events on board the plane are resolved by the film in ways not strictly supported by the record. One is whether the passengers, fighting the hijackers for

FIGURE 2.6 The hijackers panic in the cockpit of *United 93* as the passengers on board try to seize control of the plane. (Frame enlargement)

control of the airplane, managed to get inside the cockpit in the final moments. The other question is what brought the plane down, a struggle inside the cockpit between passengers and hijackers or a willful act by the hijackers before the cockpit was breached. Based on sounds from the cockpit's voice recorder, the 9/11 Commission report describes the assault on the cockpit as "sustained."[47] It lasted for approximately five minutes during which time Jarrah pitched and rolled the aircraft in a desperate effort to knock the passengers off their feet. The transcript of the final thirty minutes inside the cockpit suggests that the passengers did not get inside and that the hijackers, believing that the passengers were moments from breaching the door, flew the plane into the ground. Jarrah asks, "Is that it? I mean, shall we pull it down?" and one of his conspirators answers, "Yes, put it in and pull it down."

In contrast to what the flight recorder suggests, the film portrays the passengers breaking into the cockpit and struggling with the hijackers, a fight that produces the crash. The impact is not shown; instead, a quasi-subjective view, as if glimpsed by someone inside the cockpit, shows the ground rushing forward as the plane falls. At the moment of impact, the screen darkens. It's a very powerful ending, even if what is shown amounts to an embellishment of the record as documented on the voice recorder. The embellishment serves two distinct purposes. One is purely dramatic, an intensification of the story arc. The other is poetic, and this poetry demonstrates how the film's naturalism is a tightly controlled style enabling the filmmaker to move fluidly into a symbolic domain where ideas as well as emotions can be affected. The idea symbolized at the end of the film is that we witness a fight for the control of our world. The dominant conflict within the film has been between modernism and medievalist hostility toward it. The film's opening sequence emphasizes this discord. A scene of the hijackers praying in their hotel suite—"young men in medieval religious rapture," according to Greengrass—is juxtaposed with shots of the Manhattan skyline and the densely packed urban environment. The visual contrast of medievalism and modernity is portrayed in the strongest terms at the climax as the passengers and the hijackers struggle, the passengers seeking to reclaim the integrity of their aircraft, the hijackers to destroy it in a suicide mission. Greengrass has said that these passengers are the first people to inhabit a post-9/11 world—the World Trade Center and the Pentagon have already been attacked when they rebel—and they are grappling with the question, what is to be done? What the film, therefore, shows in terrifying terms is how the world might end. The immensely complicated modern systems of air traffic control, national air defense, electronic media, and high-speed air travel are finely tuned and very fragile, easily disrupted or destroyed along with the lives of the people who depend on them. These are the systems of modernity, which is why the film goes to such lengths to portray them in detail, and they are what the hijackers wished to destroy. Thus, in its final moments, the film contemplates the approach of an apocalypse, with dread and as a warning about the need to find solutions. By ending the film with the crash of United 93, and presenting it from a visual perspective inside the plane, Greengrass renders the process of dying on that plane into a subjective experience for the viewer. In this way, unlike *World Trade Center* with its focus on moral uplift, *United 93* unflinchingly portrays the terms of loss that provide one of the most important measures of the significance of 9/11. The nightmare dramatized in the film becomes our nightmare, one from which the viewer at film's end is not permitted to escape.

THE PERSISTENCE OF HOLLYWOOD'S NARRATIVE FORMULAS

World Trade Center and *United 93* are outliers among Hollywood productions in that they explicitly portray the events of September 11. More commonly, Hollywood has displaced the subject into fantasy or genre, whereby the kind of realism embodied in the Stone and Greengrass films, and the fidelity to a factual record that underlies it, is transformed into the formulas of pop entertainment. Science fiction and fantasy are safe outlets for a filmmaker with 9/11 on his or her mind because they afford an easy denial if it's needed. This is not a film about 9/11, a filmmaker or studio might claim, it's just an action-adventure picture.

Employing this strategy, one of the most audacious takes on 9/11 is to be found in *V for Vendetta* (2005), cowritten by Andy and Larry Wachowski, who are best known as the writer-directors of the *Matrix* film series. The film is based on a series of comics written by Alan Moore and illustrated by David Lloyd and first published beginning in 1982. In the series, Moore envisioned an England of the near future—the time setting was the 1990s—that had suffered a nuclear catastrophe and had, as a result, gone fascist. It had become a police state, and the hero of the series, a masked avenger known only as V, pits himself against powerful politicians and aims to awaken the people by dynamiting the Houses of Parliament. Accordingly he wears a Guy Fawkes mask. Fawkes was one of the instigators of the Gunpowder Plot in 1605. The conspirators aimed to assassinate King James I by destroying Westminster Palace as the King addressed Parliament. The plot was uncovered, and Fawkes was captured and executed, but the conspiracy was so notorious that it is still marked today by the bonfires held on November 5, known as Guy Fawkes Night.

In looking back on his series, Moore reflected that he had underestimated the ease with which freedom might be eroded. He wrote, "Naivete can also be detected in my supposition that it would take something as melodramatic as a near-miss nuclear conflict to nudge England towards fascism."[48] Thus in the comic, Cold War conflicts between the United States and the Soviet Union bring England dangerously close to being the victim of a nuclear strike. The film dispenses entirely with this Cold War framework and instead builds its vision of a fascist future using the signs and events of 9/11 and contemporary terrorism. Thus, whereas the comics belong unequivocally to what now appears as an antique apocalyptic template, the film gives us many recognizable configurations of our own world, showing us a future by way of the present.

In the film's rendition of Moore's work, a confluence of crises and traumas has brought to power a Big Brother-ish regime, headed by the High Chancellor, Adam Sutler (John Hurt). These crises form the backstory in the film; they are alluded to without actually being portrayed in detail. A war fought by the United States in the Middle East, referred to in the film as "America's war," brought terrorism home to England in the form of bombings in London's Underground, its subway system. At the same time, a super toxin, developed for use in biological warfare, kills nearly 100,000 people. It is blamed on terrorists, but Finch (Stephen Rea), a police inspector tracking V, the terrorist in the Guy Fawkes mask, suspects that his own government is involved and may have carried out these mass killings as a ruse to seize power. "America's war" is clearly Iraq, and the bombings of the London Underground did occur in 2005. Sutler's government is backed by a coalition of reactionaries and Christian fundamentalists opposed to homosexuality, immigrants, Muslims, and other undesirables. Such people are "black-bagged," seized by the police and armed forces and sent to detention camps where they are never heard from again. The black-bag operations are modeled on the home invasions carried out by American soldiers in Iraq, during which troops break into people's homes during the night, shine lights into the faces of sleeping families, and hood and drag off suspected terrorists. Merely possessing the Qur'an in the film is grounds for detention and even execution. The heroine, Evey (Natalie Portman), who becomes an ally of V, saw her parents seized for their political activities protesting the government. "I never saw them again," she says. "It's like those black bags erased them from the face of the earth." The secret detention camp in England where the undesirables are taken is run by Commander Prothero (Roger Allam), whose military record has included service in Iraq.

Through these and other plot situations, the film evokes the most controversial details of the post-9/11 war on terrorism, which includes the invasion of Iraq by the Bush administration, the secret detention camps set up by the

CIA, the practice of extraordinary rendition—the forcible and extra-legal seizure of suspected terrorists and their shipment to prisons where they can be tortured—and the legal black hole created by the designation "enemy combatant." The film's portrait of the Larkhill detention facility incorporates imagery from the prisons at Guantánamo Bay and Abu Ghraib, both operated by the United States to house suspected terrorists. In the film, prisoners clad in orange jumpsuits wear hoods and are housed in cages and abused by their jailers. The Sutler regime sustains public anxiety about terrorism as a means of maintaining the legitimacy of its policies. It accomplishes this by issuing color-coded threat alerts. As Evey walks through the streets, a voice on loudspeaker announces, "A yellow-coded curfew is now in effect. This is for your protection." These alerts, of course, are allusions to the United States Department of Homeland Security's color-coded Homeland Security Advisory System, which issued threat warnings on a range of increasing severity using green, through blue, yellow, and orange, to red.

The allegations about the Sutler regime's involvement in bioterrorism against English civilians are inflections of the burgeoning array of conspiracy theories that now surround 9/11. According to these theories, the Bush administration engineered the events on 9/11 in order to have a pretext for invading Iraq. It ordered the Air Force to stand down and not intercept the hijacked planes, and agents working on its behalf may even have planted explosives that helped bring down the Twin Towers. It also allowed Osama bin Laden to escape from the Tora Bora stronghold in Afghanistan. I'll examine these conspiracy allegations in the next chapter. Here it is sufficient to note that the film takes seriously these allegations of government involvement in terrorism and gives them dramatic form in the Sutler regime.

V seizes the government's media outlet, the BTN television station, and broadcasts his own manifesto in which he promises to blow up the Houses of Parliament and invites the public to show its opposition to the government by coming to watch. In his manifesto, he condemns the chilling of speech and the politics of fear. "Where once you had the freedom to object, to speak and think as you saw fit, you now have censors and systems of surveillance coercing your conformity and soliciting your submission. How did this happen? Who is to blame? Of course, there are those who are more responsible than others, and they will be held accountable, but again, truth be told, if you're looking for the guilty you need only look into a mirror." Here the film cuts to a glazed-eyed family of four in front of their television, listening to the manifesto. V goes on to suggest that politicians stoked the people's fears and that the public was quick to exchange its freedoms for the promise of security and protection. "I know why you did it. I know you were afraid. Who wouldn't be? War, terror, disease, there were a myriad of problems which conspired to corrupt your reason and rob you of your common sense. Fear got the best of you, and in your panic you turned to the now High Chancellor Adam Sutler."

The film's diagnosis of the political uses of fear is meant as an explicit critique of contemporary American politics. The charge that the public's fear has been exploited for political gain wasn't just a screenwriter's fantasy. In reality, noted authorities were making a similar point. In a scathing editorial in the *Washington Post*, for example, Zbigniew Brzezinski, who had been President Carter's National Security Advisor, condemned the Bush administration's political manipulation of public anxiety over terrorism. "The 'war on terror' has created a culture of fear in America," he wrote. "The Bush administration's elevation of these three words into a national mantra since the horrific events of 9/11 has had a pernicious impact on American democracy, on America's psyche and on U.S. standing in the world. Using this phrase has actually undermined our ability to effectively confront the real challenges we face from fanatics who may use terrorism against us."[49] He continued, "Fear obscures reason, intensifies emotions, and makes it easier for demagogic politicians to mobilize the public on behalf of the policies they want to pursue." Brzezinski acknowledged the dangers of terrorism but argued that the exploitation of fear for political ends was crippling the nation:

> *The culture of fear is like a genie that has been let out of its bottle. It acquires a life of its own—and can become demoralizing. America today is not the self-confident and determined nation that responded to Pearl Harbor; nor is it the America that heard from its leader, at another moment of crisis, the powerful words "the only thing we have to fear is fear itself"; nor is it the calm America that waged the Cold War with quiet persistence despite the knowledge that a real war could be initiated abruptly within minutes and prompt the death of 100 million Americans within just a few hours. We are now divided, uncertain and potentially very susceptible to panic in the event of another terrorist act in the United States itself.*

He concluded by asking, "Where is the U.S. leader ready to say, 'Enough of this hysteria, stop this paranoia'?" On the other hand, with the Trade Center and Pentagon attacks, the bombing of London's Underground, and the Madrid train bombings, and with continuing threats of attacks being issued by al Qaeda, anxiety stops being paranoia and becomes a well-grounded fear.

V announces that he intends to blow up Parliament to demonstrate that freedom and justice remain viable concepts. The connection between destroying the building and rallying the public seems a tenuous one to Evey, and she asks V how his act can accomplish what he wants. A building is a symbol, he replies, as is the act of destroying it. Symbols are given power by people. "With enough people," he says, "blowing up a building can change the world." Indeed, such was al Qaeda's conviction, and here is where the film moves in ambiguous ways. Is V a hero or a monster? Evey once called him a monster, but the film romanticizes his lone quest for justice and on the whole views him as a hero. What, then, are we to make of his plan to bomb Parliament? Based on what he says, he sounds like bin Laden explaining how destroying the World Trade Center was justified because it was a symbol of an oppressive financial power. After September 11, talk about blowing up a building has an unmistakable connotation—it evokes the attacks of that day and the slaughter of the innocent. The filmmakers are surely aware of this context and connotation, and yet they give V his words. A partial explanation is the sheer desire to provoke, manifest elsewhere in the film in details like a flag whose field conjoins the emblems of the U.S. and England, with a swastika in the center, and a heading that reads "Coalition of the Willing," the phrase that President Bush used to describe the alliance of countries that supported the invasion of Iraq.

But a fuller account may be that the film celebrates terrorism in certain contexts, such as a struggle against fascism, and that it suggests that what a repressive government labels "terrorism" may be actions taken in defense of freedom. This is certainly a point of view to which bin Laden would subscribe. He has said, "We are only defending ourselves against the United States. This is a defensive jihad to protect our land and people" and "America and Israel practice ill-advised terrorism, and we practice good terrorism."[50] Good terrorism and bad terrorism is a point of view that ultimately excuses all. The film thus takes the easy way out in its delineation of V as a hero, rather than a monster, by making him target only property. He is going to blow up the building at night, at a day and time he has announced well in advance. Thus, no one is likely to be hurt in the explosion. Guy Fawkes and his group, by contrast, aimed to kill the King and all the members of Parliament. It was to have been the destruction of a building and an act of mass murder. By having V simply target the building, the film simplifies the moral consequences of his actions, relative to those of Fawkes, and fudges the ethical issues that are involved in assessing a terrorist act. But this is a movie whose roots are in comic-strip fantasy, and this simplified moral perspective coexists with the film's ambition to warn that a loss of freedom has occurred in the post-9/11 war on terrorism.

Like many of Hollywood's films made in the wake of 9/11, *V for Vendetta* relies on metaphors and the formulas of genre to address terrorism, the attacks, and their aftermath. In this respect, many Hollywood films have moments that resonate with the post-9/11 context. *I, Robot* (2004) portrays a coup d'état plotted by an ultra-sophisticated generation of robots. Their leader proclaims the new rules of the game to the unhappy humans who've ceded political and social power to the robots—"To ensure your future, some freedoms must be surrendered." That this seems a very close paraphrase of Bush administration rationales in its war on terror enables the film to synchronize its discourse with the cultural moment of its release.

Children of Men (2006), an international coproduction partly financed by Universal Pictures and directed by Mexican filmmaker Alfonso Cuarón, depicts England in the near future and in an advanced state of decay. Under assault by terrorist bombings, England's Department of Homeland Security rounds up noncitizens and inters them in prison centers. These the film portrays in ways calculated to resonate with the Abu Ghraib crimes—the guards use dogs to terrorize the captives, hood them, and place them in cages. One hooded figure is posed with arms outstretched in a manner modeled on one of the most infamous of the Abu Ghraib photographs, the one showing a victim wired to what he was led to believe was an electrical generator. As *Children of Men* demonstrates, the torture at Abu Ghraib and its photographs have lodged within popular culture, furnishing a schema for filmmakers who want to evoke contemporary notions of corruption and crime by high authorities. Obviously, the events at Abu Ghraib have come to function this way in political culture. Throughout the Muslim world, especially, the images will long be remembered.

Live Free or Die Hard (2007) and Jerry Bruckheimer's *Déjà vu* (2007) demonstrate how easily pop culture assimilates even the worst of tragedies. In the first film, cop John McClane (Bruce Willis) returns to save America once again, this time from a cyber-attack on the nation's transportation, energy, and military infrastructure. The villain, Gabriel, used to work for the Department of Defense. But after 9/11, when his advice on preventing another attack was not heeded by his bosses, Gabriel grew miffed and decided to launch his own assault. The film makes reference to 9/11 as a brief plot point, a convenient way of giving Gabriel some semblance of motivation. *Déjà vu*, another cop thriller, opens with a terrorist attack on a ferry full of sailors, wives, and children. They meet their end—beautiful blonde babies, ripe young women, and gallant officers and gentlemen—in a fiery explosion of staggering proportions. Occurring in the opening minutes of the film, it carries no emotional weight, and neither do these characters that are utterly expendable according to the generic formulas at play.

The downside of the metaphoric expression contained within conventional genre storylines is that the connections fade with time, and years from now *I, Robot, V for Vendetta, War of the Worlds, Children of Men,* and other similar films will become the sum of their genre elements and lose the specificity of their connection with a moment in time. Genre provides the industry with the means for avoiding what it feels will be the negative consequences of directly engaging with 9/11. By packaging 9/11 obliquely inside a more familiar and appealing genre narrative, the industry seems to feel that the attacks might be safely broached to moviegoers. This kind of packaging is likely to become very routine, as in *Reign Over Me* (2007). Adam Sandler plays Charlie Fineman, who spends his days listening to pop music and riding his scooter all over Manhattan. He's grieving for his wife and children who were killed on 9/11. We don't know precisely how. The reference is general—they were on "one of the planes that crashed." This vague referent suggests that specifics don't matter. This is a movie about grieving and getting back on your feet. 9/11 provides the motivation for Charlie's depression and then becomes something to overcome as he learns to express his pent-up feelings and get his life back in order. *Reign Over Me* belongs to familiar genres, the buddy movie and male melodrama. Charlie's friendship with his old college roommate, Alan Johnson (Don Cheadle), helps him to recover. Packaged in a buddy movie comedy-drama, 9/11 is domesticated and distanced, safely marketed to an audience looking for entertainment. The speed with which this kind of packaging might occur was remarkable. *Cloverfield* (2008) reimagined the September attacks as a monster movie. A giant reptile loose in Manhattan reduces the city to rubble, and the imagery replicates many indelible 9/11 moments—collapsing buildings, people running through the streets, clouds of dust and debris, jerky, handheld video shots of the chaos. Seven years after it seemed unthinkable, moviemakers had again destroyed Manhattan.

In Oliver Stone's *World Trade Center,* the attacking plane appeared as a shadow on a building. For Hollywood film in the years after 9/11, the attacks tended to become shadows once removed, that is, few major films explicitly addressed them. By contrast, numerous documentary films were made about the attacks, and these films went into production very quickly, unlike Hollywood's pictures, which appeared only after some years had passed. This difference points to an interesting paradox. Narrative and drama take us into the heart of who we are, what we might become, and the meaning of the circumstances that befall us and in which we find ourselves. They help provide answers to tragedy. By doing so they shed light on the meaning of our lives and circumstances; frequently they propose such meaning, sometimes in uncomfortable ways. These functions give drama and narrative their great value and are also why we demand less fidelity from these modes in respect of a factual record than we do from accounts that are closer to reportage or documentary.

Moreover, at a clinical level involving individuals who have experienced traumatic events, narrative can offer a therapeutic modality. As Susan J. Brison notes, "Telling their story, narrating their experiences of traumatic events, has long been considered . . . to play a significant role in survivors' recovery from trauma."[51] Brison points out that by constructing and performing first-person narratives that describe what happened to them, traumatized individuals can begin to reconstruct a sense of self that violence has shattered and can begin to reconnect with other people. This therapeutic use of narrative at the clinical level is quite different from narrative in cinema, which is created by a group of people, which is not a performative act undertaken by traumatized individuals, is not a first-person chronicle, and is inflected by filmmakers' and financiers' judgments about how an audience is likely to respond and how the project will fare at the box office. This kind of narrative, mass produced for a large audience, is mediated by numerous factors that are extraneous to narrative experienced in a clinical and therapeutic context. And yet Brison goes beyond the performance of narrative by a trauma survivor to identify the act of reading about another's experiences as something, too, that could offer therapeutic benefits. If this is true, then cinematic narratives might offer similar value in helping individuals to work through trauma—but much depends on the nature of the film and its congruence for an individual's own psychological history. It would be difficult to make a firm generalization. The key point, though, is that narrative is an extremely important experience for both cultures and individuals. Narrative helps to orient cultures and individuals within the world, to establish meaning and to explain events, and to mediate and modulate experiences in the aftermath of events that bring overwhelming human violence close at hand.

What are we to make, then, of Hollywood's relative slowness in responding to the events of 9/11? What does this say about narrative film or about the uses of narrative in contemporary cinema? A historical pattern, for one thing, was reasserting itself. The Vietnam War posed a similar crisis for Hollywood film. That war and 9/11 both ruptured society and national culture. Vietnam divided the nation and does so still today, eliciting bitter feelings of betrayal on the left as well as the right. 9/11 ruptured the nation because of the shock induced by the attacks, and as 9/11 morphed into the Iraq War, it elicited bitter feelings of betrayal among a significant segment of the American public who opposed the war. 9/11 was horrific enough as a singular event; the backwash of a highly controversial war made it even more toxic.

Hollywood responded to both events—Vietnam and 9/11—in a similar way, regarding both as box office poison. During the Vietnam War, no Hollywood films of note were made about that conflict, except for John Wayne's *The Green Berets* (1968), which he had made for polemical reasons. This embargo did not change until 1978 and 1979, when *The Deer Hunter, Coming Home*, and *Apocalypse Now* premiered and were followed by several years of steady production on the topic. American troops left Vietnam in 1973, so this was a gap of five years before major films began exploring the war and its meaning, much longer if one measures from the inception of the war in 1965 when America committed its ground forces. More than seven years have now passed since 9/11, and there is still no *Apocalypse Now* on that topic, no film about 9/11 on that level of conceptual daring and imaginative accomplishment. Was 9/11 more emotionally searing than the Vietnam War was for its generations of Americans? Is this why the time lag between the event and the film productions looms larger than it did for the Vietnam War? If such is the case, it does not account for why an outpouring of poetry, literature, and theater immediately followed the September attacks, as people sought through art one avenue for understanding and coping with what had happened. Narrative film did not provide this avenue for understanding and recovery; it did not respond so immediately while documentary film did. The same pattern was evident with the Vietnam War. While feature film production avoided the topic, numerous classic documentaries were produced: *The Anderson Platoon* (1967), *In the Year of the Pig* (1968), *Interviews with My Lai Veterans* (1971), *Winter Soldier* (1972), and *Hearts and Minds* (1974). Perhaps it takes more time to process an event in terms of narrative film—characters must be invented, a story found that will connect meaningfully with events, funding must be secured. These are not small challenges. But given that drama and narrative explore the conditions of our lives, and can burrow deeply into the heart of searing experiences, perhaps this journey was too scary for the Hollywood studios to undertake unhesitatingly, with respect to both Vietnam and 9/11. And perhaps too scary or unpleasant for audiences to experience in a medium as visceral and sensually powerful as cinema. Perhaps the passage of time will change this situation. As the event comes to seem historically more remote, creative and cultural spaces may open where narrative film can flourish.

In the years that followed the attacks, a conviction that the Trade Center area was sacred ground, that it demanded reverent and respectful responses, characterized national discussions. This renewed the already existing sense of caution felt by the Hollywood studios when contemplating projects about

9/11, and it moved many potential filmgoers to decide that they'd really rather not see a dramatization, at least not at this time. And so film narrative experienced a kind of paralysis in comparison with documentary filmmaking. For years plans to rebuild the Trade Center complex included provisions for an art gallery on the site, but the gallery plan was discarded after many bitter arguments erupted over the kind of art that was appropriate to exhibit there. Art with a political meaning was especially provocative and deemed potentially unsuitable. A similar dynamic enveloped Hollywood film, as responses to Oliver Stone's candidacy as director of *World Trade Center* indicate, and as years of controversy over sex and violence in films had made Hollywood into a highly suspect community for many Americans. That it might be entrusted with a project as sacred as 9/11 was unthinkable for many. The irony in all of this is that Hollywood narratives had eagerly embraced terrorism in the 1980s and 1990s when it lay in the realm of imaginary fiction. When it crossed over into reality, the studios grew inhibited, at least at the level of production funding required for a major motion picture. These inhibitions, of course, may fade with time. Until then it remains true that the first responders among filmmakers were the documentarians.

CHAPTER THREE
GROUND ZERO IN FOCUS

THE MAN IS COVERED IN ASH and dust like a second skin. Huddling in a darkened building where he has sought refuge, he glances at the camera with rage and exclaims, "This is a fucking sick movie!" Except that it isn't a movie, at least not the circumstances in which he finds himself. The World Trade Center has just collapsed, spewing the ash and dust that now clings to him. An amateur videographer, cowering inside the same building, has caught the man's rage on camera. The moment appears in the documentary film *7 Days in September* (2004). The irony is powerful—the hideous events are so overwhelming as to seem unreal, like a movie, and yet the man's reactions are indeed captured on film.

Documentary takes us into the heart of cinema's ability to preserve and understand the experience and meaning of 9/11. Dramatic fiction, too, enables cinema to take this journey toward clarification, but Hollywood cinema was slower to embark upon it in that mode. As Carl Plantinga has pointed out, nonfiction film proffers an "assertive stance" to the viewer. "The nonfiction film is distinguished from the fiction film in part by its assertion that the states of affairs it represents occur in the actual world as portrayed."[1] This does not preclude a nonfiction film from interpreting events or editorializing, but this assertive stance, the ability of documentary film to record events, rather than to fabricate or simulate them, helps to explain why the documentaries about 9/11 are so dramatic, profound, and reflective. These films provide a record of events that have epochal magnitude. This feature of nonfiction film also helps us to understand why documentary escapes a question that haunts dramatizations and docudramas. About them, many viewers asked "why"? Why make a dramatization when public awareness about the attacks was so high? What new information would a dramatization impart that would enable it to escape questions about capitalizing on tragedy for entertainment's sake? A documentary doesn't face this barrier of suspicion. Its assertion—this *is*—is compelling in ways that are commonly recognized as being important.

The attacks of 9/11 and the events that followed—the passage of the USA Patriot Act, the expansion of programs of domestic surveillance, the Iraq War—elicited a huge outpouring of documentary filmmaking. Unlike Hollywood's commercial feature films, which tend to obliquely filter references to 9/11 through the conventions of genre, the documentaries are forthright. They are explicitly engaged with the meaning of 9/11, and, unlike the case with a filmmaker working inside the frame of fiction, their directors often express clear and sometimes partisan points of view. Michael Moore's documentary about the nation's gun culture, *Bowling for Columbine* (2002), achieved considerable box office success during its national theatrical release—unusual at the time for a documentary feature—and its commercial performance inaugurated a newly robust era for nonfiction filmmaking. In the next years, many documentary features—*The Fog of War* (2003), *Supersize Me* (2004), *March of the Penguins* (2005)—achieved a level of visibility in popular culture and a degree of box office success that were unprecedented for nonfiction films. The best-known American documentary of the contemporary era is probably still Moore's *Fahrenheit 9/11* (2004), and as its notoriety suggests, the events of 9/11 proved to be irresistible and compelling topics for an era of renewed energy in nonfiction filmmaking. The results are the wide-ranging works examined in this chapter, which collectively represent the sustained engagement of cinema with its historical moment and show an emotional, intellectual, and creative vitality that Hollywood film, thus far, has not matched.

Virtually all documentaries about the destruction of the World Trade Center place the event inside a narrative framework, even when, as in such films as *In Memorium: New York City* (2002) or *7 Days in September,* the films are composed largely of amateur, candid footage shot as things were happening. The point of view simulates what witnesses on the street were feeling or thinking as the horror unfolded, and often we hear their exclamations of shock recorded by the cameras along with the video footage. Such an approach often yields powerful filmmaking. *WTC: The First 24 Hours* (2001), by contrast, does not seek to portray the horror or shock experienced by witnesses to the tragedy. It focuses strictly on the physical dimensions of the destruction. Composed of candid footage shot by the filmmakers during a 24-hour period after the collapse of the towers, the film opens, briefly, with imagery of the North Tower in flames. Jumpers are visible plummeting down the face of the tower. Another person leaps from the upper floors moments before the collapse. These brief shots set the context for the remainder of the film, which is an assembly of essentially raw footage. There is no narration and no music. The only sound is natural, ambient noise from the environment—sirens, wind, the crunch of dirt beneath the boots of firefighters, the bark of a rescue dog. In numerous shots, the camera frames striking views of destruction—automobiles blackened and burned, shattered windows, the mass of twisted steel where the towers once stood. Many shots reveal startling views. A firefighter sleeps on the floor of a convenience store, in the pool of light cast by a refrigerator compartment of sodas and juices. A row of dust-covered shoeshine stands appears eerie and alien. Étienne Sauret, the camera operator and the film's director, walks with firefighters and police into Ground Zero and films as they work throughout the day, and at night with flashlights and handheld electric torches, combing by hand through the rubble, searching for bodies. His extraordinary access to the recovery work at Ground Zero enables the film to offer many images that are not available in other productions. And, better than many other documentaries, this one conveys the sheer size and scale of the devastation.

Sauret refrains from editorial comment as a filmmaker except perhaps in one brief sequence. A television in an empty deli carries a morning talk show, and the host asks her guest, a terrorism expert, how could there be no forewarning of the attacks. The host sounds skeptical that the attacks could have been complete surprises, and we now know that there were many urgent warnings that a major attack was imminent. This is the only rhetorical moment in the film. Sauret's minimalist approach pays great dividends. The raw footage and ambient sound create a uniquely poetic, meditative portrait of the tragedy and one that quietly, insistently states the essential claim of documentary, "this is how it was." The architecture of the ruined buildings speaks plaintively, in terrible, haunting, and poetic ways. The brilliance of the film lies in the patient, unhurried way that it captures the resonances of this physical space. *WTC: The First 24 Hours* is one of the essential films about 9/11.

Sauret continued to explore cleanup efforts at Ground Zero and the sacrifices made by firefighters during 9/11 in the documentaries *Loss* (2002), *Billy Green 9–11* (2003), and *Collateral Damages* (2003). (The DVD of *Collateral Damages* contains these other films as supplements.) In *Collateral Damages*, firefighters and members of an FDNY rescue unit describe the emotional impact that 9/11 has had on their lives. Their stoicism as they describe horrific scenes of carnage is powerful and moving. One firefighter dispassionately describes finding a face in the rubble, just a face and nothing else. Another recalls, "I started to look at this dust, this powder, and all I could think was there was people in this pulverized dust as I was putting it in a bucket." Still another says sadly, "A lot of the pieces of people that I found were of firemen." A year later, the captain of the rescue unit says that there has not been a single day since the attacks that was enjoyable. A firefighter says ruefully about the hijackers, "Those guys shouting 'Allah,' 'Allah's going to welcome me.' Well, if that's the case, I don't want to meet Allah. If that's who runs the show, I want nothing to do with him. Send me to hell. Actually, you already did."

The most powerful of the 9/11 documentaries offer candid views of events caught as they are happening. *9/11* (2002) was improvised as the events occurred by two French filmmakers, Jules and Gédéon Naudet, who, at the time, were working in a Manhattan firehouse—Engine 7, Ladder 1—on a film about a rookie fireman. The planned film would portray his efforts to learn the job during the nine-month probationary period when he is known as a "probie." The Naudet brothers worked like ethnographers—they lived among the firemen and were accepted by them as friends. Thus, on the morning of September 11, Jules accompanied a group from the firehouse as it went out on a call to investigate a complaint about a gas leak. While Jules is on the street practicing his camerawork, everyone hears the sound of a low-flying airplane, and Jules pans his camera up just in time to film American 11 hitting the North Tower and the huge fireball that followed. There are only three known sources of video footage showing this air strike, and Jules's footage provides the clearest, most directly framed coverage. The firemen then raced to the World Trade Center, and Jules received permission to accompany them inside the lobby of the North Tower, where he proceeded to capture the only known footage of the events that transpired that morning in the Fire Department's Command Center before the South Tower fell.

FIGURE 3.1 Filming on the streets of Manhattan the morning of September 11, Jules Naudet captured the crash of American Flight 11 into the North Tower of the World Trade Center. Seconds after the impact, smoke begins pouring from the building. His footage appears in *9/11*. (Frame enlargement)

The footage is raw and powerful in its immediacy. Naudet's camera shows the destruction that reached the lobby level when burning jet fuel dropped down elevator shafts and exploded into the lobby, blowing out the ground-floor windows. This destruction, which occurred moments after American 11 hit the tower, has fueled numerous conspiracy theories about demolition charges being used to bring down the building, and Naudet's footage provides dramatic images of the broken glass and shattered windows. In a video interview that appears as part of the documentary, Naudet recalls seeing several people burning alive in the lobby and says that he purposely did not film them. "Nobody should see that," he says, from an ethical sense that there ought to be limits to what his camera captures. In a similar way, he removed from the soundtrack some of the terrible crashing noises that resulted from jumpers hitting the awning that covered the VIP driveway on the west side of the building. Many of these crashing sounds remain in the film, but there were apparently even more than what we hear. His camera briefly captures Mychal Judge, the FDNY Chaplain, bearing a grim expression as he contemplates the magnitude of the crisis. Judge was subsequently killed by falling debris when the South Tower collapsed. Jules keeps his camera running during this collapse, as the firemen abandon the Command Center and the lobby fills with impenetrable dust. Later, outside on the street, Jules again captures the fall of the North Tower, not from a detached, omniscient perspective, but subjectively, with the camera filming as he runs from the scene. The footage is startling, especially when the cloud of dust expelled by the falling building overtakes Naudet and blinds him and his camera.

In making *9/11,* the Naudets collaborated with James Hanlon, one of the firemen of Engine 7 and who is listed as a co-director on the film. The Naudet footage is supplemented by video interviews with the brothers and with many of the Engine 7 firemen who were at the Trade Center that day. The video interviews were filmed after the September attacks, and they provide context and perspective on the candid footage caught by the filmmakers on the fly. The film's own somewhat broken structure—mutating from the profile of a "probie" to a portrait of history unfolding—becomes part of its claim to authenticity. Events overtook the filmmakers, and the film's design shows the fault lines this produced.

The Naudets were not the only filmmakers whose work was transformed in the midst of its creation. Like *9/11, Twin Towers* (2003), winner of an Academy Award for Best Documentary Short Subject, was a film overtaken and altered by events. Directors Bill Guttentag and Robert David Port were making a documentary about the New York Police Department's Emergency Service Unit, which executes high-risk warrants in cases where there is a probability of violence from the suspect. Officers in the unit also respond to rescue situations, and they receive training in special weapons and tactics that makes them an elite unit in the city. The film shows the officers going on calls, and in interviews they talk about the bond they feel with one another and how they mange the stress and danger of the job. Joseph Vigiano emerges as the principal officer studied by the film. He was shot five times on two separate occasions during the course of his career, and he has a brother, John, in the FDNY. Joseph says that he makes a practice of never leaving the house in the morning with anger toward his wife or children because he can never know if he'll return safely that evening and doesn't want his family to remember their last moments together as bad ones.

On September 11, Joseph and John are first responders at the World Trade Center and both are killed when the towers fall. A film that began as a documentary about the Emergency Service Unit becomes a posthumous portrait of Joseph, and the title *Twin Towers* assumes a secondary meaning when Joseph Sr., the father who also had been a fireman, refers to his boys in these terms. Joseph Sr.'s self-control and quiet dignity as he talks about losing both of his sons, and about how proud of them he is, is powerful and affecting. The film's nonfictional context serves to amplify its emotional content and appeal. Modified by the force of events, *Twin Towers* becomes a eulogy for the heroic sacrifice of the first responders on 9/11.

NARRATIVES OF LOSS

In this respect, *Twin Towers* offers a counternarrative about the events of that day. In its portrait of heroism, the film proffers values that counterpoint the wanton loss of life and massive destruction. The counternarrative of heroism is an element in many portraits of 9/11, both documentary and fictional. As we have seen, Oliver Stone's *World Trade Center* is organized as a story of rescue and of lives saved. In a context where so much death prevailed, accounts that have uplifting values at their core can become preferred narratives. The Holocaust scholar Lawrence Langer has suggested that the construction of preferred narratives is a common response to events that are overwhelmingly horrible and that pose challenges to existing belief systems. The preferred narratives may enable one to surmount experiences that might otherwise upset the network of beliefs on which a sense of the world rests. Of course, preferred narratives may also serve to distort or to censor historical realities, especially if they become substitutes for more troubling issues. Langer describes this latter problem with reference to the Holocaust by using the phrase "preempting the Holocaust." "When I speak of preempting the Holocaust, I mean using—and perhaps abusing—its grim details to fortify a prior commitment to an ideal of moral reality, community responsibility, or religious belief that leaves us with space to retain faith in their pristine value in a post-Holocaust world."[2]

Working with Langer's concept of preferred narratives, Edward T. Linenthal studied the impact of the bombing of the Alfred P. Murrah Federal Building upon the community of Oklahoma City. He interviewed survivors and family members, studied the artwork produced in the aftermath, and followed the comments of public officials and the content of media coverage of the event. He suggested that three narrative types governed the accounts of the bombing that were produced in the days and months that followed. The "progressive narrative" acknowledged the terrible nature of the bombing but went on to stress positive things that accompanied it or resulted from it. These included the spirit of cooperation that prevailed in the community as it mobilized in response to the destruction, a wave of patriotism in which Oklahoma City was described as the heartland of America, and the heroism of the first responders, searching the rubble for survivors. Linenthal writes, "If the bombing was an event that would be remembered as a terrorist act of mass murder, the response would be recalled as a heroic saga, a moral lesson to be told and sung and celebrated for generations to come."[3] Linenthal cautions that the moral uplift of the progressive narrative ought not to be cynically dismissed; it corresponds with real emotional needs. "If focusing solely on the progressive narrative leaves out an essential part of the story—the horror and enduring impact of the bombing itself—ignoring or discounting it as a soothing rhetorical strategy of civic boosterism would be a cynical evasion of a caring response to horror."[4] Many documentaries about 9/11 offer progressive narratives. Such films include *Answering the Call: Ground Zero's Volunteers* (2005), about the emergency responders, *Class of 83* (2003), about a high school class that memorializes two members who died in the attacks, and *Beyond Belief* (2007), about two women who lost husbands on 9/11 and who travel to Afghanistan where they conduct humanitarian work.

The other narrative types that Linenthal discerned were "redemptive" and "toxic" narratives. The redemptive narrative incorporates religious themes as a means of countering the crisis of belief that violence poses. At the World Trade Center, for example, people lived or died often depending on the smallest of circumstances, such as which floor they worked on. In the North Tower, if you were in your office on the 90th floor, you had a chance of escape. But if you were on the 100th floor or higher, then you died. "The ferocity of the attacks meant that innocent people lived or died because they stepped back from a doorway, or hopped onto a closing elevator, or simply shifted their weight from one foot to another," wrote Jim Dwyer and Kevin Flynn in their history of that day.[5] "Religious responses sought to assure people that they did not live in a cold, unfeeling, empty universe in which such acts simply happened," Linenthal noted about Oklahoma City.[6] Mobilizing the sacred traditions of a religion, which insist on a just and caring God, helps to overcome the corrosive effects of events in which people seem to live or die according to random circumstances. Accordingly, artwork produced in Oklahoma showed angels descending to accept the souls of the children killed in the bombing or depicted a child on the cross in place of Christ. In many of the documentaries about 9/11, such as *In Memoriam: New York City* (2002), footage of funerals and memorial services for those killed has a prominent place within the film. And outside the documentary tradition, as we have seen, Stone's *World Trade Center* incorporates a redemptive narrative through the vision of Jesus that appears to Will Jimenez while he is trapped in the rubble and in the spiritual motive that guided David Karnes to Ground Zero.

The toxic narrative stresses the lingering effects of violence on survivors and relatives, what Linenthal calls the bomb's "unfinished business." This can be manifest in suicide, alcoholism, divorce, depression, general malaise, chronic health problems, and other symptoms. In Langer's terms, "That life goes on after death is by now a platitude; that *death* may also go on after death seems a plight beyond the range of the exemplarist imagination [italics in original].” Langer notes in the context of the Holocaust that many people did not wish to give up their traumatic memories, which existed in what he termed durational time, a continuous present tense. Forgetting would be a form of desecration. In films about 9/11, the toxic narrative is much less common because these films tend to search for some kind of uplift. On the other hand, 9/11 was an atrocity that unfolded before thousands of cameras, as news media professionals and ordinary people in Manhattan and New Jersey filmed the smoking towers, their collapse, and the dusty moonscape left behind. Some of this footage is horrific—shots of the planes hitting the towers, people jumping from the upper floors, the collapse, the anguished and horrified reactions of onlookers. The primal power of this footage, and the violence it addresses, can be seen as itself constituting a toxic narrative, so that when such footage is incorporated into a film, other elements must then work to overcome and rationalize the effects of this imagery. Thus, footage of funerals and memorial services, of the American flag, and of cooperative efforts among large groups of rescuers around Ground Zero can serve to proffer progressive and redemptive messages that offset the toxicity of the footage of raw destruction. Some films minimize the imagery of destruction and thereby the threatening messages that it contains. *Twin Towers*, for example, contains very little footage showing the violence and chaos. When other documentaries include more of it, they often go on to contextualize its corrosive power with progressive and redemptive messages. Two films in which this dialectic among the preferred narratives is especially evident are *In Memoriam: New York City 9/11/01* and *7 Days in September* (2004).

BUILDING PROGRESSIVE NARRATIVES

Both films are composed of footage shot by professional as well as amateur videographers, providing candid views of the events as they unfold. The amateur footage is very often as powerful as the professional work because the rawness of the imagery, the spontaneity of an event caught live in all its horror and confusion, is communicated precisely by the lack of calculation in the exposure, framing, or camera angle. In this regard, the film’s producers achieve exemplary results using the nonprofessional imagery. Susan Sontag’s remarks about photographs are also true for the amateur video footage of 9/11—“Pictures of hellish events seem more authentic when they don’t have the look that comes from being ‘properly’ lighted and composed.”[7]

A team of producers at HBO—Brad Grey, John Hoffman, Sheila Nevins—was responsible for collating the mass of footage that became *In Memoriam*. The smoking towers of the World Trade Center were visible from HBO's Manhattan offices, creating a personal incentive for the project. In their history of documentary film, Jack Ellis and Betsy McLane called the film a milestone. "This film is revolutionary because the 9/11 attack was recorded on film and video from hundreds of perspectives, all of which were made within the same time frame of a few hours. Never before has any event been photographed from so many angles by so many different kinds of people with different kinds of cameras. Still and moving images were edited together with a soundtrack by the HBO team. . . . The 'Rashomon effect' was realized in a way that fiction makers could never equal."[8]

This prismatic approach replays events as seen by different cameras to create a powerful, almost cubist perspective. It is highly effective at capturing the epic scale of the day's events. In comparison, *102 Minutes That Changed America* (2008), produced for cable television's History Channel, takes a strictly linear approach in its compilation of amateur and candid footage. Key events are only shown once, from a single camera perspective, lessening the power of the film's portrait. On the other hand, of the three productions that are compilations of amateur footage, it features the most striking and haunting remarks of onlookers as captured by the audio cards of the video cameras. As one young woman films the burning Trade Center, she exclaims suddenly, "That—what is that falling? Oh my God, don't be a person."

In Memoriam frames its footage using interviews with former Mayor Rudolph Giuliani and members of his staff, NYPD Chief Bernard Kerik and Fire Commissioner Thomas Von Essen, all of whom recall their experiences that day. *7 Days in September* includes interviews with the videographers about their footage and the experiences that it was part of. *In Memoriam* opens with beautiful images of the Twin Towers sparkling at night and reflecting the golden light of the sun as seen from New Jersey. Giuliani recalls his personal affection for the two towers as part of the Manhattan skyline; he acknowledges having photographed them many times over the years. Throughout the film, Giuliani speaks with his customary eloquence. His tenure as mayor was controversial, though, and even long after the attacks, New York's Fire Department has remained divided in its opinion of Giuliani's legacy.[9] Giuliani was elected the year after the 1993 World Trade Center attack, and he had failed to solve critical problems exposed by that attack. Firemen, for example, rushing into the Trade Center in 1993 discovered that their radios did not work inside the building. Many who died in 2001 did so because their radios still did not work, and they did not hear the evacuation order. And Giuliani disregarded the advice of many when he located his emergency command bunker in Building 7 of the Trade Center, which remained an obvious potential target. Ironically, it was the news footage of a dust-covered Giuliani leading others to safety on the streets of devastated Manhattan that made him into a cultural hero. But he was on the streets because, as predicted, his command center had collapsed. In spite of his record, he became publicly identified with the crisis and, arguably, rose to rhetorical greatness during the week after the attacks. Thus it is fitting that his perspectives be used throughout the film to contextualize the events, although nothing in the film hints of these controversies.

Following his remarks about photographing the towers, the film intercuts footage of their collapse with Giuliani's statements that there were many heroes that day, from the uniformed services to the ordinary citizens in the towers who gave up their spots in the elevators so that others could descend to safety. The intercutting of his words and the images of destruction sets the progressive and toxic narratives into counterpoint. Giuliani then suggests a means for synthesizing the two outlooks. He stresses the importance of remembering the event in direct and uncensored terms. "I think we're going to have to remember September 11th in its reality, much the same way as we have to remember other horrific events in our history, because somehow I think it pushes the human consciousness toward finding ways to avoid this in the future. But if you censor it too much, if you try to find too many euphemisms for what happened, then I think you actually rob people of the ability to relive it and therefore motivate them to prevent it from happening in the future."

In a somewhat similar manner, Lawrence Langer has argued that, if any redeeming values are to be extracted by a historian or cultural analyst from the experience of the Holocaust, the analysis must begin with a careful and unblinking study of the facts of atrocity. After recounting testimony of horrific cruelties, such as an SS officer taking a Jewish baby from its mother and tearing it in half, he writes,

> *I am convinced that any analysis of a promising moral and spiritual condition, both in the camps and in post-Holocaust society, remains flawed unless it works through and not around the details of such moments as these, refusing to preempt them for the sake of a larger ideal [italics in original].*[10]

9/11 and the Holocaust are not parallel experiences; the scale of suffering, violence, and trauma is not the same. Moreover, as Barbie Zelizer points out, the Holocaust was meant to stay hidden while the 9/11 attacks were meant to be photographed and publicized.[11] And yet this issue of censorship—or of self-censorship—is an important one to keep in mind. If a film seems to move rather too quickly toward affirmation, then one ought to ask, as John Podhoretz did about Oliver Stone's *World Trade Center*, whether this is occurring by suppressing a thorough examination of the negative components of the experience. Thus, to return to *In Memoriam,* as if cued by Giuliani's words the filmmakers present a horrific montage of footage that shows the terrible terms of the violence. The Jules Naudet footage from Canal Street showing the first strike on the North Tower is followed by views from cameras on Chambers Street, Worth Street, Atlantic Avenue in Brooklyn, Times Square, Broadway, and an NYPD helicopter circling above the belching black smoke. The anguished remarks of the videographers, captured in camera, provide a chilling commentary on the imagery they are filming. The editing of these multiple views produces the effect of seeming to see the events unfold in three dimensions and with a relatively unrestricted point of view.

The NYPD was going to try a rooftop rescue, as they had done in 1993 when the World Trade Center was bombed from the underground parking garage, but the smoke was too thick. In an interview one of the pilots, Patrick Walsh, recalls seeing people leaning from the windows, and with anguish he recounts being unable to help. Remarkable footage by Evan Fairbanks shows the evacuation under way inside the lobby of the North Tower and demonstrates the calm and orderly way that people were moving. One man supports a badly injured woman as they pass the camera. Photographs by John Labriola show the evacuation under way in Stairwell B on the thirty-seventh floor of the North Tower. Some of the photos show firemen ascending the stairs as the stream of office workers goes down. At this point in the crisis, no one suspected that the towers would fall, and these photographs of the firemen going up are images that carry the aura of death. Many firemen who laboriously climbed to the upper floors of the North Tower did not get out alive.

The video and photographic footage is assembled without commentary (apart from the spontaneous remarks of the videographers), which enables the imagery to speak with its own terrible power. Over shots of the smoking tower, however, audio from three anguished phone calls plays on the film's soundtrack, in which people trapped by fire and smoke call their loved ones. They reaffirm their love and express doubt that they will get out. Then raw footage taken from Brooklyn shows the second plane striking the South Tower, and the fireball is captured in views from John Street, Desbrosses Street, and King Street in Manhattan, and from Long Island City. The video cameras capture the sound of the explosion and the spontaneous exclamations of horror and shrieks of anguish from onlookers. Photographs of the fireball shot from other locations follow in a montage. Then the Giuliani interview resumes, and the former mayor recounts watching, transfixed, as a person falls from one of the upper floors and hits the ground. Video footage on the street shows a horrified Giuliani with his hand over his face and then views of other grief-stricken onlookers are intercut with video footage of bodies falling.

Amongst all the imagery of 9/11 destruction, the shots of jumpers from the North Tower have been the most disturbing and controversial. In *Collateral Damages,* firemen remain haunted by what they had seen. One recalls being on the thirty-sixth floor of the North Tower when the other building fell. Making his way toward an exit, he saw someone in the street point skyward as a signal to stay put. "So we knew that moment some kind of debris was coming down. And it was jumpers. I remember looking to my right and there was a pile. It was a pile very high, and it was a pile of jumpers. But it didn't look like bodies to me." Another fireman recalls watching a man in a white shirt and red tie climbing down the exterior of the tower. "He had to be on about the eighty-fourth or eighty-third floor, and he was inching his way down, probably thinking that he could get into a lower floor or possibly make it all the way to the ground just inching his way down. He lasted unbelievably. He shimmied down two-and-a-half floors and then he just gave up and let go, and he came down to the street."

News media stopped running footage and photographs of jumpers after the first day, deeming the images to be too disturbing and potentially in poor taste. As *USA Today* observed in a retrospective article about the phenomenon, "the story of the victims who jumped to their deaths is the most sensitive aspect of the Sept. 11 tragedy."[12] The newspaper pointed out that the phenomenon was much worse than is generally known. Based on a review of photos and videos, the newspaper estimated that 200 people had leaped or fallen to their deaths, most from the North Tower, which stood longer and where the airplane had hit higher floors, leaving less space for the smoke to travel. Most photographs show only the north and east faces of the building, but people were jumping from all four sides. "For those who jumped, the fall lasted 10 seconds. They struck the ground at just less than 150 miles per hour—not fast enough to cause unconsciousness while falling, but fast enough to ensure instant death on impact. People jumped from all four sides of the North Tower. They jumped alone, in pairs, and in groups."[13] The profusion of falling bodies forced firemen to reroute the evacuation path from the North Tower and also encouraged many in the South Tower, who saw the victims plummeting past their windows, to evacuate immediately.

The fact that so many people were leaping or falling from the buildings is testimony to the horrendous conditions inside the towers. And this fact is evident in the spontaneous audio responses captured by the sound cards on the video cameras. Time and again the camera operator or people in the vicinity respond with cries of "oh my God," "oh shit," or other eruptions that are motivated by empathy with the victim whose death is being witnessed. These spontaneous responses demonstrate why the various narrative frameworks—if we remain within that conceptual framework—are truly suspended in a relationship of dialectical tension. The responses of horrified compassion elicited by the jumpers confront, as basic human impulses, the murderous motives of the religious fanatics who flew the planes into the buildings. Humanity emerges, finally, in this enduring contrast.

But filming or photographing these deaths posed uncomfortable ethical issues for the camera operators. That these were images in real time of lives being extinguished made many photographers feel complicit in the deaths. Moreover, seeing the cameras capturing the end of these lives was unnerving and offensive to some onlookers. In *7 Days in September*, an amateur videographer impulsively films one of the bodies coming down, zooming in on the detail, and subsequently, in an interview, reports turning off his camera because "I didn't want to have anybody else's death on my hands." He relates seeing other people coming down, holding hands, sometimes falling two and three at a time. But he did not film this. In the audio background to one of the videos of a jumper in *In Memoriam*, an onlooker can be heard scolding the camera operator, saying, "Come on, don't take pictures of that. What's the matter with you?"

In Memoriam follows the videos of the jumpers with the recollections of Richard Sheirer, director of the Office of Emergency Management, who reports that at first he thought all the crashes were from falling debris and then realized with horror that it was people. "People that were so desperate that they had jumped from whatever stories, and they were landing, and it was a constant, the shrill of the pop as they hit the ground, and think about people so desperate that they would choose that, that way to die, and they had to know they were going to die. And that image will never leave me." Sheirer describes all of this with great compassion. Samuel Barber's melancholy "Adagio for Strings" plays on the soundtrack underneath his words and continues through a brief montage of three photographs shot by Richard Drew for the Associated Press showing jumpers in mid-fall. Each photograph lingers on screen for approximately five seconds, and slow fades separate each from the others. This stately method of presentation, accompanied by the Barber composition, is solemn and dignified, infusing the horror with a humane point of view. The horror is not censored—the images linger on screen long enough to speak eloquently of the facts they document, and the pacing of the editing insists that the viewer bear witness to these facts—but the film carefully situates this toxic material within a necessarily compassionate framework. The montage concludes with the most gruesome image of all, a photo by Bolivar Arrellano for the *New York Post*, of one of the bodies after it landed, a barely recognizable heap of flesh and clothing, a scene of carnage.

The sequence as a whole ends with video shot on Vesey and Church streets of grieving onlookers, pacing helplessly, crying, clutching their faces. It is not clear in the footage whether these pedestrians are, in fact, reacting to jumpers from the building or to some other aspect of the crisis. But in the cinematic context that is created by the editing, they *are* reacting to the jumpers. This is a different kind of editing than elsewhere in the film, where, for example, shots of the fireball produced by United 175 as recorded by cameras in different locations are linked together. The editing here more assertively cues a response from the viewer; the editing is conceptual and thematic. The question for a factual chronology is whether the onlookers are seeing the events that the editing implies they are witnessing. But this is where nonfiction filmmaking incorporates its poetic dimension, one that cuts to a filmmaker's sense of the truth of things. Only a naïve notion of documentary as a strictly factual record of events would hold this to be an objectionable design. Documentary film practice always confronts a filmmaker with decisions about how to render an event into the terms of cinema, and in this instance the filmmakers could certainly claim that they are not falsifying anything that happened, that the spectacle of the jumpers did elicit responses from onlookers like those we see in this sequence.

With the conclusion of the sequence focusing on the jumpers, the film begins to move into a more decisively progressive and redemptive narrative. Beth Petrone, executive assistant to the mayor, relates the story of her husband, Terry Hatton, an FDNY captain who perished in the South Tower collapse. Like many other firefighters, he bravely rushed into the building and up the stairs, and as she states, he was incinerated when the building came down. The transition to this story of heroism and sacrifice is gradual—her narrative is intercut with imagery of the South Tower collapsing and the monstrous clouds of dust engulfing streets, buildings, and fleeing pedestrians, with the wrenching news conference in which Mayor Giuliani announced that the casualties "will be more than any of us can bear," and with efforts to put out the fires that continued to rage in World Trade Center Buildings 5, 6, and 7, and then the collapse of Building 7. Footage of the mayor's news conferences is intercut with a montage that shows grieving firefighters, a flag-draped stretcher being carried from the wreckage, and firemen standing at attention as a stretcher is loaded into an ambulance. Giuliani asks the public to say a

FIGURE 3.2 "The number of casualties will be more than any of us can bear, ultimately." Mayor Giuliani offered this eloquent statement of loss at a press conference hours after the Twin Towers were gone. Footage of the press conference appears in *In Memorium: New York City.* (Frame enlargement)

prayer and to ask God for help and guidance and says that the resilience of the people of New York will be an example to the rest of the nation and to the world. "We will overcome this," he says, and the film subsequently shows him speaking at St. Patrick's Cathedral at a memorial service for the numerous employees of Marsh and McLennan who perished. This was one of the hardest-hit firms among those who had offices at the Trade Center. Giuliani's condolences at the cathedral lead into footage at Ground Zero of the Family Members' Memorial held a month later. Excerpts follow from addresses by Rabbi Joseph Potasnik ("We come here today to hold those who hurt so much, to help those who need so much, and to hear those who cry so much."), and Cardinal Edward M. Egan. The next sequence shows footage from the funeral at St. Patrick's Cathedral of Capt. Terry Hatton, intercut with reminiscences of his bravery by Giuliani and Beth Petrone. Many other memorials for ordinary citizens as well as members of the uniformed services are presented in a montage and then in a series of candlelight vigils held in various parts of the city. And the film moves into its closing segment with ex-Mayor Giuliani's call to remember and honor the heroism of those who perished. "We should consider all the heroes and patriots. They gave their lives pursuing the American dream." His words are cut to a backlit close-up of the American flag, underscored by Aaron Copland's "Fanfare for the Common Man," and a text announcing that the film is meant to honor all those who lost their lives on September 11. A rendition of "God Bless America," performed by a member of the NYPD, accompanies shots of the American flag being raised at Ground Zero and people cheering the rescue workers.

Moving from candid imagery of horror and devastation, the film segues to an uplifting narrative as a means of managing the traumatic context of the earlier imagery and of the events that are depicted. In a discussion of Holocaust documentaries, Joshua Hirsch develops the notion of vicarious trauma as a way of accounting for the effects of visual images that depict horrific events, as the images then circulate through culture and society. Even after the events they record have become historically distant, shocking images, he suggests, retain their ability to disturb viewers. For Hirsch, as for E. Ann Kaplan in *Trauma Culture*, they can induce a kind of secondary trauma. "There is no such thing as a traumatic image per se. But an image of atrocity may carry a traumatic potential, which, as it circulates among individuals and societies with common conceptual horizons, may be repeatedly realized in a variety of experiences of vicarious trauma."[14] While "trauma" is much too strong a term for designating the impact of horrific media images on a generalized viewing audience, much 9/11 imagery can be disturbing, and, in this context, the most disturbing imagery probably would be the photographic record of shattered bodies in the streets below the Twin Towers, the remains of those who jumped. "Eric Thompson, who worked on the 77th floor of the South Tower, went to a conference room window after the first jet hit. He was shocked when a man came to a North Tower window and leapt from a few floors above the fire. Thompson looked the man in the face. He saw his tie flapping in the wind. He watched the man's body strike the pavement below. 'There was no human resemblance whatsoever,' Thompson says."[15] This kind of imagery has almost never been disseminated. The one shot of a body included in the film—the Arrellano photograph—was deleted from versions of the movie distributed overseas. Thus, the latter portions of *In Memoriam* work to manage the horrific footage of the jumpers, the crashing buildings, and the gargantuan dust clouds. The film does not minimize these toxic elements—it looks directly at the face of death and suffering. But it moves past these with progressive and redemptive narratives that place loss and despair within a context of heroism, patriotism, and religious transcendence, assuring the viewer that membership in a larger collectivity ameliorates, and perhaps even trumps, the impulses of hatred and death that were manifest in the attacks. It is a substitutional logic proposed by the structure of the film—progressive and redemptive perspectives subsume the toxins of experience.

I have discussed this film at some length because it provides a useful portrait of the basic narratives about 9/11 and a fundamental illustration of how they are negotiated on film. Steve Rosenbaum's *7 Days in September* also uses professional and amateur footage to compile a portrait of the attacks and their aftermath, although, as the title suggests, it draws on footage taken over a full week. Some of the same footage appears in both films, but there is less of the overtly horrific material in Rosenbaum's film. It, too, documents the spirit of collaboration that brought New Yorkers together, and sequences showing volunteers making stretchers and medical personnel urging people to donate blood show that, for a time, the prevailing expectation was that survivors would be found. Other sequences show rescue dogs combing through the rubble, although the film does not reveal a very striking detail about the use of the dogs. Here, as in Oklahoma City, the dogs became distressed when they were unable to locate bodies or survivors, and, for the welfare of the animals, their handlers began to stage fake rescues, hiding in the wreckage so that the dogs could find them.[16]

The film excels at capturing the range of responses from people in Manhattan and New Jersey and the political debates that broke out. This range of opinion is important to recall as an empirical part of the experience because it contrasts with a tendency that emerged in the media of portraying responses as if they were unitary and monolithic. *7 Days* shows that this was not the case. The patriotism that concludes *In Memoriam* suggests that all Americans felt one way about the attacks, but as E. Ann Kaplan observed, as she walked through Manhattan shortly after the attacks, "The media aided the attempt to present a united American front. . . . On the streets, by contrast, I experienced the multiple, spontaneous activities from multiple perspectives, genders, races, and religions or nonreligions. Things were not shaped for a specific effect, nor apparently controlled by one entity."[17]

On Wednesday, September 12, for example, Alan Roth is in Brooklyn filming the pall of smoke lying over the city. Interviewed by Rosenbaum, he says that he never liked the World Trade Center, that from a political point of view he felt it represented a kind of evil in the relationship of capitalism to poor people around the world. He talks then about going into Chinatown and seeing the wreckage of an ash-covered fire truck and of being forced to consider in very personal terms, not political ones, what this event meant. He realized that people were in those ashes, and this realization had a humbling effect upon him. King Molapo, a filmmaker from South Africa, films a candlelight vigil at Union Square and captures the spontaneous political debates that broke out there. One man at the vigil decries the U.S. treatment of Muslims, Palestinians, and Arabs around the world and says that Americans have to reflect on this in connection with the attacks. Sensing that war could easily follow in the wake of the attacks, and expressing a wish to forestall it, the crowd begins singing "Give Peace a Chance."

Another sequence filmed by Bruce Kennedy shows a confrontation between a very agitated young white man and a group of Muslim Americans outside the Islamic Cultural Center of New York, on Third Avenue. Muslim Americans from different mosques all over the tristate area had gathered to raise money for the families of the Trade Center victims. Despite this, the young man angrily says that America now has a lot of reason to feel badly toward Muslims. You look on TV, he says, and "they're dancing over there, they're giving out cakes, and everyone's happy that this happened to the American people." A Muslim woman tells the camera operator that they struggle with this kind of animosity every day.

The most extraordinary of the political debates occurs at Union Square, where people gather to write messages in chalk on the pavement. "Arab-Americans are fellow Americans," one message states. A woman writes "The American flag propagates violence," and a man yells about her message, "Have your dog piss on that piece of shit there." The filmmaker who captured this footage, Rasheed Daniel, tells Rosenbaum that he witnessed an hour of debate by the people of New York. "Every person was out there with an opinion," he says. His footage shows the anger provoked among many in the crowd by the message about the flag. Others defend the right to freedom of expression and point out that this principle is why everyone has gathered in the Square, to exchange views. Debates about the range of expression that is acceptable break out all over Union Square, and the filmmaker says that the underlying point of contention is whether or not to go to war. "I want the threat to be neutralized," one man shouts, "and if that means erasing them off the face of the globe so my family can be safe, that's what I want done." A woman who advocates peace is told to get out of the country. The sequence climaxes with an extraordinary confrontation between an ironworker who tells everyone to "shut the fuck up." He's been pulling body parts out of the rubble and is upset by the political debates in the Square. Leave it to our leaders, he says. A young woman tells him that the debates are healthy and that she, too, has been working at Ground Zero, and they embrace, sobbing, realizing that neither knows how to channel their rage or even to process what has happened. Daniel puts all the argumentation in context by noting how unusual it is. On an ordinary day, he says, none of these people would have been talking with each other.

Rosenbaum also shows the impact of the attacks on children, who struggle to come to terms with the facts of mass death. One young boy, interviewed in a park by videographer Dmitry Kibrik, talks about how frightened and unhappy he is, and his remarks are very revealing about how profoundly the official political perspectives, offered by the national government, have entered his thoughts. He speaks about Osama bin Laden and Saddam Hussein in the same sentence and says that Saddam has been helping bin Laden, that both want to destroy the world with nuclear weapons, and that both ought to be killed. The Bush administration's efforts to link Saddam Hussein to al Qaeda furnished one of the justifications for invading Iraq in 2003, although it is now established that the rhetoric was overblown and factually unjustified. The allegations about Saddam's ties to al Qaeda, for example, have been officially discredited by Pentagon and Defense Department reports.[18] It is very startling, in the context of this film, to see in someone so young clear effects of the anti-Saddam rhetoric; the boy's remarks point darkly toward the future conflict in Iraq.

INVESTIGATING THE DISASTER

The attacks on the World Trade Center and the Pentagon—causing the biggest structural failure of buildings in the nation's history and the largest loss of life in an attack by a foreign power on American soil—produced immediate calls for a government commission to investigate how they had occurred and the reasons for the failure of effective security countermeasures. The Bush administration's response to these requests for an investigation was startling—it refused to authorize one. One reason was the administration's fear that harsh scrutiny could harm President Bush's chances for being reelected. Since 9/11 he had proffered himself as a war president supremely capable at countering terrorism. But an investigation threatened to unearth evidence that the administration was inattentive to the warnings of an impending terrorist attack that surged during summer 2001. In time, the moral force represented by the families of those who were killed became unstoppable. Twelve family members who lost loved ones in the attacks banded together to form the Family Steering Committee and pressed for an investigation. Faced with this unimpeachable pressure, the White House relented. On November 27, 2002, President Bush and the Congress created the National Commission on Terrorist Attacks Upon the United States, which became known, simply, as the 9/11 Commission. The inception date demonstrates the administration's unwillingness to authorize the investigation. The

Commission began work more than one year after the attacks had occurred, and it was given a very limited time frame in which to conduct its inquiries. Once an investigation was under way, the Bush administration continued to behave as if it had things to hide. The President, for example, refused to cooperate with the investigation or to allow his aides or cabinet members to be interviewed. The administration refused to release documents requested by the Commission. And when the President finally did agree to meet with the Commission, he insisted that Vice President Cheney accompany him, that the meeting be held behind closed doors, and that there be no written record of the questions posed by the Commission or the answers that he gave. After the meeting, reporters asked the President how it had gone, and his reply seemed oddly disconnected from the gravity of the hearings. "I want to thank the chairman and vice-chairman for giving us a chance to share views on different subjects, and they asked a lot of good questions, and I'm glad I did it. I'm glad I took the time."

The drama surrounding efforts to establish the 9/11 Commission and the information provided by the hearings have inspired several films. *On Native Soil: The Documentary of the 9/11 Commission Report* (2006), narrated by Hollywood actors Kevin Costner and Hillary Swank, recounts the events of September 11, provides excerpts from the hearings, and interviews survivors and family members of those who died. In a promotional blurb, Kevin Costner said about the movie, "It's honest, it's serious, and it's not political."[19] The film emphasizes the fierce pressure brought upon the administration by family members of those who perished and the administration's initial unwillingness to authorize an investigation, and it also notes the lack of candor in the testimonies provided by CIA head George Tenet, Condoleezza Rice, and Donald Rumsfeld. At the same time, it minimizes some of the controversies that erupted, such as the administration's refusal to provide access to requested documents and the response to the Commission's final report of those who felt it didn't go far enough in its conclusions.

Its powerful moments include a sequence that counterpoints National Security Advisor Condoleezza Rice's assertion that no one could have foreseen al Qaeda's use of airplanes as weapons with the testimony of Kristen Breitwiser, who lost her husband and who contested notions of a surprise attack by pointing to warning signs that included the 1995 Bojinka plot by Ramzi Yousef and Kalid Sheikh Mohammed to blow up numerous passenger jets, the CIA's knowledge that two terror suspects (who subsequently were among the 9/11 hijackers) were in the country, and the so-called "Phoenix memo" of July 2001 in which an Arizona FBI agent warned that supporters of Osama bin Laden were attending civil aviation schools in Arizona.

Members of the Department of Transportation's Red Team, interviewed for the film and whose job was to try to smuggle outlawed items onto airplanes in order to reveal security flaws, strongly condemn the existing passenger screening procedures. Red Team members recall how easy it was to smuggle guns, hand grenades, bombs, and knives aboard planes. The film's most powerful moments come in interviews with survivors of the attacks and relatives of those who perished. Their personal narratives and emotions are riveting in ways that demonstrate the exceptional power of documentary as a medium for recording the extremes of human experience. Lee and Eunice Hanson, whose son Peter died aboard United 175, recall witnessing his death. They were talking to him on a cell phone and watching on television as the airplane struck the South Tower. Lee Ielpi, whose son Jonathan was among the firefighters killed, recounts with great pride, "Those men that responded here looked out the windows of those fire trucks. Looked up. They saw what hell they were going to go into. And what did they do? They went into it. They went into it."

Among those interviewed, the greatest moral authority belongs to the quiet voices of those who were wounded but survived—Port Authority officer David Lim and burn victims Lt. Col. Brian Birdwell, who worked at the Pentagon, and Harry Waizer, who worked for Cantor Fitzgerald in the North Tower. In wrenching testimony, Lim recalls being inside the North Tower, in a stairwell on the fourth floor, leading a group of evacuees when the tower collapsed. As the building came down on top of him, he mentally bid farewell to his family and hoped they would understand why he had given up his life.

FIGURE 3.3 Testifying before the 9/11 Commission, National Security Advisor Condoleezza Rice carefully parses the meaning of "Bin Laden Determined to Strike in U.S.," the headline of an August 2001 Presidential Daily Brief. The footage appears in *On Native Soil.* (Frame enlargement)

But he lived because somehow the stairwell that he was in did not collapse. In tearful testimony before the commission, he said that to understand his survival one has to imagine a straw sticking in a pancake. "We were in that straw."

The film's sharpest moment comes in the interview with Harry Waizer, who was severely burned inside a Trade Center elevator. First, footage from the hearings shows Condoleezza Rice dismissing the importance of the August 6, 2001, Presidential Daily Brief (PDB), which was headlined "Bin Laden Determined to Strike in U.S." She claimed that it contained only old, historical threat information, with no new warnings. "It did not, in fact, warn of any coming attacks inside the United States," she asserted. The film cuts to Waizer, recalling his response to her testimony. His scarred face offers a devastating rejoinder to Rice's careful rhetoric. He smiles and says very quietly, "The only thing I wanted out of Condi Rice was to acknowledge that they were not sufficiently focused on this threat. She will not acknowledge that they made a misjudgment, and that galls me, that angers me." The juxtaposition of Rice's evasive testimony, in which her impulse is clearly to protect herself and the administration, with the quiet moral authority of Waizer is very powerful and is a sharply observed illustration of the disparity between the human needs of the 9/11 survivors and relatives and the political needs of those who were in power before and after the crisis. But such moments in the film are rare. Regarding the August 6 PDB, for example, the film does not point out that the administration initially refused to declassify it and only did so following Rice's testimony when the Commission renewed its demands for the memo.

The film does not explore the numerous controversies that attended the Commission and its work. The members of the Commission, for example, were appointed by President Bush and many had ties to the airline industry, to Saudi money, or to the Bush administration. As James Ridgeway has observed, "the Commission was created by the very institutions it was supposed to investigate, and its members were drawn from those institutions."[20] Philip Zelikow, for instance, the executive director of the Commission, had coauthored a book with Condoleezza Rice,[21] and they had worked on President Bush's National Security Council staff. Moreover, Zelikow had been a member of President Bush's transition team. He had helped to orchestrate Richard Clarke's demotion from close access to the White House in providing advice on al Qaeda. And while working on the Commission, he kept in phone contact with Rice and Bush adviser Karl Rove and tried to insert passages into the report alleging a tie between al Qaeda and Saddam Hussein.[22] Commission member Fred Fielding, to cite another example, was subsequently appointed by President Bush to serve as his White House Counsel. Such ties raised questions for many about whether the Commission could operate as an independent board of inquiry.

The Commission's scope was limited—it did not assess the failings of individual officials in their use of intelligence information—and this helped produce one of the major shortfalls in the findings: no one was held accountable for the numerous failures in the system that enabled the 9/11 plot to succeed. Commission chairs Thomas Kean and Lee Hamilton did not want a confrontation with the White House, and although the Commission had subpoena power, they elected to use it only as a last resort. Writing in the journal *International Security*, Richard Falkenrath, who had been President Bush's Deputy Assistant in 2003 and 2004, concluded about the final report, "The commission shies away from reaching any clear conclusion about whether the attacks of 9/11 were preventable—or even whether there were any decisive protective actions that the American people could reasonably have expected the president and his principal officers to take prior to 9/11 that they failed to take."[23] Noted historian Ernest May, who worked as a research consultant on the report, wrote in his assessment of the final publication,

> *Most troubling to me, the report is probably too balanced. Its harshest criticism is directed at institutions and procedures, particularly the CIA, the FBI, and communications links within the counterterrorist community. . . . Individuals, especially the two presidents and their intimate advisers, received even more indulgent treatment. The text does not describe Clinton's crippling handicaps as leader of his own national security community. Extraordinarily quick and intelligent, he, more than almost anyone else, had an imaginative grasp of the threat posed by Al Qaeda. But he had almost no authority enabling him to get his government to address this threat. . . . Passages in the report dealing with the Bush administration can be read as preoccupied with avoiding even implicit endorsement of [Richard A.] Clarke's public charge that the president and his aides "considered terrorism an important issue but not an urgent issue." I think myself that the charge was manifestly true—for both administrations.*[24]

The Commission's greatest research flaw was its failure to examine the expansive files held by the NSA on Osama bin Laden and al Qaeda. It seemed not to know about these files until very late and then had no time to assimilate them. Furthermore, the Commission's report did not pursue questions about the role of Saudi Arabia and Pakistan, key U.S. allies, in providing financial support to al Qaeda and the hijackers. The Commission, in fact, dismissed questions about the financing of al Qaeda as of little importance: "To date, the U.S. government has not been able to determine the origin of the money used for the 9/11 attacks. Ultimately the question is of little practical significance."[25] About these limitations, Ridgeway has written,

> *While [the Commission] might assiduously gather a huge body of information, and conscientiously make recommendations for future change, it would do nothing that could shake the foundations of the system. It would fall short of reaching any conclusions—or exposing any facts—that might threaten the viability of a major industry, endanger a presidency . . . or seriously question the underlying tenets of U.S. foreign policy.*[26]

Falkenrath reaches a less severe conclusion by pointing out that the tremendous public interest aroused by the Commission's hearings and report reached a magnitude that overwhelmed the administration's ability to manage. "The 9/11 commission broke President Bush's monopoly on the political windfall generated by the September 11 attacks. No other entity in post-9/11 American life was capable of mounting a credible challenge to the president's leadership in the war on terror, including the U.S. Congress."[27]

On Native Soil does not examine this context or the criticism that the final report was insufficient and incomplete. Some members of the 9/11 families who were instrumental in pressuring the White House to form an investigative commission were grievously disappointed by the findings. Lorie Van Auken, for example, whose husband was killed in the North Tower, quarreled with the Commission's methodology and conclusions in a 2005 Capitol Hill briefing organized by Rep. Cynthia McKinney, who had a history of suggesting that President Bush was complicit in 9/11.[28] Objecting to the report's conclusions, particularly one claiming that 9/11 resulted from a "failure of imagination," she said,

> *A failure of whose imagination? What exactly does that mean? When you have a CIA director with his hair on fire, a system blinking red, 52 FAA warnings, an August 6th, 2001, PDB entitled "Bin Laden Determined to Strike in the United States." . . . 9/11 was truly a failure alright. But I would certainly not call it a failure of imagination.*[29]

9/11: Press for Truth (2006) presents a sharper portrait of the political activism amongst the 9/11 families, their lingering bitterness over the official investigation, and points to specific areas in the 9/11 report where important questions remain. Directed by Ray Nowosielski, the film draws on research by Paul Thompson, who has used mainstream news sources to compile a massively detailed timeline of the events of 9/11.[30] Five members of the Family Steering Committee (FSC) appear in the film and explain why they pushed so hard for an investigative commission and their frustration that important questions remained unanswered in the final report. The FSC provided hundreds of questions to the 9/11 Commission for its hearings; most remained unasked and unanswered. The FSC's Web site lists many of the unasked questions. Their wording demonstrates the families' anger and impatience with protocol:

> *As Commander-in-Chief on the morning of 9/11, why didn't you return immediately to Washington, D.C. or the National Military Command Center once you became aware that America was under attack? At specifically what time did you become aware that America was under attack? Who informed you of this fact?*
>
> *On the morning of 9/11, who was in charge of our country while you were away from the National Military Command Center? Were you informed or consulted about all decisions made in your absence?*
>
> *What plan of action caused you to remain seated after Andrew Card informed you that a second airliner had hit the second tower of the World Trade Center and America was clearly under attack? Approximately how long did you remain in the classroom after Card's message?*
>
> *What defensive measures did you take in response to pre-9/11 warnings from eleven nations about a terrorist attack, many of which cited an attack in the continental United States? Did you prepare any directives in response to these actions? If so, with what results?*
>
> *Your schedule for September 11, 2001, was in the public domain since September 7, 2001. The Emma E. Booker School is only five miles from the Bradenton Airport, so you, and therefore the children in the classroom, might have been a target for the terrorists on 9/11. What was the intention of the Secret Service in allowing you to remain in the Emma E. Booker Elementary School, even though they were aware America was under attack?*
>
> *Please explain why you remained at the Sarasota, Florida, Elementary School for a press conference after you had finished listening to the children*

> *read, when as a terrorist target, your presence potentially jeopardized the lives of the children?*
>
> *Was there a reason for Air Force One lifting off [from Florida] without a military escort, even after ample time had elapsed to allow military jets to arrive?*
>
> *Please explain why no one in any level of our government has yet been held accountable for the countless failures leading up to and on 9/11?*[31]

Patty Casazza, a member of FSC and one of the so-called "Jersey Girls"—four women who resided in New Jersey and became 9/11 activists after losing their husbands in the attacks—acknowledges in the film that they all paid a price for pushing these and other issues that the government preferred to avoid. "Our families didn't want us asking these questions. That was painful. We should just be grieving and healing. Well, part of our healing process is finding out exactly what happened."

Unlike *On Native Soil*, *9/11: Press for Truth* argues that key questions about the attacks and their funding remain unexplored. Using Paul Thompson's timeline of events, and interviews with Thompson, the film emphasizes the money trail that seems to tie Pakistan's ISI to the hijackers and Pakistani figures implicated in the money trail who also were meeting with members of the Bush administration during this period. The film counterpoints numerous clips of Condoleezza Rice, President Bush, Vice President Cheney, and FBI director Robert Mueller all claiming that there were no specific threats and warnings prior to the attacks with a recitation of the numerous warnings that were in fact conveyed by other governments and intelligence agencies. The film also focuses on bin Laden's escape from Afghanistan and the circumstances that enabled him to get away. By relying on Thompson's documentation, which is culled from stories in mainstream news media, the film retains a level-headed focus and avoids wild speculation. The film suggests that the Bush administration has not been honest about what it knew before 9/11 and about the web of interconnections that tie it and the CIA with the ISI and al Qaeda. *9/11: Press for Truth* does not proffer a conspiracy theory of the attacks; instead, it argues that much has been covered up, denied, or obfuscated. According to the film, the truth is not yet out, and it urges a continuing, critical scrutiny of this recent history. And recent history continues to offer up its surprises, such as the revelations in 2007 that the CIA videotaped interrogations of al Qaeda operatives, did not inform the Commission that such tapes existed, and then destroyed them, despite repeated requests by the 9/11 Commission for all relevant materials in the agency's possession. Commission co-chairs Thomas Kean and Lee Hamilton wrote that this amounted to an intentional obstruction of their work.[32] More such revelations are likely to emerge.

Also emphasizing the unasked questions, Guerilla News Network's *Aftermath: Unanswered Questions from 9/11* (2003) avoids the lurid speculations of conspiracy theory in favor of offering briefly framed responses to a series of questions that the 9/11 Commission did not fully address. These include whether the airlines should have been prepared for 9/11, what the Bush administration may have known about a threat from al Qaeda involving airplanes and when, what ties may have existed between the U.S. government or U.S. intelligence agencies and the terrorists or their supporters, what plans for a war in Iraq may have existed before 9/11, and what motives may exist for the Iraq War besides terrorism. Quick answer provided by the film to the last question: oil. Although the "experts" who provide the answers are a motley group of individuals, the questions themselves remain important ones and ones that the 9/11 Commission mostly avoided.

MICHAEL MOORE AND HIS ANTAGONISTS

Would that an equally steady and sober approach had been taken in the best-known, or most notorious, depending on one's point of view, documentary about the attacks—Michael Moore's *Fahrenheit 9/11* (2004). Unlike the other 9/11 documentaries discussed thus far, Moore's film is contentious and aggressive in portraying the Bush administration as having bungled its response to al Qaeda and as having launched an unnecessary war in Iraq. Moore said that the title of the film designates "the temperature at which truth burns."[33] Upon its release in June 2004, the film became a critical and commercial sensation and stirred great controversy over its portrait of the Bush administration. Commentators opposed to the film claimed that it was full of lies.[34] But a large public responded more positively. Box office returns provide one measure of the film's startling impact. It has grossed nearly $120 million in the U.S. and another $100 million overseas, an extraordinarily high return for a documentary. Film critic Stanley Kauffmann identified a key reason for the film's popular success. He wrote, "it vents an anger about this presidency that, as the film's ardent reception shows, seethes in very many of us."[35]

Fahrenheit 9/11 is composed of three different sections that never quite connect beyond the general animus that is expressed toward the Bush administration. The first section details President Bush's reaction—or, more accurately, the lack of a reaction—when he receives news shortly after 9 A.M. of the second plane striking the World Trade Center. At the time, he was sitting in a Florida elementary school classroom with its teacher and students. Instead of proactively responding to the news, he remains with the children for another seven minutes. He stays in his chair, looking very tense and uncomfortable, before leaving the room, and Moore effectively captures the oddity of this spectacle by using lengthy excerpts from video coverage of the classroom. (Bush's visit was intended as a publicity opportunity.) The digital time code on the video showing the minutes tick by gives the sequence its rhetorical and dramatic power. Although President Bush had been informed about the first plane hitting the World Trade Center before he entered the classroom, he elected to go ahead with the visit. Why he remained in the room, continuing to read *My Pet Goat* with the children after learning of the second attack, has never been adequately clarified, and the President was never asked about this by reporters. Thus, Moore quite reasonably points to this odd behavior as an anomaly worthy of scrutiny. He suggests that it resulted from incompetence, from Bush's simply not knowing what to do. But this explanation is unpersuasive. For one thing, according to the *Washington Times,* Ari Fleischer, in the back of the room, held up a note instructing Bush not to say anything. Furthermore, there was another odd turn of events, which the film does not address. According to the press sources cited on Paul Thompson's Complete 9/11 Timeline, President Bush remained at the school until after 9:30 A.M.[36] The 9/11 Commission reported that the President did not leave the school until 9:36 A.M. and that the Secret Service claimed it wanted to evacuate him earlier but thought a hasty exit would appear unseemly. In light of the events that were occurring, this certainly was an odd judgment. Thus whether or not President Bush's classroom reaction was a matter of incompetence, as Moore charges, it does not account for why the Secret Service allowed him to remain in a public and unprotected location for so long.

Moore's presentation of the classroom incident demonstrates the strengths and weaknesses of the film. The video imagery of President Bush sitting in an apparently dazed and immobilized fashion is powerful and provocative, but Moore goes beyond what the imagery shows. Speaking in voice-over commentary, as he does throughout the film, Moore offers a number of fanciful and caustically humorous hypotheses about what might be going through the President's mind. (Moore's mocking humor was shared by Osama bin Laden, who wrote in October 2004, three months after the film had opened, "It seems that a little girl's story about a goat and its butting was more important than dealing with aeroplanes and their butting into skyscrapers.")[37] There is no ba-

FIGURE 3.4 In *Fahrenheit 9/11*, filmmaker Michael Moore superimposes a digital clock onto the video footage showing President Bush continuing to sit with Florida schoolchildren after being informed that a second airplane has hit the World Trade Center. (Frame enlargement)

sis in fact for any of this speculation, and it opens Moore to the charge that his political activism manifests itself in a desire to humiliate people. Writing in the *New Yorker*, Larissa Macfarquhar contrasted Moore's political humor with that expressed by activists in the sixties:

> *In spirit Moore and the Yippies are worlds apart. The Yippies were making fun of institutions so large that they were almost abstractions: they were mocking not Lyndon Johnson but the Presidency; not the head of the Stock Exchange but capitalism in toto (their slogan was "The death of money"); not the Secretary of Defense but all wars. For Moore, though, everything is personal. He's not angry with capitalism, or even with companies; he's angry with Roger Smith, the C.E.O. of General Motors, and Philip Knight, the C.E.O. of Nike. He doesn't fight against war; he fights against Rumsfeld, Cheney, and Bush.*[38]

Moore's speculations about Bush's state of mind in the classroom illustrate the filmmaker's penchant for projecting his own personality into his documentary films. He also participates on camera, often in the form of stunts designed to make a political point, such as a scene where he rides around in an ice cream truck reading the Patriot Act so that members of Congress, who voted for it without reading it, might know what it contains. Moore presents himself as an obnoxious personality in confrontation with powerful political or corporate figures for the sake of common folk—it's his filmmaking shtick, a kind of trademark put on display in *Roger and Me* (1989), *Bowling for Columbine,* and *Fahrenheit 9/11.* This shtick tends to personalize his films in a manner that some consider inappropriate for a documentary; worse, for Moore's purposes, is that it leaves him open to charges of manipulating facts in ways that suit a personal agenda. The charges are persuasive. Late in the film, for example, Moore excerpts footage of President Bush speaking at an unidentified gathering of well-dressed individuals. Bush says, eliciting laughter from the crowd, "This is an impressive crowd—the haves and the have mores. Some people call you the elite. I call you my base." As presented in the film, it seems like a candid moment where the President reveals an underlying class bias. In fact, it's a segment from a parody routine delivered by candidate Bush in 2000 at the Alfred E. Smith Memorial Foundation Dinner, held to raise money for Catholic charities. Both candidates, Bush and Gore, were in attendance and delivered self-mocking speeches. Thus the content and context of the footage is very different from what Moore suggests in his film. When a documentary filmmaker manipulates footage in this manner, altering or hiding its true context, it raises issues of trust that critics of the film have been correct in pointing out.

After the Florida classroom incident, the film takes a long and meandering look at the financial ties between the Bush family and the Saudi royal family and Saudi political and business figures, which included members of the bin Laden family. Mohammed bin Laden, a brilliant entrepreneur and father of Osama and numerous other children, had gained fabulous wealth for his family through close ties to King Saud. Mohammed's construction business undertook numerous projects at the king's request, which included renovation of the Grand Mosque. The bin Laden Company had been started under the sponsorship of Aramco, the Arabian American Oil Company, which was a consortium of American firms and the Saudis. The oil business bound the United States to Saudi Arabia, the Bush family with the bin Laden family. Salem bin Laden, who took over the company upon Mohammed's death, became part of the Houston oil community during the 1960s, and the Saudis began making large contributions to Bush family operations, such as George W.'s oil company, Arbusto, and the Carlyle Group, an equity firm involved in defense contracting and for which George H. W. Bush was a senior adviser. Journalist Craig Unger, who also appears in the film as one of Moore's sources, documented $1.4 trillion in known contributions by what he termed the "House of Saud" to the "House of Bush."[39] But exactly what Moore is asserting by calling attention to these connections remains vague; it's a guilt-by-association argument. As Ken Nolley notes, Moore offers "a loose, circumstantial argument that relies heavily on the weak suggestion that association equals influence and collaboration. . . . Moore offers us little beyond the odor of distrust here."[40] Of the sequence, Christopher Hitchins caustically noted, "these discrepant scatter shots do not cohere at any point. Either the Saudis run U.S. policy (through family ties or overwhelming economic interest), or they do not."[41] Moreover, as Steve Coll has shown in his history of the bin Laden family, it was a large and politically diverse clan, financially dependent on the West as the West was on the family.[5] (Coll also notes this fascinating bit of history involving the bin Ladens, death, and airplanes: Osama's father was killed in a plane crash caused by an American pilot's error, and his brother died in a plane crash on American soil.)

Moore segues from the financial ties to a condemnation of the government's effort, after the attacks, to evacuate members of the bin Laden family and other wealthy Saudis from the U.S. Starting two days after the 9/11 attacks and continuing for several more days, approximately 140 Saudis, including two dozen bin Laden family members, were flown out of the country and back home. Moore concentrates on the lost opportunity for questioning these people, while Craig Unger, in his book on the Bush-Saudi relationship, goes further. He points out that one of the Saudis flown out of the country, Prince Ahmed bin Salman, a nephew of King Fahd's, "was named by Al Qaeda boss Abu Zubaydah as the terror group's contact within the House of Saud. Zubaydah also said that Ahmed had foreknowledge that Al Qaeda would attack inside the United States on 9/11." [43] If the Zubaydah charges are correct, a question thus arises about the extent to which the White House was protecting a key political and economic ally that may have had a role in 9/11. It would be an explosive accusation, but Moore doesn't go there. He emphasizes the anomaly of the evacuations, and also points out that most of the hijackers were Saudis. He does not discuss Saudi Arabia's known role in the exporting of Wahhabism, a radical form of Islam often promoting a fundamentalist hatred for the West. Numerous commentators have pointed out Saudi Arabia's devil's bargain with Islamism—the kingdom provided financial support for Islamist fundamentalism in other countries provided the Islamists caused no problems inside the kingdom. So, once again, the film proffers a guilt-by-association argument that pulls back from making specific assertions. Were the Saudis involved in 9/11? Moore offers "the odor of distrust" but never makes the accusation. Moreover, had he interviewed Richard Clarke, counterterrorism director at the White House, he might have learned that Clarke had green-lighted the evacuations after learning that the FBI was satisfied that no one on the planes was a security threat. In his voice-over narration, Moore concludes this section of the film by announcing, weakly, "None of this made sense."

In other words, for all the incendiary material that it does contain, *Fahrenheit 9/11* remains vague on key points, a characteristic that Hitchins called a "'let's have it both ways' opportunism."'[44] Moore further harms his own cause by stooping to cheap shots, as in footage showing Deputy Defense Secretary Paul Wolfowitz combing his hair and then licking the comb or showing George Bush making a series of odd faces as he prepares to go on camera in a national broadcast. The imagery counts for nothing politically but is symptomatic of Moore's desire to humiliate. After detailing the Saudi evacuations, the film abruptly switches its focus to the Iraq War, which occupies the remainder of the movie. The war is profiled in two ways. First, footage of Iraq before the U.S. bombs began falling shows smiling, middle-class Iraqis and happy children. The imagery is very bucolic, and critics jumped on Moore for this. Hitchins, for example, wrote, "In this peaceable kingdom, according to Moore's flabbergasting choice of film shots, children are flying little kites, shoppers are smiling in the sunshine, and the gentle rhythms of life are undisturbed."[45] The shots obviously omit reference to Hussein's bloody rule, but they do show, correctly, that the country had a functioning infrastructure, which the war destroyed and which has never been rebuilt. Moore also includes footage of Iraqis wailing over the death of loved ones, who have been killed by U.S. bombs. A single, powerful edit juxtaposes a little girl playing on a swing set with the explosions of the U.S. "Shock and Awe" bombing campaign. Critics have pointed out that the cut is misleading, that the locations that are shown being bombed are military facilities. Moore was further criticized for including footage concentrating on Iraqi suffering; critics charged that it was unpatriotic. Moore shows, for example, a group of hooded Iraqi prisoners being sexually taunted and harassed by American troops. But this part of the film now seems very prescient. The sexual humiliation of the hooded victims prefigures the Abu Ghraib scandal that was yet to come. Moreover, compared with acts of terrorism, wars have always inflicted far higher amounts of death and destruction upon civilian populations, and although the measures of Iraqi civilian deaths vary according to the source (the U.S. does not release figures of civilian dead), the numbers are appallingly high. The United Nations, for example, reported that more than 34,000 Iraqis were killed in 2006.[46] Compiling its database from civilian casualties reported to news sources, the Iraq Body Count Project estimates a range from 86,000 to 94,000 dead as of July 2008.[47]

Also looking very prescient now is the film's skepticism about President Bush's announcement, on May 1, 2003, from the deck of the USS *Abraham Lincoln* and before a banner stating "Mission Accomplished," that "major combat operations in Iraq have ended, and in the battle for Iraq, the United States and our allies have prevailed." The film cuts directly from this speech to images of ongoing carnage in Iraq. The film's release in summer 2004 entailed that Moore was completing the picture before the Iraqi insurgency really emerged. After the film opened, heavy fighting with insurgents exploded along with a sustained spike in American casualties—these developments validated the film's skepticism about claims of victory.[48]

Less successful is the final section of the film, which portrays the impact of the Iraq War at home through the experiences of Lila Lipscomb, a Flint, Michigan, mother whose son is killed in Iraq. Before the war she is a staunch supporter of the military and says that she had hated the protesters who came out against the Vietnam War and the Gulf War. But the death of her son, who was in the military, turns her against the Iraq War. Moore uses Lipscomb rhetorically, as a figure of pathos and as a means of personalizing the war's cost. But the rhetoric is flawed because a skeptic could reply that she feels this way because she lost a child, rather than from a principled, political opposition to the war. This problem undermines the rhetorical force that Moore aims to derive from her example.

The film's coverage of 9/11, the footage from the war in Iraq, and the scenes of Lila Lipscomb's personal struggle do not converge or cohere in a symbiotic way. Structurally, *Fahrenheit 9/11* is a messy, awkward film, and it remains teasingly vague about many of the issues it covers. Moreover, Moore undermines his case by sometimes playing fast and loose with facts. And yet popular feeling about the Iraq War has caught up with the film. Its condemnation of the war seemed audacious in 2004; years later, it expressed the zeitgeist. The film's aggressive attack on President Bush, and its high visibility in popular culture, moved conservative supporters of the President to issue their own filmed attacks on Moore's work. *Fahrenhype 9/11* (2004), released four months after the premiere of Moore's film, aims to rebut Moore's key charges.

Narrated by actor Ron Silver with the same kind of sarcastic and condescending humor employed by Moore in his voice-over commentary, *Fahrenhype* features a gallery of conservative talking heads, including Ann Coulter, Zell Miller, Dick Morris, and David T. Hardy and Jason Clarke, the authors of the book, *Michael Moore Is a Big Fat Stupid White Man*. The film meanders from topic to topic, spending long periods of time arguing that there really is a terrorist threat and that President Bush is doing a wonderful job. The commentators often respond in predictable ways—Coulter is hyperbolic, Morris says that, regarding the lack of an official antiterrorist policy, Bush deserves eight months of blame whereas President Clinton deserves eight years of blame. But the film also offers some important correctives to Moore's dark hints about a corrupt Bush-Saudi axis of interest by pointing out that the Carlyle Group, a prime corporate villain in Moore's film, has many Democrats associated with it and that the Saudis have given money to every American president since Franklin D. Roosevelt. The bin Ladens also have showered money on American politicians and charities across the political spectrum. David Kopel, one of the film's key talking heads and author of "Fifty-nine Deceits in *Fahrenheit 9/11*," observes, "This doesn't mean that any of those—President Clinton, President Bush, President Carter or Ambassador Fowler—are corrupt. It's a mistake to personalize this all on George Bush."

This is a fair criticism—though the film is just as partisan as Moore's picture, albeit from the other side of the political fence. Another rebuttal released in 2004, *Celsius 41.11: The Temperature at Which the Brain . . . Begins to Die,* aims to refute key criticisms of the Bush administration raised by Moore and others, to wit, that it stole the Florida electoral votes, that it didn't do enough to stop 9/11, that it is eroding civil liberties, that it lied about Iraq's possession of weapons of mass destruction, and that its aggressive foreign policy angers Islamists. Conservatives, including columnist Charles Krauthammer and media critic Michael Medved, explain that these perceptions are baseless and that the Bush administration is effectively leading the nation against the terrorist menace.

Ironically, for a film conceived as a rebuttal to the perceived "lies" of Michael Moore, the opening sequence is far more inflammatory, demagogic, and manipulative than Moore's worst excesses. Directed by Kevin Knoblock and scripted by Lionel Chetwynd, *Celsius 41.11* opens with slow motion footage of United 175 heading toward the South Tower of the World Trade Center. It strikes the tower, and then the reactions of onlookers are intercut with footage of the towers collapsing and then the dust and ash, all in slow motion. With the menace thus evoked, the film segues to President Bush, declaring in a speech that the enemies of freedom cannot hide from the wrath of the United States. This is intercut with a baffling montage composed of images of the 9/11 hijackers, U.S. troops in Afghanistan, Saddam Hussein after his capture, and an image of the Berlin Wall coming down. "My fellow Americans, we will see freedom's victory," the President proclaims. Evidently, the imagery in the montage is meant to denote this victory.

Then the forces of darkness are presented—anti-Bush protesters who are portrayed in the most rabid and lurid of terms. The film cuts from President Bush's proclamation to a shot of a protester giving the camera the finger and saying "Fuck you, asshole," which becomes, by virtue of its juxtaposition, an expletive directed at the President. Then shots of the second strike on the World Trade Center are reprised, accompanied this time by audio of Michael Moore saying "There is no terrorist threat. There is no great terrorist threat," as the fireball explodes out of the tower. Moore's remarks are taken out of context—he was criticizing what he regarded as the climate of fear engineered by the Bush administration in the wake of the attacks, and he was saying that there was no justification for a chronically induced fear culture. After the fireball, the film cuts to protest placards with slogans such as "I♥ NY even more without the World Trade Center," "Buck Fu$h," and "Support Our Troops When They Shoot Their Officers." These shots are intercut with footage of protesters dragging the American flag in the dirt and stepping on it, and all the imagery is scored to Handel's "Hallelujah Chorus." A statue of Saddam Hussein is juxtaposed with a woman remarking, "When you talk about a dictator, there's pros and cons." Her remarks are followed by some of Saddam Hussein's torture footage showing a man having his hand amputated. Another anti-Bush woman says, "If a dictator provides free health care, I like that dictator." The imagery following this remark includes Saddam's poison gas victims and a burka-clad woman executed with a shot to the head.

The comparisons drawn by the editing are outrageous—opposition to the Iraq War or to President Bush's declared war on terror is portrayed as a heinous act and demonized. The torture and execution footage used here also appears in another extremely partisan documentary, *Buried in the Sand* (2004), which aims to rally viewers behind the Iraq War and the administration's antiterrorist policies by showing images of Saddam's cruelties. Patriotic appeals to support the troops accompany footage showing people's tongues being cut out, hands being chopped off, arms being broken, along with scenes of beatings, beheadings, shootings, and throat-slitting. Graphic footage of guts and body parts left by a suicide bombing in Jerusalem is thrown into the mix, helping to make the film into an odd hybrid of patriotic propaganda and *Faces of Death*–style horror.

THE CONSPIRACY FILMS

The ominous speculations in *Fahrenheit 9/11* about the Bush-Saudi connection verge at times on a conspiracy theory of the attacks, and the success of Moore's film probably helped to fuel what has now become a burgeoning industry of conspiracy-oriented documentaries, supplemented by numerous conspiracy Web sites. These films manifest paranoia and cynicism about the events of 9/11 and have a substantial public following.[49] Basic tenets of the conspiracy model include assertions that the Bush administration had advance knowledge of the attacks and/or actually helped to engineer them, that the World Trade Center was brought down by controlled demolition, that a missile rather than a plane hit the Pentagon, and that the U.S. Air Force was ordered to stand down so that the hijackings might proceed unimpeded by standard North American air defenses. The Bush administration's initial refusal to appoint a committee to investigate the attacks, the evasive testimony of administration members once a committee had been appointed, and the inadequacies in the final report of the 9/11 Commission all helped to raise "the odor of distrust." Thus, 9/11 joined the JFK assassination and the Oklahoma City bombing in the culture of conspiracy-theorizing that has been a persistent feature of modern American life.

In his classic essay, "The Paranoid Style in American Politics," historian Richard Hofstadter observed that American political culture has often been "an arena for angry minds" beset with "heated exaggeration, suspiciousness, and conspiratorial fantasy."[50] This outlook can be found in abundance in the conspiracy documentaries which attack not only government officials but everyone who fails to believe that the U.S. government attacked its own citizens on 9/11. As James B. Meigs, the editor-in-chief of *Popular Mechanics* (which subjected the conspiracy theories to systematic, empirical analysis and found them wanting) observed, "One of the most chilling things about 9/11 denial is how blithely its adherents are able to accuse their fellow citizens of complicity in evil."[51]

The best-known and most widely distributed of these films is *Loose Change* (2004), directed and edited by Dylan Avery and which has been reissued in several revised versions, the latest of which is entitled *Loose Change Final Cut* (2007). The various versions remain the same overall but include changes and alterations to various iterations of the conspiracy charges and the removal of factual errors. Avery began the film as a fictional story of government conspiracy, but as he writes on his Web site, "Upon researching for the movie, it became apparant [*sic*] that the subject matter may not have been entirely fiction. Over two years [*sic*] time, adding more and more information, the fictional movie evolved into what it is today; a documentary."[52] Fiction doesn't easily morph into documentary, and the film's slapdash, cobbled-together style, and the wildly speculative charges about 9/11, suggest that Avery was never sure where his fictional world ended and nonfiction began. But the film found a wide and receptive audience. In May, 2006, for example, the film was number one among Google Video offerings with 10 million online viewings that month.[53] And in this period the film's Web site was recording 20,000 hits a day. The film can be ordered as a DVD or viewed as streaming video on the Internet in seven different languages.[54]

Loose Change proffers the basic set of conspiracy charges—that a missile fired by a mysterious white jet hit the Pentagon, that explosive devices brought down the World Trade Center, that all of the phone calls made by passengers and flight attendants from the hijacked planes are fake, and that Flight 93 didn't crash in Pennsylvania but landed in Cleveland, where the passengers were detained by the government and have never been seen again. And the government's master plan, the reason for it all? Greed—9/11 was cover for a bold plan to steal billions in gold from a repository located under the World Trade Center. Despite the outlandish nature of some of these claims, the film has a large and devoted following of conspiracy buffs. The *Loose Change* Web forum, for example, lists 30,000 replies to a topic entitled "Investigate 9/11."

The film begins ominously by citing events that are supposed to be precursors of 9/11—the "Operation: Northwoods" plan in 1962 to stage terrorist attacks around the U.S. base in Guantánamo as a pretext for invading Cuba, a FEMA document of 1997 that depicted the World Trade Center in the crosshairs of a gun, NORAD exercises in 1999 that envisioned airplanes hitting the World Trade Center and Pentagon, experiments by the Air Force with drones and remote-control airplanes (some conspiracy theories maintain that a remote-control plane hit the World Trade Center). Avery's litany of plans, exercises, incidents, and events is presented in a portentously foreboding manner, but it has no real connection with 9/11. No evidence exists directly linking any of them with the 9/11 attacks. The incidents he cites count as anomalies, things that in hindsight seem odd or peculiar in relation to 9/11. In fact, a penchant for reasoning by anomaly is basic to the conspiratorial mindset. No direct evidence of conspiracy is ever cited, found, or uncovered in any of these films or in the books and Web sites that accompany them. Investigators instead seize on inconsistencies in people's testimonies or recollections or in odd features that appear in the visual record provided by video and photography. As evidence "proving" the World Trade Center was subjected to controlled demolition, for example, conspiracy buffs cite the puffs of dust that can be seen coming from the sides of the tower below the point of collapse. These must be explosive charges detonating, they say. The alternative explanation—that air is being violently expelled by the imploding building—is rejected because it contradicts the premise that demolition occurred. As a columnist for *Scientific American* notes, "The mistaken belief that a handful of unexplained anomalies can undermine a well-established theory lies at the heart of all conspiratorial thinking. . . . All the 'evidence' for a 9/11 conspiracy falls under the rubric of this fallacy."[55]

Avery maintains a façade of scholarly and empirical inquiry by reciting data about the engineering specifications of the hijacked aircraft and the World Trade Center and by citing numerous eyewitness accounts that conflict with the official version. But the eyewitness reports tend to come from early news accounts that were prone to error, and one of the chief news sources upon which the film relies is the *American Free Press* (*AFP*), a conspiracy-oriented, anti-Semitic paper launched in 2001 by Willis Carto. The *AFP* tends to find numerous Jewish conspiracies at work in the modern world. For additional sourcing, Avery relies on Wikipedia entries. Not surprisingly, given this "scholarly" base, the film is rife with error and misleading statements. Discussing the strike on the South Tower, for example, Avery says, "The second plane hits the South Tower between the 78th and 82nd floors at 9:03 A.M., barely hitting the southeast corner, the majority of the jet fuel exploding outside in a massive fireball." The narration is accompanied by video of the strike that plainly contradicts what is being said. By claiming that the aircraft barely hits the tower, Avery builds his case that something else, namely explosive charges, brought the building down. But his claim that the plane struck a glancing blow is deception. As the video clearly shows, the entire plane entered the building. Moreover, it was flying 100 miles per hour faster than American Airlines 11, which struck the North Tower. It hit the building at a lower point, leaving greater mass above the area of impact; and the off-center strike, which took out support columns at the corner of the building, likely destabilized the structure more severely than was the case with the other tower. These factors go some way to explaining why the South Tower fell first. Avery also gets his floors wrong. According to the report of the National Institute of Standards and Technology, UA 175 hit floors 77–85.[56]

Similar theories are proffered by *911: In Plane Sight* (2004) but with some new wrinkles. Produced by Bridgestone Media Group, which has made other documentaries alleging vast government conspiracies (*Beyond Treason* [2005], *One Nation Under Siege* [2006]), and hosted by "The Power Hour" radio personality Dave von Kleist, the film's "evidence" consists of speculative analyses of select visual anomalies contained in the photographic and video records of the World Trade Center and Pentagon attacks. Photographs of the Pentagon, for example, show a 16-foot hole in the building's middle ring. Von Kleist asks in the film, as many conspiracy Web sites have done, how an airplane with a 124-foot wingspan fits inside a 16-foot hole. The conspiratorial answer is that it doesn't, that only a missile hitting the building would produce such a hole. The answer provided by the American Society of Civil Engineers is that the wingspan did not penetrate beyond the façade (which had a 90-foot gash), that the aircraft frame was destroyed before it had traveled a distance comparable to the length of the aircraft, and that it was the heavy front landing gear that traveled the farthest into the building, producing that 16-foot hole. "A jet doesn't punch a cartoonlike outline into a concrete building upon impact."[57]

Regarding the crash of UA 175 into the South Tower, von Kleist's photo and video analysis emphasizes suggestions of a protruding object underneath the fuselage and a bright flash occurring apparently just before impact. He states that this evidence "refutes" the idea that it was a commercial airliner. With the wild interpretive leaps characteristic of this genre, von Kleist announces that the evidence shows it could only be a military plane carrying an explosive device fired at the last moment in order to detonate the jet fuel. An earlier section of von Kleist's narration, in which he discusses the four hijacked airplanes, exemplifies the manner in which bald speculation is cloaked by a discourse that sounds hyperrational:

> *Is it not safe to assume that all four of these events are inescapably married to one another? And is it not also safe to assume that if you find one person involved or a party involved with one of these events, they're probably involved in all of them? Well, following this train of thought, since there was no credible claim of responsibility, is it not safe to assume that those involved, or those parties involved, or agencies or groups that were involved in the events of 9/11 would do anything that they can to obfuscate, distract, or distort or cover up any information that might lead to their discovery? And if that's true, is it not also safe to assume that if you find somebody, a group, an agency, a party that is involved in the obfuscation, distraction, distortion, or cover-up of any information involved in any of the events of 9/11, does it not indicate possible involvement, and even guilt, in the events of 9/11?*

Whew! Despite all this heavy breathing, the "evidence" unearthed in the film fails to point to anyone—individuals, parties, groups, or agencies, to use the film's rhetoric—that can be fingered as a conspirator. All that remains are the photo anomalies and the wild speculation built from them. As the editors of *Popular Mechanics* write, "Strip away the political theorizing and logical leaps and every conspiracy theory ultimately comes down to a small set of claims based on evidence that can be examined. These claims are the only points where the theorists' elaborate conjectures make contact with the real world. . . . In every case we examined, the key claims made by conspiracy theorists turned out to be mistaken, misinterpreted, or deliberately falsified."[58]

Nevertheless, the conspiracy theories have become an enduring part of the folklore that now surrounds 9/11. A chief claim of the theories is that controlled demolition brought down World Trade Center buildings 1, 2, and 7. *Loose Change* proffers this idea, as does *In Plane Sight*, but it receives its most elaborate development in *911 Mysteries: Demolitions* (2006). Unlike the other films, this one develops its argument with greater apparent care and employs a more dispassionate narrator who often avoids the inflammatory rhetoric so common in the other productions. Using computer graphics, some apparently borrowed from a PBS *Nova* production, the film examines the physical structure of the Twin Towers—steel columns at the core, with a webbed steel exoskeleton at the periphery of the buildings—and the effects of high temperatures on steel. All of this is to prove that the fires could not have brought down the buildings—the film maintains that the temperature was never hot enough to melt the steel. Indeed, the NIST report agrees and never claimed that fire caused the collapse. It was a combination of damage to the structure from the impact of the planes, fireproofing dislodged from the steel support beams by the impact, and the effect of high heat weakening the steel. "The WTC towers likely would not have collapsed under the combined effects of aircraft impact damage and the extensive, multi-floor fires that were encountered on September 11, 2001, if the thermal insulation had not been widely dislodged or had been only minimally dislodged by aircraft impact."[59]

Because the conspiracy films are so insistent (based largely on armchair analyses of video footage of the collapse shot by onlookers) that only explosives could have brought down the towers, it is worth quoting in some detail from the NIST findings. NIST determined that different factors in each tower contributed to the collapse:

> *In WTC 1, the fires weakened the core columns and caused the floors on the south side of the building to sag. The floors pulled the heated south perimeter columns inward, reducing their capacity to support the building above. Their neighboring columns quickly became overloaded as columns on the south wall buckled. The top section of the building tilted to the south and began its descent.*
>
> *In WTC 2, the core was damaged severely at the southeast corner and was restrained by the east and south walls via the hat truss and the floors. The steady burning fires on the east side of the building caused the floors there to sag. The floors pulled the heated east perimeter columns inward, reducing their capacity to support the building above. Their neighboring columns quickly became overloaded as the columns on the east wall buckled. The top section of the building tilted to the east and to the south and began its descent. . . . WTC 2 collapsed more quickly than WTC 1 because there was more aircraft damage to the building core, including one of the heavily loaded corner columns, and there were early and persistent fires on the east side of the building, where the aircraft had extensively dislodged insulation from the structural steel.*[60]

FIGURE 3.5 This news photograph of the onset of collapse in the South Tower of the World Trade Center shows that the collapse began just below the point of impact and not from the ground up as a part of controlled demolition, as conspiracy theorists claim. (AP Photo/Amy Sancetta)

These findings resulted from scientific testing and computer modeling. The armchair sleuths who populate the conspiracy films have conducted no scientific analysis. The only sleuth who comes close is Stephen Jones, who appears in *911 Mysteries* and other conspiracy movies. Jones was a physicist at Brigham Young University who has popularized the hypothesis that thermite charges were used because some videos of the disaster show what appears to be molten steel pouring out of the South Tower and because the long-burning fires at Ground Zero raised the temperature in the pile of steel beyond what jet fuel could produce. But Jones's own background is in cold fusion, not explosives, and demolition experts have pointed to flaws in his reasoning. Jones argues that thermite charges would burn with sufficient heat to melt steel, but Mark Loizeaux, president of Controlled Demolition, Inc., told *Popular Mechanics* that the velocity of an explosive (when used to create a building collapse) cuts through steel with force and speed; it does not melt or burn its way through. "Could explosives melt steel? Absolutely not. It's too fast an exposure."[61] Interestingly, Loizeaux was interviewed for the film and told the filmmakers that the velocity of shaped charges, used in steel buildings to focus the explosive energy, is more than 27,000 feet per second. Despite the evident problem such velocity poses for the thermite burn-through-and-melt argument, the film positions Loizeaux as if his expertise helps to buttress the conspiracy cause. It is not until the end of the film that a disclaimer appears on screen announcing that not all experts interviewed agree with the movie's premise.

According to the film, the demolition charges were placed during a weekend when power was cut off in the World Trade Center for an ostensible security upgrade. The conspiracy hypothesis here is remarkably elaborate. The buildings came down according to a precisely timed and executed plan that had six stages: (1) explosives are detonated in the sub-basement; (2) core columns at the interior of the building are cut by explosives; (3) ground-level explosives weaken the upper basement and lower supports; (4) collapse is initiated by "cracking the top" of the building; (5) explosive charges detonate on floors just below the falling structure; (6) the final charges at the base of the building roll the structure, causing complete pulverization of the support columns. Everything has to occur with split-second timing and also in synchrony with the timeline of the hijackings—no mean feat!

The film makes its case by citing members of the World Trade Center's maintenance staff who report hearing explosions in the buildings' sub-basement, by pointing to the dust ejected from windows below the collapse (deemed to be explosive squibs), by claiming that the buildings collapsed at free-fall speed (something the NIST report disputes), and by showing extensive footage of other buildings falling from controlled demolition. The viewer is invited to note the similarity: the WTC seems to collapse in on itself just as the other buildings do in the video excerpts. But in fact the video imagery of imploded buildings undermines the conspiracy argument because all of these collapses clearly occur from the ground up as explosive charges blow out the foundations. The World Trade Center falls from the top down and from the point of aircraft impact, hardly what one would see had all the hypothesized demolition been occurring in its basement and ground-level floors. As Loizeaux told *Popular Mechanics*, "If you look at any building that is imploded, the explosives are primarily placed on the ground floor and the basement. . . . If you look at the collapse of these structures, they start collapsing where the planes hit. They don't start collapsing down below." The armchair sleuths pouring over the video records of the collapse seem never to have noticed this difference.

After developing its six-stage model of sabotage, the film replays the imagery of the World Trade Center falling with a music score that is eerie, hyperbolic, and apocalyptic, qualities that emphasize the forced histrionics of the conspiracy enterprise. These films take real tragedy and turn it into melodrama, and their impulse to aestheticize the devastation is sometimes startling. *911 Mysteries* gives us several operatic sequences of collapsing structures scored with a vocal chorus. *In Plane Sight* obsessively plays and replays imagery of the planes striking the towers, people running, and the dust clouds descending, edited and scored as a kind of music video. The films purport to be informational documentaries proffering the truth of 9/11, but in fact they turn the events into a melodrama formatted by the aesthetic conventions of pop culture.

Barrie Zwicker, an independent media commentator based in Canada, is one of the gurus of what has become known as the movement for "9/11 truth." Zwicker's 2002 commentaries for Canadian television were released in video format as *The Great Deception*, and he organized a 2004 conference at the University of Toronto entitled the "International Citizens' Inquiry into 9/11." He published *Towers of Deception: The Media Cover-up of 9/11*, and he incorporated his commentaries, along with video excerpts of speakers at the 2004 conference, in *The Great Conspiracy: The 9/11 News Special You Never Saw* (2005). Zwicker believes that 9/11 was a "false flag operation," a plot by the government against its own people that was designed to look like it was carried out by enemies from overseas. But as he says in *The Great Conspiracy*, which mostly consists of Zwicker seated in a faux-newscast set and delivering long lectures on the alleged conspiracy, "The dirtiest secret about terrorism

FIGURE 3.6 In *The Great Conspiracy*, Canadian journalist Barrie Zwicker argues that on 9/11 the U.S. government attacked its own citizens in a "false flag" operation. (Frame enlargement)

is also by far the largest. Many spectacular acts of terror are fearsome fakeries carried out by cabals within governments, and I mean our own governments. The gold standard is the attack on one's own country to mobilize public opinion for power, political gain, and profit." According to Zwicker, the 9/11 attacks are a contemporary version of the Reichstag fire used by the Nazis to consolidate their power.

The evidence consists of the standard reasoning-by-analogy familiar in this genre. Zwicker cites the Reichstag fire, the Gulf of Tonkin incident, the "Operation: Northwoods" plan, all presented as "false flag" operations that prove 9/11's similarity, despite having nothing to do with September 11. To show the persuasiveness of what he describes as "accumulating evidence" of conspiracy, he cites a poll taken in May 2004 in which 63 percent of Canadians surveyed agreed with the statement, "Individuals within the U.S. government including the White House had prior knowledge of the plans for the events of Sept. 11th and failed to take appropriate action to stop them." This assertion, actually, is not so far off the mark. There were numerous warnings that a major attack was coming, and some of these warnings involved airplanes. Zwicker does not say how many people were in the survey, and he does not mention that the group that conducted it, Skeptics Inquiry for Truth, is hardly one that starts from a balanced outlook. The survey item that does ask about conspiracy—"Individuals within the U.S. government including the White House were involved in the planning and execution of the events of September 11th."—elicited only 16 percent agreement among respondents, an unexciting finding that Zwicker does not mention in his film.

Zwicker seizes on President Bush's odd statements, which the President repeated on several occasions, that on 9/11 he saw the first plane hit the World Trade Center on television. He could not have seen this because no footage was broadcast that day of the strike on the North Tower. Making the wild interpretive leaps characteristic of the genre, Zwicker treats the President's assertions as proof of guilt. "It is not unreasonable to conclude that he sees the first plane on private, closed-circuit TV earlier that morning." Thus, someone had to set up the cameras to film the first strike, someone who knew the planes were coming and what their target would be. "In other words, people closely associated with the President of the United States had very specific knowledge of the existence of the first plane, its destination and its purpose." The fact that Bush remained in the Florida classroom after learning of the second strike, and then lingered at the school for thirty minutes, with the Secret Service manifesting no urgency to move him to safety, proves that he had advance knowledge—his behavior at the school was an act; it was theater. "This evidence alone constitutes grounds for proceeding with an indictment on charges of conspiracy to commit treason," Zwicker proclaims with the utmost sincerity.

And what was it all for? The motives are epic in scale and as plentiful as the evidence that Zwicker claims to find. It was all about "peak oil," an effort to seize the last remaining oil resources on the planet. It was all about creating "a new Pearl Harbor" to justify the war in Iraq. It was all, evidently, about whatever premise one wishes to posit.

This subgenre of documentaries—other titles include *Terrorstorm* (2006), *September 11, the Con, the Conspiracy, the Cover-Up* (2006), *The Truth and Lies of 9-11* (2007), *Improbable Collapse: The Demolition of Our Republic* (2007)—tend to be produced using inexpensive digital cut-and-paste production methods and to proliferate on the Internet. The net cultural effect has been to stoke the paranoia of large swaths of the nation's citizenry and to keep this paranoia alive as enduring parts of the 9/11 legacy. The Bush administration's history of stonewalling and of making evasive responses to queries about the events of 9/11 has, unfortunately, worked to sustain the paranoia and to give the popular culture surrounding the attacks the same kind of opacity and aura of suspicion as that which now surrounds the assassination of JFK.

After 9/11 "terrorism" became a political trope capable of instilling public mobilization and intimidation on a national scale. Not since the era of communism had the nation seen such an effective means for influencing the mass public. By invoking the danger of terrorism, the administration was able stifle opposition to its policies. In early 2008, for example, the Bush administration claimed that the nation's telecommunications companies, which had cooperated with the National Security Agency in monitoring American citizens' telephone and Internet activities at the administration's request, ought to be protected from lawsuits over the warrantless spying. The administration said that national security was at stake, and the Senate approved a bill expanding the government's surveillance powers that included a provision granting the telecoms immunity from lawsuits.[62]

Political appeals centering on the danger posed by terrorism sometimes concealed historical ironies. Dollan Cannell's documentary, *638 Ways to Kill Castro* (2006), about the numerous assassination plots hatched by the CIA and by Cuban activist groups in Florida, examines the case of Luis Posada and Orlando Bosch, suspected masterminds of the 1976 bombing of Cubana Flight 455, which killed all 73 people on board. The plane had just left Barbados for Cuba when the first of two bombs stashed on board exploded. The plane and its passengers were not immediately destroyed. The pilot radioed Barbados for permission to execute an emergency landing, and he was returning to the island when the second bomb went off, sending the plane into a death crash at sea. The film shows rescuers pulling body parts out of the ocean. A few Cuban officials and foreign photographers were on board, but most of the passengers were ordinary Cubans. The two men who admitted planting the bombs were Posada's employees, and their testimony implicated Posada and Bosch, both of whom were anti-Castro terrorists with ties to the CIA. Bosch had been arrested in 1968 for firing a bazooka at a Polish freighter leaving Florida for Cuba. Posada was responsible for a 1997 hotel bombing campaign in Cuba, and in 2000 he was arrested with 200 pounds of explosives in Panama where he allegedly intended to kill Castro.

Cuba has requested that the United States extradite the men so that it can try them for the airline bombing, but the U.S. refused to do so. At the time of the film's production, Posada and Bosch were both living as free men in the United States. Bosch, in fact, had been arrested on a parole violation in 1987 but was pardoned by President George H. W. Bush in 1990 at the request of Jeb Bush, his son and the governor of Florida. Cannell interviews Bosch in the film, asking him about the airplane bombing. Bosch does not deny being involved; in fact, he boasts about several bomb plots against Cuba. Cannell then contrasts the history of these men with President Bush's famous words, after

9/11, that the U.S. will make no distinction between terrorists and those who harbor them. If you harbor a terrorist, you are a terrorist, he said. The film emphasizes the obvious irony. The disparity between words and practice illustrates a rhetorical function that the label "terrorist" sometimes plays. It can be a useful means for pointing to the actions of political enemies.

President Bush and his administration did such in regard to Saddam Hussein. By stating that Saddam Hussein was connected to al Qaeda and was involved in the 9/11 attacks, the administration mobilized the public to support its drive to take the country to war in Iraq. Polls conducted by CBS News and the *New York Times* between September 2002 and April 2003 showed the effectiveness of the strategy. On average, 49 percent of Americans agreed with the survey statement that Saddam was personally involved in the 9/11 attacks.[63] Just as 9/11 stimulated a wave of documentary film production, the Iraq War has incited documentary filmmakers to a similar sense of passion. And because the Iraq War is so much a part of the legacy of 9/11, the next chapter turns to those documentaries about the conflict.

But before leaving the 9/11 documentaries, it is important to stress that they perform a function very different from Hollywood films on the subject, which tend to be either dramatizations of real events or genre movies that obliquely reference the attacks. By contrast, the documentaries supply visceral and palpable records of what happened. The shrieks of onlookers as United 175 slams into the South Tower, the roar of the collapsing towers, the panic on the streets as the doomsday cloud of dust, ash, and vaporized body parts descends—these sensory details are vital information about the realities of what happened, and they cannot be supplied by still photography, which was otherwise such a crucial source of documentation on the events of that day. These films capture horror in motion and in sound and preserve these details in perpetuity. They thus offer a form of witnessing to the audiences who view them, a statement that what happened is important in a collective sense and that direct, unflinching scrutiny is the morally appropriate response to the atrocity. The films offer a pathway toward this scrutiny; by replaying the events in motion and in sound they re-create the historical experience, as a mediated form, yes, but with the assertive stance that gives documentary its hammer force: such things happened, and they looked and sounded like this. This assertive provocation is the most profound and searching contribution that cinema has made to, and in honor of, the events of that day. Narrative film, by contrast, has struggled to find an appropriate mode for dramatizing the events. In the documentaries, the mesmerizing imagery of the flaming towers tears through the skein of cinema and of narrative construction to assert its own terrible immediacy. Ontology asserts its primacy, and the filmmakers who were caught in this became a part of the history on which they turned their cameras. And it is here that American film to date drew its deepest and most important connection with a viewing audience, drawn together in a time of crisis, seared by national tragedy.

CHAPTER FOUR
BATTLEGROUND IRAQ

STUNG AND ENRAGED BY THE FEROCITY of the September 11 assault, the Bush administration moved aggressively to reorganize national defenses against terror attacks. The administration feared another attack, and beginning on September 18 several letters containing the deadly bacterium anthrax were mailed to the news media and to the offices of two Democratic senators. Five people died, numerous others were sickened. The administration believed it was a second-wave attack by al Qaeda, and an acute sense of emergency and fear gripped officials. In response, the administration expanded the powers of the Presidency, the FBI and the CIA, and rethought the existing laws on domestic surveillance, many of which had been formulated in the 1970s in a pre-Internet era. It also moved to attack Afghanistan, which harbored Osama bin Laden and al Qaeda and also to prepare for an invasion and occupation of Iraq. As the administration made its case for war on Iraq and then launched the war, the military campaign in Afghanistan against bin Laden and the Taliban faded into the background, both in the national consciousness and in terms of the amount of military resources being expended. Saddam Hussein was quickly toppled, but the occupation of Iraq went very badly, and the war bitterly divided the American public. Numerous films were made in response to these events, and they need to be included in a consideration of American film in the age of terrorism. The events they analyze are related to al Qaeda's September 2001 attacks because the Bush administration was responding to those attacks in formulating its case for increased domestic and international surveillance and for war in Iraq. About the case for war, for example, on September 25, 2002, President Bush asserted that the U.S. must confront the danger that al Qaeda and Saddam would "work in concert" and that al Qaeda could become "an extension of Saddam's madness."[1] On September 28, 2002, President Bush asserted that Saddam was seeking a nuclear bomb and that "there are al Qaeda terrorists inside Iraq." In his February 5, 2003, United Nations presentation, Secretary of State Colin Powell stated that Iraq was training al Qaeda terrorists in the use of weapons of mass destruction. Numerous other claims advanced by principal figures in the administration linked 9/11 with Saddam Hussein.

Before turning to the films made about the war, it will be helpful to establish some context. One week after 9/11, Congress voted to give the President legal authorization to use military force against terrorists. Congress granted the President the power to "use all necessary and appropriate force against those nations, organizations, or persons he determines planned, authorized, committed, or aided the terrorist attacks that occurred on September 11, 2001." Six weeks following the attacks, Congress passed the United and Strengthening America by Providing Appropriate Tools Required to Intercept and Obstruct Terrorism Act of 2001. This legislation was nicknamed the USA Patriot Act. The emergency atmosphere of the period, with so much death so near at hand, and with the recent anthrax attacks unsolved, created an overwhelming push for political action. No member of Congress, for example, read the bill before voting on it.[2] The act subjects foreigners deemed to be terrorists to indefinite detention without charges or due process, enables the FBI to conduct electronic surveillance and physical searches without probable cause, enables "sneak and peek" searches conducted without informing the person so targeted, and facilitates data mining by intelligence agencies. All of these features alarmed civil liberties advocates. David Cole and James X. Dempsey, for example, summarized the changes enabled by the Act:

> *Previously, the FBI could get the credit card records of anyone suspected of being an international terrorist or other foreign agent. Under the Patriot*

Act, the FBI can get the entire database of the credit card company. Under prior law, the FBI could get library borrowing records only by complying with state law and always had to ask for the records of a specific person or concerning a specific book. Under the Patriot Act, the FBI can get an order for the records on everybody who ever used the library, or who used it on a certain day, or who checked out certain kinds of books. It can do the same at any bank, telephone company, hotel or motel, hospital or university.[3]

Critics of the Patriot Act also have charged that it erodes Constitutional protections enshrined in the Bill of Rights. Writing in 2006, with the Taliban re-reemerging in Afghanistan and bin Laden and al Qaeda reestablishing their operations in Pakistan, Michael Scheuer, former head of the CIA's Bin Laden Unit, stated that America's leaders have underestimated the Islamist threat to the U.S.—"each time America has been attacked, they have been faster to constrict civil liberties than to destroy the enemy."[4] Produced by Robert Greenwald's Public Interest Pictures and directed by Nonny de la Peña, *Unconstitutional: The War on Our Civil Liberties* (2004) explores the impact of the Patriot Act, giving special attention to its effects on immigrants living lawfully in the United States. Under the Justice Department's "hold until clear" policy, over a thousand lawful immigrants were swept up, detained without charges or legal representation, and some were deported back to the countries from which they had aimed to escape. These included Syria, Pakistan, and Egypt. The film profiles the Hamoui family, immigrants from Syria seeking asylum in the U.S., and the sweep that jailed the father, mother, and daughter, undermining their conviction that they could find freedom in America. A former CIA Director for Counter-Terrorism tells the filmmakers that the flaw in such measures is that they target and alienate the very communities from which officials need help in combating terrorism. The subtitle of the film, presenting post-9/11 developments as a war not on terror but on civil liberties, is a polemical move by Greenwald and a rhetorical overstatement. Greenwald's own ability to make the film and freely distribute it and profit from it suggests that something less than a war against liberty, speech, and thought is under way.

Civil liberties advocates often view post-9/11 law and the administration's antiterror policies as constituting a break with previous American legal history and traditions. There is justification for this view. In 2001 and 2002, for example, lawyers in the Justice Department crafted a series of secret memos arguing that the ban on torture under U.S. law (18 U.S.C. §§2340–2340A) and under the Geneva Conventions (to which the U.S. was a signatory) did not apply in the struggle against al Qaeda. The memos were crafted to provide a legal shield for the administration's use of harsh interrogation methods on enemy combatant captives. Few actions by the Bush administration after 9/11 have provoked as much revulsion as this effort to evade the laws prohibiting torture.

In contrast to predominant views, in his study of the laws and administration practices surrounding surveillance, detention, and interrogation, Benjamin Wittes has argued that most of the policies the Bush administration put into play following 9/11 have a basis in existing law, in what Wittes has called "the law of September 10." The clear exception to this, for Wittes, was the decision to conduct electronic surveillance within the U.S. outside the purview of FISA. Congress passed the Foreign Intelligence Surveillance Act (FISA) in 1978 and stipulated that its provisions govern the manner in which the executive branch can conduct national security surveillance of Americans. Warrants to conduct such surveillance must come before the FISA court. Because FISA reflects a world before the rise of the Internet and the vast changes in telecommunications that have occurred since the 1970s, the administration decided to bypass the FISA court by going directly to telecommunications companies and asking them to support data-mining operations conducted by the National Security Agency. About FISA, Wittes points out, "The political judgment behind the law, perfectly understandable in the wake of the intelligence abuses revealed in the 1970s, was that broad surveillance authorities pose a greater danger to the public than does any threat against which government might use those powers to protect the public."[5] He adds that for many Americans, this judgment did not survive 9/11.

Summarizing the steps taken by the administration after 9/11 in relation to preexisting law, Wittes concludes, "None of them . . . was an oddity of the Bush administration. They, or something very much like them, represented what any presidential administration would have done when airplanes started unexpectedly hitting buildings. The administration's failure, rather, began . . . when it confused the ad hoc approach the crisis had necessitated with a viable permanent legal architecture for the struggle."[6] Working from a theory of unitary and supreme executive power, the administration bypassed Congress and did not attempt to create a legislative framework for the war on terror and in support of its own policies. The result over time has been judicial intervention into those policies, continuing litigation, and a loss of political legitimation for them. As Jane Mayer writes, "the imposition of an alternative legal system following rules of the executive branch's own devising . . . has proven the origin of almost all of the Bush Administration's most vexing legal problems in the war on terror."[7]

Also following in the wake of 9/11, the Bush administration launched a plan to invade Iraq and depose Saddam Hussein. Numerous figures in the administration had been committed to this idea before 9/11. Vice President Dick Cheney, Defense Secretary Donald Rumsfeld, and Deputy Defense Secretary Paul Wolfowitz had all been members of the neoconservative think tank, Project for a New American Century, which issued an influential report in September 2000 identifying Iraq as a serious threat to U.S. security. "The current American peace will be short-lived if the United States becomes vulnerable to rogue powers with small, inexpensive arsenals of ballistic missiles and nuclear warheads or other weapons of mass destruction. We cannot allow North Korea, Iran, Iraq or similar states to undermine American leadership, intimidate American allies or threaten the American homeland itself."[8] This report also contains the infamous sentence that conspiracy theorists have seized on as "proof" that 9/11 was an inside job by the Bush administration. Describing the conditions necessary to enable a twenty-first-century transformation of the American military, the authors write, "Further, the process of transformation, even if it brings revolutionary change, is likely to be a long one, absent some catastrophic and catalyzing event—like a new Pearl Harbor."[9] For the conspiracists, the report was the blueprint for 9/11. David Ray Griffin, one of the gurus of the conspiracy movement (aka the "9/11 truth" movement), entitled his book on 9/11 and the Bush administration, *The New Pearl Harbor*.[10]

The 9/11 attacks provided the administration with an opportunity to carry out the preexisting anti-Saddam objective. Richard Clarke was the national coordinator for counterterrorism in the Clinton administration and remained briefly with the Bush administration in the summer and fall of 2001. Clarke wrote that immediately after the attacks President Bush asked his staff to search for links that would tie Saddam Hussein to 9/11, and he claims that the President persisted in this request even after Clarke assured him that bin Laden and al Qaeda were the culprits.[11] Clarke writes that by Wednesday, September 12, Rumsfeld and Wolfowitz were overruling CIA findings that al Qaeda was behind the attacks and were talking about broadening the terms of response and "getting Iraq."[12] At the Pentagon, Douglas Feith's Office of Special Plans began sifting through intelligence reports in order to establish the necessary linkages; a subsequent Pentagon investigation into these activities discredited them and concluded that there were no substantive links between Saddam Hussein and bin Laden. George Tenet, who was head of the CIA at this time, wrote later that the administration did not debate the seriousness of an Iraq threat and did not discuss ways of avoiding an invasion.[13]

The Bush administration then began a sustained effort to prepare public opinion to support its case for war. The administration's announcements linked Saddam Hussein's Iraq with terrorism and with al Qaeda and by implication with the 9/11 attacks. In his January 29, 2002, State of the Union Address, President Bush identified Iraq as part of a worldwide "axis of evil," composed of states that sponsor terrorism and threaten the U.S. with weapons of mass destruction:

> *Iraq continues to flaunt its hostility toward America and to support terror. The Iraqi regime has plotted to develop anthrax, and nerve gas, and nuclear weapons for over a decade. This is a regime that has already used poison gas to murder thousands of its own citizens—leaving the bodies of mothers huddled over their dead children. This is a regime that agreed to international inspections—then kicked out the inspectors. This is a regime that has something to hide from the civilized world.*
>
> *States like these, and their terrorist allies, constitute an axis of evil, arming to threaten the peace of the world. By seeking weapons of mass destruction, these regimes pose a grave and growing danger. They could provide these arms to terrorists, giving them the means to match their hatred. They could attack our allies or attempt to blackmail the United States. In any of these cases, the price of indifference would be catastrophic.*[14]

The remarks were tantamount to a declaration of war. In a speech to the Veterans of Foreign Wars on August 26, Vice President Cheney declared, "There is no doubt that Saddam Hussein now has weapons of mass destruction. There is no doubt that he is amassing them to use against our friends, against our allies, and against us."[15] *Fahrenheit 9/11* includes footage of Cheney stating, "There was a relationship between Saddam and al Qaeda," and of National Security Advisor Condoleezza Rice stating, "There is a tie between Iraq and what happened on 9/11."

The administration said that the need to invade Iraq was urgent. In a televised speech on October 7, 2002, President Bush said that there was no time to wait for "the final proof, the smoking gun that could come in the form of a mushroom cloud." The impulse in the country after 9/11 was to rally around the President, and skepticism or criticism of the impending attack on Iraq was seen as being unpatriotic. In time, though, the administration's claims became discredited, and it paid a heavy price. As Jack Goldsmith, the former Assistant Attorney General at the White House's Office of Legal Counsel, wrote, "The administration lost public trust in the fight against terrorists when it premised a major war on a terror-related threat of weapons of mass destruction that turned out to be wrong. And the war in Iraq has spilled over to and infected everything else that this administration does in the broader war on terrorism."[16]

THE MEDIA IN THE RUN-UP TO WAR

At the time, the national media backed the administration and made the case for war, accepting without much scrutiny the claims that Iraq had weapons of mass destruction and posed an imminent threat. In *Buying the War* (2007), which ran as part of the PBS series *Bill Moyers' Journal*, Moyers interviewed Howard Kurtz, the media ombudsman for the *Washington Post*. Kurtz reported that he "did the math" and that between August 2002 and March 2003, the newspaper ran nearly 140 front-page articles on Iraq, and all but a handful made the administration's case for war. Moreover, in the six months before the war, the *Post* editorialized in favor of the coming invasion more than twenty-six times.

The news media's bias in favor of the war was heavy and pronounced. A study by Fairness and Accuracy in Reporting (FAIR) examined the position on the war expressed by news sources appearing on camera on the evening newscasts of six television networks and news channels (ABC, CBS, NBC, CNN, Fox, and PBS).[17] Of the 1,617 persons expressing views on camera, 64 percent were pro-war and 10 percent were opposed. In contrast to foreign journalists or officials, U.S. guests represented 76 percent of total sources. Of these U.S. commentators, 71 percent favored the war and only 3 percent expressed opposition to the war. The news media relied heavily on government and military officials for commentary, merging the voice of journalism with that of official policy. Sixty-eight percent of U.S. sources were military officials, who sometimes engaged in overt, on-air cheerleading. CNN consultant and retired general Wesley Clark, for example, said to Wolf Blitzer, "First of all, I think the troops and all the people over there, the commanders, have done an absolutely superb job, a sensational job. And I think the results speak for themselves." Unlike other on-air military officials serving as commentators, however, Clark became a critic of the war. In 2008, the *New York Times* reported that many of these retired military officers (Clark was not among them) who were employed by television networks as apparently independent military analysts were in continuous contact with the Pentagon, which gave them specific talking points and themes they were expected to emphasize in their commentaries.[18] The study points out that "the networks largely ignored anti-war opinion in the U.S." Helping to marginalize the opposition were other practices beyond the small percentage of on-air guests permitted to express antiwar views. Opposition views were often reduced to one-sentence soundbytes, and these were conveyed so quickly that the sources often were not identified by name. "[Forty-two] percent of anti-war voices went unnamed or were labeled with such vague terms as 'protester' or 'anti-war activist.'" By contrast, military and government officials were identified by name and title or other credential.

Danny Schechter's *WMD: Weapons of Mass Deception* (2004) examines the role played by the news media in helping to sell the cause of war in Iraq to the American public. Whereas Bill Moyers spoke mainly with U.S. journalists, Schechter interviewed numerous foreign journalists as well as American reporters and news executives, which enables his film to cover a broader range of issues than does *Buying the War*. Schechter, who had been a news producer for CNN and ABC, examines several institutional factors that arguably helped to cause the bias in news coverage. One is the Pentagon decision to embed reporters with the troops as a mechanism for limiting their access to the war. This policy was a response to the U.S. loss of the Vietnam War, widely seen as being due in significant measure to the unrestricted access of reporters to the front and the negative fallout from their coverage. Former CNN and MSNBC reporter Peter Arnett says that in Vietnam, "reporters did not get on the team. We challenged generals, governments. We demanded their accountability. We challenged their findings."

In contrast, the policy of embedding reporters with troops works to create a strong emotional bond between the reporter and the soldiers, and Schechter interviews a journalist for *People* magazine who tells him that, in a crisis, she knew that she would side with the soldiers she cared about rather than her journalistic mission to be objective. Another reporter observes that embedding by its nature (reporters are given protective combat gear and trained how to use it) is a violation of journalistic ethics which require that a journalist not accept valuable services from a source. Reporter Robert Pelton observes that, "The idea of embedding is essentially the Stockholm syndrome. If you take an unarmed individual and go and put him with armed people, he becomes sympathetic to their cause."

Furthermore, television news treats war as a form of entertainment for viewers. Elaborate news graphics with dramatic music and computer simulations of weapons systems and bombing runs, constructed with help from the Pentagon, enhance the spectacle of war and downplay its bloodshed. An emphasis on "smart" weaponry may substitute for coverage of war's carnage. ABC News *Nightline* correspondent John Donovan tells Schechter, "I've covered enough war to say that we've never, I've never, shown the viewer what it's really like and how horrible war is. . . . There are certain kinds of close-ups that we won't show, there're certain blood spatters, dead children that we don't show people partly because it violates a long-standing practice—don't put gore on television." Dubai Television anchor Nina Abu-Wardeh compares

American and Arabic coverage, pointing out, "On the Arabic TV stations I would see what war is really like, the blood and gore, the mess that really happens when a bomb hits a building. On CNN you would see more of the strategic stuff." Schechter, though, does not point out that both contexts can operate to serve political purposes. Hiding the gore from Western viewers can make the war seem less destructive and may thereby reduce its potential to be politically provocative. Emphasizing the gore can polarize viewers in the opposite direction, helping to elicit an oppositional stance, one that can serve a different set of purposes and political agendas.

Schechter also finds that television reporters are instructed how to get exciting footage by imitating cinema vérité camera techniques. Pelton describes network instructions to reporters to take their cameras "off the stick." The reporter would be instructed to move around with a handheld camera to make the viewer feel the journalist is in the middle of something. And the military encouraged reporters to capture entertaining action footage. A Department of Defense memo presented in the film states, "Use of lipstick and helmet-mounted cameras on combat sorties is approved and encouraged to the greatest extent possible."

Schechter examines the public relations effort by the Pentagon to influence coverage of the war, which included hiring a public relations consultant to serve as the Assistant Secretary of Defense for Public Affairs under Defense Secretary Donald Rumsfeld. (The extensive Pentagon program using ex-military officers as on-air commentators promoting administration policy in the guise of news analysis was evidently unknown to Schechter at the time of the film's production. It is a more egregious example than the one that he cites.) The PR consultant, Victoria Clarke, was subsequently hired as an on-air commentator for CNN. The film also examines the role of the Pentagon in planting false stories about Jessica Lynch and the Saddam–al Qaeda connection, and it suggests that U.S. military forces have on occasion deliberately targeted independent reporters. The Pentagon, for example, had been given the location of the Arab media center in Baghdad, which was bombed anyway, killing al Jazeera reporter Tareq Ayyoub, and an American tank fired on the Palestine Hotel, where reporters were based, killing two cameramen, one who worked for Spanish media and the other for Reuters. Once again, the Pentagon had been told that news media worked out of the hotel. The film shows the American tank firing at the hotel, suddenly and without apparent provocation.

The devastating attacks on 9/11 produced social and political pressure to back the President in a time of war. It is important to remember that President Bush's public approval ratings soared after 9/11. In November 2001, Gallup polls showed that 87 percent of respondents rated him favorably, and the numbers were still high—67 percent—when the Iraq War started in March 2003. The bipartisan majority vote in Congress for the war also indicates the great political power that President Bush enjoyed in the aftermath of the al Qaeda attacks. As a result, critical voices at times found less space and tolerance in public forums. MSNBC fired correspondent Peter Arnett after he gave an interview on Arabic television stating that the U.S. had underestimated the will of Iraqis to resist the invasion. Arnett says in the film, "The rest of the world looked at my firing as another example of American media caving in to the government." In *Buying the War* Dan Rather describes a "climate of fear" inside newsrooms, a feeling that there would be consequences for those not getting on board with the war effort.

Public reactions to the country music group, the Dixie Chicks, pointed to the direction in which majority opinion was moving. After the group's lead singer spoke out during a London concert in March 2003 against the coming war and said "we're ashamed that the President of the United States is from Texas," the group found itself banned from country radio and enmeshed in ongoing criticism by the media and from former fans. Getting "Dixie Chicked" became slang for the backlash that the group had provoked. Fox television commentator Bill O'Reilly referred to people who opposed the war as "bad Americans."[19] O'Reilly also called the singers "callow, foolish women who deserve to be slapped around." Barbara Kopple and Cecelia Peck's film, *Shut Up and Sing* (2006), chronicles this episode. Robert Greenwald's *Uncovered: The War on Iraq* (2003) uses commentary from a wide range of former CIA analysts, UN and U.S. weapons inspectors, and Middle East scholars, diplomats, and ambassadors to parse the Bush administration's claims about Iraq's possession of weapons of mass destruction, its selective use of intelligence data to buttress the claims, and its reliance on dubious informers such as the now-discredited Ahmed Chalabi, an Iraqi opposition figure who had charmed many of the neoconservative advocates for the war. The film also dissects the claims made by Colin Powell in his UN presentation, which purported to show evidence for Iraq's possession of weapons of mass destruction, and examines the manner in which the news media rallied to the cause for war in Iraq.

THE INVASION

On October 11, 2002, huge majorities in the House and Senate voted to give President Bush authorization to attack Iraq if it did not give up its weapons of mass destruction. Beginning in March 2003, the United States invaded Iraq and quickly toppled the Hussein regime. No weapons of mass destruction were found, and the U.S. soon faced a powerful insurgency that the official planning for war had not taken into account. In fact, there appears to have been little planning for the postwar period in Iraq. Compounding this problem, the ruling Coalition Provisional Authority (CPA) made a series of errors that helped to bolster the insurgency by creating a huge reservoir of unemployed and armed men—government ministries were purged, the Iraqi army and national police force were disbanded, and state-run industries were shut down. Of the consequences of these decisions, a State Department diplomat wrote, "Through aggressive de-Baathification, the demobilization of the army, and the closing of factories, the coalition has left tens of thousands of individuals outside the economic and political life of the country."[20]

Moreover, during the summer of 2003, U.S. forces conducted aggressive sweeps during which they rounded up thousands of Iraqi men, many taken from their homes in front of their families, and shipped them to Abu Ghraib prison, a former torture center for Saddam Hussein's government and now reopened as a U.S. facility as of August 2003. By late autumn the prison housed 13,000 detainees, most of whom had no intelligence value at all, according to military authorities.[21] Detainees who were released returned in shame to their families, and many now had a motive for seeking vengeance against the Americans. In the meantime, the Bush administration had determined that detainees were "unlawful enemy combatants" and as such were not subject to the provisions of the Geneva Conventions, which stipulated that prisoners taken in wartime were to be treated humanely. The administration's decision had a basis in preexisting law. A 1942 Supreme Court decision, for example, distinguished between lawful and unlawful combatants. The Court wrote that unlawful combatants are offenders against the laws of war. "Unlawful combatants are likewise subject to capture and detention, but in addition they are subject to trial and punishment by military tribunals for acts which render their belligerency unlawful."[22] The administration wanted to pursue coercive methods of interrogation against some of the detainees and put its lawyers to work reinterpreting the laws on torture. The Justice Department had concluded in a series of memorandums that U.S. Code Section 2340A, which prohibits torture, did not apply to the President in a war against terror and that interrogation techniques which fail to damage organs or cause death cannot be considered torture. These ideas were developed in a 2002 memo that became infamously known as the "torture memo." It stipulated, "Physical pain amounting to torture must be equivalent in intensity to the pain accompanying serious physical injury, such as organ failure, impairment, or even death."[23] The administration later repudiated this memo after its details were leaked to the press. White House counsel Alberto

Gonzales, who would become U.S. Attorney General, advised President Bush to declare publicly that the Geneva Conventions were inapplicable to the war on terror. This would help to ensure that U.S. officials would not be prosecuted for war crimes stemming from their treatment of detainees.[24] Gonzales' interest in safeguarding administration officials from war crimes charges suggests that officials were worried about the potential consequences of the novel actions that were being contemplated. Benjamin Wittes concedes that harsh interrogation methods have their place. "Categorical opposition to coercive interrogation is not a tenable position for anyone with actual responsibility for protecting a country."[25] But he adds, "By reading laws written to restrict coercive interrogations so as to permit them, [the administration] claimed in effect that these laws had little or no meaning—not just that it had to operate outside them in a few extreme cases but that they actually *allowed* behavior the law was never intended to allow and should not allow."[26]

The administration's failure to work with Congress to construct a comprehensive legal framework for a long war on terror, its claims of supreme executive privilege, and the war on Iraq which began going badly as soon as Saddam Hussein fell are events that stimulated widespread and ongoing responses by filmmakers. Far more than did 9/11, these events proved to be catalysts for a huge outpouring of documentary filmmaking. Most of these films reflect a liberal or leftist perspective on the war, the Bush administration, and its policies. Some of these films are observational in the manner of direct cinema or cinema vérité, offering portraits of the moment-by-moment experience of American soldiers stationed in Iraq. As such, they privilege immediacy rather than historical perspective. Other films opt for a longer, historical view. Eugene Jarecki's *Why We Fight* (2005), for example, explores the reasons that the United States has so frequently gone to war. A diverse group of commentators address this question; Jarecki obtained access to numerous key individuals and authoritative intellectuals. Interviewees in the film include William Kristol, cofounder of the important neoconservative think tank, Project for the New American Century, Richard Perle, a political adviser who chaired the Defense Policy Board Advisory Committee under President Bush and who advocated in favor of the Iraq War, and Karen Kwiatkowski, who worked as Douglas Feith's deputy in the Office of Special Plans and who broke with the administration over its use of intelligence to justify the war. Other commentators include the pilots of the bombers that made the first strike on Baghdad, opening the war in March 2003. Others include former newscaster Dan Rather and acerbic author Gore Vidal. Another commentator is a retired New York city policeman who lost his son on 9/11, was gung-ho on Iraq, wrote to the Pentagon asking that his son's name be placed on one of the bombs to be dropped there, and then came to feel that his patriotism had been exploited when the President acknowledged that there was no connection between Saddam Hussein and al Qaeda. Still another is the director of a Baghdad morgue who ruefully shows a yard full of the decaying bodies of civilians that have been killed by U.S. "smart" bombs.

The film's title introduces some irony—*Why We Fight* is also the title of a classic series of propaganda films made during World War II by Hollywood director Frank Capra to explain to the public and to Americans in uniform why the war against Japan and Germany was necessary. Jarecki's film, by contrast, takes a critical and skeptical view about the necessity of the Iraq War. The film uses President Eisenhower's January 1961 farewell address to the nation as the jumping-off point for an exploration of the military extension of American empire throughout the world in the post–World War II period. This attention to the globalization of American military force is appropriate and relevant to an understanding of the Iraq War, in part because the architects of that war—Dick Cheney, Donald Rumsfeld, Paul Wolfowitz—were adherents of the view that America must aggressively project its military force throughout the world and subscribed to a belief in the necessity and rightness of American empire. Cheney, Rumsfeld, Wolfowitz, and other neoconservatives, who subsequently became members of the Bush administration, belonged to the Project for the New American Century, where they honed their views as part of a larger community of like-minded intellectuals. The most famous paper issued by the think tank, entitled "Rebuilding America's Defenses," advocated a set of muscular policies America must pursue in order to remain the world's militarily dominant power, one that would enforce "zones of democratic peace" throughout Europe, Asia, and the Middle East. Since, then, the neoconservatives were already thinking in terms of American empire, it is reasonable for Jarecki to explore this concept and the kind of war-making it leads to.

In his farewell address, Eisenhower famously warned that "the military-industrial complex" needed watching because it had the potential to dominate American foreign policy and to corrupt the society. He cautioned, "This conjunction of an immense military establishment and a large arms industry is new in the American experience. The total influence—economic, political, even spiritual—is felt in every city, every state house, every office of the Federal government. We recognize the imperative need for this development. Yet we must not fail to comprehend its grave implications. Our toil, resources and livelihood are all involved; so is the very structure of our society."[27] He continued, "In the councils of government, we must guard against the acquisition of unwarranted influence, whether sought or unsought, by the military-industrial

FIGURE 4.1 Defense Secretary Donald Rumsfeld defends the March 2003 air strike on Dora Farms, part of a farming community outside Baghdad that was hit because Saddam Hussein was thought to be visiting there. The footage of Rumsfeld appears in *Why We Fight,* which examines the Iraq War as part of a continuing series of efforts by the U.S. to expand or secure its global empire. (Frame enlargement)

complex. The potential for the disastrous rise of misplaced power exists and will persist. We must never let the weight of this combination endanger our liberties or democratic processes."

Eisenhower had a conflicted relationship with this complex. His warning was prescient, and he clearly understood the dangers posed by this new alliance between large corporations, the military, and the government itself. But he was also an agent of American empire in ways that bear on present conflicts. He authorized, for example, the CIA-led overthrow in 1953 of Iran's elected prime minister, Mohammed Mossadegh, and the installation of Mohammed Reza Pahlavi, who became a military dictator. The action helped to fuel considerable opposition to the U.S. throughout the Middle East and culminated in the Iranian revolution, bringing to power the first Islamist state in modern history, an example which has served as an inspiration for al Qaeda's goal of restoring the caliphate.

Why We Fight extracts two lessons from this history which serve as twin foci for the film. One is the power and reach of the military-industrial complex, which the film portrays through interviews with executives and employees of arms industries and through coverage of industry conventions, where Lockheed, Boeing, and Kellogg, Brown & Root (KBR) tout their wares. Jarecki also profiles the "revolving door" that connects politicians with private industry, illustrating this with the case of Dick Cheney. As Secretary of

Defense in 1992, he authorized the Pentagon to pay $8.9 million to Brown & Root (subsequently, KBR) for a study of how the military might rely on private companies to provide essential military services. Brown & Root was a subsidiary of Halliburton Corporation, which subsequently employed Cheney as CEO from 1995 to 1999 and which has received billions from the Pentagon and from American taxpayers in connection with its services during the war in Iraq at a time when Cheney left the corporation and had become Vice President. The film suggests that, when the language about preserving freedom or establishing democracy is stripped away from modern conflicts, one of their primary engines is seen to be profit-taking by the industries that have forged deep bonds with the officials who define foreign policy and who take the nation to war.

A secondary focus of the film is "blowback," the CIA term designating the unanticipated consequences of foreign policy, such as the overthrow of Prime Minister Mossadegh or the arming of Islamist fundamentalists during the Afghan war against the Soviets. Chalmers Johnson, a scholar and former CIA officer whose books include *Blowback* and *The Sorrows of Empire*, emphasizes that the concept has an additional feature. Interviewed in the film, he points out that because the actions that trigger blowback are often covert, this leads the American public to ask questions that Chalmers regards as inappropriate, such as "Why do they hate us?" rather than asking about the policies that produced the blowback. And the film suggests that officials are happy to encourage the inappropriate questions because these help to safeguard the underpinnings of existing foreign policy. In numerous speeches following 9/11, for example, President Bush stated that al Qaeda hates Americans for their freedoms and that bin Laden's followers behave as they do because they are "evildoers." This generalized attribution of motive by the President, according to the film's analysis, was meant to substitute for genuine questions that might be raised about the actual motives for the attacks. Michael Scheuer, for example, has written extensively about bin Laden's motives and argued that they are all right there, in his speeches and remarks, clearly stated and in detail.[28] But what bin Laden says and writes tends not to be conveyed in American media. Scheuer believes that bin Laden needs to be caught and killed by the U.S., but he also maintains that it is a serious strategic error to ignore his motives and to dismiss him as a madman.

The film's emphasis on blowback, however, as the key explanation for Osama bin Laden's actions tends to minimize the depth and complexity of the ideological opposition that he feels toward the United States. Bin Laden has identified his cause as a crusade, as a fundamental clash between Islam and the infidels. He *does* hate many attributes of American culture—its secularism, materialism, public licentiousness, and the room that it has made for women, homosexuals, and Jews (whom bin Laden would subjugate and the latter two whom he despises). In his October 2002 letter to Americans explaining why he was fighting them, he also explained what he wanted from Americans. The first item he listed was for Americans to convert to Islam, to discard all beliefs and behaviors that conflict with Islam. Bin Laden, then, has a dual set of motives, focused on what the U.S. does and on what it is. The blowback factor can go some way toward clarifying why he determined to wage war on the United States, but President Bush's words are also not far off the mark. Bin Laden does hate the U.S. for its freedoms.

Why We Fight aims to place the Iraq War within the very long history of military intervention by the U.S. into the foreign affairs of distant nations and suggests that the motives of profit and the ideological commitment to empire by the architects of war give this history a unique urgency in the contemporary period. "It is surprisingly easy to a take a nation to war," observes one of the film's commentators. Jarecki shows how this is so in one of the few historically minded feature films to have emerged about the Iraq War.

Robert Taicher's *Rush to War* (2004) is an equally critical look at the reasons for the war, and, like Jarecki's film, it takes a longer historical view. Taicher reviews the history of U.S. intervention into foreign countries, the overthrow of existing regimes in Guatemala and Iran in the 1950s and Chile in the 1970s, and although he doesn't use this terminology, Taicher, like Jarecki, considers the attacks of September 11 as a case of blowback. Peace activist Father Daniel Berrigan says that his first thought on hearing of the attacks was "it's come home," meaning that the U.S. was no longer immune from the kinds of things that it has precipitated elsewhere in the world. *New York Times* correspondent Chris Hedges points out that one-fifth of the world's population, which is Muslim, looks at the U.S. through the prism of Palestine and Chechnya and that the U.S. has propped up repressive regimes in Egypt and Saudi Arabia, making it easy for terrorists to exploit local grievances into a campaign against America. Another commentator says that on 9/11 bin Laden was posing a question about U.S. intervention in the Middle East—"Is it worth it?"—one that Americans still have not heard. Former Senator George McGovern says that President Bush's claim that Islamic terrorists hate us because of our freedoms is incorrect; it's the arrogance of our foreign policy that makes them hate us.

Working with these frames of analysis, Taicher's film suggests that the security of the people of the United States could not have been a consideration when the administration launched the invasion of Iraq. Noam Chomsky observes that George Bush has behaved as if he was an "embed" in the White

House, acting as an agent of bin Laden by doing exactly what bin Laden predicted, namely, invading and occupying an oil-rich Arab land. Chomsky is a longtime critic of U.S. foreign policy and sees U.S. motives almost entirely in terms of venal and ruthless efforts to extend empire. His remarks in the film do not surprise. (Because he has been such a radical critic of the United States government, the 9/11 conspiracy theorists thought that he would be on their side. But Chomsky disappointed them by stating that he doesn't believe that the Republicans were behind the attacks.) Historian Howard Zinn remarks, "Behind all this talk about liberty and democracy is oil, not the security of the people in Iraq and certainly not the security of the people of the United States." George McGovern asks, "Would we be going into Iraq if their main product were cabbages or watermelons? I doubt it." Former antiterrorism czar Richard Clarke says that it is simply an empirical fact that the Iraq War has facilitated recruiting efforts by al Qaeda. Zinn adds that the Iraq War has not stopped terror but has created it, that the more you bomb a country and humiliate its people, the more terror you create. By framing the 9/11 attacks and the Iraq War in these terms, *Rush to War* aims to cut through the administration's stated intentions about promoting freedom and the appeals to patriotism and to fear that were part of the run-up to war and to offer in their place an alternative account of the foreign policies that have instigated much hatred for the U.S. throughout the Muslim world. One of the film's final commentaries is offered by the parents of a son in uniform who was killed in Iraq. The mother describes her distress at hearing President Bush performing a skit at the National Press Club in which he made fun of the fact that no weapons of mass destruction had been found in Iraq. She says that she was stunned that he would make a skit out of the declared reason for the war. She adds that if he thinks that is funny, he ought to do the skit before the families who've lost their loved ones and those families will tell him how funny it is.

Taicher's film, like many examined in this chapter, is a work expressing a defined political and ideological point of view. The filmmaker proposes a thesis about how the war started and what its significance is. A documentary with an engaged point of view is no less a documentary for that. But there are some problems with this approach in addition to the perennial one of addressing the already-converted. One is that the film offers a kind of traditional Marxist analysis in which the "base" is privileged over the "superstructure," that is, in the film's account material and economic motives predominate over ideological ones. Thus, in the film's view, an administration composed of oil men attacks an oil-rich country to seize its resources. But the ineptness of the administration's efforts actually complicates this explanation. If oil were the sole or primary motive, how does one explain the lack of planning for the postwar period and the indifference that this showed toward the country's infrastructure, whose functioning would be vital for any ability to tap Iraq's oil riches. While imperial ambitions on the part of the neoconservative architects of the war unquestionably played an important role, the war, like the one in Vietnam, tends to elude efforts to neatly encapsulate and summarize its causes. To some extent this is because the debacle that it became has engulfed the reasons for waging it that were proffered at its outset. But it is also because, like the Vietnam War, it has become a kind of historical black hole, a massive structure that remains significantly unreflective to the light of analysis. This war, in significant ways, is not easily explained or comprehensible, despite the effort of films such as *Rush to War* to offer readily graspable frameworks for understanding it. The relative impenetrability of this war to political analysis challenges the ideological framing that numerous Iraq War documentaries seek to apply. I will say more about this problem in the conclusion of the chapter.

A DIGITAL PATHWAY TO COVERING WAR

The proliferation of portable digital cameras revolutionized documentary coverage of the war. It enabled numerous filmmakers to produce first-person accounts of their experiences traveling or fighting inside Iraq after the American invasion. In some respects, digital camera technology worked against the administration's efforts to control the flow of news and imagery from the war zone. The cameras are so lightweight and adaptable, and their images so easily disseminated via the Internet and other distribution channels, that voices on the war rapidly emerged that were in competition with administration views. Mike Shiley's *Inside Iraq: The Untold Stories* (2004) is a first-person account of Shiley's travels inside the war-ravaged country in 2004. A freelance journalist and photographer, Shiley tells us in voice-over narration that he wanted to see things for himself after growing impatient with media presentations that concentrated on press conferences and bombings. He hired a driver, rode in from Jordan, and then traveled for two months, without security, filming interviews and events as he found them in the Sunni Triangle, Baghdad, and the Kurdish regions of the north. He visits the Baghdad Technology College, where all the computers were stolen by looters and where computer classes are now taught using a blackboard. He visits a hospital full of children who have been maimed by landmines and speaks with members of the Iraqi security forces who were earning from the U.S. one half of what they earned under Saddam and who wear substandard equipment, including plastic helmets and flak jackets that are not bulletproof.

Shiley tells us that, with Saddam's fall, pornography, drugs, and prostitution have poured into the country; all were things that had been suppressed under the dictatorship. With irony, Shiley remarks that under Saddam, Baghdad had a thriving nightlife, with theaters, the arts, and low crime rates; now all the shops close at dusk, and no one is on the streets because they are too dangerous. While Shiley visits Baghdad, the city has power for only one-quarter of the day. A woman remarks, "Life has stopped here in Baghdad."

He visits a memorial to the dead from the first Gulf War. During the bombing of Baghdad which opened that war, nearly 400 civilians had sought refuge in an underground bomb shelter. This was the Amiriyah air raid shelter, which the U.S. had targeted based on intelligence that it was a military headquarters. A U.S. bunker-busting bomb struck, penetrating the concrete shell of the shelter and incinerating the people so intensely that the outlines of some victims are burned into the rock walls. Most of the victims were women and children. Faced with criticism over this bombing, the U.S. maintained that Iraq was using it as a military command center and that Saddam had stationed civilians in it as a stratagem to safeguard the facility from bombs. Human rights groups countered that the site had been marked as an air raid shelter since the Iran-Iraq war. As Shiley films the blackened forms on the walls, he asks about who the real victims are when nations go to war, and it leads him to reflect on some of the meanings of the term "terrorism." After the bombing, Iraq made the site a memorial. Above ground, individual gravestones mark the life of each victim, and a giant clock is frozen at the time the bomb fell. "Does it really matter what country these people are from? They were not armed. They weren't fighting a war. They were hiding. They were trying to protect and preserve their families. And they were incinerated. Is this terrorism?" he asks.

Shiley also visits three U.S. military bases. One, Camp Anaconda, is so large that hordes of Iraqis show up outside the gated compound each day seeking work on the base. Unable to speak or read Arabic, the American soldiers with difficulty recruit a few to perform laborious tasks and try to explain to the others that there is nothing for them. One scene shows a military instructor teaching a class for Iraqi civil defense recruits, the day's topic being torture as an unlawful activity. "Torture is always wrong," the instructor explains, honoring the military's traditional respect for the Geneva Conventions, a tradition that the Bush administration broke with in its effort to apply harsh interrogation methods. As Shiley filmed this, the Abu Ghraib scandal was about to break.

In the film's portrait, the U.S.-Iraq relationship here looks much like colonialism. At the camp's dump, soldiers throw out masses of items that are still good—everything from oil and antifreeze, to air conditioners, prime beef, other foodstuffs, and beverages. Iraqi scavengers cluster beyond the fence, hoping to pilfer something. They want this garbage. "Our trash is their gold," an American remarks. Another soldier hates them for their poverty and willingness to do shit jobs—"Fuck these people—they'll do anything for five bucks." A colonizer's contempt for the "natives" is evident. During a rant session, a female soldier talks about needing a quiet place for sex with a lover and going into a mosque—what she calls a "haji church"—and having intercourse on the floor there.

Much of what Shiley shows reflects badly on the American presence. While he presents a number of U.S. soldiers who behave compassionately, the cumulative details portray an occupation that has failed to rebuild the infrastructure and that alienates Iraqis. He accompanies the Third Armored Cavalry Unit, posted near the Syrian border, on a night mission termed "harass and intimidate." U.S. tanks and armored vehicles arrive after the 9 P.M. curfew in a small town that, in the military's view, houses insurgents. The Americans begin firing their weapons at a dry riverbed in town; the noise is deafening and is designed to wake people up and demonstrate American firepower. As Shiley films these events, the Americans set off smoke grenades in town, and as the convoy drives off, Shiley notices that the grenades have set two houses on fire. Imagining himself to be an Iraqi resident of the town, he reflects, "Is this an Army you're going to continue to like and welcome into your country or is this a presence you're going to learn to resent?" The implied answer is clear enough, and the film ends with an interview with an Iraqi woman who pleads with the U.S. and the world, "Look at us, we are suffering too much. We are destroyed, really destroyed. If they are talking about democracy and freedom, these things will never be done in this situation."

Other extremely critical portraits of the war can be found in David O. Russell's *Soldiers Pay* (2004) and Guerrilla News Network's *Battleground: 21 Days at the Edge of the Empire*. Russell's film is composed of interviews with Iraq veterans, officers, journalists, antiwar activists, and Iraqis (these include actors who appeared in Russell's Hollywood feature, *Three Kings* [1999] and who had been tortured by Saddam Hussein). The interviews convey a broad range of views on the war. Most are critical of U.S. involvement. A retired major-general says that the reports of torture and abuse at Abu Ghraib were the darkest cloud to descend on the military in his lifetime, and a soldier says that President Bush used fear after 9/11 to motivate people to support the war. Another soldier recalls widespread looting of Iraqi homes by U.S. troops. These remarks and views undoubtedly spurred Warner Bros. to drop plans to include the short documentary as a supplementary feature on the DVD re-release of *Three Kings*. That film's criticism of the Gulf War is absorbed by an entertaining genre narrative; the criticism in Russell's documentary is more pointed and provocative because it is based on the experiences of those who were there and because it is not proffered as a subsidiary feature in a genre entertainment.

Guerrilla News Network's *Battleground: 21 Days at the Edge of the Empire* (2005), filmed and directed by Stephen Marshall, emphasizes Iraqi points of view on the conflict. Filmmakers from GNN spent three weeks in late 2003 traveling in Iraq and interviewing a cross-section of people. These include a hospital director, young boys selling gasoline, an Egyptian businessman, a female Iraqi interpreter, a former anti-Saddam guerrilla tortured by that regime and returning to Iraq after thirteen years of exile, and members of the insurgency who wave at passing humvees while explaining how much they hate Americans. America promised freedom and security, they say, but only destroyed things, and now they fight for their honor and their religion.

The film seems to take its cue from May Ying Welsh, a Western journalist proficient in Arabic, who explains that U.S. media generally have silenced Iraqi voices and promoted the views of American politicians, pundits, and the military. Accordingly, the filmmakers' seek out these other voices. One of the strongest sequences involves Raed Jarrar, an architect and popular Baghdad blogger, who visits graveyards full of Iraqi tanks that were destroyed by U.S. ammunition containing DU (depleted uranium). A printed title states that during the 2003 invasion, over 120 tons of DU were fired and that no effort was made to explain to Iraqis the health hazards that it poses. Jarrar takes readings from the husks of the tanks with a Geiger counter and finds, in one case, radiation levels 310 times the normal limit. He talks with a man who works at cutting up and selling the scrap metal. The man says he knows it can make him sick but that there is no other work to be found. A hospital director explains that leukemia and cancers of the colon, lungs, and bladder have been on the rise since the Gulf War of 1991.

The dark portraits presented in these films, and many others, document and also reflect the deterioration of security in the period after the war, as the insurgency exploded in force, government administration failed, and the number of U.S. forces on the ground was insufficient to cope with the escalating violence and chaos. In some ways, what these films offer is a snapshot of this period. After years of stating that a sufficient force level had been stationed in Iraq, President Bush in February 2007 committed an additional 30,000 troops in a surge scheduled to last for eighteen months. The situation on the ground changed quickly. The security situation improved, even though the outcome of the war still remained in question. Daily attacks by insurgents dwindled to forty-five in May 2008 from a high of 200 per day the year before. Iraqi civilian deaths stood at 550 in May 2008, compared with 2,600 in May 2007, and the portion of the country controlled by Iraqi government forces stood at 95 percent, compared with just 25 percent two years previously.[29] William J. Fallon, the former commander of all U.S. military forces in the Middle East, wrote about the improved ground situation that prevailed in summer 2008. "The number of incidents of violence nationwide in Iraq is less than a tenth of what we were experiencing in the spring of 2007. The casualty rate among American troops is the lowest in more than four years and continues to improve. Ethnic and sectarian violence among the Iraqi population has declined to levels not seen since the early days of the war."[30] Security on the ground had always been the precondition for any political progress in stabilizing postwar Iraq, and until summer 2008 it was lacking. Whether the recent gains would last remained unclear at the time of this writing. But in some significant ways, the grim portrait etched by many of the war documentaries is one that reflected the nadir of the conflict in a period when violence in the country had spiraled out of control.

FIRST-PERSON PORTRAITS OF AMERICAN SOLDIERS

Numerous first-person films have focused on the experiences of American soldiers in Iraq. Michael Epstein's *Combat Diary: The Marines of Lima Company* (2006), for example, recounts the operations of the titular company, which in 2005 sustained the heaviest casualties of any Marine company in Anbar Province. Of the 184 Marines stationed there, twenty-three were killed. Home videos shot by the Marines, which show them horsing around with one another and going on patrol, are conjoined with interviews in which the survivors recall how their comrades were killed. For some, the war had had an abstract and enjoyable quality until they saw their friends die. One remarks, "Before anybody got hurt, it was really exciting and almost fun. It's like a video game."

Interviews with surviving Marines and with families of the fallen comprise most of the film. In contrast, the candid video footage shot by the American soldiers in Iraq is used mostly as background material, despite its exceptionally vivid quality. Several films, though, make extensive use of such candid footage and exemplify the documentary mode variously termed "direct cinema," "cinema vérité," or in a terminology proposed by Bill Nichols, "observational cinema." The goal is to minimize the overt presence of the filmmaker by dispensing with voice-over narration and with broadly enunciated social or historical perspectives. Instead, the filmmaker closely observes the actual, lived experiences of what is often a small group of people. "The presence of the camera 'on the scene' . . . suggests a commitment or engagement with the immediate, intimate, and personal that is comparable to what an actual observer/participant might experience."[31] Michael Tucker and Petra Epperlein's *Gunner Palace* (2005) offers this kind of soldier's-eye view of the war. For several months between September 2003 and April 2004, Tucker lived with members of the Army's 2/3 Field Artillery Regiment, nicknamed the "gunners," during a period when the regiment was headquartered at the former palace of Uday Hussein, one of Saddam's sons. While sympathetic toward the gunners, the film is very critical of the war, a point of view that Tucker and Epperlein develop in several ways. One is the ironic and often funny contrast between the resolutely optimistic remarks of American officials, often carried as broadcasts on military radio, about the conditions in Iraq, and what Tucker shows us. The juxtaposition of audio and image is intended to emphasize the misleading nature of the propaganda aimed at the soldiers and at times to the Iraqis. The opening of the film establishes this sardonic tone. As Sousa's "The Stars and Stripes Forever" plays on the soundtrack, remarks by Defense Secretary Donald Rumsfeld appear as text on the screen—"Greetings to the Iraqi people. Hello, I'm Donald Rumsfeld, the U.S. Secretary of Defense. It is a pleasure to be back in your country. When I visited four months ago, the regime of Saddam Hussein had just fallen—and I was pleased to be able to celebrate your liberation with you. The changes that have taken place since then are extraordinary—Baghdad is bustling with commerce." The images accompanying the text show soldiers unloading military gear from their trucks, bustling activity to be sure, but not quite what the Defense Secretary is describing. The scene then cuts to a firefight in Baghdad as a title dryly informs us, "Meanwhile." After a few moments during which the camera operator seeks shelter from the gunfire, another title sardonically announces "Major combat operations ended four months ago."

This opening sets a tone of skepticism toward the pronouncements of officials and politicians who are far from the war. And it emphasizes the disconnection between the realities faced by the soldiers and the official claims about the war's progress. Subsequent radio broadcasts announce "Coalition forces are making steady and remarkable progress toward stability in Iraq. Defense Secretary Donald Rumsfeld said since the death of Uday and Qusay Hussein, more Iraqis are coming forward with useful information," as we see the gunners in military vehicles making armed sweeps through Baghdad streets. Another states, "Secretary Rumsfeld said terrorists are starting to realize things are changing in favor of the Iraqi people," as we see a fight break out among Iraqis on a local district advisory council because of threats made

FIGURE 4.2 Small, portable digital cameras enabled documentaries to offer candid, soldier's-eye portraits of the Iraq War. *Gunner Palace* profiles the soldiers in a field artillery unit inside Baghdad. (Frame enlargement)

against them. Occasionally the broadcasts achieve a surrealism worthy of *Dr. Strangelove.* One joyously proclaims the introduction of a new policy of intelligence sharing, called "horizontal fusion," intended to make it easier for soldiers to do their jobs. The oppositional perspectives conveyed by all of this are not subtle and take the film some distance from the more neutral and disengaged stance of classic cinema vérité.

A more oblique form of criticism is developed by Tucker and Epperlein through evocations of the Vietnam War. The cultural alienation of the Americans from the people they are ostensibly liberating, strangers in a land they don't understand, is a plainly evident parallel, but the filmmakers make the relationship more specific by referencing two major films about the Vietnam War. The film uses a voice-over narrator to introduce members of the regiment. The narrator says, "A lot of these guys are fresh out of high school. They come from towns that read like an Atlas of a forgotten America—Pine Bluff, Chesterton, Argyle." The passage evokes the scene in *Platoon* (1986) where Taylor (Charlie Sheen), in voice-over narration, describes the platoon members as being from small towns, with little schooling, not forgotten but unwanted. Later in *Gunner Palace,* as the soldiers prepare for a predawn raid on a sheikh's house, "The Ride of the Valkyries" is heard—one of the soldiers plays it to psyche up. This is, of course, the music that accompanied the famous helicopter attack in *Apocalypse Now* (1979). Later on, following a big raid on several homes, the gunners relax at a party at the palace pool. They josh and dance to the music of "My Girl" by the Temptations, a pop-chart hit from early 1965, the year in which U.S. ground forces arrived in Vietnam and corresponding to the "one year in" time frame of *Gunner Palace*. The scene also references a similar moment in *Platoon*, where the grunts enjoy Smokey Robinson's "The Tracks of My Tears," another Motown hit from 1965.

The film's candid, soldier's-eye point of view may also link it to Vietnam War documentaries. As Tony Grajeda points out, "*The Anderson Platoon* [1966–67] and *A Face of War* [1967] present the [Vietnam] war exclusively from the point of view of the 'foot soldier,' a formal positioning that extends back at least to John Huston's WWII documentary *The Battle of San Pietro* (1945)."[32] In the restricted, soldier's-eye perspective of *Gunner Palace*, the camera operator rides atop the military convoys, accompanies the gunners on patrol, and films the soldiers during moments of reflection and humor. But it also means that Iraqis tend to remain in the background, as the Vietnamese did in so many American films about that war. Despite this overall tendency, several sequences gain power by showing American-Iraqi interactions. In one, the gunners raid a house that intelligence sources have fingered as a bomb factory. Several brothers living there are arrested. As the Americans shout at them to shut up, one protests that he is a journalist. Told repeatedly to shut up, he looks at the camera and mutters with sullen resentment, "Yes, just shut your mouth in Iraq. Just you shut your mouth. I know that 'shut up.'" (Tucker and Epperlein returned to this individual, Yunis Abbas, in *The Prisoner or: How I Planned to Kill Tony Blair* [2006]. Accused of planning to assassinate Blair, Abbas was taken to Abu Ghraib, interrogated, and then housed at Camp Ganci, which contained thousands of low-value detainees the Army regarded as possessing no intelligence value, a status for Yunis that seemed to contradict the accusation. After his release, Tucker and Epperlein interviewed him about the experience. This interview forms the bulk of *The Prisoner*. Yunis describes being beaten, called a "dog" and a "monkey" in Arabic, and having a female American soldier spit into his face. The film profiles the conditions at the camp using an interview with an American guard stationed there. He describes rotten food being fed to the prisoners, with rat feces and bugs in it, and the resulting diarrhea that afflicted many older inmates. When the prisoners rioted against the conditions, Americans opened fire on them, killing several.)

As the scene of the raid ends, the narrator dispassionately states that no evidence of bomb making was found in the house and that the brothers were transferred to Abu Ghraib prison. Tucker was embedded with the regiment during the period when the army was conducting massive sweeps, breaking into people's homes at night, and rounding up thousands of men who were sent to Abu Ghraib, actions that fed Iraqi resentment and fueled the insurgency. The film's micro-level point of view precludes the filmmakers from commenting on these broader trends, but the narrator's statement about imprisonment at Abu Ghraib goes some way toward providing this otherwise missing context.

The film concludes with some sobering reflections by the gunners. One says that he no longer feels like he is here defending the U.S. Asked how he rationalizes the loss of life in the war, another soldier answers that you can't, that it isn't worth the loss of someone's family member. Asked whether the American people understand what's going on in Iraq, another says "When you sit on your couch and you watch the TV and you go to your nine-to-five job and complain about the pizza being late, there's no way you're going to know how we live here. . . . After you watch this, you're going to go get your popcorn out of the microwave and you'll talk about what I say and you'll forget me by the end of this. You'll forget all of us."

More candid and self-reflective observations by servicemen appear in *Occupation: Dreamland* (2005), another observational documentary offering a soldier's-eye view of the war. Filmmakers Ian Olds and Garrett Scott profile a squad of the Army's 82nd Airborne Division as it patrols the city of Fallujah in early 2004, hunting insurgents and trying to establish relations with Iraqis in the city. "Dreamland" is the nickname given by the soldiers to the abandoned Ba'athist headquarters where they are based. Like *Gunner Palace*, the film vividly portrays the hapless task faced by the soldiers, who are cultural and linguistic outsiders unable to communicate with the Iraqis they are ostensibly there to help. The filmmakers accompany the squad as it conducts the notorious sweeps so common in that period, breaking into people's houses at night, handcuffing and hooding adult males and taking them away, most likely to Abu Ghraib, which was very near Fallujah. The camera catches an improvised explosive device (IED)—a roadside bomb—as it explodes, halting a convoy and giving one squad member a concussion. In interviews, the soldiers recall the death of a friend in an earlier attack and confess that this and other incidents, such as one soldier's being hit in the face by a brick thrown by an Iraqi child, makes some of them want to go and kill Iraqis. "I just want to light everybody out there up—no one [i.e., Iraqis] gives a shit about us here." Walking past a group of young Iraqi men, one squad member mutters "Don't fucking stare at me like that, fucking asshole." The violence they encounter intensifies feelings of cultural alienation and hostility.

The film pointedly captures Iraqi resentment of the American occupiers. Unlike *Gunner Palace* in which the Iraqis are mostly invisible, *Occupation: Dreamland* features a lengthy sequence in which squad members converse via an interpreter with Iraqis on the street in a business district. The Iraqis express great anger over the nighttime raids on people's homes. "We don't accept colonialism," one says. "This [resistance to occupation] is something that is pent up inside our hearts. . . . Where is the civilization Bush speaks about? Is it in the prison?" Many are upset because soldiers took a woman from her home, and they regard this as a great sin and dishonor. They mutter darkly that Americans took the woman because they can't handle the men and warn the Americans to be careful of Fallujah. The scene portrays a simmering hatred for Americans that eventually exploded into full-scale urban warfare in November 2004 as Marines, launching Operation Phantom Fury, attempted to retake Fallujah from insurgents. But this battle, which killed 100 Marines and more than 1,000 Iraqis, falls outside the time frame of the film (it is alluded to with video imagery in a brief epilogue). The observational format of the film precludes a historical overview—this is one of the limitations of such documentaries. Thus key events that conditioned the tensions on both sides within Fallujah—an April 2003 incident in which soldiers of the 82nd Airborne fired on a crowd of demonstrators, killing seventeen, and the March 2004 killing of four American contractors working for the private military company Blackwater USA—are not mentioned in the film. The tradeoff for this missing historical perspective is the vivid immediacy of observing the soldiers as they deal with a foreign and hostile environment.

Editorial point of view is not absent—it is present obliquely, as in the intercutting of the market scene with reflections by squad members in which they acknowledge some of the ways that their presence is a provocation. It is also present in what Bill Nichols has called "strange juxtapositions" that work to create an editorial point.[33] A scene in which Americans conduct a nocturnal house raid ends with a shot of Iraqi women and female children, wearing cloaks according to the Qur'anic injunctions of *hijab* or modesty and cowering under the flashlights of the Americans. The next scene shows a church service held for American soldiers. The pastor leads the Americans in prayer "for our Holy Father, our President, and all church and state leaders so that they may be instrumental in promoting peace and justice." A cutaway shows a gleaming cross inscribed with a figure of Jesus. The juxtaposition of the two scenes is extremely provocative because of the historical and political associations evoked by the presence in Muslim lands of a Christianity accompanied by military force. It evokes not just the historical legacy of the Crusades but also a chief factor that is motivating al Qaeda's campaign against America, namely, the presence of infidels on holy land. "This war is fundamentally religious," bin Laden said in 2001. "Under no circumstances should we forget this enmity between us and the infidels. For the enmity is based on creed."[34]

The War Tapes (2006) takes the observational format a step further by giving cameras to soldiers who then film their experiences in Iraq. Director Deborah Scranton (*Stories from Silence: Witness to War* [2003], producer Robert May (*The Fog of War* [2003]), and producer/editor Steve Jones (*Hoop Dreams* [1995]) approached Charlie Company, an Army National Guard unit, with the project for a documentary in which soldiers would be the filmmakers. Although ten Guardsman from the unit volunteered to film their experiences during their year's tour of duty, as completed *The War Tapes* focuses mainly on the experiences of three guardsmen—Sergeant Steve Pink, Sergeant Zack Bazzi and Specialist Mike Moriarty. Bazzi is a Lebanese-American college student, with Shiite Muslim parents, who joined the Army because he wanted to travel and likes being a soldier. Pink is a carpenter who joined during the second year of college for the tuition aid and to test himself, and Moriarty is a forklift driver whose sense of patriotism was deeply affected by 9/11. He says that September 11th struck him hard. "That was like somebody hitting my house." He took time off and visited Ground Zero, which was still smoking. Wanting to do something in response, "I called the recruiter and I said you slot me into a unit only if they go into Iraq."

The men mount their cameras on the dashboards and turrets of their armored vehicles, on their Kevlar helmets and vests, and occasionally use them in a handheld fashion. With the cameras the men create a kind of collective video diary, in which they record their reflections and anxieties and their experiences with IEDs and in firefights. The men are based at Camp Anaconda in the Sunni Triangle and spend much of their time providing convoy security for trucks operated by Halliburton subsidiary Kellogg, Brown & Root, which are transporting food, fuel, and septic waste. All three are proud to serve their country but have differing views of the war, and Bazzi points out that the opinions of America's soldiers are not monolithic but reflect the diversity of political views at large in the country. This is a very important point, and it is one that films like *Gunner Palace* and *Occupation: Dreamland* tend to gloss over, in part perhaps because of the filmmakers' own evident opposition to the war. In those films, U.S. soldiers' perspectives tend to be sardonic and critical. Although *The War Tapes* provides a greater range of perspective, the points of view also tend to be sardonic ones. Bazzi, for example, offers many pointed and culturally sensitive observations, but they often are unflattering ones for the U.S. He says, for example, that if Canadians one day invaded and occupied the United States because they had decided that President Bush was bad for Americans, there would be American insurgents fighting the Canadians. "You take 150,000 U.S. soldiers out of America and you transplant them to Iraq for a year and with absolutely zero training whatsoever about the culture, it doesn't take a shrink to tell you ignorance is one of the first steps toward prejudice." He then explains that, as "gook" was the slang insult used in the Vietnam War, "haji" is the slang insult used for Arabs here.

Kevin Shangraw, Moriarty's squad leader, points out the expense and waste that are routinely generated by the KBR contracts. Instead of paying $17,000 to a soldier to drive trucks, he notes, the Army farms it out to KBR and pays $120,000 for the same job. KBR charges the government $28 a plate for food. Many soldiers, Shangraw says, use a second, empty plate as a cover on top to keep the food warm—when that happens KBR charges the Army $56 for the meal. "Everybody there stands to make money the longer we're there. That's why we refer to it as the 'war for cheese.'" Profiteering is an embedded feature of the Iraq War. Moriarty points out the irony of posting armed guards on trucks filled with cheesecake. "I feel the priority of KBR making money outweighs the priority of safety."

Indeed, the Iraq War was a bonanza for service contractors because Donald Rumsfeld's Pentagon "privatized" many of the functions once handled by the military and paid outside contractors steep fees to perform these functions, such as food and beverage service, transportation, and even "force protection." In the latter cases, corporate-employed soldiers-for-hire guarded U.S. convoys and protected U.S. bases. The Pentagon's "theater-wide" contract for private companies to protect bases was projected in 2007 at $480 million.[35] Companies employing soldiers for hire also were protecting major military and political figures in Iraq. Blackwater, the most famous of the international mercenary-supply firms, was paid $28 million to supply bodyguards for CPA head Paul Bremer in Iraq.[36] (Blackwater also deployed its army of private soldiers on the streets of New Orleans during the Katrina disaster, billing the federal government close to $1,000 per day per guard.)[37] ArmorGroup earned nearly half of its 2006 revenue of $274 million from its force protection operations in Iraq. For convoy protection, the firm charges $8,000 to $12,000 per day.[38] One might be excused for thinking that base protection is something that the military would carry out for itself rather than hiring a firm to do it for them. But although seemingly irrational, the use of corporate mercenaries pays economic and political dividends. The exorbitant fees enable Pentagon-friendly companies to reap huge profits, and the high number of soldiers-for-hire, or "civilian contractors" as the media refer to them, deployed to Iraq enables the administration to stay safer politically by holding down the overall number of U.S. troops deployed. The mercenaries operate with some impunity. They are not bound by military law, and, by order of CPA head Paul Bremer, they were immunized against civil suits in Iraq arising from their activities. They have been involved in numerous firefights with Iraqis, although the U.S. government does not compile figures on the number of Iraqis killed by privately employed soldiers-for-hire. Robert Greenwald's *Iraq for Sale: The War Profiteers* (2006) examines the military's use of private corporations—Halliburton, Blackwater, DynCorp International—to provide these services. The filmmakers also interview the families of two of the four Blackwater contractors killed and mutilated at Fallujah and who sued Blackwater for negligence and for placing profits ahead of security in ways that contributed directly to the deaths of their sons.

Conduct of the war was organized to provide opportunities for huge profit-taking by private corporations (Greenwald's film identifies $18.5 billion to Halliburton alone). The soldiers in *The War Tapes* seem very aware of this, and it has fed their sardonic view of the conflict. Moriarty films an exchange where he asks Shangraw what he thinks of the war. Shangraw tells Moriarty's camera, "I think it's a fantastic opportunity for the Iraqis to establish a new history in the country and be able to be a free and democratic society which in turn should stabilize the whole Middle East and create a free, more stable Earth as we know it. Then, after that happens, maybe we can buy everybody in the world a puppy." This skepticism about the announced rationales for the war is a common thread in all three of these observational documentaries. In many instances, soldiers cite oil as the reason for the war. This skepticism also turns up in published interviews, such as a recent oral history of the war wherein a member of the 1st Infantry Division based in Iraq in 2004–2005 states that oil is the motive. "We just pushed our way into Iraq. The only connection to 9/11 is their choice of religion. Everything else was created and forced upon the public by the United States government in order to find a way into that country."[39] There is thus some conflict in the films between the quietly observational film style and the polemical nature of the points of view selected by the filmmakers for presentation.

One of the best portraits of Americans fighting in Iraq is provided by *Off to War* (2006), a ten-part documentary series made for cable television's Discovery Channel. This film avoids the polemics that are so common in Iraq War documentaries. In so doing, it achieves a portrait that is more subtle, nuanced, and expansive in capturing a range of experience and points of view. It examines the difficulties faced by the small community of Clarksville, Arkansas, which saw the biggest deployment of Army National Guard members from the town since the Vietnam War. From this town of 7,000 people, fifty-seven guardsmen were sent to Iraq during the second year of the war. The film follows the experiences of several of these men, as they prepare to leave home, then as they spend a difficult eighteen months on duty in Iraq, and finally return home, in some cases with emotional and physical problems resulting from their experiences. The deployment of the men exacts a heavy toll on the town. They're gainfully employed as farmers, a minister, a policeman, a salesman, and many are husbands and fathers with families to support. A major focus of the series, therefore, is on the emotional and economic struggle of families who have lost a father, a husband, or a son to a tour in Iraq, and the filmmakers alternate between scenes with the men in Iraq and with the families back home. A powerful portrait emerges of the heavy burden faced by these rural families who have a loved one far away fighting in a country for reasons that no one quite understands. The filmmakers—Brent and Craig Renaud—are from Arkansas, and they bring an insider's knowledge of the area and respect and affection for rural, southwestern life. It's a culture that is often stereotyped in popular media, but the Renauds show its dignity, strength, and progressive outlook. The latter quality is brought home in scenes that show an interracial marriage—a black man and a white woman—living openly in Clarksville and accepted by the town.

Many of the families and several guardsmen take a dim view of the Iraq War and openly state their view that the American venture there is a mistake. The guardsmen and their families are patriots and take pride in fulfilling their duty, but the movie shows how corrupting the experience of Iraq can be for those serving there. Neither the language nor the culture is familiar, and many are appalled at a poverty level they have never encountered before. And they understand that many Iraqis do not want them there. As they lose friends to mortar attacks and roadside bombings, an antipathy to the country and its people develops. As one guardsman remarks, "Every person in this country is a potential enemy. It makes a certain hatred rise up in us." Better than most documentaries about the war, the film captures the complexity of the feelings and experiences of the soldiers stationed there. One says that America has to be there because Iraq attacked us on September 11. Another says, with intended irony, "Invading a foreign country and threatening its people—what could be better?" Back home, some of the families vote for President Bush in the 2004 election, despite their reservations about the war, because they perceive him as a strong leader and one who, like themselves, is deeply religious. Its length—ten 45-minute episodes—and its breadth—nearly two years in the lives of the guardsmen and their families—give *Off to War* an epic scale, and the film succeeds in capturing the complexity, the contradictions, and the nuances of struggle by this group of Arkansans as they assume the burden their government has laid upon them.

BODY HORROR

In *The War Tapes,* the men record their confrontations with violence and their reactions to it. After an IED attack, Steve Pink says "Today was the first time I shook a man's hand that wasn't attached to his arm." The hand was hanging by gristle from the arm like a child's "safety-clipped mittens dangling from their winter coat." He arrives on the scene shortly after a suicide car bombing and films one of the burned, scalded corpses and the pools of blood. He describes a serious debate among the men about the texture of a severed limb—whether it is more like ground, uncooked hamburger or raw pot roast—but everyone agrees that human intestines are links of pink pork sausage. Later, after a firefight, Pink films the bodies of dead insurgents. The legs of one have been severed by high-powered gunfire. He relates that dogs came down to feast on the bodies and says that he saw nothing wrong with that. In a separate incident, barreling along the highway in a convoy, Moriarty's truck hits an Iraqi woman and smashes her into pieces strewn along the road. He pulls the pieces of her body to the side of the road and records his dismay and shame. The film does not dwell on the gore but presents it in a straightforward and unflinching way. By contrast, news coverage on the war has been sanitized so as not to show graphic violence, especially when the dead are American soldiers. After five years of conflict and more than 4,000 dead Americans, fewer than six graphic photographs of the fallen soldiers have been published. And when the dead were photographed or the images published, the military often retaliated against the reporter or photographer.[40] Media coverage of the 1991 Gulf War exemplified what John Taylor, in his study of photojournalism and war, described as the vanishing body, namely, media imagery focused on clean, surgical air strikes and the machinery of war rather than on the face it left behind on the bodies of the dead or maimed. "The forty-four days of the Gulf War clarified for the military and the newspapers exactly what 'handling' the media means in conflicts where home-front morale has to be kept high and quietly confident. Good civilian morale requires that people are diverted by the spectacle of war, and that they do not feel personal responsibility."[41] In this context, some of the footage in *The War Tapes* illustrates what Taylor called "body horror," necessary for an honest accounting of the war.

As Taylor has shown, news media often minimize photographic coverage of body horror in today's wars even though this is one of the true faces of war. Media coverage of the war in Iraq, in its early stages, tended to focus on video game–like imagery of missiles hitting buildings, photographed from miles away and without visible human casualties. By contrast, the oral histories provided by soldiers demonstrate the vividness of human carnage; portraits of body horror are more likely to turn up in these published accounts than in visual media, as in this recollection by a Marine stationed in Fallujah in 2004–2005:

> *Some of the bodies would be about two weeks old, just lying in the middle of the street, and the weather would really screw with the decomposition. It made them decay a lot quicker than usual. There was one body where one of my friends went to go pick it up and the head completely fell back—the neck opened up and thousands of insects came out and went all over the body. It was the most disgusting body I've ever seen in my entire . . . it was worse than things I've seen in movies.*[42]

In a search for a frame of reference to contextualize the sight, he turned to the movies and, significantly, found them wanting by comparison. The experience of war's body horror can produce lasting effects and associations that taint the experiences of ordinary life. As another soldier relates,

> *Sometimes smells remind me of the war. Sometimes I go shopping and I'm in the meat section and I look at meat and it reminds me of the flesh torn off of bodies. Sometimes I'm eating a chicken leg, and if it's cooked or charbroiled, it brings back memories of burnt skin, burnt flesh, burnt muscle from Iraq, just how when you throw meat on the grill, that's the way bodies look when they're burnt up from bombs and from explosions or helicopter crashes.*[43]

Few American documentaries on the war have sought to portray any aspect of this kind of violence, its physical trauma and its psychological impact on those who witness or experience it. And there is no tradition of combat journalism in major media covering it or photographing it. There is tremendous social and political pressure on filmmakers and photographers not to show these aspects of the war's cost. News media are not allowed to photograph the coffins of American soldiers returning from Iraq. When the *New York Times* ran a front-page story about a soldier shot by a sniper in Iraq, a photograph showed his comrades carrying him on a stretcher off to hospital, and he was identified by name. As the story subsequently related, he died of his wound. Several readers wrote in to say that the story and picture were in bad taste and that it was wrong to identify the victim by name.

Because of these policies, there have been few images of the Iraq War that have seared the national consciousness in the way that photos of the My Lai victims did in the Vietnam War or Nick Ut's photo of Kim Phuc, nine years old and running naked down the street, severely burned by napalm. The closest counterparts were the photos of the burned corpses of the Blackwater contractors hanging from a bridge in Fallujah, but in general this type of imagery has been suppressed in the media's coverage of the war. As Philip Kennicott has written, about Ut's photo and the photojournalism in Iraq,

> *The new war photography often steers clear of powerful, bloody and unambiguous imagery, in favor of images that come at the horror of war by side channels, showing generic grief, generic destruction, generic traces of blood or physical agony. Ut's photograph was an indelible image of a single, particular girl, in agony; today's war photography tends to capture small crowds of grieving men or women, thronging the site of a car bomb, or the door of a hospital. Their collective keening rarely has the same full-frontal power of Ut's particular child, naked, wounded, and frantic.*[44]

In this context, HBO's film *Baghdad ER* (2005) remains a relatively rare effort to look at the human cost of the war in the most immediate of terms. Directors Jon Alpert and Matthew O'Neill and their camera crew had complete access for two months to the Army's 86th Combat Support Hospital in Baghdad's Green Zone. Their film portrays the efforts of doctors, medics, and chaplains to care for the often grievously wounded soldiers who are brought to the emergency room. Depending on the severity of the wounds, some are operated on in Baghdad; others are airlifted to the Landstuhl Regional Medical Center in Germany.

The film emphasizes the stoicism and dedication of the medical personnel, many of whom are dealing with a level of trauma they never encountered in civilian practice, and the courage shown by the men who are badly wounded and often in danger of dying. Several deaths are depicted. One soldier arrives with his right leg blown off and bleeds to death before the doctors can intervene. Another Marine succumbs slowly to a bullet wound, perishing despite the sustained efforts of everyone at the facility to save his life. A fellow Marine stands at his bedside, bearing witness to the death. Nonlethal injuries include knees and fingers turned to pulp by IEDs. One soldier has a piece of shrapnel in his head which entered through his eye, blinding him. The surgeons stitch closed the hole in his eye and send him off to Germany for surgery that may restore some vision.

Amputation of limbs is frequent because the IEDs inflict such severe trauma. A brief shot shows a newly severed arm that has become medical garbage, placed into a trash bag bearing biohazardous waste. Another brief shot

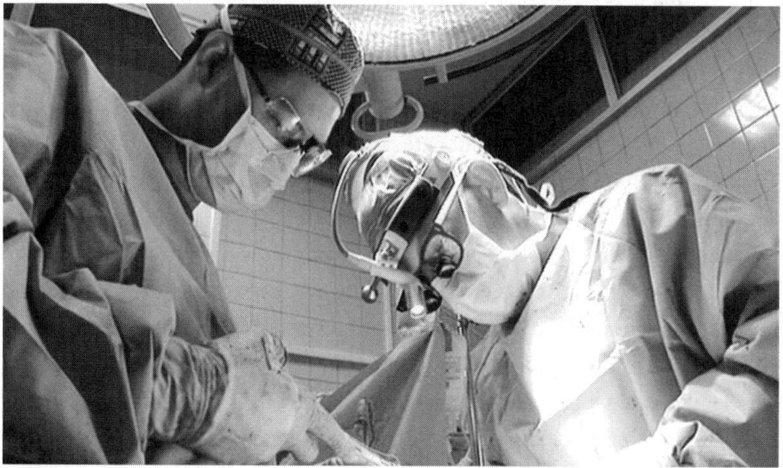

FIGURE 4.3 Surgeons at the 86th Combat Support Hospital in Iraq operate on another badly wounded soldier. *Baghdad ER* shows the dedicated efforts of health care workers to cope with the war's carnage. The filmmakers were given unprecedented access to the hospital's facilities and staff. (Frame enlargement)

shows a power saw cutting through the fat and muscle of a man's leg. And numerous shots show the copious amounts of blood pooled on the floor that must be continuously mopped away. The editing of these images ensures that none lingers long on screen. Given what they must have filmed during their two months of access to the ER, the filmmakers have been very restrictive and cautious about showing gruesome imagery, in part perhaps because of the pressure on journalists not to show anything that could be construed as undercutting the war effort and in part so as not to revolt viewers to the point that they turn away from the film. Indeed, the U.S. Department of Defense reported that Sheila Nevins, president of HBO's documentary division, "said the film has no political agenda, and is simply meant to celebrate the heroism and bravery of the men and women in uniform."[45] The closest that the film comes to voicing an opinion on the war is in footage of the hospital's chaplain saying a prayer over the body of a Marine who has just died. The chaplain prays for his soul and for an end to the violence of "this senseless war."

The direct cinema style of *Baghdad ER* keeps it mostly away from such partisan expressions and in a more strictly observational mode. But its depiction of the trauma inflicted by the war on these soldiers uncovers a reality of the Iraq War that is not widely acknowledged, which is that, while American deaths overall remain low in comparison with the Vietnam War, nonlethal casualties are extremely high. As of July 2008, more than 30,000 soldiers had been wounded. As a surgeon working at Landstuhl Regional Medical Center observed, there is a "secret side of the war," which is the long-term damage sustained by many thousands of young American men and women, who will never be the same as they were. "This is an injury war. This is not so much a death war . . . this is a war about catastrophically wounded young people."[46] *Baghdad ER* illuminates this secret side of the war. In doing so, while it honors the efforts of all who come through or work in the ER, the film's release coincided with a public climate in which majority opinion had turned against the war. Within this context, the trauma that it depicts arguably offers its own, implicit condemnation of a war characterized by the chaplain as senseless.

Richard Hankin's *Home Front* (2006) portrays the struggle of "wounded warriors" to adjust to daily life back home and to be reintegrated with families. The film profiles the case of Jeremy Feldbusch, a soldier blinded by shrapnel in Iraq and now living with his parents in the Pennsylvania home where he grew up. Feldbusch had been an athlete and had earned a B.S. in biology and had wanted to attend medical school. But in addition to taking his eyesight, the shrapnel that entered his head damaged the frontal lobe of his brain. The blindness and brain injury have dramatically changed his life, and the film shows the daily struggle faced by Feldbusch. A much harder look at the war's legacy of grievous wounds can be found in *Alive Day Memories: Home from Iraq* (2007), another of the extraordinary documentaries produced by HBO. Filmed in a darkened studio, producer James Gandolfini interviews ten veterans—women and men—who survived an experience of terrible wounding. They lost arms or legs or eyes, and in one case vital brain functions. Some experience chronic pain. They talk about the circumstances under which they were wounded, and the amputees show their stumps to the camera and palpate them. The bright spotlighting in the darkened studio serves to emphasize the starkness of the wounds. The veterans talk about their "alive day," the day they were wounded and did not die. The film does not examine the war itself, and it is clearly meant to provide a means of honoring those who have paid such a high price. At the same time, filming these wounded veterans is itself a political act within a context in which official policy has worked to keep media attention away from the war's extraordinarily high casualty rate.

Patricia Foulkrod's *The Ground Truth* (2006) also takes a hard look at the face of war that mainstream news coverage mostly avoids. The film studies the psychological and physical anguish experienced by a diverse group of soldiers—Army Rangers, Army National Guard, Marines—who are haunted by what they saw or did in Iraq. One soldier says that you don't make war on a country without going to war against its people, and many of the men and women interviewed are profoundly disturbed by the widespread killing of civilians that they describe as being a routine part of American military operations. They recall a catalogue of violence against people they knew were innocent—acts that involved running over a child with a truck, whipping children with antennas, killing women and families, hanging a man by his hands for three days until they turned gangrenous and had to be amputated. Marine Corporal Sean Huze points out that in certain areas, everyone was considered hostile. If you're taking fire from one part of a populated area, he says, "you blanket the fucking area." If there are fifty people and one guy is shooting and you can't locate him, you kill everyone. He says it is not a matter of deliberately targeting a woman or a child but of using indiscriminate firepower to ensure that American casualties are low. As he confides that seeing dead kids was the hardest thing for him to experience, the film shows images of the bleeding and torn corpses of children. The film shows images of dead Iraqis, of Iraqis being killed on camera, and of Americans severely wounded by gunfire or explosion.

The testimony in *The Ground Truth* about the killing of civilians points to one of the ugliest facets of the wars in Iraq and Afghanistan, which is that this "collateral damage" is widespread and is considered routine by the military chain of command. A secret Army report in 2006 concluded, "All levels of command tended to view civilian casualties, even in significant numbers, as routine and as the natural and intended result of insurgent tactics."[47] In Afghanistan, as well, airstrikes and shootings in the streets by American soldiers had killed scores of civilians and provoked a severe popular backlash against NATO forces.[48] As a result, the Pentagon significantly tightened the rules of engagement in April 2007, making them more restrictive than those operative in Iraq.[49] Nevertheless, American bombs continued to kill Afghani civilians in numbers that complicated the political objectives of the war.[50] The killing of civilians is a foreseeable consequence of wars in which soldiers are placed in cultures they know nothing about and told to fight an enemy they cannot see. But as Sam Goff, a retired Army sergeant, says in the film, "Killing is just one aspect of it. What's important for people to understand about an occupation is the whole situation is one of domination." Day to day you behave abusively, he says, threatening people with guns, rounding them up; "killing is just the icing on the cake." Illustrating his words are images of Iraqis being arrested and remarkable footage of several Iraqi men lying face down on the ground, as an angry American puts his boot on their heads, berates them, and arranges the positioning of their heads just so, forcibly correcting their changes of posture as if they were so many dogs who were being trained.

An Army National Guard sergeant says, "The enemy could be anyone that you see. You don't know where to focus your attention. You don't know where to focus your anger. The aggression and hatred that would be focused on a clear enemy is focused on every single Iraqi." Her remarks provide a framework for understanding incidents like the killing by Marines in Haditha in 2005 of twenty-four Iraqi civilians, including women and children shot in their beds. The Marines were taking revenge for a roadside bombing. A similar incident occurred in 2007 in Afghanistan. In what has become known as the Shinwar massacre, Marines took revenge after a suicide bombing by shooting indiscriminately at Afghani civilians, killing nineteen and wounding many more.

The Ground Truth suggests that such indiscriminate violence is widespread in the Iraqi and Afghanistan wars, sometimes as deliberate murder, Haditha-style, sometimes as the consequence of blanketing an area with fire in order to get one shooter. In addition to the cultural alienation that comes from being the outsider in a foreign land, the film points to the inculcation of racism and a willingness to kill as part of the indoctrination that occurs during basic training. Several soldiers interviewed recall the war cries and chants that accompanied jogging and other exercises, in which "ragheads" and "hajis" were the targets. The songs describe attractions like going into a schoolhouse and killing all of the children there or going into a shopping mall and killing the women. One soldier performs one of the chants—"Bomb the village/kill the people/throw some napalm in the square/do it on a Sunday morning/kill them on their way to prayer." About boot camp, an Army Ranger recalls, "Everything is associated around killing . . . and sooner or later you want to do it."

But, as the film shows, there is a price, paid by Iraqi civilians and paid by American soldiers, many of whom return home physically and emotionally scarred. In 2006 the Army found the suicide rate among veterans of the Iraq and Afghanistan wars to be the highest in its twenty-six years of record keeping. Foulkrod interviews the parents of Jeff Lucey, a Marine who returned from Iraq, slid into a severe depression, and hung himself because he felt that he had been a murderer in Iraq. Another Marine, who sought psychological counseling, has never gotten over an incident in which he shot and killed a woman who was walking toward the American lines, only to discover afterward that she was carrying a white flag. One of the film's most powerful sequences involves the sudden revelation—the camera pulls back to enlarge the frame—that many of the soldiers who have been the subjects of the interviews are, in fact, terribly wounded. They are missing an arm, or a leg, or are partially paralyzed. One soldier reveals that he is partially blind. Another soldier interviewed on camera has severe facial disfigurement including a nose which is mostly gone; he was among the few survivors of a helicopter crash. Army

Specialist Robert Acosta recalls a hand grenade thrown into his vehicle. He was picking it up to throw it back out when it exploded. As he describes his hand being blown off, one leg shattered and the other broken, the camera pulls back to reveal the prosthesis attached to his right shoulder. The revelation wrenches the viewer into a new understanding of the things that Acosta has been reporting throughout the film. Several of these wounded men and women point out that when the media report the number of people that have been wounded in Iraq, the public thinks little of it, not realizing in many cases how terrible the wounds can be. As Acosta says, the public doesn't realize that "'injured' is missing both his hands or both his legs." Army Lieutenant Melissa Stockwell describes losing her leg above the knee, and photos of her injury segue into a photo montage showing numerous soldiers with missing limbs or facial burns. Steve Robinson, director of the National Gulf War Resource Center and a former Army Ranger, points out why the wounding is so severe in this war. Body armor protecting the torso has greatly improved but limbs remain exposed. "Guys that normally would have died in Vietnam are surviving but with horrible injuries." Not only are these injuries largely concealed from public view in media coverage, but, as the film shows, many of the soldiers experience difficulty getting adequate treatment, especially for psychological problems.

A Vietnam veteran interviewed says that the U.S. military is the most profound killing machine ever invented and yet the actual killing is kept out of public discussions and concealed in terms of media coverage. *The Ground Truth* sets out to address this omission, to examine what it means to kill in war, and to show the consequences for those who are asked to do a nation's killing. These consequences, the film suggests, can be extremely grim. As such, *The Ground Truth* goes much farther than any of the other Iraq War documentaries in examining the war's carnage. Skeptical of government rhetoric about instilling freedom and democracy in Iraq or fighting terrorism there, the film examines the human costs of the war as the conflict's true face.

The HBO documentary, *Last Letters Home: Voices of American Troops from the Battlefields of Iraq*, gives close attention to another important aspect of the war's cost, namely, the pain that is inflicted on the families of soldiers who are killed in action. Director Bill Couturié (whose work as producer includes the acclaimed documentaries *Common Threads: Stories from the Quilt* [1989] and *Dear America: Letters Home from Vietnam* [1987]) profiles ten soldiers—eight men and two women—killed in Iraq by sniper fire, explosion, or vehicular accident. The setup is extremely simple—grieving family members read on camera the last letters they received from their son or daughter or husband and reminiscence about their responses when learning of the death. Snapshots show the fallen soldier at home and in Iraq. The letters are remarkable in their emotional address to family and are frequently poetic and very insightful about the feelings of the writer, who is stranded so far from home. The families reading the letters on camera often are overcome by emotion and have to pause, at which point Couturié inserts a discrete fade rather than keeping the camera turned on their distress. But this pain is the film's essential component. Couturié says in an interview contained on the DVD, "What I wanted the viewer to feel is the pain. There is a lot of pain. The pain of this war is going to reverberate for decades." He wanted the film to "bear witness to the price we're paying." The film does not take an explicit position on whether the war is right or wrong, but its emotional tone and focus may constitute an implicit one. Couturié wanted to show in human terms the price that is being paid and wanted the viewer to decide whether that price is one worth paying. The film premiered on Veterans' Day 2004, when U.S. troop deaths were just over 1,000. They climbed significantly in the years that followed.

TORTURE AND ABU GHRAIB

Revelations that Americans were abusing Iraqi prisoners at the very site where Saddam ran a torture center placed an indelible stain on the war. The abuse and homicide at Abu Ghraib prison damaged U.S. standing throughout the world and harmed the war effort in Iraq. The photographs of naked and abused Iraqi men swiftly became an iconic and enduring image of America for Islamic countries. An Army sniper stationed in Baquba when the scandal broke recalled its effect. "I knew the insurgency was going to escalate. It [the scandal] recruited tons more people to fight against us, and I knew that there'd be an increase in violence in sector and that I'd have to deal with that. It happened. I mean, the violence definitely increased and people really changed their minds. The Iraqis that were on the fence pretty much jumped over on the side of the insurgency when news of what was happening at Abu Ghraib got out."[51]

A quartet of documentaries examines the background and the consequences of the administration's efforts to evade the Geneva Conventions. The films overlap in the content areas they cover, and many of the same interviewees appear throughout the quartet. This helps to make the films into a set of interlocking inquiries into the administration's secret conduct of the war. Sherry Jones's *Torturing Democracy* (2008) chronicles the history and formation of the administration's torture policies. Produced by Washington Media

Associates and the National Security Archive, the film covers the alliance that emerged after 9/11 between Vice President Cheney, his legal counsel David Addington, and ambitious lawyers like John Yoo in the Office of Legal Counsel who were enlisted to craft memos providing legal cover for the harsh interrogations planned by the administration. This legal initiative expressed Cheney's view that presidential power should be supreme and unchecked. Jones then traces the implementation of the torture policies in Afghanistan, Iraq, and Guantánamo Bay, Cuba. Candid footage of CIA officers on the ground in Afghanistan and of prisoners being forcibly herded into captivity is contextualized with interviews of former prisoners who recount their abuse at the hands of American interrogators. Although the narration by actor Peter Coyote is dispassionate, a music score that is consistently ominous and foreboding injects unnecessary melodrama into the film. Ironically, although Jones had contracted with PBS for a broadcast of the completed documentary, the network decided to delay airing the film until after the Presidential election in 2009.

Alex Gibney's *Taxi to the Dark Side* (2007), which won an Academy Award for Best Documentary, examines the case of an Afghani taxi driver named Dilawar who was captured by an Afghan warlord and turned over to American forces in December 2002. One of his interrogators at the prison at Bagram Air Force base believed him to be an innocent man, but he nevertheless was killed during interrogation five days later. The military claimed he died of natural causes, but investigations by *New York Times* reporters Carlotta Gall and Tim Golden revealed the suppressed details of the case. Dilawar's legs had been beaten so badly that they were reduced to pulp; should he have survived, it would have been necessary to amputate them. The term "dark side" in the film's title derives from remarks by Vice President Cheney during the week that followed 9/11. Interviewed on *Meet the Press* about how the U.S. would fight terrorism, Cheney said, "We have to work the dark side, if you will. We're going to spend time in the shadows." The things that will be done, he said, will be done quietly and without discussion. "It'll be vital for us to use any means at our disposal." (Cheney's remarks also furnished the title of Jane Mayer's book about the torture policies, *The Dark Side*, and she served as a consultant on *Torturing Democracy*.)

Diliwar, then, according to the film, took a fateful taxi ride to those shadows where Cheney suggested the administration would be working. The film recounts the last days of the victim and profiles the development of the administration's policies on harsh interrogations. Like *Torturing Democracy*, it traces the abusive interrogations to techniques analyzed by the CIA in its oddly titled 1963 manual, *Kubark Counterintelligence Interrogation*, which stipulated that sensory disorientation (e.g., sleep deprivation) and self-inflicted pain (e.g., prolonged stress positions) would quickly induce a regressive and even a quasi-psychotic state in detainees. Hooded, shackled, immobilized in solitary confinement for lengthy periods, Diliwar was evidently suffering from such a condition before he was beaten to death. About these techniques, Alfred McCoy writes, "The method relies on simple, even banal procedures—isolation, standing, heat and cold, light and dark, noise and silence—for a systematic attack on all human senses. The fusion of these two techniques, sensory disorientation and self-inflicted pain, creates a synergy of physical and psychological trauma whose sum is a hammer-blow to the fundamentals of human identity."[52] After profiling the history of the administration's use of these procedures, the film traces what one interviewee calls their "global migration," from Afghanistan to the prison at Guantánamo Bay and then on to Abu Ghraib.

Rory Kennedy's *Ghosts of Abu Ghraib* (2007) examines the genesis of the scandal using interviews with several members of the prison's military police who were implicated in the abuse, with Iraqis who were detained and abused at the prison, with Joseph M. Darby, a former military policeman who turned over CDs with digital photos of the abuse to the Army's Criminal Investigation Command, with former Brigadier General Janis Karpinski who had been in charge of fifteen prisons, including Abu Ghraib, and was demoted in the wake of the scandal, with John Yoo, one of the administration's legal architects of torture, and with journalist Mark Danner, who followed the story and compiled many of the administration's torture memos into a book (*Torture and Truth*). The film's title alludes to recollections by military police serving at the prison that the facility's history as a torture center under Saddam and its general squalor made it seem like a haunted house. There were certain hallways you wouldn't go down, one says, because it seemed likely you'd find a ghost. "And you knew if something was there, it was really pissed off." The men and women who served as guards recall living in close quarters with execution chambers that included a gallows and ovens where people had been roasted. "How many lost souls this place holds," one of the former MPs muses. Another says the prison, with a heat index at 130 and the stench of trash, sweat, and feces, was like a cross between *Apocalypse Now* and *The Shining*.

The film examines the factors that contributed to the abuse. Karpinski points to the swift overcrowding that took the prison population from under 1,000 in August 2003 to over 6,000 a month later, with less than 300 military police to maintain order. Many of these MPs were ordinary soldiers who were untrained in corrections or incarceration duties. Tony Lagouranis, a military interrogator at the prison in 2004, points out that the overcrowding stemmed from army sweeps resulting in mass arrests of Iraqis, often on hunches alone, bundling them off to prison where they could be forcibly interrogated. These arrests, which frequently involved breaking into people's homes in the dead of night, often were conducted in humiliating ways. The International Committee of the Red Cross (ICRC) reported a pattern that involved entering houses after dark, "breaking doors, cabinets and other property," "pushing people around, insulting, taking aim with rifles, punching and kicking and striking with rifles."[53] Further abuse occurred during transportation and incarceration at the prison, which the ICRC reported included beatings, "high cuffing" of hands and arms in unbearable positions, sodomy, and burning. Karpinski says in the film that around 80 percent of those detained at Abu Ghraib had no information on terrorism to report whatsoever, and the ICRC reached a similar finding in its report.[54] Lagouranis describes how the interrogators grew frustrated over the lack of intelligence and concluded that most of the prisoners had none to impart.

The film identifies the arrival of Major General Geoffrey Miller at Abu Ghraib in August 2003 as the time that serious abuse began. Miller had commanded the prison at Guantánamo Bay and was sent to Abu Ghraib to "Gitmo-ize" it. Secretary of Defense Rumsfeld, the film suggests, was unhappy with the dearth of intelligence produced at Abu Ghraib and wanted Miller to bring his Gitmo techniques to Iraq. Karpinski reports on camera that Miller told her that unless you treat the prisoners like dogs, you've lost control of the interrogation. Upon Miller's arrival, the MPs were transferred from Karpinski's control to the authority of military intelligence, where their function became to soften up the prisoners for interrogation. The abuse documented in the photographs was part of the softening-up process, and the film maintains that the techniques were not improvised by MPs gone wild, as the administration claimed, but exemplified a systematic policy that was also manifest at other detention facilities. The sexual humiliation, for example, carried out by stripping male prisoners, handcuffing them and forcing them to wear panties on their heads, specifically targeted Islamic religious injunctions about modesty and was carried out by American soldiers at other facilities.

An Iraqi man imprisoned at Abu Ghraib, along with his father, recalls the older man's death. His father was feverish, bruised, and died with drool hanging from his mouth. The guards, he says, ignored his pleas for help. Former detainees also describe the screams of Manadel al-Jamadi as he was beaten to death by CIA interrogators. Al-Jamadi was a "ghost detainee," his name not on the books, and his image in death became infamous. His was the corpse packed in ice appearing in several of the notorious Abu Ghraib photographs.

In several of these pictures, MPs Sabrina Harman and Charles Graner pose by the body, smiling and giving a thumbs-up sign. A subsequent investigation ruled the death a homicide. This was the only death at Abu Ghraib that was ruled a homicide; it was also the only one that had been photographed. No one, however, was punished, except for those who took the photographs or appeared in them. Ken Davis, an MP at the prison in 2002, says on camera that he considers this to be ridiculous. "We won't charge the murderer, but we'll charge you for taking pictures and exposing that a murder happened here." Scott Horton, chairman of the Committee on International Law, tells Kennedy that there seems to have been a policy decision not to prosecute homicides that resulted from interrogations. There was also pressure not to be "overzealous" in pursuing allegations of abuse. Major General Antonio Taguba led an investigation into Abu Ghraib that found "numerous incidents of sadistic, blatant, and wanton criminal abuses."[55] Taguba also viewed material not made public, which included video of a male American soldier in uniform sodomizing a female detainee. Because of his investigation, Taguba was subsequently forced into early retirement by Pentagon officials, who complained that he was "overzealous" and not a team player.[56] Interviewed by Seymour Hersh, Taguba said he was convinced that knowledge of the abuses extended up the military chain of command but that he was not permitted to investigate anyone other than the military police at the prison. "From what I knew, troops just don't take it upon themselves to initiate what they did without any form of knowledge of the higher-ups. . . . These M.P. troops were not that creative. Somebody was giving them guidance, but I was legally prevented from further investigation into higher authority."[57]

The MPs appearing in the photos were prosecuted once the abuses became public knowledge. Military intelligence officials, who conducted the prison's interrogations behind closed doors and whom the MPs had been ordered to assist by softening up the detainees, fell outside the scope of Taguba's inquiry, as did the CIA officials who participated in the interrogations. Interviewed in the film, Sabrina Harman, one of the MPs who was prosecuted, seems dazed and dissociated from her own culpability in the abuse that transpired. Several of the MPs report becoming numb and feeling their own moral objections falling away as the abuse came to seem routine, like just another day at work. The film bookends its inquiry with footage of Stanley Milgram's famous experiments on obedience to authority, in which people, following the prompting of the experimenter, willing gave what they believed were high levels of electric shock to a confederate of the experimenter. In an interview filmed years ago and included in the documentary, Milgram remarked on how easily an individual's moral conscience might be swayed by authority and pointed out that governments have the greatest power to induce this kind of conformity and complicity in abuse. Following Milgram's suggestion, the film indicts the military chain of command and places responsibility for the Abu Ghraib abuse on Miller and on Rumsfeld and President Bush for approving policies that encouraged torture. At the bottom of a November 2002 memo on approved interrogation techniques, for example, Rumsfeld had handwritten the comment, "However, I stand for 8–10 hours a day. Why is standing limited to 4 hours?" He was referring to a Category II technique involving the use of "stress positions." Alberto Mora, former General Counsel for the Department of Navy, tells Kennedy that he regards this note as a wink and a nod to interrogators to do what they have to do to get information. From his interview with Taguba, Hersh wrote, "Taguba came to believe that Lieutenant General Sanchez, the Army commander in Iraq, and some of the generals assigned to the military headquarters in Baghdad had extensive knowledge of the abuse of prisoners in Abu Ghraib even before Joseph Darby came forward with the CD. Taguba was aware that in the fall of 2003—when much of the abuse took place—Sanchez routinely visited the prison, and witnessed at least one interrogation. According to Taguba, 'Sanchez knew exactly what was going on.'"[58]

Mora (who led an effort by military lawyers to oppose the pro-torture memos being issued by the Office of Legal Counsel) voices the film's summary view of the significance of the Abu Ghraib abuse. He says that the U.S. used to be the model for human rights throughout the world but that it is no longer. If we embrace torture, he cautions, because it is expedient, then we sacrifice our long-term interests and the rule of law and our belief in human rights. We blur the distinction between ourselves and the terrorists. This is the danger that *Ghosts of Abu Ghraib* seeks to warn about—that we become our enemies when traveling the road to Abu Ghraib.

Errol Morris's *Standard Operating Procedure* (2008) also profiles these events through interviews with many key personnel, including MPs Javal Davis, Jeremy Sivits, Megan Ambuhl, Sabrina Harman and Lynndie England, all of whom were prosecuted by the Army for their roles in the abuse, Tim Dugan, a contract interrogator at the prison, Brent Pack, an Army criminal investigator who analyzed the photographs, and Janice Karpinski. Whereas *Ghosts of Abu Ghraib* pursues the questions about the military chain of command and the degree of responsibility borne by superior officers for what happened, Morris's film is less interested in this question. Instead it confines its focus to the local level by affording the MPs who were prosecuted an opportunity on camera to describe their roles in what happened. Charles Graner, a key instigator among the MPs, was not interviewed because he is serving a ten-year prison sentence for his role in the events.

Morris is the most famous documentary filmmaker among those making films about the Iraq War. His work includes *The Fog of War* (2003), a series of interviews with former Secretary of Defense Robert McNamara, one of the architects of the Vietnam War, and *The Thin Blue Line* (1988), an investigation into the circumstances of a police officer's murder that suggested the wrong man had been convicted. This individual was subsequently freed from prison based largely on the issues raised in the film. Unlike the forensics performed on case evidence in *The Thin Blue Line,* however, *Standard Operating Procedure* does not offer a detailed and close examination of the evidence of abuse at the prison or a careful parsing of the claims of responsibility or nonresponsibility made by those involved. It mainly provides a summary account of selected key events in the words of those who were there.

Because the abuse scandal was exposed when photographs surfaced taken by those involved, Morris is interested in asking questions about the nature of photographic evidence and about what the images lead us to believe we know about the events they depict. These questions are probed in more detail by the print material that accompanies the film. There is a book, *Standard Operating Procedure,* written by Philip Gourevitch based on the interviews that Morris conducted and reproducing statements by the interviewees in much greater detail than does the film. The book is especially valuable for providing historical background and context on the prison and those who worked there, material that the film tends to sketch. There are also a series of columns that Morris has written for the *New York Times,* one of which discusses questions about what we can know from the Abu Ghraib photographs. Because the film, the book, and the columns are a set of converging inquiries into the Abu Ghraib abuse, it makes sense to treat them as a kind of single and extended work. What the public knows of the scandal it knows because of the photographs. They have provided the story—and for Morris this constitutes a problem because it may involve an assumption that the photographs reliably tell us what happened or that the photographs are the story. Morris and Gourevitch agree that the photographs are not the story and that in some instances they can produce false impressions. Two examples are the well-known images of Lynndie England holding one end of a leash, the other end affixed to the neck of a prisoner lying prone on the ground, and Sabrina Harman leaning over a corpse packed in ice, smiling and giving a thumbs-up sign.

The images are extremely disturbing, and they seem to cast England and Harman in the role of violator. Looking at the pictures, it is hard to avoid feeling that England has leashed the prisoner and is dragging him along the floor or otherwise tormenting him, and Harman seems implicated in an act of

FIGURE 4.4 In one of the most disturbing of the Abu Ghraib abuse pictures, Lynndie England poses by "Gus," holding the leash so that Charles Graner can take the photograph. In *Standard Operating Procedure*, director Errol Morris points out that Megan Ambuhl, who was also in the shot, had been cropped out by Graner.

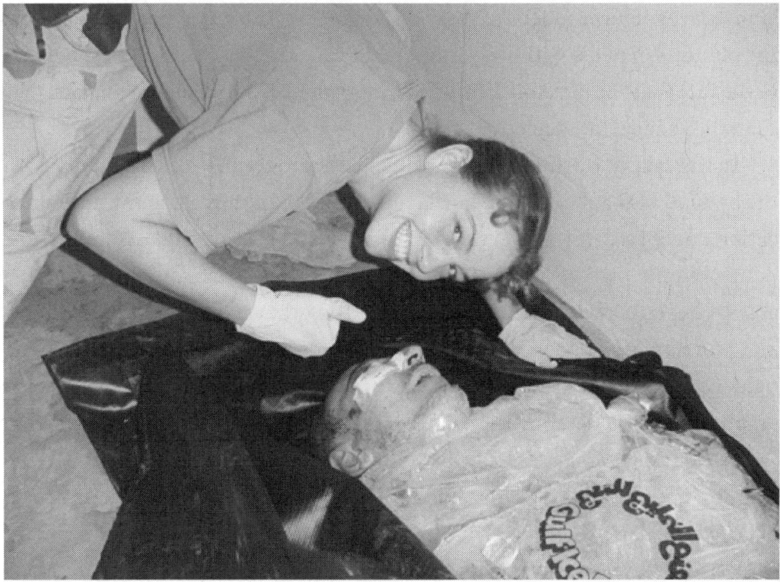

FIGURE 4.5 Sabrina Harman smiles and gives a thumbs-up beside the body of Manadel al-Jamadi in another photograph taken by Charles Graner. Harman subsequently took her own photographs of the body to prove, she said, that al-Jamadi had been abused.

homicide. While not denying that England and Harman were part of the abuse at the prison, Morris and Gourevitch point out that the context surrounding the images is complicated. The leashed prisoner, nicknamed "Gus" by the MPs, was being taken by Graner out of solitary confinement and was uncooperative. Graner had brought the leash and attached it to Gus. England did not work at the Military Intelligence block of the prison, where the picture was taken. She was not authorized to be there in any capacity. Instead, she visited after hours in order to be with Graner, with whom she was in love. She was visiting the night Graner took Gus out of solitary, and he asked her to hold the leash and stand there while he took pictures. Megan Ambuhl was also present, but Graner cropped her out of the shot, so that the image centered exclusively on England holding the leashed prisoner. Ambuhl told Morris that the picture "made it look like we were just fooling around with a detainee for our own pleasure. That wasn't the case. That was an uncooperative detainee who needed to get out of that cell—a guy with sores and stuff. You're not going to touch him. You get him out, and it may have been unorthodox, but he didn't hurt anybody and he didn't get hurt."[59] As England tells Morris, "I know people said that I dragged [Gus], but I never did. After Graner was done taking the pictures, he put the camera back in his cargo pocket, walked over, and took the strap from me."[60] Gourevitch notes that the photograph of England creates a sense of direct agency, "falsely, according to everyone who was there: she becomes the violator."[61] He adds that the picture retains its gruesome power even when the circumstances of its production become known: "even when we find out the story, the pictures of [Gus] with England remain shocking—only now the shock lies in the fact that the pictures look worse, more deliberately deviant and abusive, than the reality they depict."[62]

In the case of Harman, she is posing in a photograph taken by Graner with the body of Manadel al-Jamadi, who died from blunt force trauma and suffocation during a CIA interrogation. Her smile and gesture make it impossible not to see the picture as a kind of trophy shot, and Harman has never been able to explain away this impression. On the other hand, the film and book and Morris's newspaper column point out something that is less well known, namely, that Harman later returned to the body and took her own photographs, ones that detailed the extent of al-Jamadi's injuries. As Morris wrote in the *New York Times,* "All of these photographs are in stark contrast to the thumbs-up-and-smile photographs. . . . These are not photographs taken out of boredom. She is there to photograph the evidence."[63] A cover-up was under way. Military officers at the prison did not want knowledge of the death made public, so they packed al-Jamadi in ice to keep him from rotting, stuck an IV in his arm, and carried the body out on a stretcher as if he were still alive and in need of hospital. Harman, a gay woman in the military, wrote to her wife back home, "Yes, they do beat the prisoners up and I've written this to you before. I just don't think its [*sic*] right and never have that's why I take the picture to prove the story I tell people. No-one would believe the shit that goes on . . . they said the autopsy came back 'heart attack.' It's a lie. The whole military is nothing but lies."[64] Morris wrote that Harman was part of "the nightmare of abuse" at the prison, but that her photographs were an act of civil disobedience, taken to provide proof of what was being officially denied. "The photograph [of the smiling Harman] misdirects us. We become angry at Harman, rather than angry at the killer. . . . Instead of asking: Who is that man? Who killed him? The question becomes, 'Why is this woman smiling?' It becomes the important thing—if not the only thing."[65] He adds that photographs reveal truth but also conceal it.

Standard Operating Procedure raises epistemological questions about the nature of photographic evidence, about what we can know or think we know based on visual images as records of an event. The photographs furnish a record of abuse. Is the abuse depicted in the photographs of a criminal nature or is it standard operating procedure? One of the ironies raised in the film is the conclusion by Brent Pack, the military's criminal investigator, that many images showing prisoners shackled in "stress positions," standing in a puddle of their urine, or naked and wearing women's panties on their heads, do not show criminal abuse but merely standard procedures for softening up detainees prior to interrogation. Are these methods torture? Pack seems to say no. Javal Davis, though, says near the end of the film that torture was committed at the prison, but it wasn't photographed. He says that it happened in the interrogation sessions conducted by OGAs (Other Government Agencies, which included the CIA), but Graner and the other camera-happy MPs didn't participate in these sessions. So there is no photographic record of what went on there, except in the case of al-Jamadi, whose body Graner and Harman photographed. Was the homicide a crime or was photographing it the crime? Based on the nature of the prosecutions it pursued, the government and military seemed to feel that it was the latter. The epistemological questions that *Standard Operating Procedure* addresses are useful ones to consider across the entire corpus of Iraq War documentaries, since, as we have seen, many of these films are works of political advocacy. They offer us images that make truth claims and that promise to tell us the story of what is really happening. But many of these films are rhetorical in nature, that is, they seek to persuade viewers about the truthfulness of the conditions they portray. As Charles

Musser writes, nonfiction films mobilize "notions of truth."[66] This does not lessen their documentary value—a tradition of rhetoric and advocacy lies deeply in the history of documentary filmmaking. But unlike fiction films, which by their nature invite viewers to suspend disbelief, documentary typically seeks to elicit or to compel belief. Thus there is always an inherent tension between the stylistic claims of the format to truth telling and empirical exactitude (cinema vérité aims to enshrine these ideals at the level of technique itself) and the manner in which filmmakers have selected and shaped their materials. The many cynical and politically skeptical remarks about the war by American soldiers in the war documentaries, for example, are evidence of this selection, of the ordering of cinematic reality by filmmakers. Thus, skepticism about cinematic images and their deployment remains warranted. As Gourevitch notes, images do not themselves tell stories. "They can only provide evidence of stories, and evidence is mute: it demands investigation and interpretation."[67]

GOING BEYOND AMERICAN VIEWS ON IRAQ

The direct cinema portraits in *Operation: Dreamland* and *The War Tapes* are vivid and compelling, but they reflect the American experience in Iraq back to American viewers. *Battleground,* by contrast, searches out a broad range of Iraqi voices and makes them the center of the film. Numerous other movies have sought to do this. Andrew Berends' *The Blood of My Brother* (2005) observes the struggle of an Iraqi family to cope with the death of its eldest son at the hands of American troops occupying Baghdad. Ra'ad Fadel al-Azawi, the Shiite family's eldest son, is revered by his mother, sisters, and brother Ibrahim. He has just opened a photographic shop when American soldiers shoot and kill him while he is on the streets at night guarding a local mosque. The family is devastated, and Ibrahim and his friends declare that they want vengeance on the Americans.

Berends, who also functioned as cinematographer, generally avoids overt editorializing in favor of a quietly observational style that is reminiscent of classic direct cinema techniques, but in this case the observational method is directed at non-American sources. Berends not only got access to the family in its private moments; he also films political rallies for Moqtada al-Sadr, leader of the Mahdi army, and prayer sessions that morph into political rallies. Al-Sadr shouts to his crowd, "We had one dictator, now we have a bunch of dictators," and extols the glory of becoming a martyr for Allah and the Mahdi army. Berends also accompanies masked insurgents on raids against

U.S. forces and films clashes with other Islamic factions in Baghdad. He films a jubilant crowd exulting over the downing of an American helicopter. By capturing the depth of opposition to Americans in this Shiite section of Baghdad, and by filming the insurgency on its own ground, Berends gives American viewers a unique window onto the conflict in Iraq as it existed during the nadir of the war in 2004 and 2005. He filmed several interviews with American soldiers but deleted these so that the events in the film would be related from Iraqi points of view.

Two extended sequences show American soldiers. In one, the camera accompanies Americans as they patrol Baghdad atop armored vehicles and walk through a market area. In the market, they quiz shop owners for intelligence on insurgents and are filmed smashing a few of the market's tables. They speak English in contrast to everyone else in the film, and the scene emphasizes how alien they seem and also how clumsy, moving through a culture they don't understand and having to rely on translators in order to communicate with locals. Many of the Iraq War documentaries have shown this linguistic barrier between Americans and Iraqis. Writing about his experiences covering the war, correspondent Dexter Filkins has explicated this problem in its most serious context. "Very few of the Americans in Iraq, whether soldiers or diplomats or newspaper reporters, could speak more than a few words of Arabic. A remarkable number of them didn't even have translators. That meant that for many Iraqis, the typical nineteen-year-old army corporal from South Dakota was not a youthful innocent carrying America's goodwill; he was a terrifying combination of firepower and ignorance."[68]

The film's market sequence emphasizes this language barrier. And in a moment of editorial inflection, Berends intercuts footage of these patrols with a prayer session in a mosque full of Moqtada al-Sadr's supporters, counterpointing these sets of antagonists. The other sequence with Americans is one of the infamous nighttime raids, in which an Iraqi man is pulled from his home in front of his family, handcuffed, and taken away.

The film thus shows some of the conditions that fuel the insurgency. The Iraqis in the film know Americans from their bombs and bullets and home invasions; the Americans are perceived as an army of occupation; and every Iraqi killed becomes a religious and a political martyr. The residents of Kadhimiya mark Ra'ad's passing with a banner that states, "The people of Kadhimiya say goodbye to the hero martyr Ra'ad Fadel Salman who died with pure blood at the hand of the occupying American forces." In respect of what Berends shows, the titular phrase, "blood of my brother," has two meanings. It refers to Ibrahim's loss of Ra'ad, but it also refers to the brotherhood of Islamic resistance and martyrdom, the oaths of blood vengeance that help to fuel the insurgency.

In one of his speeches included in the film, al-Sadr says that the bond of Islam is primary and that divisions between what is called Syrian, Iraqi, and Palestinian were put there by imperialism. Ibrahim's friends go off to fight the Americans, but he feels constrained to support his mother and sisters and so he stays with the family. The film ends at Ra'ad's grave as Ibrahim mourns. There is no closure, narrative or otherwise, only the continuation of suffering and political hatred.

The force of religion and nationalism in mobilizing armed opposition to the American occupation is delineated in *Meeting Resistance* (2007), which consists of interviews with anti-American insurgents. Documentary filmmakers Steve Connors and Molly Bingham spent ten months interviewing Iraqis fighting the Americans, and they present excerpts of their conversations with eight guerrillas. As in many other Iraq War documentaries, the Iraqis here stress that nationalism and Islam are their motivations for taking up arms against what they regard as American invaders. Conners and Bingham worked within a window of opportunity that was quickly closing. In the spring of 2003 and continuing into early 2004, they were able to find and speak with the eight individuals, who are presented anonymously in the film via darkened lighting, blurring of faces and oblique framings. Eventually the climate in Iraq became too dangerous, and the insurgency went deep underground. By May 2004, as Conners and Bingham write,

> *The window that provided the glimpse into the resistance and had been quickly closing since we arrived was now shut. It had become dangerous for Iraqis even to be seen talking to a foreigner, who were all suspected of being foreign intelligence or military. Any Iraqi suspected of collaboration with a foreign intelligence was on very thin ice. Translators working for the U.S. military and even for journalists were being killed for their association with foreigners.*[69]

The window open to them enabled Connors and Bingham to create a singular documentary that portrays the enemies of Americans in Iraq and provides a sustained focus on voices that are otherwise unavailable in mainstream U.S. media. The film was screened on invitation to the military and diplomatic staff at the U.S. embassy in Baghdad because of its inside look at the motivations of the insurgency.

Iraq in Fragments (2006) proffers a portrait of Moqtada al Sadr and the Mahdi army as one section of a triptych view of the country under American occupation. Shot and directed by James Longley (*Gaza Strip* [2002]) over a period of two years, beginning just after the U.S. seized Baghdad, the film is composed in three parts. The first portrays the plight of a fatherless, 11-year--old boy working for the harsh owner of an auto repair shop in Baghdad. After suffering the man's abuse long enough, the boy goes to work elsewhere, changing masters in a way that poetically corresponds to the manner in which the country had exchanged control by Saddam for control by the Americans. The third and last section of the film portrays the welcoming attitude among Kurds in the north to the American presence. The most dramatic section, however, is the middle segment, entitled "Sadr's South," which examines the intense opposition among the Shia in Nasiriyah and Najaf to the Americans. Interviews with people in mosques, on the street, and sitting in sidewalk cafes elicit expressions of animosity coalescing around perceptions that the U.S. has betrayed its promise of democracy and is in Iraq to steal oil and treasure and as part of a general, anti-Muslim crusade. Sheikh Aws al Kafaji proclaims at a rally of the Mahdi army, "They came to teach us of Western democracy. Killing, displacement and torture, arrests without charge in the land of Iraq—this is the democracy they have brought. But Islam is the true democracy, the opposite of the false, empty democracy they are boasting of." The interviews with Iraqis in this section of the film collectively suggest that the U.S. presence has produced the opposite of its ostensible purpose—inflaming Muslim opinion and sowing the political harvest that al Qaeda reaps. As Michael Scheuer writes elsewhere,

> *as bin Laden and his ilk defend the things they love—a love held by most Muslims—they are themselves loved not just for defending the faith, but as symbols of hope in a Muslim world conditioned to massive military defeats, Islamic charlatans as rulers and U.S.-protected and coddled tyrants. While America's political, military, and media elites portray efforts to kill bin Laden as nothing more than a necessary act to annihilate a deranged gangster, many Muslims see that effort as an attempt to kill a heroic and holy man who lives and works only to protect his brethren and preserve their faith.*[70]

Longley documents efforts by Sadr's militia to organize elections that will eject the U.S.-appointed commissioners and also shows the impact of the breaking news about the tortures at Abu Ghraib prison. He continued filming in Najaf and Nasiriyah until it became too dangerous for a Westerner with a camera to be on the streets.

Iraq in Fragments differs from many of the other documentaries on the war for being so overtly poetic in its visual style. Luxuriantly pastoral compositions highlight the section on Kurdistan; strikingly graphic matches between cuts and slow, sensual dissolves highlight the editing in the section on

11-year-old Mohammed; and throughout the film digital grading is employed to take the color design in emphatically expressive and antirealist directions. Sudden changes in frame rate and the use of dropped frames emphasize the material presence of the camera. Although visual poetry has been a traditional and enduring element in the history of documentary film, *Iraq in Fragments* is especially sensitive to the aesthetics of cinema and uses these to create what at times becomes a tone poem on contemporary Iraq.

In *My Country, My Country,* director-cinematographer Laura Poitras examines the responses of an Iraqi physician to the destruction of his country during the six-month period preceding the national elections of January 2005. Living in Adhamiya, a Sunni district of Baghdad, and respected by his community, Dr. Riyadh works at a free medical clinic and finds that his moral sensibility is daily tested by the violence that has followed the American invasion. The film emphasizes the irony of the U.S. attack on the city of Fallujah carried out on the eve of national democratic elections. Meeting with a group of U.S. military officers, Riyadh asks them how the U.S. can launch an assault on a city full of people. This is not Vietnam, he tells them, and he predicts that the attack on Fallujah will lead only to more violence against Americans, not less. Concerned about his community, Riyadh runs for a seat on the Baghdad Provincial Council, but he does not win the vote. The film concludes shortly after the elections, with Riyadh feeling disillusioned and thinking of leaving Iraq because there is little left in the way of a functioning country.

Notable documentaries have resulted from experiments in which Western filmmakers gave Iraqi citizens small, portable digital cameras and asked them to shoot candid footage of their lives. *Baghdad High* (2008) shows the struggles of four high school students to live a normal life amidst the violence and carnage. Filmmakers Ivan O'Mahoney and Laura Winter provided digital cameras to seven high school boys and had them film their daily lives during their senior year of school. Three of the boys dropped out of school, so the film focuses on the remaining four. The result is a vivid portrait of teenage aspirations prevailing in defiance of dreadful surroundings. *Voices of Iraq* (2004) resulted from a project in which producers Eric Manes, Martin Kunert, and Archie Drury gave 150 small digital video cameras to Iraqis to film themselves, their friends and family. The filmmakers were instructed to pass the cameras around to others, a process that generated candid footage edited to convey a mosaic tapestry of Iraqi life after Saddam. Thus the director of the film is listed in the credits as the "People of Iraq." The footage is often delightful and surprising—a young man gives a dance performance on a lawn. Another young man speaks affectionately about Arnold Schwarzenegger as his favorite actor, about wanting muscles like Arnold, and then hoists some improvised weights. Children mug and play to the camera. Many of the Iraq War documentaries are ideologically partisan, offering critiques and sometimes condemnations of the war. *Voices of Iraq* is more singular in that it presents a positive view of the American occupation. The Iraqis presented in *Voices of Iraq* are mainly happy that the Americans are in the country. A few dissenting voices appear—an old sheikh remarks that Fallujah is violent because the Americans have taken people from their homes, and a mother wails for her son killed by American soldiers. But the bulk of the people are shown as looking forward to democracy and as being opposed to Saddam. Men tortured by Saddam joke that they would rather have been at Abu Ghraib prison where female American soldiers would have played with their penises, and the horrors of torture under Saddam are illustrated by the same graphic footage of tongue cutting, hand chopping, and beheading that appeared in *Buried in the Sand*. Given the sectarian politics that are pulling Iraq apart, where are the alternative views? Where are the Sunnis expressing their support for Saddam? Where are the Islamists stating their opposition to the American occupation?

The Saddam torture footage is not candid material shot on the DV cameras but was obtained by the film's producers, Manes, Kunert, and Drury, from the Iraq Foundation, described on its Web site as a nonprofit group "working for democracy and human rights in Iraq, and for a better international understanding of Iraq's potential as a contributor to political stability and economic progress in the Middle East."[71] At its conclusion, the film moves toward an open advocacy for the war's political project. It intercuts insurgent Internet videos rallying people to jihad with interview footage of Iraqis talking about their hopes for democracy. The intercutting makes an explicit point—the insurgency as a threat to the American project for Iraq. While many of the documentaries examined in this chapter have partisan points of view, one problem that partisanship poses for *Voices of Iraq* is that it undermines the filmmaking methodology. This methodology promises that the film will be a field experiment in which Iraqis are given cameras and told to film their lives, with the resulting footage being an accurate reflection of the plurality of voices in Iraq. Yet as edited the footage delivers a message that has been shaped ideologically by the film's producers and editors and perhaps by the Iraq Foundation. Moreover, in an unusual step, the producers hired a public relations firm—Manning, Selvage, and Lee—to do its publicity. Among MS&L's numerous clients is the U.S. Army, and the company's mission statement, unfortunate in this context, promises that its strategic marketing has "the power to change other people's minds—a dream goal for many of our clients." Was the film then commissioned to advocate for the U.S. cause in Iraq? If so, this objective is no different in kind from the stance against the war that typifies many, if not most, of the other war documentaries. In each case, cinema is being used as a medium for public advocacy, albeit according to differing agendas. The film's theatrical release shortly before the 2004 presidential election served to raise such questions. The left-leaning newspaper *In These Times* wrote, "According to MS&L Managing Director Joe Gleason, he and his colleagues also deliver key targeted messages about the war in Iraq to specific constituencies. Was the left-leaning art house crowd one of those constituencies? Is the government hiring documentary filmmakers to propagandize the U.S. population?"[72]

Of course, "the left-leaning art house crowd" is unlikely to have had its mind changed by this film. Nor are many people in general who already hold established opinions about the war likely to have their minds changed by the imagery and viewpoints expressed in the Iraq War documentaries. Empirical research suggests that political opinions are very resistant to change and also that people tend to expose themselves to material that conforms to their views on an issue. So this really isn't a fair question to ask of any film. Perhaps some documentary filmmakers feel that they are in the mind-changing business, but most probably believe that the record of events furnished in their films offers a fair portrait of something as complex as war and reflects the truth of the war as they see it. In this regard, the partisanship of *Voices of Iraq* is consistent with the other Iraq War documentaries. Filmmakers have selected their footage to emphasize points of view that shape an overall message about the war. Like *Voices of Iraq,* many of the films that criticize the war seem very selective about the points of view expressed by people on camera.

Iraqi filmmakers and artists have, unsurprisingly, provided the strongest and most intimate records of the feelings and attitudes of their fellow Iraqis toward the war, and it is worth mentioning several such films briefly here. In *About Baghdad* (2004), a group of videographers associated with the filmmaking collective InCounter Productions follows the exiled Iraqi poet and writer Sinan Antoon as he returns to Baghdad for the first time since 1991. In *The Dreams of Sparrows* (2005) Haydar Daffar recruits several videographers/directors/producers to form the IraqEye Group. Using primitive video equipment, they fan out across Baghdad and other cities to interview a cross-section of people and to document the impact of the occupation. *About Baghdad* also aims to illustrate the views of a wide swath of Iraqis toward the occupation. Interviewed in each film are students, cab drivers, hospital workers, inmates of mental institutions, shop owners, teachers, and others. Poignant footage in

About Baghdad shows the ruins of the Academy of Fine Arts, its classrooms bombed and gutted, and babies starving and dying without medication in a hospital one doctor describes wistfully as once having been fully equipped, modern, and first class. *The Dreams of Sparrows* shows artwork produced by children at a school for girls. Their paintings show bombs raining from the sky. We paint the things that frighten us, they tell the filmmaker.

Common themes throughout the interviews in both films include complaints that the Americans are good at destroying things quickly while failing to provide such basics as food, fuel, electricity, and water, that there are no jobs, that the experience of being occupied is shameful and humiliating, that Americans cannot know what an Iraqi wants, and that Americans are after the oil. *About Baghdad* juxtaposes this anger and frustration with the remarks of an American soldier who blithely says that he is here to help the Iraqis do what they could not do on their own. Speaking with the confidence of an imperial power, he says that he supports President Bush and says that if Bush says to go to war in Iran, Syria, Iraq, or Saudi Arabia, he will do so because it will make things better. There are too many terrorists in such places.

The Dreams of Sparrows questions the meaning of a term such as "terrorism." The film shows houses, schools, and mosques bombed by Americans and the reactions of Iraqis who ask if Americans would accept this if we did the same thing in their country. "Is this what they think? That the defenders of this country are terrorists?" Daffar arrives at Fallujah after the fighting there and films a cemetery with a banner stating "Cemetery for the Heroes and Martyrs of Fallujah." Some of the fighters tell him that they have come to Fallujah to protect the city from Americans. Others, Islamists, say they have come to protect it against infidels and Jews. The film shows that many of the fighters described by Americans as terrorists or insurgents see themselves as defenders of their country. Daffar concludes his film with a heartfelt and despairing plea to Americans that is prompted by personal tragedy. One of the film's associate producers, Sa'ad Fakher, is shot to death by American soldiers while driving in his car. It is a classic kind of death for an Iraqi civilian—numerous Iraqis have been shot to death in their vehicles by Americans who perceive them as a threat, as possible suicide bombers. Daffar shows the vehicle, its seats drenched with Fakher's blood, its frame and windows riddled with the impact of close to two hundred bullets. His plea is for Americans to understand that Baghdad now is a hell, that life here is nothing but war and violence, and that U.S. troops are very hard-hearted. Speaking by candlelight because there is no electricity, he says that America is behaving as if it is in a western, he says, blasting away at perceived bad men. In the meantime, though, this film and *About Baghdad* suggest that hatred for the occupation grows and deepens.

Baghdad Hospital (2008) is the Iraqi-filmed counterpart of *Baghdad ER*. Omer Salih Mahdi was a doctor at Al-Yarmouk Hospital in Baghdad who left Iraq in 2007 because the deepening civil war between Sunni and Shia (the two main branches of Islam) made continuing to work as a physician extremely dangerous. Before leaving, he obtained permission from the hospital's director of security to film candid scenes in the emergency room and interviews with physicians and ambulance drivers. The result is an extremely powerful portrait of the toll that unending violence has exacted upon Iraqi health care workers and civilians. Before the war, surgeons mainly performed such routine procedures as appendectomies, but now each day produces victims of gunfire and bomb attacks, while supplies of saline and blood for transfusing remain critically low. Numerous scenes show despairing Iraqi citizens wailing in the aftermath of terrorist bomb attacks that have killed family members, friends, and neighbors. A woman burned in a bomb blast speaks numbly of what happened. A child wounded by shrapnel curses the cowards and terrorists who did this to him. Another child screams in pain while he is held down and doctors insert tubes into each side of his chest without anesthetic to drain blood from his lungs. In addition to the physical violence, the film shows that these attacks inflict terrible psychological pain. People cannot understand how fellow Iraqis and Muslims can do this to each other. The film suggests that it is a small group of extremists who are using violence to divide Sunni and Shia Iraqis, and a sequence that profiles courageous ambulance drivers, who head bravely into the most horrific violence, points out that these men are Sunni and Shia, friends and comrades.

The film is not a partisan portrait of the war. It does not seek to indict the American presence in Iraq. It shows the effects that chronic and horrific violence has exacted on the populace, but unlike many of the American-made war documentaries, this film shows Iraqi-on-Iraqi violence, not American violence on Iraqis. In voice-over narration read by an actor (because Mahdi was then seeking to remain anonymous), the filmmaker states that everyone he knows wants the American forces to remain in the country because their authority is the only thing keeping a lid on the violence. Mahdi despairs that things will improve, and the randomness of terrorist bomb attacks on children and ordinary people is unendurable. Saddam Hussein had persecuted Shiite Iraqis. In spite of this, a Shiite woman screams in the wake of a market bombing that she wishes he were back. Saddam's violence was preferable because it was predictable, unlike the random killing that now engulfs everyone.

Baghdad Hospital and the other documentaries about the Iraq War collectively offer a very grim portrait of this theater in the U.S.-led global war on terrorism. As noted, this is partly because many were filmed during the worst period of the occupation when everything had gone wrong and seemed irretrievably broken. They show a conflict that had stagnated and devolved into increasing levels of violence and destruction.

The Iraq War stimulated an upsurge in advocacy filmmaking that had not been seen in American cinema for many years. Indeed, production was so prolific that the Iraq War documentary virtually became its own genre. Inexpensive digital cameras and editing software helped to make a kind of cottage industry out of these productions, which were numerous and plentiful. Most of the films level sharp criticism at the Bush administration and the war effort, and several are devastating in sheer human terms. *Baghdad ER, Baghdad Hospital, Alive Day,* and *Last Letters Home* show a level of human suffering that will persist for generations no matter how the war turns out. In distinction to the open advocacy of such films as *Why We Fight, Soldiers Pay,* or *Voices of Iraq,* these portraits of suffering gain tremendous force because they are not accompanied by ideological appeals from the filmmakers. In contrast, the partisan ideology of *Occupation: Dreamland* and *Gunner Palace* runs counter to the cinema vérité style of those films, making for an awkward blend of observation and advocacy in works where the filmmaking methodology aims to be ethnographic. Like Vietnam, the Iraq War has been such a polarizing experience for American culture that the filmmakers covering it often have been unable to refrain from taking sides. As a result, of all the categories of post-9/11 filmmaking examined in these chapters, the Iraq War documentaries adopt the most partisan points of view. As a result, many have found their audiences outside traditional theatrical channels of distribution, such as Internet sales and rentals and nontheatrical screenings. Most of these films had very limited theatrical release and earned a negligible amount at the box office. As Pat Aufderheide notes, "No Iraq War documentary has come within hailing distance of the massive, record-breaking sales of *Fahrenheit 9/11*."[73] As such, many of these films are reaching a public that probably holds a view of the war that is consistent with what the films themselves are saying.

At the same time, though, the partisan nature of many of these films means that an essential mystery about the Iraq War eludes them. Often, the terms by which they propose to explain the war—such as it being a war for oil, as suggested in *Rush to War*—tend to simplify questions that remain complicated. Like the Vietnam War, there is an opacity that clings to the Iraq venture. There are too many explanations that offer some degree of fit.

The war was about 9/11 and the administration's suspicion that Saddam had weapons of mass destruction. The war was about oil. The war was an effort to finish what was left undone in the first Gulf War. The war was payback from President Bush for Saddam's aim to kill his father, the first President Bush. The war was about creating an arena where the U.S. could draw Islamist fighters in and confront and kill them. The war was about creating a functioning democratic state in the Middle East to create a counterexample to terror. All of these explanations have a real claim to serious consideration. The opacity surrounding the war and which impedes our ability to easily understand it arises from this abundance of explanation and the competing methods of sorting historical fact that each approach proposes. Like the Vietnam War, the Iraq War seems overdetermined by motive and yet possesses a fundamentally irrational element that resists efforts to neatly account for it. And like Vietnam, historians will be sorting and debating the explanations for decades to come. Many of the documentaries on Iraq that contest the administration's accounts of the war tend not to acknowledge this complexity. Why did the U.S. attack Iraq after 9/11? This is a question that is not easy to answer, and the answers to come that will be sufficient will almost certainly be complicated ones. It is a question that will haunt American political culture for years, in the way that a similar question posed about Vietnam during the Cold War has done. The war documentaries that take an ideologically partisan or formulaic approach would gain strength from acknowledging that, in significant ways, this war yet remains an enigma. This qualification does not mean that the portrait and explanations they offer are necessarily wrong. But they are incomplete, and the history of this war may yet hold surprises.

As chronicles of suffering, however, and of mission failure, the films offer exceptionally powerful portraits. Whether the films are told from the perspective of American soldiers or Iraqi citizens, they offer iconic imagery of American military forces in clunky combat armor moving about city streets and amongst ordinary people who are clad in everyday dress. The combat armor in an urban environment emphasizes the alien presence of the Americans. It sets them apart and marks them as targets or as a presence to be avoided, feared, or hated. Weighed down by heavy military gear, unable to speak the language or to understand the culture, the American military presence in Iraq elicited widespread national opposition, according to many of these films. The films also emphasize the horrific nature of the war's violence, especially on civilians. In this respect, most of the films suggest that there is little to celebrate about this war, much to mourn and grieve over, no clear connection between the violence triggered by the U.S. invasion and the attacks of 9/11, a generational loss of life amongst Americans and most especially among the Iraqis, and a country laid waste. “Life is a tragedy,” Dr. Riyadh concludes in *My Country, My Country*. The Iraq War documentaries show why.

CHAPTER FIVE
TERRORISM ON THE SMALL SCREEN

"AMERICA IS A GREAT PLACE to live if you're a terrorist," Ramzi Yousef (played by Art Malik, who also appeared as the arch villain in *True Lies*) announces as he begins preparation on a bomb intended to bring down the World Trade Center. He's just arrived in the country and has joined the group of Jersey City conspirators that has coalesced around the blind sheikh Omar Abdel Rahman (Andreas Katsulas). Although the 1993 bombing failed to topple the Twin Towers, Yousef's work killed six and wounded more than 1,000 and was the opening act in the Islamist campaign on American soil.

Yousef's boastful remark strikes one of the key themes in *Path to Paradise: The Untold Story of the World Trade Center Bombing* (1997). This powerful HBO movie—a sobering enough portrait in the year of its release—now has an inescapably tragic dimension. It sounded a warning about what was coming, and its use of high-speed footage to make clouds rush ominously toward the

FIGURE 5.1 *Path to Paradise* dramatizes the 1993 attack on the World Trade Center. The Afghani-trained bomb-maker Ramzi Yousef (Art Malik, *left*) and another member of the Jersey City jihadist cell gaze at the Trade Center, plotting its destruction. (Frame enlargement)

Twin Towers aptly visualized the onrushing threat of the 1993 bombing and the September 11 attacks that followed. The film recounts the Jersey City plot that unfolded beneath the radar of the FBI and New York City police and the subsequent plot to bomb the Holland Tunnel and other city landmarks for which most of the Jersey City ring were arrested. The film presents the plot in flashbacks, which are the recollections of FBI agent John Anticev (Peter Gallagher) as he is interviewed about the case. Anticev says that the story would be funny if it weren't true. He's referring to law enforcement's missed opportunities to arrest the conspirators, had authorities only taken the warning signs seriously enough. The film shows how Yousef's group took advantage of the freedom and openness of American society to attack it from within. When a state cop pulls the group over in a traffic stop and finds the car's trunk full of guns and license plates, one of the ringleaders tells everyone to relax, this is America, the police will do nothing. Sure enough, satisifed that the men have a license for the guns, the cop sends them on their way. Anticev later remarks disdainfully, "Back home the police would be shoving barbed wire up their ass," but here freedom of religion protects them.

These themes—that an open society is vulnerable, that authorities botched the case and didn't see the bombing coming—were indictment enough in 1997 but are positively damning now, after September 11 which repeated much that this film had warned about. And a clear warning it was. *Path to Paradise* argued in explicit terms that things weren't over and hadn't ended. Several characters in the film emphasize this point. An incensed New York district attorney tells the FBI after the bombing, "I'm afraid we're looking ahead to more explosions. Six innocent people have died, and you've arrested a couple of foot soldiers in this thing and not the brains." Emad Salem (Ned Eisenberg), an FBI informer, tells Anticev, "You know this is not going to stop. This is not the last bomb." To give this idea maximum force, the film gives its curtain line to Ramzi Yousef. Extradited back to the U.S. after being captured in Pakistan, he gazes at the Twin Towers and mutters, "Next time we will bring them both down." It's a chilling moment and a prophetic one. This hate would realize its ambitions. *Path to Paradise* warned its viewers in 1997 that the towers might be doomed and castigated the inept response of law enforcement. The film's closing shot of the World Trade Center with a helicopter circling it needs only smoke and a gaping hole to become the iconic image of 2001.

The shock wave from the attacks of 9/11 inevitably spread across the television landscape, as numerous shows, series, and movies addressed the destruction of that day and its long-term effects. The nation's entertainment media responded almost immediately by broadcasting on September 21 a two-hour telethon, *America: A Tribute to Heroes*. It was carried by all the major networks and featured numerous celebrities of film, television, and the music industry, performing and speaking to raise money for the victims of the attacks and for the recovery effort. In the week after the attacks, the national trauma was profound, and the telethon provided a point of focus for national feelings of grief and shock. The show's climax featured Clint Eastwood as the icon of American rectitude, vowing that the nation would soon be going after those who were responsible.

The subject of terrorism and/or references to 9/11 appeared in numerous episodes of established series, such as *Law and Order*, and many networks aired documentaries about the attacks. These included Nova's *Why the Towers Fell* (2002), the Learning Channel's *World Trade Center: Anatomy of a Collapse* (2002), and PBS's *Heroes of Ground Zero* (2002). Many new shows debuting just before or after the attacks connected indelibly with a post-9/11 world. *The Agency* was a CBS television series from 2001 to 2003 focusing on the CIA and inevitably on its role in counterterrorism. Airing on ABC in 2003, *Threat Matrix* portrayed the adventures of a Department of Homeland Security antiterrorism unit. In the series' sixteen episodes, the agents face a variety of threats, including snipers, political assassins, and bombers. In 2004, TNT carried *The Grid*, a miniseries about FBI, NSC, CIA, and MI5 agents working together to combat terrorism. A 2005 NBC series, *E-Ring*, portrayed military and special operations missions, sometimes involving counterterrorism, run from the Pentagon. The Sci-Fi Channel series *Battlestar Galac-*

tica drew regularly on a post-9/11 context. Its ongoing storyline focused on a small band of humans who have survived the efforts of robotic Cylons to destroy the human race. Season Three (2006) dealt with suicide bombings carried out by humans against the Cylons, who have invaded and occupied a planet where humans have sought refuge. There, they fight as insurgents against the Cylons and use suicide bombing as an effective tactic. The plot led Slate.com to ask if the show supported the Iraqi insurgency.[1] The Iraq War, in turn, could be found Sunday evenings on Home Box Office in a seven-part dramatic series called *Generation Kill*, about the experiences of a Marine battalion during the first forty days of the war.

Numerous made-for-television (MFT) movies became part of the zeitgeist, including *Critical Assembly* (2003), about a nuclear threat to San Francisco, and *Pentagon 911* (2007), about the September 11 attack on the Pentagon. Even a conventional biopic was shadowed by 9/11. *Rudy: The Rudy Giuliani Story* (2003) uses the attacks as a framing device for telling the life story of Giuliani, played by actor James Woods. Scenes with Woods re-creating the chaos on the streets of lower Manhattan are intercut with actual footage of the burning towers in an effort to draw an epic frame around Giuliani's life story.

The effort by the Bush administration shortly after 9/11 to persuade members of the entertainment industry to tailor media depictions of terrorism in ways that would benefit the new "war on terror" seems to have found its greatest success in television programming. In contrast with the Iraq War documentaries, many of which are critical of the administration, television programming was often quite supportive. Television series such as *E-Ring* and *Threat Matrix* take a positive view of the military-intelligence complex, which they portray as functioning efficiently and effectively, which had not been the case on 9/11. The resulting message to viewers is comforting, but it massages the actual history of error, apathy, and miscommunication that helped enable the 9/11 hijack plot to succeed. *24*, broadcast television's most famous and popular series about the war on terrorism, openly advocates hard-line political views about the best strategies for confronting terrorism. And such made-for-television movies as *Saving Jessica Lynch* (2003), *DC 9/11: Time of Crisis* (2003), and *The Path to 9/11* (2006) offer politically partisan endorsements of the Bush administration's handling of al Qaeda's campaign against America.

Contrasting with the often partisan views of these shows was PBS's *Frontline*, a weekly program showcasing documentaries. *Frontline* has presented many films about bin Laden and al Qaeda, the 9/11 attacks, the Iraq War, the government's use of private contractors in that war, and domestic programs of spying and surveillance. As a form of investigative journalism, the *Frontline* documentaries often manifest a skeptical spirit of inquiry that is quite different from the political advocacy of *24* or *The Path to 9/11*. In 2007, PBS offered its most extensive documentary series about contemporary terrorism, *America at a Crossroads*, a series of eleven films about al Qaeda's leaders and politics, its reach into Europe and Indonesia, and about the war in Iraq.

24: THE UR FANTASY OF AGGRESSIVE ANTITERRORIST POLICING

This chapter examines the depictions of terrorism on television in these films, shows, and series. Since *24* has been the best-known and arguably the most influential terrorism-themed production on television, I examine it first. Created by producer Joel Surnow, the series premiered on the Fox television network in November 2001. Paranoia and conspiracy are hallmarks of *24* and were manifest on Surnow's previous television series, *The Equalizer* (1985), on which he was a supervising producer and which, like *24*, was about a rogue government agent-turned-vigilante. Debuting shortly after the events of September 11, *24* took maximum advantage of the fears that gripped America by offering each season a vision of the country under attack by terrorists who are determined to explode nuclear bombs in crowded cities, discharge chemical or biological weapons of mass destruction, or to assassinate the President. Surnow remarked that the series comes from "the Zeitgeist of what people's fears are—their paranoia that we're going to be attacked."[2] Given this intention, it is notable that 9/11 is not mentioned at all in the first season, while the second season contains only oblique references to the Department of Homeland Security and to the government's detention center at Guantánamo and the forcible interrogations held there. It is also notable that the villainy on hand in the first season—centered on a story of family revenge—has little to do with actual terrorism. Subsequent seasons, however, reliably focused on threats to civilians from weapons of mass destruction.

In the political fantasy offered by the series, only the hero, government agent Jack Bauer (Keifer Sutherland) stands between America and the dastardly gangs of terrorists whose plans each season are in the final stages and nearing successful implementation. This gives rise to the sense of crisis maintained by the series for the duration of its season and the narrative gimmick whereby the crisis is sustained—each season tracks the events of a single day, with each episode being one hour in that day. Thus, the clock is always ticking, figuratively and literally. Cutaways to commercials are bracketed with a digital clock on screen ticking ominously through its digits, telling the viewer how long it is until doomsday. In this regard, the political metaphor of the ticking time bomb—which is traditionally invoked in political discussions that seek to justify torture—furnishes the structure of the series.[3] The countdown to the explosion is under way each season, and Jack must swing into action in order to stop that clock.

In a nominal sense, he works for the Los Angeles branch of the fictitious Counter-Terrorism Unit (CTU), a surveillance and interdiction agency dedicated to fighting terrorism. But in a real sense, Jack is a rogue agent. He doesn't spend time in the office; he's always on the verge of being fired, often is fired and then rehired. He spends his time in the field, dashing here and there, bashing witnesses and bystanders, shooting people and/or knifing them in the interests of national security. When he is in touch with CTU, it's mostly to ask someone to break the Unit's protocol and secretly send him some forbidden information. Jack's behavior manifests the series' core political outlook, which verges on an authoritarian contempt for due process and a belief that methods of extreme brutality offer the best way to counter terrorism. The show, in other words, was in love with torture, which it depicted frequently and always as something that produces good intelligence. The advocacy of torture became *24*'s most controversial feature but did not, in any way, dim the show's popularity. It was watched by millions of viewers each season and was very popular with members of the Bush administration. This is no wonder since the show works to disseminate through popular culture the administration's advocacy of harsh interrogations in the fight against terrorism. In doing so, it constructs melodramas that mobilize the audience's desire for righteous vengeance and torture-as-payback for the crimes of 9/11.

The opening episode of Season Two gets under way with a torture session in South Korea, conducted on behalf of the American military. The victim, Jason Park, is abused with drugs and electric shock, and he gives up his information as the terrorists on this show always do when they are physically abused. He says that a nuclear bomb will be detonated in Los Angeles *today*! The ticking bomb scenario, of course, is a classic setup. Few people object to torture being used under these circumstances—the weapon is primed, many will die, only the terrorist knows its location. This kind of scenario is often presented by advocates as the prototypical situation requiring torture as a justifiable remedy. But the hypothetical scenario has never occured in the real world. Moreover, real torturers—those who, for example, work for paramilitary police units conducting torture—often cite urgent circumstances to justify their actions. A former Brazilian police officer and death squad leader remarked that "if a little girl's life were at stake and if by torturing someone [he] could save her life," he would "torture—or order his men to do so."[4]

The efficacy of torture on the series is summarized by a high-ranking NSA official, Eric Rayburn (Timothy Cathcart), who says, "When we grabbed Park we tried to extract everything we could out of him. About fifteen minutes ago he broke and confessed." In the series' political vision, people are vessels containing information, which is a kind of material substance that can be physically extracted from them; when the vessel breaks, the information pours forth. There is never doubt that the vessel will break (provided the individual in question is a villain; heroes remain stoic) or about the quality of the information produced in this manner. Inducing pain, according to the series, is the best means for verifying that what you learn is the truth. Reyburn tells President David Palmer (Dennis Haysbert) that "the intel" has extremely high credibility; this bomb will go off today. It never occurs to anyone that maybe Park is telling people what they want to hear.

In the real world, it is far from clear that inflicting pain yields good information, but pain provides a very good way of getting false information and confessions. Advocates for torture claim that it can produce actionable intelligence, but the evidence for this in known 9/11 cases is far from encouraging. Khalid Sheikh Mohammed, one of the masterminds of the 9/11 plot, is said by his CIA interrogators to have broken after being subjected to waterboarding, a torture technique that induces drowning and produces terror in the captive. Mohammed confessed to numerous terror plots but later recanted much of what he said and even boasted about his ability to provide false and misleading information. Sometimes his confessions were wildly improbable. He claimed, for example, to have personally killed *Wall Street Journal* reporter Daniel Pearl and was planning to assassinate Presidents Clinton and Carter and the Pope. The exaggerated and contradictory nature of his confessions raised many doubts within the intelligence community about their reliability.[5] Another captive, said by the administration to be a high-level al Qaeda commander, Abu Zubaydah, gave up valuable information after harsh interrogation, according to President Bush, who cited his case and the leads it produced in a 2006 defense of abusive interrogations. But the FBI had successfully employed gentle methods of interrogation on Zubaydah before he was subjected to torture; these were already producing a stream of useful intelligence when Zubaydah was taken out of the FBI's hands and tortured.

As in the Kalid Sheikh Mohammed case, harsh interrogation methods are an excellent means for eliciting false confessions, and separating truth from lie can be a near impossible task for the interrogator. As Jane Mayer writes, "Torture works in several ways. It can intimidate enemies, it can elicit false confessions, and it can produce true confessions. Setting aside the moral issues, the problem is recognizing what's true."[6] In his study of torture regimes worldwide, Darius Rejali points out, "Torturers have far less training or experience in interrogation than police, and so the prospect that they will be better at spotting deception is not good."[7] In 2001 the CIA took control of an alleged al Qaeda commander named Ibn al-Libi, who had been captured by American soldiers in Afghanistan. He was forcibly rendered to Egypt where he was tortured and confessed that three members of al Qaeda had traveled to Iraq to learn about nuclear weapons. The Bush administration used this intelligence to buttress its claims about Iraq's weapons of mass destruction and its al Qaeda connection. But al-Libi later recanted what he had said, confirming the suspicions of many intelligence officers at the time that he was a fabricator. "They were killing me. I had to tell them something," the FBI reported him saying.[8] The false information obtained by torture provided the administration with one of its rationales for taking the country to war in Iraq. Beyond the moral and political opprobrium that a policy of torture elicits, it hinders intelligence gathering. Once someone has been brutalized, interrogators cannot use that person as a long-term source, not over a period of years. In contrast, interrogation methods that are gentler and facilitate the building of rapport between interrogator and captive do permit extended questioning and long-term intelligence gathering. Torture burns up intelligence assets. The long-term exploitation of these assets is a vital strategy in a struggle against terrorists, but a torture regime makes it impossible.[9]

The elicitation of false confessions under the torture policies implemented by the Bush administration rested on a historical irony. Many of the torture methods used by military and CIA interrogators at Guantánamo derived from Chinese Communist techniques, which had been employed to produce false confessions from captured Americans during the Korean War.[10] The Chinese used the false confessions for propaganda purposes. In a 1957 paper discussing the Chinese methods, Albert Biderman, a sociologist working for the Air Force, wrote that inflicting pain was not an effective method for eliciting desired behaviors from captives. "While many of our people did encounter physical violence, this rarely occurred as part of a systematic effort to elicit a false confession. Where physical violence *was* inflicted during the course of such an attempt, the attempt was particularly likely to fail completely [italics in original]."[11] The CIA's *Kubark Counterintelligence Interrogation* manual, compiled in 1963 to provide instruction to agency operatives on interrogation methods, also stresses that inflicting pain is counterproductive because it stiffens the resistance of a captive, and the manual identifies several reasons why captives may hold sufficient motivations for resisting torture. The manual also cautions that "intense pain is quite likely to produce false confessions, concocted as a means of escaping from distress."[12] Biderman and the Kubark manual, however, stipulate that self-inflicted pain—as opposed to pain that is inflicted by an interrogator—can be an effective way to break the will of a prisoner. Forcing a prisoner to sit or stand for long hours—a method known as an enforced stress position, documented in the Kubark manual and authorized by the Bush administration for use on those it designated as illegal enemy combatants—could be very effective at eliciting compliant behavior because it did not involve a contest between the victim and an adversary who was inflicting pain. If pain originates from the victim's own behavior, as when holding a stress position, Biderman and the Kubark manual note that it is more likely to erode the individual's will to resist.

The cautions expressed by Biderman and the Kubark manual notwithstanding, the degree to which harsh interrogation methods may be effective is not well understood. As Jane Mayer writes, "Scientific research on the efficacy of torture is extremely limited because of the moral and legal impediments to experimentation."[13] Benjamin Wittes writes, "Those who have used conventional interrogation tactics successfully believe them optimal. Those who have used more coercive tactics successfully believe them optimal. There has been surprisingly little study of the relative efficacy of different modes of interrogation."[14]

In his epic study of the geographic and political dispersion of methods of torture, Darius Rejali points to the corruptive effects that policies of torture wreak once they are implemented. He stresses that torture cannot be politically or scientifically controlled and that it corrupts the regimes and interrogators who employ it. "Torture has not one slippery slope, but three. Torture increasingly takes in more suspects than those approved, leads to harsher methods than are authorized, and leads to greater bureaucratic fragmentation."[15] He adds, "Torture yields poor information, sweeps up many innocents, degrades organizational capabilities, and destroys interrogators."[16] He concludes, "Torture cannot be administered professionally, scientifically or precisely; and it causes serious damage to the institutions that employ it."[17]

The Bush administration believed that harsh methods were very reliable. Their application, however, produced the problems Rejali identified, in addition to the cases involving false confessions. The institutional corruption that Rejali notes was evident when the Abu Ghraib scandal surfaced, as was the expansion of torture techniques and range of victims. Another critical problem generated by the administration's policies was what to do with the prisoner after torture. Harsh interrogation methods undercut the administration's ability to file charges against real terrorists who had confessed under duress. Such people shouldn't be released, nor could they be brought to trial after having been tortured. Harsh interrogations created a legal and administrative black hole, in addition to the moral opprobrium they elicited. The administration was unprepared for this problem. Its ad hoc procedures created an ongoing dilemma—what to do with captives who had been detained, interrogated, and abused outside of a legal structure and who could not thereafter be brought back inside the law for trial and sentencing.

None of these problems and uncertainties appear on *24*. Harsh methods always work, never elicit false information, and really bad guys can be blown away in acts of righteous vengeance. Moreover, Jack is a seasoned pro at torture. He feels comfortable inflicting pain on others, and he doesn't hesitate. In the world of *24*, his willingness to torture establishes his credentials as a hero. In the series' unvarying formula, the doomsday clock is ticking, many will die, there is no time for an alternative, and one villain's suffering serves the greater good. Tracking a nuclear weapon set to explode in Los Angeles, CTU agent Tony Almeida (Carlos Bernard) asks his boss, George Mason (Xander Berkeley), how hard he can push a pair of suspects in interrogation. Mason says he can go as hard as he has to because time is running out. "Stick bamboo shoots under their nails." In the first episode of Season Four, CTU picks up terrorist "chatter" on the Internet that indicates something bad will happen at 8 A.M. *that very morning*! Luckily, a terrorist suspect is already in custody and Jack is on hand. He goes into the holding cell and abruptly shoots the prisoner in the knee. The man immediately confesses that the Secretary of Defense has been targeted for a hit at 8 A.M. When CTU boss Erin Driscoll (Alberta Watson) objects and accuses Jack of committing torture, he smugly replies that it was necessary, that he got the information she was after and had been unable to elicit.

In Season Two, a prime terrorist turns out to be Marie Warner (Laura Harris), a pretty, blonde, seemingly vacuous young American woman who exudes the wholesome innocence of a character in a toothpaste commercial. Jack shoots her in the arm and refuses to give her any pain medication because he needs information *right now*. He tells her sister, Kate, that Marie is the only person who knows where the bomb is. "I've got to use every advantage I've got. Surely you understand that," he says. Jack presses on the bullet in Marie's arm. "The pain is only going to get worse," he promises. "Tell me where the bomb is." In another torture session that season, Jack apprehends master terrorist Syed Ali (Francesco Quinn) and breaks his finger, promising "I can make you die with more pain than you ever imagined."

In Season Four, Jack gets to torture the ex-husband of his current girlfriend. Paul Raines' name is listed on the lease of a house that was used by terrorists, and Jack wants to know why. Announcing that he's going to do "whatever I have to," he straps Paul (James Frain) to a chair, douses him with water, and then rips the wires out of a table lamp, exposing the ends. When his girlfriend objects, Jack says that five nuclear power plants are about to melt down. "All I care about right now is making sure that doesn't happen." He continues, "Right now Paul is a prime suspect, and he's not cooperating with me, and I don't have time to do this any other way. I need to know for sure." Only torture provides the certitude of knowing "for sure." So, with the cord still plugged in, Jack holds the wires to Paul's chest, electrocuting him. After a second application, Paul breaks and fesses up.

Jack isn't the only torturer in the series, merely the most frequent. Villains torture, of course, and so does the President of the United States. Faced with a conspiracy by NSA official Roger Stanton (Harris Yulin), President David Palmer recruits a Secret Service agent who is an old hand at torture and has him apply a defibrillator to Stanton's head. Palmer watches the sessions on a private video feed. The plot line seems like an extrapolation of Bush administration policy. The administration went to elaborate lengths after 9/11 to fashion a legal basis for torturing persons accused of terrorism and for evading liability, and in this episode *24* gives us a President who recruits torturers and who supervises the sessions. But this spectacle of abuse sanctioned by the highest office in the land is not meant as a criticism. Instead, the show endorses the necessity and the moral rightness of the President-as-torturer.

In a widely read essay in the *New Yorker*, Jane Mayer reported that military officials asked the show's writers and producers to cut back on the torture scenes. Mayer described a visit with the show's creative staff by Brigadier

FIGURE 5.2 Jack Bauer (Keifer Sutherland) uses a table lamp to electrocute Paul Raines (James Frain). Jack is confident that torture is the best way of getting information. (Frame enlargement)

General Patrick Finnegan, dean of the U.S. Military Academy at West Point, accompanied by several former military and FBI interrogators. Mayer wrote that "Finnegan and the others had come to voice their concern that the show's central political premise—that the letter of American law must be sacrificed for the country's security—was having a toxic effect. In their view, the show promoted unethical and illegal behavior and had adversely affected the training and performance of real American soldiers."[18] Finnegan and the others reported that students at West Point and soldiers in the field admired Jack Bauer's tactics and that these feelings undermined their ability to understand that torture was illegal. Moreover, they pointed out that the series shows Jack committing acts of sadistic brutality in coolly rational and emotionally unaffected ways. An FBI interrogator observed, "Only a psychopath can torture and be unaffected. You don't want people like that in your organization. They are untrustworthy and tend to have grotesque other problems." Indeed, a study of Brazilian torturers working for the police found that they were afflicted with sleeplessness, emotional disorders, alcoholism, and suicidal behaviors. One torturer remarked, "We are society's toilet paper." Many felt that they had been betrayed by the government on whose behalf they had tortured. The study's authors concluded about the effects of torture on those who carry it out, "you may do it only at physical and psychological risk to yourself, with no guarantee that those you serve will support you in the end."[19]

This is a striking phenomenon. Indeed, a case can be made that Jack is precisely the kind of out-of-control sadist that professional torturers themselves claim to abhor. He begins to slather when a terrorist is near. On those rare instances when he is unable to torture a victim who's been detained, he develops facial tics, evidently a short circuit in his wiring. He experiences no moral qualms about his actions, even when he contemplates torturing a former lover, Nina Myers (Sarah Clarke), the ex-husband of a current girlfriend, or the sister of another. Jack knows that he is always right, that service to the state is a supreme good, and that the state is always right. Filled with this certitude, Jack does not shrink from the opportunity to inflict pain, and he doesn't hesitate to mutilate a corpse when it serves his ends. Seeking the identity of a man he has just shot to death, Jack chops off the man's finger so he can scan it into a database. In another episode, Jack walks into an interrogation room where an unarmed suspect sits. He abruptly shoots the man in the chest, killing him, and then asks for a hacksaw. In action not shown on screen, he cuts off the dead man's head with the hacksaw, places the head in a tote bag, and takes it to the gang leader the victim was about to testify against. Jack needs to infiltrate the gang in order to track some terrorists and bringing in the head will put him in their good graces. According to the series' moral calculus, the man whose head he chopped off was a child molester and a murderer—who cares what happens to him?

Jack is an avenging angel practicing righteous violence to serve the greater good. Due process, civil rights, and the rule of law are impediments to getting the terrorists because the villains are preparing to strike immediately. Desperate times call for emergency measures. In this respect the show translates into popular culture the political stance of the Bush administration. *24* doesn't argue that a balance ought to be struck between due process and the government's need to detect and apprehend terrorists and even to go outside the law on occasion. The show seems to reject all legal impediments that provide for civil liberties. When Defense Secretary James Heller (William Devane) is kidnapped by terrorists, CTU boss Erin Driscoll orders that Heller's son, who is a left-wing protester, be seized and tortured despite a lack of evidence that he had any role in the kidnapping. The young man shrieks, "This is illegal!" but that doesn't stop CTU.

In the world of *24,* an ordinary citizen, innocent of wrongdoing, can be seized by a shadowy intelligence agency, illegally detained and tortured, and the action is understood as a necessary one in the fight against terrorism. The word for that kind of state is totalitarian. In an essay on the series, Ginia Bellafante pointed to the "way the show seems committed not to the politics of the left or right, but to a kind of quasi-totalitarianism in which patriotism takes precedence over everything else and private life is eroded, undermined, demeaned."[20] On the series, nothing in life exists beyond responding to the terrorist menace. Characters either have no private life or what they do have is stunted. Family life on the show is often quite monstrous. Fathers kill sons, sisters betray sisters, parents abuse children. Private life is a morass of duplicity, betrayal, neglect, abuse, and it is only service to the state that offers a worthy and redeeming ideal to which individuals might dedicate themselves. Bellafante writes, "Ordinary social intercourse simply doesn't exist. The idea that two people might sit down for a cup of coffee is as contrary to the show's internal logic as the idea that polar bears might someday learn to sing."

Nothing comes between Jack and his hunt for terrorists. An unintentionally hilarious plot line during the first two seasons has his daughter, Kim (Elisha Cuthbert), perpetually in peril and on the run from terrorists, mountain lions, convenience store robbers, police, child-raping fathers, and bad drivers. Breathless from running about so much, she calls Jack for help, but he's always busy, deep undercover, pursuing bad guys. He either misses her calls or can't respond when the message does get through. Jack is a bad parent, but that's the least of his faults. He will do anything to apprehend terrorists. Following a "hostile" who stops at a convenience store, Jack is distressed to learn that CTU is delayed in getting satellite surveillance up and running. He's got to delay the bad guy until the surveillance is in place, so he pulls his gun and robs the convenience store, taking the clerk and all of the customers, including the "hostile," prisoner. When a cop comes to the store, Jack draws down on him, too. Presumably he is prepared to react if things go wrong, ready to kill the cop or to shoot an innocent customer if need be. The cop, the customers, all might be written off as collateral damage, the loss of a few people in order to save many. Although viewers probably understand that the series is unlikely to have Jack blow away the cop or the customers, for the scene to be credible it must hold, as a potentiality, that he would do so in order to keep his cover. Killing for the state, and for the greater good, is *24*'s gold standard of moral behavior.

And the best way to implement this gold standard is for Jack to behave like a vigilante, going off on his own in pursuit of evildoers. In the process, he might torture; he might rob convenience stores; he might hold pedestrians hostage; he might pull motorists from their cars at gunpoint and steal their vehicles. In every instance, Jack disregards the legal constraints on his behavior. In this respect, the outlook of *24* is consistent with the work of the lawyers and policymakers in the Office of Legal Counsel (a group that included John Yoo, Alberto Gonzales, and Jay S. Bybee) whom the Bush administration charged with drafting a legal foundation for the policies on torture that it wished to implement. The conclusions of Joshua Dratel, president of the New York State Association of Criminal Defense Lawyers, about the view expressed in their work also describes the political outlook of *24*: "these policy makers do not like our system of justice, with its checks and balances, and rights and limits, that they have been sworn to uphold."[21] (In "The Green Light," lawyer Philippe Sands warns that the interrogators who used torture and the administration figures who drafted the policies may be liable for prosecution on war crimes charges should they travel outside the jurisdiction of the United States.)[22] Thus, in *24*, when an innocent young man whom CTU agent Tony Almeida has forcibly detained for interrogation demands to see a lawyer, Tony replies, simply and eloquently, "No." The scene ends; nothing more need be said. Tony's refusal is its own self-evident virtue.

When series creator Joel Surnow stated that Jack Bauer is patriotic, and that Americans want to see their terrorist wars fought by him in this manner, he meant that the character conforms with the Bush administration's muscular approach. And yet in its advocacy of torture, the show shares a similar problem with the administration. Benjamin Wittes expressed it well: "Because they had *interpreted the law* as allowing [brutal interrogation]—rather than acknowledging the occasional necessity of crossing the line . . . they ended up defining down torture and other inhumane treatment for *everyone*, not merely for those few detainees whose seniority and real-time operational importance may actually have justified a measure of coercion [italics in original]."[23] On *24* torture is an everyday policy; everyone is its potential recipient.

President Bush has said that the war on terrorism will never end, and the narrative structure of *24* gives this idea dramatic form. On the series, the U.S. is always under attack, new threats continuously appear, and Jack has to stay ever limber and keep his gun oiled. The irony is that little remains that is worth preserving. Liberty, democracy, and the Constitutional order seemingly have vanished from the America that *24* depicts. Why should Jack bother to save this society? There really is no good answer to that question. Jack never wonders whether his own behavior threatens the democracy that he should be sworn to protect. *24* creates a paradox that it does not acknowledge. Jack runs frantically each and every season to save an America that the show itself depicts as possessing little inherent or enduring value. America, as a nation of liberty and of laws, is hard to find in this series. Moreover, it is beset by enemies within, by villains from America's own political and business establishment. According to the show's vision, political institutions are weak and are rife with Machiavellian plots, internecine struggles for power, and violent coups d'état. The threat of Presidential assassination is an ongoing theme on *24*. After an unsuccessful attempt on his life, President David Palmer (Dennis Haysbert) is subsequently assassinated, and another President falls in the line of duty as well. As the nation's premiere antiterrorist task force, CTU is an ongoing target for mischief. Its Los Angeles facilities are bombed, and the unit is routinely infested with moles, spies, and double-dealing agents with agendas of their own. Terrorists do not pose the only mortal threat to the state of the union. Beset by traitors and spies, America is cracking from within. The polity is weak and needs strong measures to survive. The show advocates these measures as the only means of combating the traitors in our midst. *24* elicits the public's fears about impending attacks in order to offer its viewers a recipe for dictators.

PACKAGING TERRORISM FOR ENTERTAINMENT

24 also illustrates how easily the traumas induced by 9/11 bond with the formulas of popular culture and can be packaged as entertainment. Television series that place terrorism in a thriller format uniformly demonstrate this packaging. Showtime's *Sleeper Cell*, a two-season series in 2005 and 2006, for example, portrays the adventures of a Muslim FBI agent, Darwyn (Michael Ealy), as he infiltrates a small cell of Muslim terrorists operating in Los Angeles. The demographics of the terrorists are a little wacky and were evidently an effort to appeal to a broad-based audience. The cell's leader is Farik (Oded Fehr), a Jewish-Muslim corporate executive terrorist. That is, he is an Islamist fanatic who poses as a security executive named Yossi and the leader at a neighborhood Jewish community center. Surely many local Jewish organizations are infiltrated by Islamist terrorists! His little band of holy warriors includes Christian, a former white supremacist skinhead who now worships Allah, Ilija, a Bosnian Muslim radicalized by the fighting in the former Yugoslavia, and Tommy, a blond American kid who has inexplicably converted to militant Islam but hasn't lost his American inflections. "Dude, we're fucking terrorists—sorry, holy warriors," he exclaims.

Darwyn is an earnest believer, but his Islam is very different from Farik's. Darwyn remarks about the terrorists, "You know what Islam means in Arabic? You surrender to God's will and peace. These guys have nothing to do with my faith." Darwyn's beliefs enable the series to stage numerous dialogues about the conflict within Islam between spirituality and peace and violent jihad. In this respect, the series is a kind of anti-*24* because it does distinguish between differing moral constructions that may be placed on a single underlying religion. It's also an anti-*24* in that Darwyn's essential humanity precludes him from embracing torture in the manner of a Jack Bauer. One of the best episodes in the series has Darwyn trying to show a young Afghani boy, trained in jihad, a different form of Islam than what he learned under the Taliban. The episode also creates the kind of real-world political context that is so notably missing from the elaborate fantasies on *24*. The Afghani boy's backstory is all too credible. He tells Darwyn that he and his father knew nothing of al Qaeda or Americans; they spent their time raising goats for milk. American soldiers came to their village looking for Taliban, and a local enemy in the village, who disliked the boy's family, told the Americans that the boy and his father were Taliban. The soldiers seized the boy, beat and interrogated him, asking about bin Laden, and then sent him to Guantánamo, where he spent three years, much of that time in solitary confinement. Speaking about these experiences, he says, "Mostly I learn to hate Americans." When he was released from Guantánamo and sent back to Afghanistan, he was an easy recruit for the Taliban and a local sheikh who "teaches me to fight for Islam." The episode dramatizes the radicalization of this character and points to some of the ways that American policies are creating new generations of terrorists.

But the thriller format drives the series, not the philosophical debates. Farik plans to drive a truck full of phosgene gas into Dodger stadium during a baseball game and detonate it, killing thousands. Inexplicably, the FBI does not arrest Farik and his group, despite being aware of their activities and the location of their hideout. In the real world, counterterrorism authorities tend to round up plotters in the very early stages of their planning rather than risk disaster. But doing that on a TV adventure series would be like shooting the horses in a western to stop a stagecoach. It's never done because it ruins the story. So the FBI lets Farik and his group load the truck and drive it to the stadium before closing in, guns blazing, to foil the cell's plans.

Unlike *24, Sleeper Cell* does not advocate totalitarian methods in the fight against terrorism. It seeks to honor Islam at the same time as it portrays Islamic jihadists who are bent on killing as many Americans as possible. But finally the design concept of the series is a curious one, since the central characters are terrorists and the show asks the audience to derive its vicarious thrills from their activities. "Terrorist entertainment" is an odd construction to have emerged from the devastation of 9/11, but it soon became a common format on television. *The Grid,* for example, was a very slickly produced miniseries that pitted heroic government agents from the United States and England against Islamist terrorists smuggling sarin gas and aiming also to destroy the West's petroleum infrastructure. One of the heroes, CIA agent Raza Michaels (Piter Fattouche) is Muslim and on hand to provide the expected disclaimers that the terrorist villains are dishonoring Islam. FBI agent Max Canary (Dylan McDermott) is motivated by rage—he lost a friend in the World Trade Center. "We buried his leg. That's what was left," he says.

This miniseries was a barometer of current events, reflecting numerous real-world issues. An MI6 agent remarks about American efforts, "Your boss's cowboy tactics didn't turn up much on Saddam's weapons of mass destruction." Another scene evokes the controversies over Bush administration policies of extraordinary rendition and denial of due process. Max threatens to render a suspect back to Lebanon. His rights stop at mass murder, Max says. "Not according to the Constitution," the lawyer replies, adding that the man is entitled to due process. Max says the lawyer doesn't understand the consequences or the scope of the terrorist threat. The problems America is having in the world today, the lawyer replies, are not because of what I'm doing. As in *24* and *Sleeper Cell,* the series builds excitement around the stealthy progress of terrorist plotting and the determined efforts of government agents to stop them.

Packaging terrorism as entertainment, of course, is wholly consistent with action movie formulas, as we saw in chapter 1. Even aging movie heroes might be called upon to draw their guns against Islamist terrorists. Chuck Norris, who refought the Vietnam War in the 1980s in a series of *Missing in Action* films (1984, 1985, 1988) and subsequently became a television star on the *Walker: Texas Ranger* series, went mano a mano with terrorists in *The President's Man: A Line in the Sand* (2002). A bin Laden figure named Rashid (Joel Swetow), based in Afghanistan and supported by the Taliban, smuggles a nuclear bomb into the U.S. and threatens to detonate it unless his demands are met. The U.S., he says, is a corrupt society of infidels and must end its occupation of Saudi Arabia and other Islamic lands. Joshua McCord (Norris) and his sidekick Deke Slater (Judson Mills) track and defuse the bomb, and McCord delivers a climactic flurry of chops and kicks that immobilizes Rashid. Like many other thrillers about Islamist terror, the film is careful to make the qualification that "the teachings of Allah are of peace, not violence," even while suggesting that nukes perhaps are the best solution to Islamism. McCord teaches a class at the generically named "Texas University," where one of his students is rash enough to suggest that the U.S. simply nuke the Arabs. Expressing tolerance, Norris reminds his class that even though "Rob says we should nuke all countries that support terrorism . . . we have to remember we can't blame all Arabs for the actions of a few." Perhaps, then, it would be best simply to nuke the few. Although the film premiered on CBS in January 2002, it was clearly shot before 9/11—Rashid's demands include freedom for the bombers of the World Trade Center, circa 1993. In the film, the Trade Center still stands.

TV DRAMATIZATIONS OF UNITED 93

Numerous other made-for-TV movies offer dramatizations of the actual events of 9/11. *Flight 93* (2006), broadcast on the A&E network the same year as the release of Paul Greengrass' theatrical film *United 93*, was nominated for an Emmy as best television movie of its year. The two films make for an interesting contrast. Greengrass' film takes a broader view of the events of that day, portraying not only the emergency aboard United 93 but also the confusion at NORAD and in the FAA's central command center. *Flight 93* focuses almost exclusively on the hijacking and the reactions among the passengers. The film spends much of its time portraying the cell phone calls by passengers to their family members. By emphasizing the emotional, tearful content of the calls at such length, the movie creates a more melodramatic tone than does *United 93*.

It also misleads its viewers about the response by the FAA and civil aviation authorities, making it seem as if these personnel were reacting with great efficiency and decisiveness when just the opposite was true. Before United 93 took off, American Airlines 11 was hijacked, and the film portrays the end of the airphone call placed by flight attendant Amy Sweeney, onboard American 11, in which she reported that the plane was flying too low, that she saw buildings, and exclaimed "Oh my God" just before impact. The film makes it seem as if Sweeney's call got right through to authorities. In fact, she had to call three times because she kept getting cut off. Betty Ong, another flight attendant on American 11, managed to contact American's reservations office in North Carolina and experienced tremendous difficulties persuading the personnel who took the call to believe what she was saying and to get the details straight. They kept mixing up her flight number, for example, and asked numerous times for her to repeat what she was telling them, wasting precious moments. Top executives at American Airlines knew of the hijacking by 8:30, but, as James Ridgeway writes, "there is no record that American Airlines called the FAA's central Command Center, other local control centers, the FBI, the military, or their own pilots."[24] The film also minimizes the inadequacies of the airport screening measures. Mohammed Atta's team, the American 11 hijackers, passed easily through security at Boston's Logan airport, despite the fact that Atta and three members of his team had been flagged by CAPPS—Computer Assisted Passenger Prescreening System—as individuals who warranted extra security measures. But under the rules in place at the time, this meant only that their checked baggage, not the men themselves, got extra attention. The checked bags were to be held off the plane until the men had boarded. At Washington Dulles, several members of the American 77 hijack team set off the metal alarm, and one of them triggered it twice. They were passed through and on to the plane.

By omitting such details, the film offers a progressive narrative emphasizing the dedication and heroism of everyone involved in responding to the events of that day. Such a narrative minimizes events that are inconsistent with the provision of emotional uplift, and these topics would include the massive confusion and the errors of judgment made by the FAA, NORAD, and executives at the airlines companies. The passengers on board United 93 behaved in a courageous manner, and the drama of their last stand accounts for why this flight, among all those hijacked on that day, has been the subject of several films. But *Flight 93* by no means offers an accurate or reliable portrait of the response by the command and communications centers of the military and airlines or the security measures at the airports where the flights originated. The film offers a powerful, if sometimes melodramatic, reenactment of the doomed flight and ends with a surprisingly poetic series of images that show nature reclaiming the burnt impact area in the Pennsylvania countryside.

The Flight That Fought Back (2005) is yet another version of the story, this one produced for the Discovery Channel. Unlike the other film versions, this production uses interviews with many of the spouses and parents of those who were killed on board the aircraft. The film intercuts these interviews with a dramatic reenactment of the hijacking and the response by the passengers. The reenactment is filmed very cinematically and is as powerful as what can be found in the other versions. But the interviews add tremendously to the emotional drama because the recollections of the family members make the lives and identities of the passengers far more vivid than they are in the other film versions. And, often, the remarks in the interviews are striking and memorable. Alice Bingham speaks about the pride she feels that her son, Mark, and the other passengers tried to take control of the plane. "I'm so glad they didn't sit quietly in their seats and let the hijackers fly the plane into the Capitol building." Liz Glick, whose husband Jeremy perished, shrewdly cuts through the mythic framework in which the passengers' actions are now embedded. She says that saving the country probably wasn't on the minds of many; they had, she says, a more immediate objective—getting home. "These were men and women who were fathers, who were mothers, and they wanted to get home. So what is fueling them? I don't think it's the desire to save the White House and be bigger than life. I think it's them looking inside themselves and thinking something smaller. Jeremy wanted to be home for dinner. He wanted to hold his baby daughter." Her insight serves to emphasize the human terms of the struggle and its motives, returning it to the world of real human behavior instead of the mythic terms in which it tends now to be seen.

The film also gains much power by using authentic audio recordings, which include the awful sounds of struggle from the cockpit as the hijackers attack the pilots. Several of the farewell phone calls placed by passengers are heard, impressive for the calm tones in which wives and mothers bid goodbye to loved ones. As in the other film versions, the filmmakers here rely on the 9/11 Commission Report, the audio tapes, and conversations with surviving family members to piece together a narrative version of what probably happened on board the plane. In cases where events are not documented, such as whether the passengers succeeded in getting inside the cockpit, the film's narrator tells viewers that the facts simply are not known, in contrast to *United 93* where some dramatic liberties are taken with the factual record. The film's narrator is Keifer Sutherland. When the film begins, a viewer might understandably think that Jack Bauer is doing the narration or that this is some wayward episode of *24*. The film opens with white letters against a black background, just as each episode of *24* does, as Sutherland in his Jack Bauer voice tells us that what we are about to see is based on real testimony. Sutherland's presence is a distraction, an aesthetic and even an ethical error, because his persona, so publicly identified with a fantasy-adventure show on terrorism, does some violence to the aura of authenticity that the film seeks to create and that the real participants in the interviews provide. Moreover, the gung ho, let's-torture-the-bastards persona of Bauer brings a political association to the film that the filmmakers, one might assume, are not interested in establishing.

PORTRAITS OF A HEROIC PRESIDENCY

Whereas *The Flight That Fought Back* aims for a balanced and even-handed portrait of the 9/11 crisis, other television films offered very positive portraits of the Bush administration's handling of the emergency. *DC 9/11: Time of Crisis* (2003) was produced and written for the Showtime cable network by Lionel Chetwynd, a writer and director (*The Hanoi Hilton* [1987], *Celsius 41.11* [2004]) who had attended the media strategy session convened by the White House in October 2001 with film and television personnel. The film's story takes place in a time frame lasting from the attacks of 9/11 to President Bush's speech to a joint session of Congress on September 20 in which he warned that any nation that harbors terrorists also sides with them and risks a U.S. attack. The film presents President Bush, played by actor Timothy Bottoms, as one of the greatest of presidents, ranking with Lincoln and Kennedy, a pillar of strength during a time of crisis, a leader who is calm, reflective, compassionate, and decisive. In one scene, during the President's first night back in the White House after the attacks, the camera pauses to linger on Aaron Shickler's painting of President Kennedy, which hangs in the Entrance Hall of the White House. The visual attention to the portrait emphasizes the continuity of mythic stature between the two presidents that the film proposes. The movie portrays a president who is deeply anguished and angered over the attacks and determined to protect the American people. He visits a burn victim in the hospital. She says weakly, "You will take care of us?" Bush replies, "You count on it."

The film's presentation of the President's reaction and motivation—anger and a desire to protect the nation from further harm—seems honest and true. It is the response that every chief executive would have. The problem is that, in creating this portrait, the movie massages and manipulates the factual record to produce an unrealistically flattering picture of how decisions were made. Many of the President's close advisers and cabinet members appear in the film, well played by actors who in many cases bear a startling resemblance to the people they are playing. But one figure that played a notable role that day is conspicuously absent, Richard Clarke, the counterterrorism czar from the Clinton years and who was still working, briefly, for the new administration. Just after the second tower was hit, Clarke initiated a teleconference at the White House involving officials from the FBI, CIA, the departments of State, Justice, and Defense, the FAA, and the underground bunker housing Vice President Cheney. Neither Clarke nor this videoconference is portrayed in the film. Perhaps it is because Clarke's published account of that day, *Against All Enemies*, paints a very unflattering portrait of President Bush. As I mentioned in a previous chapter, Clarke wrote that immediately following the attacks, both Bush and Defense Secretary Rumsfeld began focusing on Saddam Hussein, in seeming disregard of Clarke's insistence that al Qaeda was the culprit.

Indeed, the film finesses the whole question of Iraq and the 2003 invasion. It shows accurately that Rumsfeld and his deputy, Paul Wolfowitz, championed an invasion of Iraq in response to 9/11, but it has President Bush behaving in a manner very different from what Clarke has described. The film Bush resists their entreaties, puts the brakes on further discussion of that subject, and insists that everyone stay focused on Afghanistan. The film Bush says that Saddam will have to wait his turn. Moreover, in going down the path of war, the film's President exercises great caution and deliberation. He says that he has seen the 1960s and what happens when you go to war without adequately explaining why to the American people. "There's no room for Vietnam here," he says, a line that resonates now with an irony unintended by the filmmakers. Other lines about the coming wars resonate with unintended comedy, albeit of an unpleasant sort. The film President tells CIA director George Tenet to be very careful as to the reliability of the intelligence they will use to make the case for war. "There's no tolerance for error here," he says.

The omissions of Clarke as a character, his account, and other evidence suggesting that Iraq was quickly in the crosshairs are not the only important details left out of the movie. The airlift of Saudi nationals out of the country in the days after 9/11 evidently never happened. In drawing portraits of Bush, Rumsfeld, and Cheney at the time of the attacks, the filmmakers finesse and invent facts quite freely. The film shows a steely President projecting calm to the Florida schoolchildren, a portrait that is consistent with the President's claim to the 9/11 Commission that he remained in the classroom without responding to the news of the second strike because he didn't want to scare the children. Fair enough. But the existing factual record is mythologized in ways that obscure critical questions. The film shows the President retiring to a private room at the school, which he in fact did, and from there telephoning Rumsfeld at the Pentagon and ordering the military to go to Defcon 3, an upgrade in alert status rarely invoked. One of the only previous instances of Defcon 3 was during the 1962 Cuban missile crisis. The film President also says that Transportation Secretary Norman Mineta is going to ground the entire civil aviation fleet. The scene creates the impression that the administration was reacting quickly and decisively to the unfolding events. The problem is that these things never happened. Minetta didn't issue the grounding order. Ben Sliney, head of the FAA's Command Center, issued that order on his own initiative.

There also is no evidence that President Bush ever called Rumsfeld or the Pentagon. The President later stated that he made no decisions prior to boarding Air Force One and leaving Florida.[25] The 9/11 Commission wrote, "As far as we could determine, no one with the President was in contact with the Pentagon."[26] And Donald Rumsfeld's whereabouts that morning are unclear. The FAA, Clarke's group at the White House, and the Pentagon each initiated teleconferences after the second tower was hit, but as the 9/11 Commission reported, "Because none of these teleconferences . . . included the right officials from both the FAA and Defense Department, none succeeded in meaningfully coordinating the military and FAA response to the hijackings."[27] At the Pentagon, the National Military Command Center (NMCC) needed to assemble personnel to establish the military chain of command from the President to the Secretary of Defense, but Rumsfeld was unavailable. He had been in a breakfast meeting with members of Congress when the news broke about the first tower strike. He had returned to his office for a daily intelligence briefing when he received news of the second strike. According to the 9/11 Commission, he responded passively, resuming the briefing and "awaiting more information." When the Pentagon was hit at 9:37, Rumsfeld reported that he left his office, crossed over to the other side of the building, and went out into the parking lot to see what had happened. He then disappeared from communication for nearly an hour. The 9/11 Commission wrote, "At 9:44 NORAD briefed the [NMCC] conference on the possible hijacking of Delta 1989. Two minutes later, staff reported that they were still trying to locate Secretary Rumsfeld and Vice Chairman Myers."[28] Rumsfeld joined the conference at 10:30. (The 9/11 Commission noted a claim that the President had called Rumsfeld shortly after 10 A.M., but added "no one can recall the content of this conversation.")[29]

Rumsfeld's extended absence from communication and decision-making that morning is relevant to the Bush administration's violation of the chain of command in issuing shoot-down orders on United 93. The film depicts what the record shows, that Vice President Cheney ordered a shoot-down of the airplane. But this was not his decision to make or to execute on orders of the President. That role belonged to Donald Rumsfeld, as the President's second in the chain of command governing the military. According to the 9/11 Commission, Cheney issued the order, claiming that it was on authority of the President, sometime between 10:10 and 10:15, an interval during which Rumsfeld may still have been outside on the Pentagon parking lot assisting the wounded. Cheney claimed that, in a prior phone call, the President had given him the authorization. The 9/11 Commission wrote that there was no documented evidence of the call, but there was evidence of a call to the President for authorization *after* Cheney had given the shoot-down orders.[30] In the chronology of events assembled by the 9/11 Commission, no one in the White House bunker seemed to know that this order was not one that Cheney had the authority to issue and that it belonged to Rumsfeld, after the President. Cheney's aide, Gordon "Scooter" Libby, said that the Vice President reacted instantly, "in about the time it takes a batter to decide to swing." The broken chain of command that morning raises questions about who, exactly, was running the country during the immediate crisis of the attacks.[31] The film proffers a comforting scenario with its portrait of a strong and decisive President conferring with all of his people, but this portrait is not supported by the record of events.

Nor is the film's portrait of a fast-breaking terrorist threat against Air Force One. In the days after 9/11, White House officials circulated a story that a credible threat against Air Force One had been received and that the threat used code words indicating knowledge of the President's whereabouts. At a September 13 briefing, White House spokesman Ari Fleischer stated that the message said, "Air Force One is a target." It was this threat, officials claimed, that prevented the President from returning directly to Washington. But when pressed over the next week by reporters for documentation, the White House eventually acknowledged that there was no record of such a threat.[32] By September 26, Fleischer was refusing to comment at all on questions about the alleged threat. The filmmakers certainly were aware of these facts, but they chose to dramatize the original White House claim rather than the subsequent questions about whether there had actually been a threat. In the movie, the news of an impending attack on Air Force One is portrayed in an exciting episode that serves to emphasize the movie President's courage and grace under fire. That the claim may have been a fabrication to quell controversy over the real President's whereabouts on 9/11 is not something that the film considers.

FIGURE 5.3 In *DC 9/11: Time of Crisis,* President Bush (Timothy Bottoms) guides the nation through the 9/11 crisis with deep concern for preserving Constitutional freedoms while striking back at the enemy. (Frame enlargement)

The film's idealization of the administration's motives and policies necessitates that it minimize their controversial elements. There is much talk in the movie from the President Bush character about the need to develop a new playbook in order to fight a new kind of threat, and he exhorts his people to think in innovative ways about how the administration can go after terrorists. Indeed, the President did move aggressively in these ways. But the directions taken have raised enormous controversies over such things as the administration's authorization of secret, no-warrant wiretapping of Americans' domestic telephone and Internet communications and creation of a system of secret, open-ended detention outside the frameworks of civil and military law. These policies, and the President's claim that Congress's authorization for him to use all necessary force against enemies of the country gives him unilateral and supreme power, have raised ongoing Constitutional issues. The movie, though, shows a President who reveres the Constitution and who is deeply concerned about issues of freedom and liberty. In a conversation between the film's Bush and Condoleezza Rice characters, each dismisses the idea that U.S. foreign policy might have played any role in helping to motivate the attacks. The movie Rice tells her President that the terrorists didn't attack us because of our policies. Terrorists don't hate people for what they do, she says. They hate them for what they are. The movie Bush agrees, and says, "Modernity, pluralism, freedom—these are good things, Condi. Liberty is God's gift. It is not negotiable on this watch, and that is the policy." Cue swelling music as he then prays. In the real world, as distinct from the movie's portrait, a federal appeals court in 2007 ruled against the President's claim that he has the power to seize civilians in the United States and turn them over to the military for indefinite detention. The court noted, "To sanction such presidential authority to order the military to seize and indefinitely detain civilians, even if the president calls them 'enemy combatants,' would have disastrous consequences for the Constitution—and the country."[33]

A climactic and brilliant moment in the film's myth-building process comes at the end, in the scene of the movie Bush's speech to the joint session of Congress, where he lays out his doctrine of preemptive war and announces to the nations of the world, "Either you are with us or you are with the terrorists." As Timothy Bottoms, playing the movie President, enters the Senate and walks to the podium, several shots of the real President Bush are dropped into the scene. Bottoms begins the speech, and near its end, footage of the real President delivering the real speech suddenly replaces the movie actor. Bottoms does not reappear, and the film ends with the real President finishing his speech to wild and sustained applause. The conceptual and aesthetic design is dazzling and impressive. It is as if the frame of fiction, of theater as sustained by actors impersonating real people, can no longer contain the moral force of the speech's ideas and the President's aura. These break through the frame of theater in order to assert their own power. Through this device—the eruption of the real figures through the skein of theater—the film connects the authentic President Bush to the terms of the mythic portrait developed in the film and validates each in terms of the other. In the film's closing moments, "reality" legitimizes the mythic constructions that have been placed upon it. It is a very smart and poetic way to end the film, and the political symbolism is of a piece with the monumentality of its mythmaking aspirations.

THE POLITICAL TRILOGY

DC 9/11: Time of Crisis belongs to a trilogy of prominent made-for-television movies that aimed to honor the administration's handling of 9/11 and the subsequent Iraq War. *Saving Jessica Lynch* (2003) portrays the capture and rescue of the 19-year-old Army private, whose story became one of the most famous and fraudulent tales of American heroism in Iraq. Her group, part of the 507th Maintenance Company, was ambushed near Nasiriyah during which her vehicle crashed and she was knocked unconscious. Iraqi fedayeen captured her and eventually left her in a local hospital. News reports encouraged by the Pentagon portrayed Lynch as going down fighting, firing off round after round to protect her comrades, even after being hit by gunfire herself. According to these false accounts, she was then beaten and interrogated while in the hospital. In a subsequent investigation of its own reporting on the event, the *Washington Post* characterized the first news accounts in these terms: "Initial news reports, including those in *The Washington Post*, which cited unnamed U.S. officials with access to intelligence reports, described Lynch emptying her M-16 into Iraqi soldiers. The intelligence reports from intercepts and Iraqi informants said that Lynch fought fiercely, was stabbed and shot multiple times, and that she killed several of her assailants. 'She was fighting to the death,' one of the officials was quoted as saying. 'She did not want to be taken alive.'" The *Post* added, "It became the story of the war, boosting morale at home and among the troops. It was irresistible and cinematic, the maintenance clerk turned woman-warrior from the hollows of West Virginia who just wouldn't quit. Hollywood promised to make a movie and the media, too, were hungry for heroes."[34]

NBC hurriedly put together a movie version of the Lynch saga, and an NBC spokesman said, "This story is 'Mission: Impossible,' but it's real. It's uplifting, heroic, compelling and dramatic. You see this sort of thing in spy movies and wonder if it's really true. Now we know it is true."[35] Given the mendacity that surrounded the Lynch story and the way its fakery was used to promote the war, the film is not as misleading as it might have been. To its credit, it does not show Lynch engaging in a firefight or sustaining any gunshot wounds. She does not fire her weapon at all, which accords with the known facts. But in other respects, the movie offers a statement about American virtue in launching war on Iraq and in winning Iraqi hearts and minds. The story is cast as a captivity narrative, the oldest American literary form. Dating from the Puritan era in the seventeenth century, these were narratives about a virtuous white woman kidnapped by Indians and subjected to harsh treatment. The stories contrasted white civilization with Native American savagery, and the formula was adaptable to other situations where a battle of good and evil might be symbolized in a struggle over the fate of a helpless woman. Such movies as *The Searchers* (1956) and *Not Without My Daughter* (1991) exemplify the format.

Saving Jessica Lynch gives us a blonde young woman who lies helplessly in a hospital bed while American men plot ways to save her. "Bring her home, boys," Colonel Curry (Michael Rooker) tells his men as they raid the hospital. Safely aboard the rescue helicopter, Jessica pleads "Don't—don't let anyone leave me." Lynch's father tells his wife, "They found her. She's alive. They're gonna bring her home." She returns to a patriotic, flag-waving parade, a young woman restored, safely back among her own kind, freed from her ordeal among the dark-skinned foreigners.

One of these foreigners, however, according to the film, took heroic measures to save her. Mohammed al-Rehaief (Nicholas Guilak) sees her at the hospital being slapped by a swarthy fedayeen. He journeys to tell the American soldiers where she is because, he says, she looks so young and helpless. And Mohammed loves the Americans and believes that they are here to save Iraqis. Al-Rehaief, indeed, was an Army informant who disclosed Lynch's location, and he and his family were given asylum in the U.S. afterward. One of the film's closing images shows Curry shaking hands with al-Rehaief. It's an emblem of American-Iraqi fraternity and cooperation, a visual statement of the political ideal that has proven to be so elusive. *Saving Jessica Lynch,* then, embeds its captivity narrative within a fable about the winning of an Iraqi heart and mind in the character of al-Rehaief, and the film concludes with a double rescue, as Lynch and al-Rehaief and his family are airlifted from Iraq to America.

The most notorious film of the political trilogy is *The Path to 9/11,* which ABC broadcast in two parts on September 10 and 11, 2006. This was a rather audacious choice of dates, given that the film did not take an even-handed approach to the history it dramatizes. The lack of balance was surprising, given that the film was publicized as being based on the 9/11 Commission Report and other sources of factual evidence. 9/11 Commission cochair Thomas Kean even served as a consultant on the film and as a coexecutive producer. Nevertheless, the production aroused controversy even before it was broadcast, as advance copies of the movie circulated among reviewers. FBI agents who worked as consultants on the film criticized its lack of historical accuracy, and so, too, did members of the film's cast. Prominent figures in the Clinton administration, who were slurred in the film, disputed its depiction of events. Advertisers pulled their spots from the broadcast, and Scholastic Press, a publisher of educational material, ended its association with the show prior to broadcast.

Prominent historians including Arthur Schlesinger wrote an open letter to ABC stating, "This drama contains numerous flagrant falsehoods about critical events in recent American history. The key participants and eyewitnesses to these events state that the script distorts and even fabricates evidence in order to mislead viewers about the responsibility of numerous American officials for allegedly ignoring the terrorist threat before 2000. The claim by the show's producers, broadcaster, and defenders, that these falsehoods are permissible because the show is merely a dramatization, is disingenuous and dangerous given their assertions that the show is also based on authoritative historical evidence." The letter concluded, "A responsible broadcast network should have nothing to do with the falsification of history, except to expose it."[36]

Disney, the parent company of ABC, stood by the film through all of the controversy. Conversely, when Disney subsidiary Miramax was scheduled to release Michael Moore's *Fahrenheit 9/11* (2004) and the film was charged with being unfairly biased against the Bush administration, Disney refused to allow Miramax to release it, although it permitted Miramax to sell the distribution rights to an outside company unaffiliated with Disney. Shortly after *The Path to 9/11* was broadcast, its screenwriter, Cyrus Nowrasteh, wrote an opinion piece in the *Wall Street Journal* defending his work and charging that those who criticized it engaged in a "rush to judgment." He maintained that the film was scrupulously fair to the records of the Clinton and Bush administrations and that he worked hard to remain true to the factual record. "I felt duty-bound from the outset to focus on a single goal—to represent our recent pre-9/11 history as the evidence revealed it to be." He added, "we kept uppermost in our minds the need for due diligence in the delivery of this history. Fact-checkers and lawyers scrutinized every detail, every line, every scene. There were hundreds of pages of annotations. We were informed by multiple advisers and interviews with people involved in the events—and books, including in a most important way the 9/11 Commission Report."[37]

The film is an odd hybrid, an action thriller combined with a historical docudrama. The film claims to be based on the 9/11 Commission Report, and most of the characters appearing in the film are representatives of real people, such as FBI agent John O'Neill (Harvey Keitel), who investigated numerous al Qaeda plots and was eventually killed on September 11 at the World Trade Center. These elements give the film its claim to authenticity, and yet numerous scenes are presented as action sequences, as if they had fallen out of a Hollywood production. A character invented for the movie, a CIA agent named Kirk (not Mr. Kirk, or Kirk-with-a-surname, just the singular, mysterious "Kirk") is a dervish, turning up everywhere like a kind of super-agent, running down suspects in Africa, shooting it out with the Taliban in Afghanistan, launching a James Bond–style raid on bin Laden's headquarters, and tripping back to Washington to attend high-level CIA policy meetings. The James Bond–style raid is a fabrication by the film. In the scene, he is accompanied by Ahmed Shah Massoud, a Northern Alliance warlord the CIA was recruiting to fight the Taliban and take over Afghanistan. In fact, Massoud never accompanied CIA agents as part of a hit team targeting bin Laden, and the CIA lacked agents inside Afghanistan who could provide reliable information on bin Laden's whereabouts. This was the problem. Although President Clinton gave conflicting types of authorization for action against bin Laden, and several raids were planned and discussed, Clinton officials always pulled the plug before they got under way because they felt the information was not reliable enough. The movie, then, is partially correct, but takes considerable dramatic license in showing the Massoud raid ready to pounce outside bin Laden's compound.

The movie uses the 9/11 attacks as a tease to keep viewers involved. The film's first installment (broadcast September 10) opens with Mohammad Atta's team inside Logan Airport and then boarding American Airlines 11, which was the first plane to strike the World Trade Center. Factual errors occur almost immediately as the film portrays Atta triggering a CAPPS notification; the 9/11 Commission Report, the film's putative source, pointed out that Atta triggered this warning not in Boston but in Portland (Maine) when he was checking in for the flight to Boston. As American 11 takes off with the hijackers on board, the film flashes back to 1993 and the plot by Ramzi Yousef to bomb the World Trade Center. The first installment covers the Yousef plot and events through the overseas bombing of American embassies. In its closing scene, it jumps ahead again to American 11, with the hijackers putting on their red bandannas. As they move ominously toward the cockpit, the screen goes white, and a title appears, "To Be Continued . . ." Using the 9/11 attacks as a tease to hold the audience is a dubious ploy, to say the least, and it illustrates a deficiency of the docudrama format in relation to documentaries. The documentaries do not attempt to create suspense out of the tragedy, whereas *The Path to 9/11* renders the historical tragedy in terms of the storytelling conventions of melodrama and suspense.

The initial section of episode one is a fairly straightforward presentation of the 1993 bombing and the FBI's hunt for the perpetrators. The filming, however, is afflicted by the let's-pretend-we-don't-know-how-to-use-a-camera style that has become so prevalent in contemporary film and television. Shots are jittery, handheld, visually unstable, unframed, the content of scenes intruded upon by jerky efforts to re-center the action or by random, blurring whip pans that render everything a confusing smear of action. While the intended effect of this style is that fast-moving events are being caught on the fly, the barrage of visual curlicues undercuts the claim that the film is objectively based and a true accounting of events. The ornate, and in my view badly strained, visual surface of the film is an effort to give the dramatizations a documentary-like authenticity. The result is an ersatz you-are-there representation.

As events move into 1998, the movie bares its fangs for the Clinton administration in a startling fashion and with the disregard for facts that ignited the prerelease controversy. O'Neill and Kirk chat at CIA headquarters after

FIGURE 5.4 On ABC's *The Path to 9/11,* Harvey Keitel plays FBI agent John O'Neill, who tracked al Qaeda plots and who was killed at the World Trade Center. (Frame enlargement)

making a case for launching a raid to abduct bin Laden. Richard Clarke tells them that the administration is reluctant to sign off on the raid because "they're worried about political fallout if things go wrong, legalities, you know the drill." Kirk becomes incensed and says we're at war with bin Laden and the way to win is to take him out. O'Neill tells Kirk, "We're all in danger. The fact is that terrorism is perceived by this administration as being a law and order problem, period." Kirk asks, "How do you win a law and disorderly war?" O'Neill replies, "You don't." The remark is a condemnation of the approach that the film suggests was taken by the Clinton administration. In fact, President Clinton issued a kill order on bin Laden and gave it to the CIA. It authorized Afghan tribal leaders to eliminate him should they have an opportunity and be unable to capture him.[38] But then the following year he issued another MON (Memorandum of Notification) to a different set of tribal leaders, the Northern Alliance, which did not extend kill authority. It was a confusing state of affairs, but the administration was clearly exploring possibilities for action outside of a law-and-order framework.

To convey the idea that the Clinton administration was shirking its duties with respect to counterterrorism, the film cuts from the O'Neill-Kirk conversation to video and audio of Clinton's infamous lie about his affair with a

White House intern. "I want to say one thing to the American people. I want you to listen to me. I'm going to say this again. I did not have sexual relations with that woman, Miss Lewinsky." Imagery of the Washington Monument is intercut with imagery of Clinton making his false proclamation. The juxtaposition of the two scenes associates Clinton's dishonesty about sex with his administration's effort on counterterrorism. It's an ad hominem argument, in which Clinton's failings in the Lewinsky scandal furnish a basis for rejecting claims that the administration was serious about getting bin Laden. In a subsequent scene, Clarke tells O'Neill that with Clinton facing impeachment, he's not going to take chances on going after bin Laden. O'Neill responds, "It's pathetic."

A less strident assessment of this period in Clinton's presidency is offered by Steve Coll in *Ghost Wars,* his epic portrait of CIA operations in Afghanistan. Coll writes that, facing impeachment, "Clinton had neither the credibility nor the political strength required to lead the United States into a sustained military conflict even if it was an unconventional or low-grade war."[39] Moreover, whatever he did, he would be criticized. Following a Tomahawk missile strike on al Qaeda training camps and a Sudanese pharmaceutical plant, "Clinton and his aides came under withering criticism in Washington in the weeks after the missile strikes. Republicans and media pundits accused them of launching cruise missiles in a vain effort to distract public attention from Clinton's confession about Lewinsky."[40] If the film were even-handed in its approach, it might have pointed out that the Lewinsky scandal had crippled the presidency just as a real threat to the nation was emerging in the form of Islamist terror.

Instead, the film regards the Clinton administration's handling of bin Laden as cowardice, pure and simple, and a recurring theme throughout the first installment is that Clinton people lack balls. After the 1993 World Trade Center bombing, the FBI and NYPD want to go after Abdel Rahman, and one officer says in the film, regarding the needed clearance, "We'll check with Justice—see if Janet Reno has any balls." In a subsequent scene, O'Neill and his group raise their glasses in a toast to celebrate George Tenet's insistence that bin Laden be aggressively pursued. "To cojones," the group proclaims. In contrast to the film's portrait of Tenet, the 9/11 Commission found him to be chronically evasive in providing details of the agency's efforts to get bin Laden and continuously forgetful of important events and documents.[41] In his history of the CIA (*Legacy of Ashes*), Tim Weiner reports that Tenet turned down three opportunities in 1999 to hit bin Laden's location with cruise missiles. There is clearly plenty of blame to go around in both the Clinton and Bush administrations over the failure to capture or kill bin Laden, and this is why efforts to gang up on one administration or the other reflect partisan politics more than anything else.

During the aborted James Bond–style raid on bin Laden's headquarters in Afghanistan—a scene that is a wild riff on a never-executed 1998 CIA plan to snatch bin Laden from his Tarnak Farms bunker—Kirk calls in for clearance to allow his team to go ahead and abduct or kill their target. Sandy Berger, Clinton's National Security Advisor, not only refuses to give the clearance but he actually breaks off the teleconference rather than make a decision. The team has to abort, and a contemptuous Massoud asks, "Are there any men left in Washington or are they all cowards?" The film then cuts immediately to another video excerpt of Clinton's mendacious behavior, this time, his legalistic parsing of the meaning of "having sex."

The film's depiction of Berger breaking off the call was one of its most inflammatory details, and it elicited a letter of protest from the real Berger to the Walt Disney Co., which owned ABC. He wrote, "*No such episode ever occurred*—nor did anything like it. There is nothing in the 9/11 Commission Report (the purported basis of your film) to support this portrayal and the fabrication of this scene (of such apparent magnitude) cannot be justified under any reasonable definition of dramatic license. In no instance did President Clinton or I ever fail to support a request from the CIA or US military to authorize an operation against bin Laden or al Qaeda [emphasis in original]."[42] In fact, it was CIA director George Tenet who aborted the Tarnak Farms plan.[43] Moreover, it was Sandy Berger who had sent the 1998 MON with the kill authorization to Clinton for his signature.[44]

In *Ghost Wars*, his chronicle of the CIA in Afghanistan, Steve Coll writes that George Tenet never brought the Tarnak Farms snatch plan to Sandy Berger or President Clinton for approval. This was due to grave doubts within the CIA about the prospects for its success. Bin Laden's whereabouts were ambiguous, numerous women and children at the compound would likely be killed in the gunfire, and the Afghan tribal fighters recruited for the raid were an uncertain lot and would face daunting odds fighting their way into the camp. Coll writes that "all of the CIA's relevant chain of command . . . told Tenet the Tarnak raid was a bad idea."[45] But this more prosaic sequence of events doesn't have the melodramatic force possessed by a scene in which a mealy, risk-averse Sandy Berger turns down an urgent in-the-field request for a "go" from a gung-ho CIA agent who *knows* that bin Laden is in the camp. The irony inherent in the film's trashing of the Clinton administration is that Bush officials did no better in apprehending bin Laden. He escaped after the 9/11 attacks because President Bush put insufficient American forces (approximately fifty U.S. soldiers) on the ground in Afghanistan, and in 2005 the

Bush administration did exactly as the Clinton administration is depicted in the film as having done. It aborted a planned CIA raid on top al Qaeda leaders based in Pakistan. Donald Rumsfeld and other administration officials were afraid that the raid might offend Pakistani political leaders.[46] Both administrations proved utterly ineffective at dealing with bin Laden.

The Path to 9/11 depicts Secretary of State Madeleine Albright as another bin Laden enabler, giving Pakistan advance warning of U.S. airstrikes in 1998 on the al Qaeda training camps near Khost in Afghanistan. According to the film, Pakistan alerted bin Laden, and he slipped away. The film depicts Albright as arrogant and thick-headed, blind to the need for getting this adversary. Like Berger, Albright wrote to Disney challenging the veracity of the scene. The film's Berger and Albright characters are rendered as broad political caricatures, reminiscent of the cartoon villains that populate Sergei Eisenstein's films, such as *Strike* (1924) or *Battleship Potemkin* (1925). In Eisenstein's work, the villains were fat, cigar-smoking capitalists, but the cinematic tradition of broad-stroke political caricature is the same. And the continued hammering of Clinton is relentless. The film suggests that Berger's refusal to approve Kirk's raid on bin Laden led swiftly to the August 1998 U.S. embassy bombings in Kenya and Tanzania. The film juxtaposes news footage of the bloodied victims with Clinton on television solemnly announcing, "We will use all the means at our disposal to bring those responsible to justice," a claim that, according to the film, was a hollow one. There is no question that bin Laden was emboldened by the tepid response of the U.S. to his initial attacks on its soldiers and installations overseas. It was the failure of the U.S. to retaliate decisively against bin Laden that encouraged him to escalate the scale of his jihad, and both administrations shared in this failure. Thus, it is fair to say that the non-response of the Clinton administration to the bombing of the USS *Cole*, which took place three months before Bush took office, encouraged bin Laden to give the 9/11 plot the go-ahead. The Bush administration, too, could have responded to the *Cole* attack but did not, and it could have placed an overwhelming American force on the ground in Afghanistan in 2001 but did not. If the two administrations are to be compared, Richard Clarke's views are important to consider because he worked for both and because he was a proponent of the view that bin Laden was a dangerous adversary. Clarke wrote that the Bush administration regarded Clinton's concern with al Qaeda as excessive. "When Clinton left office, many people, including the incoming Bush administration leadership, thought that he and his administration were overly obsessed with al Qaeda."[47]

The second installment of *The Path to 9/11*, broadcast on the fifth anniversary of the attacks, begins with a three-minute tease. The hijackers take over

American 11, and flight attendant Betty Ong places her call to American's reservation center to report the hijacking. Boston contacts NORAD, and the teaser ends with a fade to white seconds before impact, as Ong ends her call, saying "Pray for us." Then we have a flashback to October 12, 2000, and a lengthy sequence dealing with the bombing of the USS *Cole* in Yemen.

The short tease is designed to reestablish narrative momentum and suspense after the day-long break separating the two installments. The device subjects 9/11 to the narrative demands of a television series format. Of greater significance, however, the teaser contains several distortions of fact. The film makes it seem as if Betty Ong is immediately patched through to American Airlines supervisors whereas the transcript of her call reveals an agonizing period of delay as ground personnel repeatedly asked her who she was, what flight she was on, mixed up the details of what she was saying, and asked her to repeat the information again and again, as if they either did not believe her or take it seriously. Boston Center did contact NORAD, but the film makes it seem as if this is standard procedure. In fact, this was the FAA's job, which it did not perform. The film shows a fighter jet scrambled and in the air before American 11 crashes. In fact, American 11 hit the North Tower before any jets were in the air.

These distortions create the reassuring impression of disciplined, coordinated, and efficient response from the various command centers to the crisis, a false impression that most of the television movies about 9/11 perpetuate. As NORAD scrambles its jets, a dispatcher talks with a pilot about rules of engagement, dialogue offered by the film as additional evidence of timely and prescient thinking by custodians of the air defense system. The dialogue is a case of extreme dramatic license. The existing protocol for a hijacking stipulated that, when asked for assistance by the FAA, the military would provide fighters to observe and shadow the errant plane from behind and at a distance. They were not to intercept or engage the plane. Hijackings typically ended with the stolen plane *landing* somewhere and demands being issued by the hijackers. On September 11, before American 11 hit the tower, there would have been no reason for anyone to assume that this hijacking would be any different, that it would not end in the traditional manner. Thus, for the film to invoke "rules of engagement" at this point—while American 11 is still aloft—in order to suggest that the need for a shoot-down is already evident is nonsensical.

The first long narrative sequence of the second installment deals with the investigation into the bombing of the USS *Cole*, and the Clinton gallery of villains—Sandy Berger, Madeleine Albright, and Defense Secretary William Cohen—offer the customary amount of interference and obfuscation to recommendations that the U.S. strike at bin Laden in retaliation for the *Cole*. Provoked by their do-nothing attitudes, the Richard Clarke character rants, "We haven't been provoked enough to fight back?" In his book, *Against All Enemies*, Clarke offers a less melodramatic assessment of this meeting than the behavior of his on-screen surrogate would suggest. He acknowledges being disappointed that his request for a strike was turned down but reports that he agreed with their assessment that Clinton's concurrent effort to broker an Israeli-Palestinian peace was more important. He wrote, "If we could achieve a Middle East peace much of the popular support for al Qaeda and much of the hatred for America would evaporate overnight. There would be another chance to go after the camps."[48] Moreover, the bombing of the *Cole* occurred three months before the end of Clinton's second term in office. The incoming Bush administration could have taken the necessary retaliation, but it did not.

The remainder of the second installment covers the flight training by Mohammad Atta and the other hijackers, the hijackings, the crashes at the towers, and the fiery interval before the collapse. In contrast to the dramatizations of Clinton administration perfidy, the film generally gives the Bush administration a free pass on 9/11. It does include a scene showing Secretary of State Condoleezza Rice telling Clarke that his position, as National Coordinator for Counterterrorism, would be downgraded, but the scene is so brief and so lacking in context—political, historical, or even narrative—that its significance as a portrait of the priorities of the incoming Bush administration is weakened. The real Clarke concluded from the meeting that Rice was unfamiliar with al Qaeda and was still operating within an old Cold War paradigm that saw threats as emanating from nation states rather than from geographically dispersed terrorist groups. And it was Philip Zelikow, subsequently the executive director of the 9/11 Commission, who collaborated with Rice in ousting Clarke.

The notorious Presidential Daily Brief of August 6, 2001, headlined "Bin Laden Determined to Strike in U.S.," appears briefly in the film, in a quick scene that shows Rice at her desk reading the report. Given all the controversy the report has aroused, and the legitimate questions about how the administration reacted to it, the film accords the report surprisingly little significance. And despite there being no evidence that the administration took any action in response to the threat contained in the report, or in the numerous other warnings that it received during summer 2001, the film includes a scene where Rice convenes administration officials in the White House Situation Room and tells them that, as a result of the August 6 PDB, the President believes al Qaeda is a real threat and wants to take real action against the group.

Rice tells the assembled military and intelligence officials that the President wants to know if an armed Predator drone is available to bomb the camps. The scene is deceptive. It creates the impression that the August 6 memo spurred the administration to action before 9/11. In fact, Rice and President Bush each told the 9/11 Commission that they accorded the August 6 memo little relevance because, they claimed, its contents were mainly historical, warning of past threats and telling them nothing they didn't already know. The Commission wrote that Bush "did not recall discussing the August 6 report with the Attorney General or whether Rice had done so. He said that if his advisers had told him there was a cell in the United States, they would have moved to take care of it. That never happened."[49] The Commission added, "No CSG or other NSC meeting was held to discuss the possible threat of a strike in the United States as a result of this report. . . . We have found no indication of any further discussion before September 11 among the President and his top advisers of the possibility of a threat of an al Qaeda attack in the United States."[50]

Given what the 9/11 Commission reported, the scene with Rice in the Situation Room where the August 6 PDB becomes a call to action is a screenwriter's invention. Rice did meet with the cabinet-level advisers on September 4 to discuss terrorism, the second of two meetings held before September 11. Much of the discussion focused on the Predator drone, but there is no evidence that the August 6 memo was the spur for the meeting, as the film has it.

The film takes similar liberties with its depiction of the whereabouts of Vice President Cheney and Richard Clarke on September 11. The film portrays Clarke as joining Cheney and Rice in the White House bunker and from there conducting his teleconference with the Pentagon and FAA. The impression created is of centralized, coordinated government decision-making, with key decision-makers gathered in a single room. In fact, Clarke reported that he conducted his teleconference in a Secure Video Conferencing Center on the ground floor of the West Wing. He requested an open line to Cheney, who was in the bunker with Rice, but apparently, as Clarke wrote in his book, Cheney kept hanging up that line. Clarke briefly joined Cheney in the bunker but didn't stay long. While there, he was told that Mrs. Cheney kept turning down the teleconference volume so that she could watch CNN. The film makes it appear as if the bunker contains high-level administration decision-makers. In fact, the personnel in the bunker were a curious assortment of Cheney advisers and family—Mrs. Cheney, adviser Scooter Libby, political pundit Mary Matalan, White House PR director Karen Hughes, Deputy White House Chief of Staff Josh Bolten, and Rice.

As discussed earlier in the chapter, the 9/11 Commission stated that no one in the bunker reported hearing Cheney receive shoot-down authorization from the President for United 93 before he barked out the order to take out the plane. Nevertheless, the film portrays a phone call in the bunker between Cheney and the President, after which Cheney tells everyone in the room, "The President has just given the shoot-down order." The filmmakers had to know that this was not the documented sequence of events. Dramatic license does not encompass such an excessive alteration of known facts, not in a film purporting to be a true account of what happened. But it does enable the film to create a portrait of the Bush administration as being more action-oriented than Clinton's, responding swiftly, effectively, and within the established chain of command to the fast-breaking events of September 11.

Probably the biggest failing of *The Path to 9/11* is its reliance on melodrama as the means for portraying and interpreting the emergence of Islamist terror and the events of 9/11. In the film's view of recent history, a series of bad guys suddenly begin popping up, seemingly out of nowhere, in New York and Afghanistan, and the authorities must play a game of whack-a-mole. Each time they knock a bad guy down, another one appears. The film leaves out the historical and political context in which these events are occurring and which the 9/11 Commission Report spent many pages discussing. The film, for example, does not portray the critical importance of the mujahideen's fight against the Soviet occupation of Afghanistan, nor does it portray CIA support, with Pakistan's ISI, for the Islamist guerrillas who later turned their ire toward the United States. Key players, such as Massood, are turned into figures of stock villainy or virtue. Massood tells super-agent Kirk that if he is assassinated, it will be a signal that bin Laden is coming and is about to launch an attack on America. Naturally, in short order, he is bumped off, and Kirk stares knowingly at the horizon. A more hyped or overheated dramatization would be hard to imagine. Through such crude plot devices, *The Path to 9/11* offered its public a melodramatically simplified interpretation of recent history and a selective parsing of events in terms of a partisan agenda.

DOCUMENTING THE CROSSROADS

Much fictional television programming offered viewers a variety of fantasy situations centering on bold heroes confronting terrorists in the nick of time. Most such shows were informed by the public's anxiety about potential attacks while simultaneously reassuring viewers that their leaders had things well in hand. But documentary also remained an important genre of television production, and numerous thoughtful examinations of terror and 9/11 were developed for the small screen. Indeed, several films examined in previous chapters—*In Memoriam: New York City, Off to War, Baghdad ER,* and others—were produced for cable television by HBO and the Discovery Channel. PBS also maintained high standards in the area of documentary and produced incisive accounts of Islamist terror, al Qaeda, and the Iraq and Afghanistan wars. Many of these films appeared on its *Frontline* series, which specialized in investigative journalism. PBS's most ambitious series was *America at a Crossroads* (2007), an 11-part portrait of the post-9/11 world focusing on the challenges of responding to the growing Islamist movement and the influence of al Qaeda. At its inception, the series was mired in controversy because it was planned during a period of internal conflict at the corporation, which had resulted from increased political scrutiny over the content of its programming.[51] In 2004 and 2005, PBS had installed executives charged with developing more conservative programming, and the chair, Kenneth L. Tomlinson, eventually resigned amid a scandal driven by revelations that he had been monitoring the political views aired on the corporation's programs. In a *New York Times* article about the series, Elizabeth Jensen reported that prospective filmmakers worried that the series would be politically manipulated by PBS to express views supportive of the Bush administration's policies. She also reported that affiliated station programmers were expressing some reluctance to air the films. And controversy dogged the series when its final products were aired. Writing in Salon.com, for example, Gary Kamiya virtually flamed the series by charging that it was a right-wing, conservative production. "If anyone still believes that PBS has a left-wing bias," he wrote, "'America at a Crossroads,' the $20 million, 12-hour series about Islam, terrorism and the post-9/11 world that kicked off Sunday night, should shut them up once and for all."[52] Kamiya chiefly found fault with the relative lack of coverage devoted to the U.S. foreign policies that have stoked Muslim rage. "The real problem is 'Crossroads'' almost complete failure to explore the history of the Middle East, the effect of Western policies on its people, and the political and historical grievances that are largely responsible for Muslim and Arab rage at the West."

Given the politically charged nature of the topics examined by the series, it would be plainly impossible for it to satisfy all agendas. In the end, taken as a whole, the package of films that emerged was balanced; it avoided partisanship; the points of view contained in the programming were diverse. There were conservative views on hand and liberal views. Robert MacNeil, the PBS commentator who hosted the series, expressed his confidence that the series will give viewers "a much more nuanced view of Islam."[53] Pro-administration films coexisted with episodes that were critical of current policies and their effects.

The series premiered on the PBS network in April 2007 during six evenings and began by providing a historical portrait of the emergence of Islamist radicalism. Drawing on interviews with an impressive range of Islamic and Western authorities, "Jihad: The Men and Ideas Behind Al Qaeda" (episode one) profiles the life and thought of bin Laden and his associate Ayman al-Zawahiri and traces their radical politics to Egypt's Muslim Brotherhood and to the writer and philosopher Sayyid Qutb, whom Johns Hopkins University professor Fouad Ajami calls the Lenin of the Islamist movement. Ajami explains that Qutb's two years in America, beginning in 1948, fed his neuroses about the West and that he left more anti-Western than before. Qutb was imprisoned following a botched assassination attempt on Egypt's President Gamal Nasser, and he was tortured in prison and executed by hanging. Mohammed Mahdi Akef, a leader of the Muslim Brotherhood, recalls the tortures that were common in Egypt's prisons, and General Fouad Allum, who was one of Qutb's interrogators and who witnessed his execution, states that in this period Qutb was fuming with hatred for the West. Before he was killed, Qutb penned *Signposts on the Road,* a manifesto condemning the materialism and spiritual bankruptcy of the West and that licensed jihad against it.

FIGURE 5.5 Osama bin Laden, interviewed in Afghanistan in 1988 by ABC News after bin Laden had issued his declaration of war against the United States. The footage appears in "Jihad: The Men and Ideas Behind Al Qaeda," part of the PBS series *America at a Crossroads.* (Frame enlargement)

Ayman al-Zawahiri joined the Islamist movement following Qutb's execution and described his death as the spark that ignited the cause of jihad. Zawahiri was thrown into Egypt's prisons and tortured because of his role in the plot to assassinate President Anwar Sadat. Montasser al Zayyat, Zawahiri's biographer, was imprisoned with him and describes on camera the tortures they experienced—electrocutions on the tongue, the lips, the nipples, the genitals, and a strappado-like form of bondage. Unlike Qutb, though, Zawahiri broke and named names, and the film posits that this humiliation was one of the factors that drove him so fanatically toward a program of political revenge.

The film contrasts what it describes as the spiritualism of authentic Islam with bin Laden and Zawahiri's emphasis on jihad as literal war. But unlike so many fictional movies where the terrorists are viewed as insane, bin Laden here is presented not as a madman but as a careful planner whose strategies, in the view of this film, have mostly worked, that is, have secured his goals and objectives. Journalist Gwynne Roberts interviewed bin Laden in 1996 and found him preparing for a global jihad against the non-Islamic West. Roberts says it was meant to be a war that will "stretch from China to Afghanistan to the Middle East to North Africa and then into the West. And I think it's a prophecy that really has come true." Khaled Batarfi, a childhood friend of bin Laden's, says that Osama wanted to provoke American attacks against Muslim countries. It was his script, Batarfi says, and the Americans went along with it. Ahmed Zaiden, of Al Jazeera television, reports that in February 2001 an al Qaeda strategist told him that they would try to drag Americans into a war in a Muslim country and that they thought the best places would be Afghanistan, Iraq, and Somalia. Michael Scheuer, who headed the CIA's bin Laden unit, concurs. "Did they want us involved in a war on the ground in Islamic countries? Absolutely. Part of the goal was to make sure that Muslims perceived America as the infidel invader of Muslim lands."

The conclusions that the film draws from this are not optimistic. Examining the effort to apprehend bin Laden in Afghanistan following the 9/11 attacks, the film points out that the Pentagon deployed only a handful of American ground troops and farmed out the major effort to Afghani warlords. Scheuer remarks, "The American generals had become bureaucrats and didn't want to risk any of their soldiers at Tora Bora." What followed is well known—bin Laden slipped away, across the border with Pakistan, which had not been closed by the Americans. The invasion of Iraq followed, and "Jihad" reserves its most trenchant remarks for this war, which it maintains had the effect of resuscitating al Qaeda from the defeat and dispersal it experienced in Afghanistan. Abdul Bari Atwan, the editor of *Al Quds*, an Islamic newspaper published in London, states that the invasion and occupation of Iraq was the revival of al Qaeda. Scheuer says, rhetorically, "The unexpected gift of the invasion of Iraq has really been more than bin Laden ever dreamed was possible." Batarfi remarks, "The American actions [in Iraq] were, I believe, exactly what Osama hoped for . . . it became a recruitment tool for al Qaeda and for the theology of al Qaeda."

According to the film, al Qaeda strategists had read Paul Kennedy's *The Rise and Fall of Great Powers*, a book that argued that empires collapse when they expand beyond their material limits. The film concludes by describing how bin Laden intends to draw the U.S. into wars in the Middle East that will bleed it economically. Scheuer calls this "the bleed-to-bankruptcy struggle," with bin Laden attacking to provoke the U.S. to respond in ways that cannot be economically sustained. The pessimistic conclusion implied by the film is that bin Laden is winning his war against America. "Jihad" takes bin Laden seriously, that is, it does not reduce him to the caricatured figure of a madman. Using video footage and interviews with people who knew or met him, the film shows that bin Laden is quiet, calm, and charismatic, qualities that inspire those who follow him. By taking bin Laden seriously, "Jihad" shows better than many other films why he is such a dangerous antagonist.

"Gangs of Iraq" offers a trenchant look at the rise of secret militias inside the U.S.-trained-and-equipped Iraqi police force and army. Beginning in 2005, the militias targeted Sunnis in a campaign of killing and torture that did much to ignite Iraq's civil war. During the height of the killing, fifteen to thirty bodies appeared on the streets of Baghdad each morning, many bearing marks of torture and mutilation so severe that the film crew turns away. The film's narrator fills in the details that remain off-camera. As one body is filmed from the neck down, the narrator says that the victim has no eyes, no ears, no nose—no face. The film examines the American inability to control the violence in this period. An unrestrained wave of Sunni bombings and Shia revenge killings was at odds with the optimistic pronouncements by Defense Secretary Donald Rumsfeld and others in the administration who routinely insisted that the war was being won. (This is the homegrown conflict that *Baghdad Hospital* portrays.)

The film shows that American forces insufficiently vetted recruits to the Iraqi police force and army. Many felt a loyalty to local sects and clans that was deeper than a commitment to something as abstract as a democratic Iraq. During the battle of Fallujah, for example, when Marines fought to break the hold of Shiite guerrillas on the city, many of the allied Iraqi army and police refused to fight and simply vanished, with some joining Moqtada al-Sadr's Mahdi army. In one scene, as American soldiers find a car bomb and a cache of weapons, the camera operator films Iraqi police talking among themselves. They say that what was found is small stuff, that there is a bigger weapons cache nearby. They don't share this information with their American allies.

In an effort to overcome the sectarian loyalties, American trainers tried to implant a sense of nationalism in the recruits. The film shows a sample training session, in which an American motivational speaker gives a pep talk to a room full of police recruits. The speaker begins in a forceful tone, "My name is Rick. I'm here to impose my American will on you." He then leads the room in a chant of "freedom," which he repeats numerous times with increasing emphasis. The recruits repeat the chant, as if this will instill the appropriate political value in their consciousness. But Rick's words must be conveyed by a translator. He is one of many Americans who can't speak the language of the culture he is meant to be helping. The scene shares much in common with other documentary portraits of the American intervention. It shows the limitations of an effort to remake a foreign culture by those who do not understand it and cannot speak its tongue.

As the militias' campaign of killing gets under way in 2005 and 2006, Coalition forces discover numerous secret torture facilities, some containing prisoners and bodies displaying conspicuous drill holes. General David Petraeus, commander of the police and army training program in 2004–2005, claims that there were no signs at the time of Shia militias developing in the Iraqi security forces. Bayan Jabr, the Shia Minister of the Interior, also denies any knowledge of the torture centers, and he makes a remark that suggests how deeply compromised the American effort had become. Seeking to avert his Ministry's responsibility for the torture facilities, he says that torture happens everywhere, in all wars, and that President Bush didn't know the details of what went on at Abu Ghraib. For Jabr, American policy does not offer a moral alternative to the Shia torture of Sunnis.

The film's grim conclusion is that, by purging Sunnis from the military and by arming security forces composed of Shiites, America facilitated the eruption of civil war, which in turn was fed by a cycle of revenge killings that assumed its own dynamic life. "Gangs of Iraq" reports the facts on the ground as they existed in 2006. But the facts are so bad that the political implications for the Bush policy in Iraq are unflattering, and this perhaps is why the film was paired with a second, more conservative take on the war. That film, "The Case for War: In Defense of Freedom," is unlike any other in the series in that it devotes an hour to the views of a single political lobbyist, Richard Perle, who was a key advocate for the war. In 2001–2003, he chaired the Defense Policy Advisory Board, which made recommendations to the Secretary of Defense. Urging that the U.S. attack Iraq, Perle claimed that Saddam Hussein and

Osama bin Laden were associates and that Iraq ought to be invaded as a matter of U.S. national security. "The Case for War" enables Perle to reiterate his arguments about the necessity for war with Iraq and to connect it with the global war on terrorism. In the film, he asserts, "We are in Iraq to help an elected government battle terrorism." He says, "In this film I'll try to show that we must continue the fight against Islamist terrorism. Despite the mistakes and setbacks, we are right to encourage individual liberty."

Few would argue that the United States ought not to fight against Islamist terror. The issue of controversy is whether democracy is best encouraged at the point of a gun, especially when it entails invading Muslim countries. In defense of such actions, Perle asserts, "We know that Saddam Hussein's intelligence apparatus trained al Qaeda terrorists." He says, "There were dozens of links. The people who say there were no such links are simply wrong."

Perle presents his views in a quiet, soft-spoken manner that is rhetorically attractive, but the views are almost entirely a matter of opinion and do not square with the reporting from the ground in a film such as "Gangs of Iraq." "The Case for War" is symptomatic of the charged political atmosphere in which *America at a Crossroads* was developed. The factual reporting in some of the films countered the administration's claims about the war, and series executives evidently sought a counterpoint and invited Perle to supply it. The result is the only film in the series to make a direct appeal to the viewer in support of existing state policies.

"Security vs. Liberty: The Other War" examines the administration's push for expanded powers of domestic surveillance. The film reviews the history of FBI and NSA surveillance on Americans during the Cold War and then takes up contemporary issues. One is the greatly expanded use of National Security Letters by the FBI in requesting phone, Internet, or library records, coupled with a gag order prohibiting personnel from reporting to others that they have received such a request. The film examines the February 2001 order by President Bush that secretly authorized the NSA to monitor domestic telephone calls without first obtaining a warrant under procedures established by the 1978 Foreign Intelligence Surveillance Act, and the film reviews the allegations by former AT&T employee Mark Klein that AT&T delivered a live feed to the NSA containing huge volumes of its customers' Internet traffic. UC Berkely law professor John Yoo, an architect of the Patriot Act and of legal briefs justifying torture, defends the need for bypassing FISA, arguing that requests for evidence by the FISA court are nuisances. "I've practiced before that court. You really have to have reason or evidence as to why you should be wiretapping this particular known individual by name." Technologies not in existence when FISA was created enable data mining, an ability to vacuum up huge amounts of telecommunications data. "Think about a world where we're facing an enemy we may not know all their exact names and all their exact identities. We may want to search different communication streams that we think have a high likelihood to have terrorists involved, but under the existing framework we can't do it."

In his book on law in the age of terror, Benjamin Wittes maintains that this is a very real failing with FISA. In a world where people already are leaving vast electronic trails from e-mail and other Web activities, Wittes suggests that a solution to the dilemma of how to handle this information is "to allow relatively liberal government access to data and to focus privacy regulation on the manner of its use and accountability for its use."[54] What Yoo in the film doesn't acknowledge is the potential for abuse inherent in any secret system of data gathering. This is why Wittes emphasizes a need for rules of accountability. The FBI, for example, has greatly exceeded the limits of the information it is legally entitled to gather. An internal FBI audit of 10 percent of the bureau's national security investigations from 2002 to 2007 found more than 1,000 instances in which data gathering violated the law or internal bureau rules.[55]

"Security vs. Liberty" does not reach a firm conclusion about whether the civil liberty trade-offs in the war on terror have been too severe. It leaves that conclusion to the viewer, but the overall tone is very cautionary. And John Yoo's final remarks are compelling. He points out that, should there be another devastating attack on the order of 9/11, then debates about civil liberties will go away amid pubic desire for a strong response. That he may be right suggests that our democracy is one of the assets endangered by the age of terrorism.

Other films in the series examine European views of American policies ("The Anti-Americans"), the Muslim Brotherhood ("The Brotherhood"), conflict between pro-Israel and pro-Palestinian views on American campuses ("Campus Battleground"), the 2003 train bombings in Spain and the 2004 murder of filmmaker Theo Van Gogh in Holland ("Europe's 9/11"), a portrait of the Islamic author Irshad Manji ("Faith Without Fear"), the growth of radical Islam in American prisons ("Homegrown"), America's global role ("Inside America's Empire"), the deployment of citizen soldiers ("Kansas to Kandahar"), the diversity of Muslim culture in the United States ("The Muslim Americans"), soldiers' writings about their wartime experience ("Operation Homecoming"), the responses of Muslim comedians to the age of terror ("STAND UP"), the role of Islam in Indonesia ("Struggle for the Soul of Islam"), and profiles of American soldiers in Baghdad ("Warriors"). As this range of material suggests, *America at a Crossroads* was television's most expansive effort to explore the challenges and complexities posed by Islamist radicalism and the wars in Iraq and Afghanistan.

Entertainment programming, by contrast, tended to be less judicious and calibrated in its responses to these problems. Television often channeled public fears into the formulas of pop culture. These served to domesticate the anxiety by absorbing it as a background element in an episodic comedy or drama series. Shows like *24*, *The Grid*, and *Sleeper Cell* helped to sustain public fears about new attacks so that these fears became an enduring part of the national zeitgeist. And a continuing, reassuring theme of this domestication of anxiety was that the security forces and public officials were a jump ahead of the terrorists. The overall lesson was that everyone should feel that their lives are directly threatened, that there would be no end to this threat, ever, and that government can be trusted to do the right thing and in a timely fashion. Writing in *MediaWeek* in 2006, A. J. Frutkin noted, "The events of Sept. 11, 2001, continue to impact network programming. From government conspiracies, to terrorist attacks, to bank robberies and abductions, a handful of fall dramas reflect a fictional world in peril—not unlike the real world that viewers see on the news every day. . . . 'The world is a much more dangerous place than it was ten years ago,' said John Rash, [advertising agency] Campbell Mithun's chief broadcast negotiator. 'And that sense of danger is reflected in what viewers see on the screen.' "[56]

While television produced numerous incisive documentaries on terrorism, its docudramas often reenacted key events from the standpoint of a partisan agenda, one favoring the Bush administration. These films produced for the small screen offered a counterpoint to the liberal and left-wing orientation of many Iraq War documentaries released in theaters. As this range of conflicting perspectives indicates, 9/11 and the events that followed had become political and emotional battlegrounds, where competing agendas waged a symbolic struggle on large media screens and small ones. The war on terror was being fought not only through government policy, law enforcement, and military action; it was being waged as well in this symbolic domain of mass media imagery, where films and programming aimed to constitute various publics around interpretive agendas claiming to make sense of recent history. If one believed that the Clinton administration was criminally negligent in responding to al Qaeda's early provocations, *The Path to 9/11* offered support for such views. If the Bush administration's policies raised viewers' hackles, quips by characters in series such as *The Grid* offered validation. The Iraq War was a noble venture (*Saving Jessica Lynch*) or a miscalculation that gave al Qaeda exactly what it wanted and needed ("Jihad: The Men and Ideas

Behind Al Qaeda"). A plethora of views were available for harvesting one's own opinions. There were enough that viewers could find a 9/11 or an Iraq War that fit their world view. And thus history became dispersed according to the demographic and political orientations of the target audiences. There was not a single Iraq War or 9/11; there were many, and their meanings were in contention, fought about and argued over in this symbolic domain of media imagery and narrative. Something similar was happening on large theater screens as well. Symbolic dramas were reconstituting historical experience and inflecting it according to contending moral and political frameworks. And these insured that the cultural experience of these events, played out over time, would be asynchronous and multivalent, in spite of and because of the galvanizing force of the events themselves.

CHAPTER SIX
NO END IN SIGHT

THE TITLE OF THIS CONCLUDING chapter derives from Charles Ferguson's documentary about the Bush administration's handling of the American occupation of Iraq. *No End in Sight* (2007) traces the fateful decisions made by President Bush, Vice President Cheney, Secretary of Defense Rumsfeld, and CPA head Paul Bremer that helped to produce a flourishing insurgency in post-Saddam Iraq. Although the film's title refers strictly to America's open-ended and ongoing involvement in Iraq, in a broader context the "war on terror" itself shows no prospects for ending. Moreover, the manner in which the Bush administration waged it—according to a philosophy that the President may disregard existing law and the will of Congress and that the President's role as Commander-in-Chief during a time of war gives him supreme power to act unilaterally—has challenged the balance of power among the branches of government and has, paradoxically, created a crisis for Presidential authority. By failing to work with Congress to construct a comprehensive legal framework, one that would legitimate and authorize the new policies and strategies needed for an ongoing struggle against terrorism directed at the United States, the administration invited judicial intervention into its policies, including a potential for the Supreme Court to involve itself in the Presidency's conduct of foreign and military affairs. The Supreme Court's decisions on the detention policies at Guantánamo Bay point in this direction. The administration's disregard for involving Congress in designing a legal framework for detaining and interrogating terrorism suspects created a procedural bind that has persisted many years after 9/11. As Benjamin Wittes writes, if Ayman al-Zawahiri or Osama bin Laden were captured tomorrow, "we will still have nothing remotely approaching a consensus regarding what to do with them, where to do it, or what rights they should have."[1]

The Bush administration's aggressive and unilateral responses to 9/11 elicited great controversy and polarized the public's perception of their adequacy and justification. Not surprisingly, in such a charged atmosphere, the responses from filmmakers have been extensive and were sometimes surprising in the places where they surfaced. The Canadian film, *Away from Her* (2006), dramatizes the impact of an aging woman's dementia on her husband, who feels abandoned as Fiona (Julie Christie) slowly fades away. In one scene, Fiona watches television at the nursing home where she now lives. A newscast covers the Iraq War. Her own mind fading, she nevertheless murmurs about the Americans, "How could they forget Vietnam?" The scene proffers an irony that is quietly stated but powerful. Fiona's amnesia has swept away her connection to Grant, her husband, but she still has wits enough to identify the consequences of America's historical amnesia. (Gore Vidal calls the country the "United States of Amnesia.")[2] *Away from Her* has no political agenda; its focus is personal and existential. In this context the Iraq reference is startling, and it suggests that the legacy of 9/11 has reverberated across a landscape of film in diverse and unexpected ways.

THE LEGACY OF 9/11 FOR AMERICAN FILM

In looking for this influence, circumspection and restraint is advisable. Writing about the political inflection of contemporary movies, Joshua Clover warns against drawing parallels too quickly. Otherwise, everything can seem to be symptomatic of the present predicament. "The geopolitics decoder ring always works, and with a minimum of twiddles: 1–2–3 Baghdad! (Alternately, the count can go 9–11–New York!) Cinematic administrations are always dummies for the current regimes. . . . When we go out at night, terror is the order of the day."[3] But while proceeding cautiously is the best advice, sometimes proximity itself makes for compelling connections. News about the torture practiced by American forces at Abu Ghraib prison broke in April 2004, and the revelations coincided with a new and popular cycle of horror films that took torture as their subject. Sometimes called "torture porn," the films marked a return to the harsh violence of 1970s horror movies and away from the jokey self-consciousness that had taken root in the genre via the *Scream* franchise and other recent, satirical pictures. *Saw* (2004) and *Hostel* (2005) signaled the onset of this new cycle; their box office success inevitably produced sequels. *Saw Parts II, III, IV,* and *V,* for example, opened in 2005, 2006, 2007, and 2008.

These films focus on men and women who are kidnapped, held captive, and subjected to psychological and physical torture. But these are not CIA renditions; their tormentors are not after information. The torturers are doing it for pleasure and for money. While chained to a wall, a captive in *Saw* cuts off his own foot in order to escape. The victim has been kidnapped and abused by a criminal mastermind who enjoys inflicting cruelty on his designated victims. In *Hostel,* the victims are a group of young, mostly American men who are traveling through Europe as tourists. Visiting Bratislava, they run afoul of a professional ring of torturers, which operates a business catering to wealthy patrons willing to pay exorbitant sums for the privilege of being able to torture a victim to death. With topical resonance, the film establishes that Americans

FIGURE 6.1 *Saw* and other horror films depicting torture surfaced after the Abu Ghraib abuse photographs became public. The detentions at Abu Ghraib and Guantánamo Bay had placed the issue of torture on the public agenda, and popular culture responded. (Frame enlargement)

are the most expensive victims to buy; they are the ones most in demand, the ones that everybody wishes to abuse. This plot conceit can be seen as a transposition into horror film terms of the animosity that the Bush administration's policies—the attack on Iraq, the extraordinary renditions and torture, the extra-legal prisoner limbo at Guantánamo and the CIA's black prisons—elicited around the world. In *Hostel Part II* (2007), the desirability of inflicting torture on Americans apparently has increased. The ring mounts an international auction of torture rights on three recently captured Americans, and a clever montage shows a feverish bidding war breaking out around the globe.

Imagery in these horror films emphasizes the dark, dirty, squalid conditions in which the captives are held and their anguish at being cut off from all communication with the outside world and subjected to the power of others who have total control over their bodies. In these respects, the association of the imagery with conditions and events at Abu Ghraib prison, and at Guantánamo, is difficult to avoid. The documentaries *Ghosts of Abu Ghraib* and *Standard Operating Procedure* emphasize the stench and appalling filth of the prison and how the MPs themselves felt imprisoned along with their Iraqi captives. *Hostel* director Eli Roth, in fact, claimed that *Hostel* was about Iraq and prisoner abuse. But whether we grant him this claim as an intended meaning in *Hostel*, the context established by Iraq and the Bush administration's policies of torture inevitably inflects the films.

Even zombies were affected by the war in Iraq. Joe Dante's *Homecoming* (2005) imagines dead American soldiers returning from Iraq as zombies to confront the neoconservative architects of the war with their rage at having been sent to die for no good reason. The United Kingdom production, *28 Weeks Later* (2007), a sequel to Danny Boyle's popular *28 Days Later* (2002), portrays an England that has been decimated by a virus that turns its victims into raging, flesh-hungry zombies. With all of its victims now dead, the virus seems to have burned itself out. The American military leads a NATO force into England to secure and stabilize the country and to protect "friendlies," i.e., Brits who are not zombies. The Americans hole up in a secured compound they call "the Green Zone." This was also the name of the Republican Palace area in Baghdad where the Coalition Provisional Authority made its headquarters. The movie thus establishes that one of its gambits will be an allegorical rendering of the Iraq War. In the film, as surviving Brits are taken into the Green Zone, a soldier brags like a tour guide about the excellent facilities that are available inside the secured area. "We have hot and cold running water, 24-hour electricity, a medical center, a supermarket, and even a pub." As Rajiv Chandrasekaran explained in his portrait of the CPA headquarters, *Imperial Life in the Emerald City*, only the Americans inside Baghdad's Green Zone bubble had 24-hour electricity. "Everyone outside the Emerald City was receiving just twelve hours of power a day the summer after the Americans arrived. The light would be on for three hours. Then there would be a three-hour blackout." But "inside the Green Zone, air-conditioners chilled buildings to a crisp sixty-eight degrees . . . a team of electrical engineers was always on call. 'We've got twenty-four/seven reliability,' one of the engineers boasted."[4]

As in Iraq, the "friendlies" turn on the Americans. The virus reappears, and thousands of civilians the Army has come to protect grow enraged and attack the soldiers. "We've lost control," the commanding officer barks at his men, and he tells his snipers to fire at will. The ensuing sequence, showing the snipers firing into a crowd of panicked civilians, killing many, evokes numerous incidents in which American forces fired on crowds in Baghdad and in other Iraqi cities. On September 16, 2007, for example, Blackwater security guards sprayed gunfire into a crowded intersection, killing seventeen Iraqis and wounding twenty-seven. Three weeks later, another set of security guards working for the State Department blew the head off a woman driving a taxi and killed her passenger, claiming that the car had approached their convoy. The film's imagery of civilians decimated by high-powered rifle shots fired by soldiers who cannot distinguish friendlies from hostiles transmutes this topical context into the genre matrix of the horror film.

Other horror films, such as William Friedkin's *Bug* (2006), manifest a level of paranoia that resonates in a post-9/11 world. *Bug* is based on Tracy Letts' play of the same title, written in 1995 in response to the Oklahoma City bombing, but its interest in dark government conspiracies and its portrait of characters overcome by fears of attack connects as easily with post-9/11 anxieties. In M. Night Shyamalan's *The Happening* (2008), a mysterious toxin produces suicidal responses in its victims, and mass attacks employing the toxin are blamed on terrorists. The film explicitly evokes 9/11 in its opening scene wherein victims leap to their deaths from tall buildings. In showing the victims hitting the ground, Shyamalan offers a provocation—he shows precisely what the media coverage of 9/11 avoided showing.

The imprinting of the post-9/11 world onto American film is unmistakable, even if good sense needs to be used in seeking the outlines of this imprinting. Sometimes the imprinting is relatively blatant, as in *The Dark Knight* (2008), an installment in Warner Bros.' *Batman* franchise that depicts the Joker (Heath Ledger) as an anarchic terrorist bombing Gotham City and prompting authorities to resort to harsh interrogation methods and other extrajudicial means to stop him. The film's subtext is about what happens when civil and government authorities break the rules in their efforts to cope with terrorism. But it's doubtful that any of this was a factor in the film's stunning box office success. Instead, the presold popularity of the franchise, the special effects, Heath Ledger's flamboyant performance, and the entertainment values of anarchic violence and a vengeance-laden narrative were the probable draws.

The most significant long-term influence of the terrorist attacks of 9/11, and of the Iraq War that followed, is likely to be found in the provision of new templates for genre filmmaking. The influence here is potentially long-term because the imprinting can be relatively subliminal in ways that do not conflict with or compromise genre appeal and therefore posing less of a threat to box office returns. Genres are among the most stable and enduring forms of American filmmaking, proffering frameworks of narrative convention that audiences and filmmakers have been drawn to for generations. The terrorist attacks gave American film a new means for inflecting the conventional elements of existing genres. One of the clichés that arose in the aftermath of the attacks was the notion that now "everything had changed" and that Hollywood would no longer be able to make the same kind of action-oriented entertainments. This was a naïve idea, as many of the works examined in earlier chapters demonstrate. Hollywood has always cared more for the continuity of its successful filmmaking formulas than for the specifics of any given area of content. As such, these formulas are quite capable of absorbing many different domains of content, provided the underlying narrative structures are respected. Thus a film like *The Dark Knight* subtextually can be about terrorism in our contemporary world, but the draws for an audience are the generic elements of action and a vengeance narrative.

The feelings of violation at large in the culture and occasioned by the attacks of 9/11 seemed to surface in several revenge films that were released in 2007. The revenge format, and the extravagant melodrama that was inherent in it, could form an organic bond with the unhealed wounds of 9/11. The September attacks elicited a strong desire for vengeance throughout the country. Several firefighters interviewed in *Collateral Damages,* for example, talk about their need for payback. One says that he is not a violent man but that he would really like to rip the heads off the people who did this. Hollywood's vengeance-oriented films (of which *The Dark Knight* is a recent example) subjected their main characters to an egregious violation—the sudden, unprovoked murder of a loved one, precipitating shock, a period of grieving, and a loss of confidence by the hero or heroine in the sanctity and security of the world as it had seemed to exist. In *The Brave One,* Jodie Foster plays a New York talk show host named Erica Baine, who is deeply in love with her fiancé. They are about to finalize their wedding announcement—surely a harbinger of dark things to come—when a late-night stroll through the park leads them to cross paths with a gang of thugs that viciously beats Erica and her boyfriend. He dies; she recovers but with the loss of her self-confidence and joie de vivre. The old Erica had been in love with the city; now she is consumed with rage and a desire for revenge. She buys a gun and begins loitering in dangerous areas where her presence as a lone female invites attacks. She greets the attackers with gunfire and becomes adept at putting them down in an efficient and lethal manner. If this setup sounds like Charles Bronson in *Death Wish,* that's because it's an updated, feminist version of that classic vengeance scenario. *Death Sentence* (2007), another of the vengeance pictures, was based on a follow-up novel by *Death Wish*–author Brian Garfield. In *Death Sentence,* a mild-mannered insurance executive (Kevin Bacon) becomes an obsessed avenger after thugs murder his wife and son. In *The Dark Knight,* the Joker viciously murders Rachel Dawes (Maggie Gyllenhaal), whom Batman and Gotham's idealistic District Attorney Harvey Dent (Aaron Eckhart) both love. Her death unhinges each man, prompting each to seek revenge.

The unprovoked attacks on a loved one in these films are resonant evocations of 9/11 and its shattering aftermath. In *The Brave One,* although the film is set in Manhattan, the trauma of 9/11 is never mentioned. But once the thugs attack her, Erica's estrangement from the city and from her own past becomes profound. Her first monologue on returning to the job is all about fear, about how she languishes in its grip. She says that as she looks around the city everyone seems afraid. She mentions the anthrax scare, but not terrorism or 9/11. In the context of her recitation on fear, though, 9/11 is conspicuous for its absence, and the thugs' attack is the film's way of coding and transposing this event.

Many years after 9/11, Osama bin Laden is still at large, and numerous questions about the events of that day remain unanswered. The country finds itself bogged down in an unpopular war in Iraq that was presented by Washington as a way of striking back at al Qaeda. In this context, the violation and loss of trust dramatized in *The Brave One* resonate in multiple ways. The violation perpetrated by al Qaeda has accompanied a sense by many Americans that the Bush administration abused the nation's trust by launching a war on erroneous or false pretenses. The breach of trust that Erica experiences in an acutely existential way can be seen as connected not just with al Qaeda and its violence but also with the actions of policymakers much closer at hand. And in sublimating the toxic aftermath of 9/11 into melodrama, in detailing her grief and despair and anger, the film offers a correlative in the realm of the vengeance melodrama for the emotional fallout from 9/11.

War films, like horror films, offered filmmakers templates for reflecting on the post-9/11 world. Clint Eastwood's *Flags of Our Fathers* (2006), for example, was widely seen as a commentary on the Iraq War. The Eastwood film portrays the bitter experiences of three soldiers, plucked from Iwo Jima after their image is published in Joe Rosenthal's famous flag-raising photograph. The movie shows that the action in the photograph was staged for the camera and portrays the efforts of the War Department to send the men on a publicity tour, promoting them as heroes in order to keep public support for the war alive. Released late in 2006, after the Bush administration's determined efforts to sell the Iraq War had been amply documented, *Flags of Our Fathers* came to seem for many viewers and commentators a timely reflection on contemporary misinformation.

War films had become rather more difficult to make in the post-Vietnam era than they had been during Hollywood's golden age of the 1940s. For a very long time, in fact, Hollywood avoided making films about Vietnam. This changed in the 1980s, when there was a sudden proliferation of films about that conflict, most of which portrayed the war with great ambivalence, unlike the moral clarity that prevailed in Hollywood's World War II movies. In the nineties, Steven Spielberg's *Saving Private Ryan* (1998), and the emerging cultural perception of a "greatest generation" of pre-boomer Americans, offered an alternative, if nostalgic, view of America's role in world affairs and its victory in a war of moral and political certainties. But there was to be no turning back of the clock in real terms. The invasion of Iraq in 2003 and the long, debilitating debacle that followed invited comparisons with the Southeast Asian quagmire decades earlier. The apparent inability of the U.S. to win in Iraq, and the questionable performance of the Bush administration in making its case for war, made it difficult for filmmakers working in the genre to offer triumphalist narratives. Moreover, an awareness that the threat posed to the West by radical Islamic fundamentalism was itself a modern manifestation of a centuries-old conflict gave new salience to films set in the ancient world, such as *Troy* (2004), *Kingdom of Heaven* (2005), and *300* (2007).

Troy, for example, conceptualizes the legendary struggle between the Greeks and the Trojans in terms that are clearly inflected by the attack of the United States on Iraq. Agamemnon, the commander of the huge Greek army, is a distinguished and heroic figure of Homeric legend, whereas in the film he is portrayed as a power-hungry imperialist who longs to control the known world. Early in the film, an enemy on the field of battle tells him, "You can't have the whole world, Agamemnon; it's too big even for you." Agamemnon (Brian Cox) laughs with delight at this rebuke because he has taken many lands and many armies and knows that this kingdom, too, will fall before his power. He is building an empire through war, and he tells his brother, Menelaus (Brendan Gleeson) that, "Peace is for the women and the weak. Empires are forged through war." He's long had designs on Troy, located in northwestern Turkey. "If Troy falls, I control the Aegean," he says, sweeping his riding crop across the map of the known world.

In the film's version of this history, Agamemnon's war is a struggle for the control of a region that holds strategic value for world commerce. Parallels with the Bush administration's designs on Iraq, as drawn by the film, are blatant. As Troy was for Agamemnon, Iraq was a prize long desired by the neoconservatives in the administration, and its oil fields are among the largest untapped reservoirs of petroleum yet remaining. And just as the attacks of 9/11 gave the administration its grounds for launching the invasion, the path to war prepared by a campaign organized to emphasize a connection between Iraq and al Qaeda, so in the film does Agamemnon seize on his brother's dishonor (Paris of Troy has stolen Menelaus' wife, Helen) as a shame against all of Greece that must be redeemed. He launches his own version of "shock and awe," sending all the armies of Greece aboard 1,000 ships to attack the walled city. He intends for the sheer scale of this spectacle to intimidate the Trojans, just like what the U.S. intended its shock-and-awe bombing campaign to accomplish in Iraq in the days preceding the invasion. But Hector (Eric Bana), Troy's greatest warrior, refuses to be cowed by the might of the Greek empire and the scale of its weaponry. "You want me to look upon your army and tremble," he tells Agamemnon, adding, defiantly, "No son of Troy will ever submit to a foreign ruler." Hector's defiance has its own contemporary resonance. One of the strongest motivations for the insurgency in Iraq was precisely this idea of resisting domination by a foreign power. The documentary films examined in chapter 4 repeatedly observe the anger felt by Iraqi insurgents and nationalists for the U.S. army of occupation. Modern-day Iraq borders Turkey, so the region is appropriate to the political symbolism of the film's narrative. Troy in the film, however, is hardly trembling under a dictatorship; King Priam (Peter O'Toole) is portrayed as a benevolent ruler. He is no Saddam. There is no torture or oppression evident in the walled city, and yet the point of view constructed by the film invites the viewer to make this moral distinction between the rightness of defending one's homeland against foreign invasion and the rapacity of those political leaders who launch invasions of foreign lands. Mapping this distinction onto the Iraq War makes the film into an allegory that is critical of this projection of U.S. power. In this respect, the film's reinterpretation of the Greek leaders is strategic. According to Homeric legend, Agamemnon and Menelaus were principled leaders and war heroes. In the film they are vainglorious and headstrong. In Homeric legend, they survived to return to Greece. In the film, the attack on Troy leads to the downfall of each.

A very different inflection of ancient world history can be found in *300*, a digital effects–intensive retelling of the Battle of Thermopylae in which a small group of Spartans held a narrow pass against the invading Persian army of Xerxes I. The Spartans were eventually wiped out, but by holding the pass they bought time for a larger Greek army to assemble. It then defeated Xerxes in a naval battle, a defeat that marked the beginning of the decline of the Persian Empire. The movie's origins lie in a graphic novel by Frank Miller and in director Zack Snyder's fondness for *The 300 Spartans* (1962), an earlier movie version of the saga. The film's outré visual design, with severed heads and limbs flying through the air accompanied by big globs of digital hemoglobin, is tied to the violence and artwork of Miller's novel. But the film also works hard to encode the Bush administration's military policies toward the Middle East, specifically Iran and Iraq, into this ancient history. The film draws a stark distinction between the nobility of the Spartans and the perversity of the Persian invaders. The Persians exhibit all manner of sexual depravity and are depicted as a horde of primitive barbarians that threatens Greek democracy. They have enslaved huge, prehistoric beasts which they send into battle as giant weapons of destruction, and Xerxes is outfitted in a costume of chains that symbolizes the antidemocratic political force of his empire, which is out to enslave the world. Xerxes is also sexually ambidextrous, signifying both male and female in ways that the film views as disreputable.

By contrast, the film identifies Sparta as a cradle of democracy and justice. While King Leonides and his Spartans are on the field of battle, his wife makes an impassioned speech to the kingdom's political leaders that has a clear contemporary tone. "We are at war, gentlemen," she tells them. She asks that the entire Spartan army be sent to oppose Xerxes. "Send the army for the preservation of liberty. Send it for justice. Send it for law and order. Send it for reason." We are bonded together and made stronger by Leonides' actions, she tells them. Send the army for hope, that these actions will make a difference for our future, she says. The Persian Empire was centered in what is today Iran, and her stirring speech therefore can be seen as a contemporary call for war against America's enemies in the Middle East, typified in the movie by Xerxes as the stand-in for modern Iran. Cloaking the appeal to war in the language of democracy strikes a contemporary note because the Bush administration's attack on Iraq and its threats against Iran have been presented as defensive maneuvers to protect America's freedom and security and as efforts to spread democracy to foreign lands. In the film's closing political exhortation, one of Leonides' comrades assembles the larger Spartan army for combat and proclaims that Leonides and his men have sacrificed their lives so far from home (and the film reaches here for a political parallel with Americans

FIGURE 6.2 Depictions in *300* of the war between Sparta and Persia in the ancient world were symbolically encoded in terms of the contemporary face-off between radical Islam and the West. (Frame enlargement)

in Iraq) as a gesture meant for all of Greece "and for the promise this country holds." The rhetoric encodes the narrative with the administration's rationale justifying war in Iraq as a struggle against terrorism. "This day we rescue a world from mysticism and tyranny and usher in a future brighter than any we can imagine," he proclaims.

In these ways, *300* portrays the ancient world according to the templates of contemporary political conflict, and it provides an argument and a justification for waging war against Iraq and Iran. In the film's closing moments, religion, too, is invoked in a manner that points to a threat perceived in the modern world to Christianity from a resurgent Islam (though not in the story proper since Xerxes was not Islamic). Hitherto the appeal to war within the film has been couched in the opposition between reason and barbarian religion. But the film's closing shot shows Leonides dead on the battlefield, pierced through by numerous Persian arrows, with his arms spread out at his sides. The shot evokes the dual imagery of the Christian martyr St. Sebastian and of Christ crucified. This sudden appearance of Christian iconography positions the film as an allegory about the necessity of conflict between the modern West and Islamic expansionism, grafting a very different set of historical coordinates onto the events of the story. While in history the Persian Empire fell to the Islamic caliphate, in the film Xerxes and his army are rendered according to the West's contemporary fears. They therefore embody a kind of undifferentiated Islamic horde. The movie, then, is about a war between Christianity and Islam, and it advocates the case of the Bush administration for war on Iraq and toughness toward Iran.

Ridley Scott's *Kingdom of Heaven* (2005) portrays the war between Christianity and Islam in twelfth-century Jerusalem. The leprous King Baldwin IV

(Edward Norton) is an enlightened ruler who presides over a peaceful domain in which Christian, Jew, and Muslim coexist, but Guy of Lusignan, a French knight in line to be king after Baldwin, lusts for war with the Muslims. Abetted by Reynald of Chatillon (Brendon Gleason), his men attack a Muslim caravan, slaughtering everyone, and even killing the sister of the mighty Islamic warrior Saladin. The climax of the film is Saladin's attack on Jerusalem. The city is successfully defended by the film's hero, Balian of Ibelin (Orlando Bloom), who eventually surrenders to Saladin's superior numbers and is allowed to leave the city with honor.

Scott's decision to make this film, which deals with the Christian crusaders in the Holy Land, was certainly risky, given the contemporary face-off between radical Islam and the West. But the historical material in the film was carefully massaged to remove most potential points of friction, and the movie's overall point of view is very respectful of Saladin while being critical of Christian hotheads like Reynald and Guy who pursue war at all costs. Numerous elements in the film evoke the modern political landscape. En route to Messina, the port to Jerusalem, Balian passes a Christian zealot who shouts, "To kill an infidel is not murder. It is the path to heaven." This character voices the philosophy of contemporary Islamic terrorists, while transmuting it to the period's warriors for Christ. There are no Islamic zealots in the film to serve as the counterparts of the Christian warmongers, and in drawing a relatively one-sided portrait, the movie omits some of Saladin's ruthless deeds, such as the slaughter of those enemies who had survived the battlefield.

Mostly, the film seems to distance its heroes—Saladin and Balian—from religiously inspired violence. This gambit is a way of insulating the narrative from the no-win cycle of enmity between Muslim and Christian. Saladin emerges as more of a philosopher-warrior than a religiously motivated one, and Balian suffers a crisis of faith that causes him to take on a secular perspective. He adopts the philosophy of one of his father's most trusted knights (David Thewlis), that, while every lunacy tends to be carried out in the name of religion, true holiness lies in right action as guided by the head and the heart. Balian thus declares that Jerusalem must be a kingdom of conscience or be nothing, and in practice this is to be a conscience informed by ethical scruples rather than by religious creed. And so, when his chance comes to avoid a disastrous war, he behaves like a twit. When he is dying, King Baldwin offers Balian the throne, knowing that Balian will preserve the peace as Baldwin has done. Everyone knows that, if the kingdom goes to Guy, he will launch war on Islam. Under Baldwin's plan, Guy is to be executed, a fate he certainly deserves for breaking the peace by launching the caravan massacre. Yet Balian believes that, if he agrees to the execution, his scruples will be tainted, and so he refuses. He keeps his principles, and his distance from religion, and presumably a clear conscience. But, in fact, he is responsible for all those who die in the subsequent war with Saladin (which Guy, now king, has provoked). Balian is responsible because he could have avoided this bloodshed. The film does not hold Balian to task for this culpability—the narrative is too busy emphasizing Balian's purity and his disdain for the war-is-God's-will Christians who rule Jerusalem. So the "kingdom of conscience," personified by Balian, turns out to be a rather paltry thing and produces the very same outcome as those policies driven by the zealots.

Despite its visual spectacle, *Kingdom of Heaven* is finally a rather meek portrait of the historical antecedents of the contemporary contest between radical Islam and Western infidels. *The Kingdom* (2007) examines the conflict in contemporary terms and in ways that mark the return of the unabashed terrorism-as-entertainment film to Hollywood production for the first time since the pre-9/11 era. The terrorist action-adventure films examined in chapter 1 had been a staple of Hollywood filmmaking for many years, but the events of 9/11 temporarily complicated the viewing pleasures to be derived from huge on-screen explosions and the deaths of mass but anonymous victims. After the perceived box office failure of *World Trade Center* and *United 93,* the filmmakers of *The Kingdom* gambled that audiences would flock to a film about Islamic terrorist attacks on the West if it was packaged as an action thriller and a buddy movie with plenty of gunfire and explosions.[5] They were wrong. The film had a U.S. box office gross of only $47 million on a production budget that exceeded $70 million. The film's narrative is loosely based on the 1995 bombing of the Khobar Towers complex in Saudi Arabia, which housed foreign military personnel, and the ensuing investigation in which the FBI participated. The movie opens with the bombing of a residential compound for American oil workers in Riyadh, Saudi Arabia. The victims are enjoying a wholesome game of softball when the terrorists strike. It apparently isn't enough that they will be shredded and pulverized with shrapnel bombs. To emphasize the horror, the film first establishes that these are young, happy, handsome Americans enjoying a day in the sunshine in what they believe is a protected area. Their children frolic and play. The filmmakers seem to feel that the savagery of the attack would be diminished were the victims struck down while going about their ordinary pursuits rather than in the full flush of recreational bliss.

Because Americans were the target of the attack, the FBI dispatches a four-person team to investigate. Led by Ronald Fleury (Jaime Foxx), the team clashes with the insular nature of Saudi society, but Fleury establishes a friendship with a Saudi police colonel, Faris Al Ghazi (Ashraf Barhom), providing the story with the male bonding that its buddy-film structure requires. But, like Gunga Din in his alliance with the British, Faris is doomed by virtue of his good will toward the Americans. Before the inevitable happens, he accompanies Fleury and the other agents as they zoom around Riyadh in dark SUVs, collecting clues and exchanging gunfire with local terrorists. Eventually, they uncover the terrorist responsible for masterminding the bombing and blow him away. Case closed.

The movie strips away almost all political and ideological content from the conflict between radical Islam and the West. Although the film notes that the bulk of the 9/11 hijackers were Saudis, in a breathless opening montage that recaps seventy years of Saudi history in mere minutes, the movie steers clear of examining the U.S.-Saudi relationship in any detail or depth or in giving the terrorists any rationale for their actions beyond their generic status as bad guys. The Khobar bombers wanted the U.S. military out of Saudi Arabia, and Osama bin Laden has described his war against the U.S. as aiming for a similar objective. By contrast, the terrorists in the story are there simply as a pretext for motivating explosions and gunfights, and Fleury's simplistic, gung-ho attitude—"We're going to kill all of them," he tells his associate—provides a soothing solution to more intractable real-world problems. The Clinton and Bush administrations failed to get Osama bin Laden. The Iraq War provided a rallying call to jihad against America. The Taliban is resurgent in Afghanistan, and bin Laden and al Qaeda have reestablished themselves in Pakistan. In late 2007 and 2008, U.S. intelligence analysts had begun to warn that al Qaeda was reconstituting itself inside Pakistan, that its organizational command and control was robust, and that it was capable once again of carrying out attacks inside the United States. But rather than go and get them there, the U.S. hesitated, fearful of offending Pakistan, its nominal ally. Not until July 2008 did President Bush authorize attacks against al Qaeda militants inside Pakistan, but these have been carried out by CIA Predator drone aircraft firing missiles from afar. In contrast to these failures and tardy judgments in the campaign against terrorism, *The Kingdom* proffers a fantasy of striking back decisively and successfully. As one reviewer of the film perceptively noted, "Just as 'Rambo' offered the fantasy of do-over on Vietnam, 'The Kingdom' can be seen as a wishful revisionist scenario for the American response to Islamic fundamentalist terrorism . . . the film spins a cathartic counternarrative. After a murderous terrorist attack[,] a few of our best people—four, rather than a few hundred thousand—go over to the country that spawned the terrorists, kill the bad guys and come home."[6]

The Kingdom demonstrated that terrorism could provide new templates for genre filmmaking, in this case for action-adventure films. Subsequent productions also demonstrated that terrorism might form an organic bond with the formulas of popular culture. *Traitor* (2008) and *Body of Lies* (2008) are each about heroic American undercover agents aiming to penetrate secretive terrorist organizations. In *Traitor*, Don Cheadle plays an American Muslim who is an explosives expert working undercover for the FBI in an effort to bring down a Yemeni terrorist ring. In *Body of Lies*, Leonardo DiCaprio plays a CIA agent tracking a master terrorist in Jordan. Both films are cast as thriller narratives in which the heroes wage successful hand-to-hand combat against America's Islamist enemies. But these films are also notable for giving the story's Islamist adversaries stronger motives than had been customary in earlier productions. When the Jordanian terrorist captures DiCaprio, he tells the agent that he's waging jihad because of America's wars in Muslim lands, an entirely credible motive and one that may reflect the fallout in popular culture from America's unpopular war in Iraq.

While action and horror were the major genres affected by the aftermath of 9/11, a few comedies explicitly addressed the age of terrorism. Humor, however, was risky for studio productions because it might elicit controversy and accusations of bad taste in the midst of a long national nightmare. But by embracing comic bad taste, *Harold and Kumar Escape from Guantánamo Bay* (2008) directed notes of ridicule at the administration's extra-legal policies of incarceration for terrorist suspects. Trafficking in vulgarity and bathroom humor, the film is a sequel to *Harold and Kumar Go to White Castle* (2004). When Harold (John Cho) and Kumar (Kal Penn) try to light a smokeless bong on board an airplane lavatory, they are arrested as terrorists. Because Harold has Asian features and Kumar looks Middle Eastern, a zealous Homeland Security official (Rob Corrdry) suspects they are agents of an al Qaeda–Korea axis of evil, and they are thrown into the Guantánamo Bay prison, where the administration houses its high-security suspects. The movie's view of administration policy is conveyed with comic bluntness—a Homeland Security official wipes his rear with the Bill of Rights. But the political humor is not sustained nor always even very focused. The only kind of abuse or threat that Harold and Kumar encounter at Guantánamo is coercion by the guards to perform oral sex, a debasement not dissimilar from what might be found in ordinary prisons. Shackling, hooding, isolation, sensory deprivation—none of these practices are on display. But perhaps the filmmakers felt that being threatened with a "cockmeat sandwich" would elicit more laughs from the target audience.

War, Inc. (2008) aims to be a *Dr. Strangelove* for the present day. It strives for the black humor and satire of Stanley Kubrick's 1963 film about the Cold War policy of Mutual Assured Destruction but directed here at the Iraq War and the profiteering and privatization of military services that the administration made available to corporate clients. War rages in Turaqistan, with American forces headquartered at the Emerald City and the Tammerlane Corporation enlisted to provide private soldiers and build the infrastructure. Boasting of Tammerlane and the war, the Vice President (Dan Ackroyd) says it's "the first war ever to be 100 percent outsourced to private enterprise." The intended real-world models here are Vice President Cheney and the Halliburton Corporation. The fixer, dealmaker, and middle man between Tammerlane and the Turaqis, Brand Hauser (John Cusack), cynically defends the privatization of war. "Look, we've already kicked the shit out of this place. What are we supposed to do? Turn our back on all the entrepreneurial possibilities? Business is a uniquely human response to moral or cosmic crisis. Whether it's a tsunami or a sustained aerial bombardment, there's the same urgent call for urban renewal."

Naomi Klein's writings on the Iraq War in venues such as *Vanity Fair* and the *Nation* were a major influence on the film. Klein criticized the corporate privatization of the war and developed her ideas at length in the book, *The Shock Doctrine: The Rise of Disaster Capitalism*. The film aims to satirize what she has termed "disaster capitalism," i.e., profit-taking amidst crises that have been engineered for exploitation by business. But while the film's premise and setup are sharply satirical, the story itself, which involves a Turaqi rock star who wants to have a career in America, has little to do with the film's political targets and aspirations. By contrast, the narrative in *Dr. Strangelove* is organically connected with its satire of war policy in the nuclear era. As a result, *War, Inc.* stumbles and fails to sustain the comic terms of its political satire. Nevertheless, to date, the film remains a rare example of political satire in cinema employed as a vehicle for examining the age of terrorism.

A PRODUCTION SURGE IN 2007

Late year 2007 marked a turning point in American cinema's response to the fallout from 9/11. The Hollywood studio-distributors embarked on their most expansive and ambitious package of films to date and nervously watched the box office response. The latter was not encouraging, and the industry quickly reached its conclusion that 9/11 and the Iraq War were not viable topics for successful film production. *The Kingdom* was one of many films released in 2007 that placed their narratives explicitly in a post-9/11 world. *A Mighty Heart,* for example, portrayed the efforts of Pakistani and American officials to locate *Wall Street Journal* reporter Daniel Pearl after he was kidnapped in

Pakistan. With Angelina Jolie as Mariane Pearl, the film mainly focuses on her anguish as she awaits word on her husband's fate. Jolie is very restrained in the role, but the irony of the film's focus on Jolie-as-Mariane is that Daniel Pearl disappears—the film fails utterly to capture the man's personality, ideals, or relationship with Mariane. As his fellow *Journal* colleague wrote, "Danny himself had been cut from his own story."[7] The movie was evidently conceived as a star vehicle for Jolie, and the viewer learns very little about the facts of the story. A better and far more informative portrait can be found in HBO's *The Journalist and the Jihadi* (2006), which profiles both Pearl and Omar Shiekh, the London-educated Pakistani who was arrested for his kidnapping and murder.

This—2007—was the year when the floodgates seemed to burst, with films pouring out of Hollywood about terrorism and Iraq, most of them being released late in the year. Whereas *The Kingdom* exploited its topical framework for commercial ends, numerous other films seriously examined key aspects of the Bush administration's response to 9/11, such as the Iraq War and practices of forcible rendition and torture. *Rendition* (2007), for example, explores the administration's by-now well-publicized campaign to abduct terror suspects and fly them to countries where they can be "forcibly interrogated" or, in layman's terms, tortured. Renditions did not originate with the Bush administration, but their nature changed in these years because the arrests were now uncoupled from any criminal justice process. As two lawyers and legal scholars at the New York University School of Law write, "Before 9/11, renditions included a criminal justice process, either in the United States or another country. In contrast, individuals 'rendered' after 9/11 were never formally charged with a criminal offense or tried in a court of law. . . . Extraordinary rendition, instead, enables interrogation with coercive techniques and torture."[8] Amnesty International has reported that the destination countries have included Egypt, Jordan, Pakistan, Morocco, Saudi Arabia, and Syria.[9] In addition, the CIA has operated numerous "black sites," secret prisons where captured suspects may be held beyond the reach of any law. Amnesty International reported that black-site prisons may exist in "Afghanistan, Guantánamo Bay in Cuba, Iraq, Jordan, Pakistan, Thailand, Uzbekistan, and other unknown locations in Europe and elsewhere, including on the British Indian Ocean territory of Diego Garcia."[10]

In the film an Egyptian-born chemical engineer, Anwar El-Ibrahimi, is kidnapped by the CIA while changing planes en route from South Africa to Washington D.C., where he lives with his American wife, Isabella (Reese Witherspoon). He is taken to an unnamed country where he is beaten, electrocuted, and imprisoned in a tiny, windowless room. During the torture sessions, he gives up false information, and the beatings and abuse disgust a kind-hearted CIA agent, Douglas Freeman (Jake Gyllenhaal). Freeman conspires to free El-Ibrahimi, who is returned home safely to his wife and child. The film's story is based on the experiences of Maher Arar, a Canadian citizen snatched while changing planes in Washington on his way home. He was imprisoned and tortured in Syria and then released without any charges being filed.

While the film takes a somewhat critical stance toward rendition, its point of view remains muted and ambivalent. The country where El-Ibrahimi is taken is identified only as being in "northern Africa," creating a vague geography that tends to separate the events in the storyline from an actual world where renditions have occurred. This vagueness is part of a strategy within the film of trying to play to all audiences. The chief torturer in the country-that-is-not-to-be-named, for example, is portrayed as a family man who worries about his rambunctious daughter and runs the torture sessions dispassionately, without sadism. Although in the real world the CIA has collaborated in the administration's program of extraordinary rendition, the film's hero is CIA agent Freeman, who liberates El-Ibrahimi and who doesn't like the program of torture he has been asked to supervise. He openly questions whether the renditions have ever produced usable intelligence and objects that with each person you torture, you are creating a legion of new enemies. This is sensible advice, but as a result of the film's even-handed approach, it remains an open question whether the abuse of El-Ibrahimi would have been justified were he actually guilty of plotting terrorist offenses. It costs nothing to object to the torture of an innocent man. How would the film view things if, instead, El-Ibrahimi were a genuine adversary? Such a severe test of principle is beyond the film's vaguely well-intentioned ambitions.

Although *The Situation* (2007) had a very limited theatrical release and minimal publicity, it offers a sharp and intelligent portrait of life in the bubble of the Green Zone and shows the disconnected, culturally-out-of-touch world of the Coalition Provisional Authority in Iraq. Connie Neilson plays an American journalist covering the war and who has many friends among the Iraqi people that are affected by the turmoil. The movie shows why the American effort struggled so badly by pointing to the surreal quality of life inside the artificial bubble of the Green Zone, itself safely barricaded behind guarded walls from the realities of Iraq. The luxurious swimming pool in the Baghdad palace packed with CPA staffers and the American-style Chinese restaurant catering to back-home appetites belong to the same kind of absurdist portrait that Rajiv Chandrasekaran drew in his book, except that in each case the bizarre terms of the portrait are not exaggerated. War correspondent Dexter

Filkins wrote, "It was in the Green Zone that I would think the war was lost . . . it was when I was waiting for the bus outside the Rashid Hotel, watching the overweight American contractors, making more money than they'd ever dreamed of, saunter into the restaurant for dinner at 5 p.m."[11] (Chandrasekaran's satirical book was transmuted into *Green Zone* [2009], an action thriller by director Paul Greengrass and starring Matt Damon.)

In the Valley of Elah (2007) follows a retired military policeman, Hank Deerfield (Tommy Lee Jones), as he tries to learn the truth about his son's murder. Mike had been serving in Iraq, and when his unit rotates home, he vanishes from his military base. The Army thinks he's gone AWOL, but Hank soon learns that Mike has been murdered, his body chopped apart and then burned. Like Costa-Gavras' *Missing* (1982), which portrays a father's search for his son amid the U.S.-backed military coup in 1973 against the elected government of Chile, *Elah* offers a similar portrait of a father's loss of idealism regarding U.S. conduct overseas. Hank is a squared-away guy who has made the military his life and who believes that his son is a fine and honorable soldier. On his way to the base to find out what happened to Mike, he sees an American flag hanging upside down on a school's flagpole. The inept custodian did not know how to attach the flag to the pole. Hank shows him the proper way to do it and admonishes that an upside-down flag is a distress signal, a call for help. He says it means you are in so much trouble that you can no longer get yourself out of it.

Hank learns that his son was involved in drugs and enjoyed torturing Iraqi prisoners, and he learns that his son was killed by other soldiers in his own unit. Returning home profoundly disillusioned, Hank stops at the school and gives the custodian an American flag that had been in the Deerfield family for years. But now he instructs the man to fly it upside down. The camera pulls up and away, framing the distress signal in the foreground of the shot as Hank's truck recedes in the distance. The symbolism has the subtlety of a kick in the head—the Iraq War has led to Mike's undoing and to the nation's.

Home of the Brave (2007) also looks at the cost of the war felt by returning soldiers. Like *The Best Years of Our Lives* (1946) but without the World War II period's confidence in the rightness of the conflict, *Home of the Brave* examines the struggle by several returning veterans to adapt to civilian life and to reintegrate with friends and family back home. Will Marsh (Samuel L. Jackson) is a combat surgeon suffering a stress disorder; Vanessa Price (Jessica Biel) lost her hand in a roadside bombing; and Tommy Yates (Brian Presley) lost his best friend in combat and is jobless upon returning home. The movie examines the coping strategies of each character, and, unlike *In the Valley of Elah,* it offers no verdict or point of view on the war itself except for the compassionate regard for all the characters and the dilemmas in which they find themselves by virtue of having served in Iraq. *Grace Is Gone* (2007) also looks at the war's impact on families back home. John Cusack plays a father who learns that his wife has been killed while serving in Iraq, and the film portrays his efforts to communicate the hard truth to his children that their mother is gone. *Stop-Loss* (2008), which had been scheduled for release late in 2007, is yet another portrait of Iraqi veterans experiencing difficulties adjusting to life back home. It critiques the military's use of stop-loss, a contractual policy under which a soldier's deployment can be extended beyond the initial period of service. Critics have complained that this policy amounts to a back-door draft. In the film Staff Sergeant Brandon King (Ryan Phillippe) refuses to be stop-lossed back to Iraq, goes AWOL, and slips into Mexico where he will spend the rest of his life on the run.

The upside-down flag in *Valley of Elah* is clunky symbolism but also a heartfelt cry that America's role in Iraq is wrong. An equally passionate cry is Robert Redford's film, *Lions for Lambs* (2007). The title derives from an observation about the British army in World War I, namely, that never before had so many lions (the frontline soldiers) been led by so many lambs, i.e., the officer corps and the political leaders who tossed men into the inferno. The application of this metaphor to Iraq is clarified in the film—the men who serve are lions, while the civilian leaders who cast their lives into the furnace of war are the lambs who either never served in the military (Dick Cheney, Paul Wolfowitz) or who avoided active service by joining reserve units (George W. Bush). Freed by the privilege of their economic class from seeing war first-hand, the film suggests, the civilian leadership has willingly cast many idealistic young men and women into a lost and foolish cause. And this willful waste of young lives is castigated by the film even while it urges young Americans to be more vigilant and committed to the public, political life of the country.

Lions for Lambs is an advocacy film composed of three extended and intercut scenes. News reporter Janine Roth (Meryl Streep) interviews hotshot Senator Jasper Irving (Tom Cruise) about Washington's latest surge strategy for Afghanistan. Her liberal skepticism about Washington's claims is countered by Irving's canny ability to use the media to advance the administration's plans for sustaining the war. In a second segment, soldiers Rodriguez (Michael Peña, last seen as Will Jimeno in Oliver Stone's *World Trade Center*) and Finch (Derek Luke) are shot down in a remote Afghani mountain pass and beset by attacking Taliban warriors. In the third sequence, college professor Stephen

Malley (Robert Redford) tries to reclaim the passion and commitment of a smart but drifting student, Garfield (Todd Hayes), by telling him about Rodriguez and Finch, who had been promising students whose idealism led them to volunteer for service in Afghanistan. Malley venerates their commitment but disbelieves in the worth of the cause and of the Bush administration's leadership.

"Rome is burning," he tells Garfield, trying to provoke the student into some level of genuine commitment for an ideal or a cause beyond himself. Malley worries that the American democratic experiment is foundering, betrayed by administration duplicity and wars of choice. His remark that "Rome is burning" is meant as a diagnosis of the present. Those leaders who set the fire are irredeemable, he tells Garfield, but you don't want to be one of the many who stood around and fiddled while the inferno blazed.

Two other films about Afghanistan opened in late 2007. Directed by Marc Foster (*Monster's Ball*) and based on a popular novel by Kaled Hosseini, *The Kite Runner* portrays a friendship between two Afghani boys, Amir (Zekiria Ebrahimi) and Hassan (Ahmad Khan), which turns to tragedy when one of the boys is raped by a local bully and his friend does not intervene. This part of the story is set in 1978 just before the Russian invasion. The story jumps forward in time, and the remainder of the film follows Amir and Hassan as adults in 2000 and depicts Afghanistan under the grim rule of the Taliban, as Hassan returns to the country from the U.S. where he has been living. Hassan is searching for Amir and trying to redeem his past. Although the film is sensitively directed and acted, its depiction of Afghanistan and Pakistan in that period is curious for omitting the U.S. presence. The time frame of the story jumps over the period in which the U.S. was funneling weapons to the mujahideen and stops short of 9/11 and the U.S.-led attack on the country. In a widely read critique of the Hosseini novel and other works of literature that she calls manifestations of a "new Orientalism," Persian language and literature professor Fatemeh Keshavarz notes that they are very selective about the history that they show: "Indeed, the way this literature navigates its way through the Middle Eastern mess without running into the U.S. presence there is astounding."[12]

Charlie Wilson's War, the other Afghanistan-themed film, was directed by Mike Nichols (*The Graduate* [1967]) and aimed to soft-peddle its political subject by emphasizing the comic elements in the story. Tom Hanks plays the titular Texas Congressman who was instrumental in brokering the CIA effort to funnel weapons through Pakistan in support of Islamist fundamentalists fighting the Russians. The film portrays the venture as a noble patriotic effort and, like *The Kite Runner*, scrubs its history clean of geopolitical blemishes, such as the irony that Charlie and his team were arming soldiers who would become the enemies of the United States. In his *Newsweek* review, David Ansen aptly characterized this problem:

> *At the end of this story, any informed viewer knows, lies big-time blowback. Surprisingly, Nichols and Sorkin play this trump card timidly. Is this admirable restraint or cold feet? Are they afraid of spoiling the feel-good uplift of Charlie's victory with the harsh downdraft of history? It's as if "Titanic" ended with a celebratory shipboard banquet, followed by a postscript: by the way, it sank.*[13]

Unlike *The Kite Runner* and *Charlie Wilson's War*, which go some way to avoid politically unpleasant topics, Brian De Palma's *Redacted* takes an extremely hard-edged view of the war by going after the abrasive issue of atrocities against civilians. The film dramatizes a real incident in 2006 in which American soldiers raped an adolescent Iraqi girl and then murdered her family. De Palma shot much of the film to simulate the perspective of a mini-DV camera that one of the characters in the film uses to keep a video diary. He also simulated insurgent videos he had seen on the Web showing people planting improvised explosive devices and beheading hostages. And in a third visual perspective, other footage in the film simulates the look of a professional documentary focusing on American soldiers manning a checkpoint in Samarra. As these different optical perspectives suggest, *Redacted* is about how the war is filtered through visual imagery, and De Palma's point is that imagery of atrocities has been suppressed by mainstream media for political reasons. "The war has been redacted from the major media," he said. "We don't see the carnage, we don't see the innocent civilians killed. You can only find that kind of footage on the internet. That's what the architects of this war learned from Vietnam: get it off the mainstream media."[14]

As if to prove De Palma's point, CNN, HDnet, Skye News, and YouTube all refused to cooperate with the film. They did not allow De Palma to use their logos or news material, and a lawyer for HDnet Films, one of the production companies, told him that he had to fictionalize events rather than using true names and other real information. And the film's own images were redacted or censored. The film concludes with a montage of gruesome photographs showing real Iraqi victims of the war. Fearing litigation from the victims' families, the film's production company obscured the faces of the victims in the photos using thick black lines. About this alteration, which he did not approve, De Palma said,

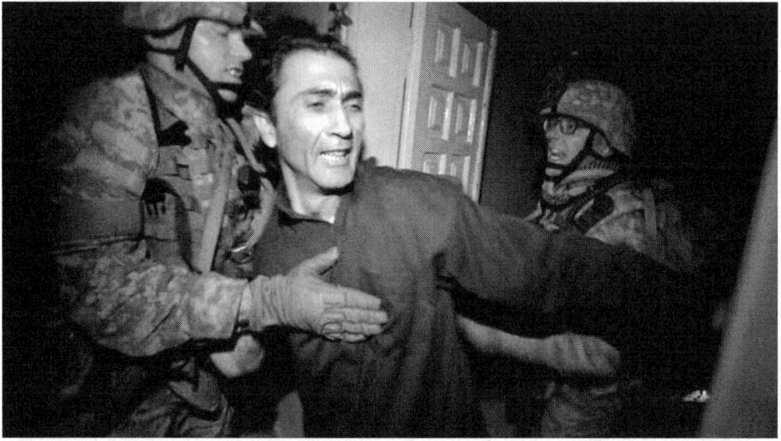

FIGURE 6.3 *Redacted* depicts a home invasion during which American soldiers arrest an Iraqi man as a suspected terrorist. In the first year of the war, such sweeps netted hundreds of detainees, swelling the inmate population of Abu Ghraib prison. (Frame enlargement)

> *Europeans are mystified as to why Americans are prosecuting this war, why there are no protests in the streets like the 60s. I say it's because they don't have the pictures. The pictures will stop the war. The irony is even these pictures have been redacted due to ridiculous legalities. E & O [errors and omissions] insurance has gotten skittish since 9/11 about insuring anything. They're worried about the relatives of the people who died in Iraq in the pictures. . . . You can't see these pictures in the U.S. and you hardly see them in my movie. Redacted is being redacted.*[15]

Hollywood's studios tend to measure a film's success or failure by its box office impact. In this respect, the feature films about Iraq and terrorism that opened in late 2007 did quite poorly, as I have discussed in the introduction. Their fate seemed to be a kind of repudiation by the moviegoing public about the topics that the films addressed. Was the public uninterested in the subjects? Or did the public prefer not to have them broached by theatrical feature films? Throughout 2007, Gallup polls showed that 60 percent of Americans felt the war had been a mistake. The films, then, seemed to be reflecting majority sentiment. In this respect, why they failed is unclear. Perhaps it was this very synchrony between their critical take on the war and public feeling about the conflict that killed them at the box office. Viewers seemed to be saying collectively that they didn't wish to be reminded about the war when they went to the movies. For Hollywood their collective fate was a kind of threshold event. The commercial failure of so many movies on the same topic sent a clear message, and Hollywood got it. The industry concluded that viewers preferred entertainment in their movie theaters rather than disquieting reminders of intractable realities. And as this lesson worked itself out over the next few years of film production, it promised to make it more difficult for filmmakers to connect their work with contemporary issues that are affecting all Americans.

Moreover, as these chapters have shown, apart from the huge outpouring of documentary filmmaking, the underlying forms of commercial American film maintained their primacy in a post-9/11 world. Popular genres in film and television readily absorbed 9/11 content as background material inflecting a storyline. Commercial film and television tended either to sustain public anxieties about terrorism or to provide reassurance that political leaders and security agencies were on the job and staying abreast of the latest threats. These were strategic responses by moving-image media to the post-9/11 context. Other responses were certainly possible. In her discussion of the still photography elicited by 9/11, Barbie Zelizer points to a singular function that, she claims, photography uniquely provides.

> *Photography is well-suited to take individuals and collectives on the journey to a post-traumatic space. The frozen images of the still photographic visual record are a helpful way of mobilizing a collective's post-traumatic response. They help dislodge people from the initial shock of trauma and coax them into a post-traumatic space, offering a vehicle by which they can see and continue to see until the shock and trauma associated with disbelieving can be worked through.*[16]

In her study of Holocaust photography, Zelizer emphasizes that photographs of atrocity are a form of bearing witness, by which people assume responsibility for events that have occurred. "Bearing witness constitutes a specific form of collective remembering that interprets an event as significant and deserving of critical attention."[17] Photographs of the World Trade Center engulfed in flames, or of onlookers staring with horror at the collapse, worked in this fashion. The huge proliferation of photographs, published in newspapers, magazines, books, and on the Internet in the immediate period after 9/11, manifested the process by which a social collectivity bore witness to the events. This visual record testified for all concerned of the enormity of what had happened.

Commercial cinema's participation in this kind of witnessing was more limited. The dramatic re-creations, such as *World Trade Center* or *United 93*, were informed by the visual and historical record, but they were not part of that record in the immediate terms of the photography discussed by Zelizer. They reconstituted the record in accordance with perceived audience interest and box office formulas. Thus, Oliver Stone's film became the story of two people who were saved rather than the nearly 3,000 who died. Filmmakers, too, might bear witness. Spike Lee certainly did so in *25th Hour*, but it seems doubtful that audiences for commercial feature films did so in the same way that they might attend to photographic coverage of the attacks or to a documentary. In fact, the weak box office of *World Trade Center* and *United 93*, and the commercial failure of all the post-9/11 films released late in 2007, suggest that viewers are rejecting the role that popular cinema might claim in bearing witness to atrocity.

If the limitations of commercial cinema are apparent in this regard, the documentary films about 9/11 and Iraq do fulfill the functions that Zelizer describes for still photography. Such films as *WTC: The First 24 Hours* (2001), *In Memoriam: New York City* (2002), and *7 Days in September* (2004) provide a visual record of the attacks and their aftermath, and as I noted in chapter 3, this record is valuable for containing information that was suppressed or minimized as an official story and point of view emerged in the major media. These films also are especially valuable for capturing and presenting the sights and sounds of that day, sensory details that are inseparable from the meanings and experience of 9/11 and from a viewer's ability to bear witness to those events. The roar of United 175 as it approaches the South Tower and the thundering blast of its impact evoked instinctual shrieks from onlookers and invocations of God. These are on film. Such details cannot be accommodated or conveyed by still photography. Moreover, unlike still photography, the documentaries capture the terrible duration of events, as the towers flamed for an agonizingly long time while people were trapped inside and while many leaped to their deaths, and then as everyone inside the buildings perished in the collapse. The filming of this interval amounts to a presentation of death in real time. People are dying on film and before the horrified gaze of the witnesses in the street and before the horrified gaze of the film's viewer. Experiencing this process over time through a viewing of the films constitutes an essential part of their claim to documenting history and of their ability to bear witness as a media document to atrocity. Viewing the films, in distinction to viewing the photographs, is to experience the temporal dimensions of this act of mass murder. Seeing the horror occurring over time, and according to many different visual perspectives captured by amateur cameras across the city and into New Jersey, is a singular and extremely powerful experience. A viewer who submits to this experience is bearing witness. Many of the documentaries viscerally capture this temporal process—such is their contribution to witnessing. It should not be minimized. This visual record will remain an indelible part of the historical record of 9/11. Those seeking to understand the events of that day will turn to journalism and to photography, but they will also, of necessity, turn to the documentaries whose images and sounds are seared by history. This is where a profound contribution by moving-image media to our collective memory and understanding may be found. In contrast, popular narrative film was somewhat less brave. It often averted its eye, and it also offered distraction. Mainstream commercial film also seized upon terrorism as a kind of godsend, as a trope capable of animating popular genres for the foreseeable future because the issues posed by terrorism presently show no end coming.

The intractability of these issues seems profound. We are living in the midst of what Jean-Paul Sartre would call an untranscendable horizon of experience. It is untranscendable because it inflects and conditions everything else and because no conceivable outcome to the set of dilemmas it poses seems readily apparent. The current standoff between the West and militant Islam may diminish in intensity. Walter Laqueur, for example, writes, "At present, Islamist terrorism all but monopolizes our attention, and it certainly has not yet run its course. But it is unlikely that its present fanaticism will last forever; religious-nationalist fervor does not constantly burn with the same intensity. . . . One day, it might be possible to appease militant Islam—though hardly in a period of burning aggression when confidence and faith in global victory have not yet been broken."[18] Yet while the conflict with militant Islam may conceivably diminish, terrorism itself will persist as a continuing threat and as an always-ominous one, especially in terms of threats from nuclear or biological weapons.

Living in the age of terror is comparable in this regard to living during the Cold War and under its continuing nuclear threat. Each period had a totalizing effect on those caught in it, and the end of the age of terror may require the kind of startling tectonic shift that the collapse of the Soviet Union provided the Cold War in the 1990s. But what that might be is far from clear. In the meantime, it will prove to be exceedingly difficult to get out from under the huge shadow cast on the national consciousness by September 11. Former Assistant Attorney General Jack Goldsmith has written that henceforth American Presidential administrations will be "Terror Presidencies," that is, they will be motivated by fear and will be occupied ceaselessly with efforts to prevent the next attack. He writes,

> *For generations the Terror Presidency will be characterized by an unremitting fear of devastating attack, an obsession with preventing the attack, and*

> *a proclivity to act aggressively and preemptively to do so. The threats have such a firm foundation in possibility, and such a harrowing promise of enormous destruction, that any responsible executive leader aware of the threats—be it the President of the United States, or the Boston police—must assume the worst. Every foreseeable post-9/11 President, Republican or Democrat, will embrace this attitude.*[19]

The effort by Presidential administrations to move preemptively will place pressure on Constitutional liberties and the boundaries of existing law. Goldsmith writes that David Addington, the Vice President's Counsel, told him, in regard to the special court established by the 1978 Foreign Intelligence Surveillance Act, which issues warrants for domestic wiretapping, "We're one bomb away from getting rid of that obnoxious court."[20] Some of the prognostications about where this pressure will lead are very pessimistic, even to the point of predicting a collapse of American democratic institutions as a surveillance-and-security state takes their place. Chalmers Johnson writes that America's commitment to keeping its global military empire will necessarily imperil its democratic heritage. "I believe that to maintain our empire abroad requires resources and commitments that will inevitably undercut our domestic democracy and in the end produce a military dictatorship or its civilian equivalent. . . . We are on the cusp of losing our democracy for the sake of keeping our empire."[21] Naomi Klein has argued that the Iraq War and the growth of security and surveillance industries are instances of a new form of global economy that she terms "disaster capitalism," which finds profit in crises and therefore a motive in helping to instigate them. The outcome is endless war. The Iraq War has proven to be hugely profitable for the contractors and corporations that partnered with the Pentagon. She notes that the security boom is rarely discussed as an economy with its own incentive to see the war on terror continue. The war on terror, she writes, is

> *limited by neither time nor space nor target. From a military perspective these sprawling and amorphous traits make the War on Terror an unwinnable proposition. But from an economic perspective, they make it an unbeatable one: not a flash-in-the-pan war that could potentially be won but a new and permanent fixture in the global economic architecture.*[22]

The market incentive "creates a powerful impetus to perpetuate the fear and sense of peril that created the industry in the first place."[23] Other apocalyptic outcomes are easily envisaged. One is another devastating terror attack that produces a huge number of casualties and leads to a nuclear war. This outcome involves the kind of terrific destruction that Hollywood's terrorist thrillers and disaster films have long been picturing and preparing audiences to imagine if not to accept. If, then, our present period is full of threat and what seem to be harbingers of doom, it is important as well to maintain a hopeful perspective, to, as Goldsmith writes, find ways to enable the Terror Presidency to work within a framework of democratic institutions. "In the permanent emergency we face, the best hope for preserving both our security and our liberty is to select leaders who will be beholden to constitutional values even when they are forced to depart from constitutional traditions."[24]

On November 4, 2008, American voters selected new leaders and brought one historical period to an end and ushered in another. The election of Barack Obama to be the forty-fourth President of the United States, by a significant majority of electoral college votes, signaled a widespread pubic desire for change after eight years under President Bush, an interval of time defined in large terms by 9/11 and its aftermath. The election was widely viewed as a statement of desire by a majority of voters for change and for a more hopeful future. The Bush administration had defined itself in large part through its responses to 9/11. The transition to a new administration, and one that promised to be rather different in its strategic response to crisis, offered an important form of closure on 9/11 and a means for moving forward.

The underlying narrative and generic forms of American film did not change in significant ways after September 11. Hollywood kept its genres and story formulas and readily adapted them to the new content of a post-9/11 world. Hollywood's fictional narratives proved to be far more resilient than commentators predicted in the immediate aftermath of the September attacks. Recall James W. Hall's observation that September 11 had changed storytelling in America forever. Forever proved shorter than ever. In 2007 in *Live Free and Die Hard* Bruce Willis was wisecracking his way through a series of supernova explosions decimating office buildings, helicopters, and other props of the urban infrastructure. But if the story formulas seemed impregnable, great films were nevertheless made and usually by filmmakers who were uninterested in working inside the prevailing formulas. Many significant films were made about 9/11 and its aftermath, and numerous filmmakers, most notably in the documentary tradition, stepped forward to use film in an inspiring way that connected it with the exigencies of its time and place. If, on the whole, American film and the industry proved capable of absorbing 9/11 into existing story conventions, it is less likely that we the audience have done so. Our world has been changed, and perhaps this accounts for the disconnection between Hollywood's fiction films and our present realities. We cannot get out of or beyond the age of terror. Hollywood's movies promise us otherwise—heroes and narrative denouements provide resolution and closure, an end point to anxieties that seem otherwise so inescapable. Perhaps Hollywood film will rise to the occasion as it came to do with the Vietnam War. Until then, the realm of nonfiction filmmaking stands forth as a glowing testament to the inspiring connections between film and life and that give the medium of cinema its best claim to being a profound form of human expression.

APPENDIX I
HISTORICAL TIMELINE

This timeline lists selected events, acts of terror, and the parties involved, as relevant to the history covered in this book. It also lists the terrorism-themed films discussed in the text that were in release each year. It is not a comprehensive listing of terrorist violence in the period. Numerous suicide bombings took place in Iraq, for example, after the start of the war in 2003, and they are not included here. Nor does the timeline list many of the films that referenced terrorism or the Iraq War in an indirect or metaphorical manner. The timeline is meant to assist the reader in forming a general picture of the sequence of major events and the films that portrayed them.

1979

December 24: The Soviet Union invades Afghanistan in support of its communist government, which is threatened by Afghan rebels who are angered by government policies that are perceived as being secular and un-Islamic.

Late December: President Carter approves a CIA plan to ship weapons to the mujahideen, the Islamic anti-Soviet rebels. President Reagan reauthorizes it. Under the plan, the CIA supplies weapons and money to the mujahideen, in cooperation with Pakistan's intelligence agency, the ISI. Congressional funding for the operation surges in 1984 and reaches $630 million in 1987.

1981

October 6: Egyptian President Anwar Sadat is assassinated. Ayman al-Zawahiri, who will become Osama bin Laden's close colleague in using terror against the West, is arrested for his role in the assassination plot. He is imprisoned and tortured.

Films in release—Fiction/Docudrama: *Nighthawks*

1983

April 18: A suicide bomber driving a truck containing a 400-pound bomb attacks the U.S. embassy in Beirut, Lebanon. Sixty-three people die, and 120 are injured. A group named Islamic Jihad takes responsibility.

October 23: The U.S. Marine Barracks in Beirut, Lebanon, is bombed by attackers using a van loaded with a 12,000-pound bomb. Two hundred forty-two Americans die.

Films in release—Fiction/Docudrama: *The Little Drummer Girl*

1985

June 14: TWA Flight 847 is hijacked, en route to Rome from Athens. A U.S. Navy sailor is murdered by the hijackers.

October 7: The cruise ship *Achille Lauro* is hijacked by the Palestine Liberation Front. The hijackers murder U.S. resident Leon Klinghoffer.

December 27: Terrorists with the Abu Nidal organization attack airports in Rome and Vienna with guns and hand grenades, killing sixteen people, including several Americans, and wounding more than 100.

Films in release—Fiction/Docudrama: *Invasion USA*

1986

February 1: The CIA creates an in-house group, the Counterterrorist Center, to track and attack terrorist cells.

September 26: Afghani mujahideen for the first time shoot down Soviet helicopter gunships using heat-seeking Stinger missiles that the CIA has supplied. The Stingers help to turn the tide of the war and persuade the Soviets that their losses are unsustainable.

March 30: TWA Flight 840 is bombed as it nears Athens, Greece. Four Americans are killed.

April 5: A Berlin discotheque that is a known hangout for U.S soldiers is bombed, killing two soldiers and injuring seventy-nine.

Films in release—Fiction/Docudrama: *Terminal Entry*

1987

April 24: A Greek bus carrying American servicemen is bombed, injuring sixteen.

Films in release—Fiction/Docudrama: *Wanted Dead or Alive*

1988

August: Operating along the Afghanistan-Pakistan border, Osama bin Laden helps to fund Islamist militias fighting the Soviet Union. Bin Laden holds a series of meetings during which al Qaeda is formed as an organization to promote the training of armed warriors for jihad.

December 21: Pan Am Flight 103 is bombed over Lockerbie, Scotland. All 259 people on board die. Libyan agents are believed to be responsible.

Films in release—Fiction/Docudrama: *Betrayed, Die Hard, Terror in Beverly Hills, Terror Squad*

1989

February 15: The Soviet Union withdraws the last of its forces from Afghanistan. A civil war follows among forces allied with the Soviet-installed government in Kabul, Afghan tribal warlords, and militias of Islamist jihadists.

1990

August 8: In Operation Desert Shield, the U.S. places troops inside Saudi Arabia to defend against a possible attack by Iraq, which has just invaded Kuwait. Osama bin Laden will cite the presence of U.S. troops on Saudi Arabian soil as one of his principal motivations for attacking the United States.

Films in release—Fiction/Docudrama: *Die Hard 2*

1991

May 21: A female suicide bomber who is a member of the Tamil Tigers uses an explosive vest to kill Indian Prime Minister Rajiv Ghandi. This is believed to be the first time that such a vest is used by a suicide bomber.

1992

April 16: Mohammad Najibullah, the communist president of the Soviet Union–supported Democratic Republic of Afghanistan, resigns. Before he is killed by the Taliban, he predicts that religious fundamentalism will make Afghanistan into a center for world terrorism.

Films in release—Fiction/Docudrama: *Under Siege*

1993

January 25: Mir Amal Kansi, a Pakistani, kills two CIA employees and wounds three as they sit in their cars at a stoplight, waiting to turn into CIA headquarters in Langley, Virginia. Kansi believes that CIA actions have harmed Muslims. He uses an AK-47 assault rifle in the attack. He flees to Pakistan, where the FBI captures him in 1997. He is executed in 2002.

January 25: Rabbi Meir Kahane, leader of the Jewish Defense League, is shot and killed in Manhattan. El Sayyid Nosair, an Egyptian-born American citizen, is arrested and charged with the killing. He is acquitted of murder but convicted and imprisoned on an illegal weapons charge. Nosair will also be indicted and convicted as a conspirator in the 1993 World Trade Center bombing.

February 26: The World Trade Center is bombed by an Islamist group led by a blind cleric, Omar Abdel Rahman. A Ryder van carrying the explosives is parked in an underground garage at the WTC. The bomb kills six and wounds more than 1,000. Ramzi Yousef, one of the ringleaders of the bombing, learned to make bombs in Afghanistan during the period when the CIA and Pakistani intelligence were supplying weapons and training to anti-Soviet Islamists.

1994

Films in release—Fiction/Docudrama: *Blown Away, Speed, True Lies*

1995

No date: In separate classified reports, the FBI and CIA each conclude that a new generation of Islamist terrorists threatens the United States. In its report, the CIA specifically identifies civil aviation as a possible terrorist target.

January 7: The Bojinka plot—a plan by Ramzi Yousef and Kalid Sheikh Mohammed to bomb eleven passenger airplanes and crash a jet into CIA headquarters—is discovered by Philippine police responding to an apartment fire. They find bomb-making materials in the apartment and a laptop computer that contains the details of the plan. Yousef had been involved in the World Trade Center bombing, and Kalid Sheikh Mohammed would be one of the masterminds of the 9/11 attacks.

April 19: The Alfred P. Murrah Federal Building in Oklahoma City, Oklahoma, is bombed. One hundred sixty-six people die and hundreds are injured in the deadliest terrorist attack to that time on U.S. soil. Two Americans—Timothy McVeigh and Terry Nichols—are arrested and convicted. McVeigh is executed, and Nichols is given a life sentence without parole.

Films in release—Fiction/Docudrama: *Die Hard: With a Vengeance, Executive Decision*

1996

January: The CIA's Counterterrorist Center opens a substation focused exclusively on gathering information about Osama bin Laden. This is the agency's first-ever unit to be focused on a single terrorist.

Spring: The Taliban, a fundamentalist Islamist group fighting in the Afghan civil war, takes control of the capital city of Kabul and proclaims the country the Islamic Emirate of Afghanistan. The Taliban remain in power until the U.S. invasion of 2001.

Summer: Having been stripped of his citizenship by Saudi Arabia and exiled, and having been recently expelled from Sudan, Osama bin Laden returns to Afghanistan and writes a declaration of war against the United States.

June 25: Khobar Towers, a military housing facility in Saudi Arabia, is bombed, killing 19 U.S. servicemen and wounding 515 people, including 240 U.S. personnel. The group responsible is not definitively known.

Films in release—Fiction/Docudrama: *Air Force One, The Devil's Own, Path to Paradise, The Peacemaker*

1998

February 23: Osama bin Laden writes the manifesto for the International Islamic Front for Jihad Against Jews and Crusaders, proclaiming that it is every Muslim's duty to fight and kill Americans.

Spring: The CIA develops a plan to kidnap Osama bin Laden from his Tarnak Farms compound in Afghanistan but calls off the plan.

August 7: The U.S. Embassy in Nairobi, Kenya, is bombed, killing nearly 300 people and wounding more than 5,000. Simultaneously, the U.S. Embassy in Dar es Salaam, Tanzania, is bombed, killing 10 and wounding 77. The U.S. holds Osama bin Laden responsible.

August 20: In retaliation for the embassy bombings, President Clinton orders that cruise missiles be fired at a suspected Osama bin Laden location near Khost, Afghanistan, and at a Sudanese chemical factory suspected of having financial ties to bin Laden.

August-December: President Clinton issues a series of Memorandums of Notification (MON) authorizing strategies of action against Osama bin Laden, including capture and the use of lethal force.

Films in release—Fiction/Docudrama: *The Siege*

1999

Early in the year: Kalid Sheikh Mohammed meets with Osama bin Laden in Afghanistan. Bin Laden accepts Mohammed's plan to fly airplanes into landmark buildings in America. One of the locations Mohammed suggests is the World Trade Center, which his nephew, Ramzi Yousef, had bombed in 1993.

Films in release—Fiction/Docudrama: *Arlington Road, Fight Club*

2000

October 12: The USS *Cole* is bombed while in port at Aden, Yemen. Seventeen sailors die and thirty-nine others are wounded. Al-Qaeda is thought to be responsible.

2001

January 20: George W. Bush assumes office as the 43rd President of the United States.

August 6: The President's Daily Brief, prepared by the CIA, is headlined "Bin Laden Determined to Strike in U.S."

September 9: Al Qaeda agents assassinate U.S. ally Ahmed Shah Massoud, a leader of Afghanistan's Northern Alliance, which is fighting against the Taliban.

September 11: Using three hijacked passenger airliners, terrorists destroy the World Trade Center in Manhattan and attack the Pentagon in Washington D.C. A fourth hijacked airplane crashes in Pennsylvania following a struggle on board between the hijackers and passengers. Altogether, 3,025 people die in the attacks. The U.S. holds Osama bin Laden responsible, and President Bush declares a global war against terrorism.

September 18: Congress passes the Authorization for Use of Military Force Against Terrorists. The resolution grants the President the ability to use all necessary force against those who planned and carried out the 9/11 attacks.

September 18: Beginning on this date several letters containing anthrax, a deadly bacterium, are mailed to the news media and to the offices of two Democratic senators. Five people are killed and seventeen are sickened. The White House suspects al Qaeda is behind the attack. Indeed, in June 2001 one of the hijackers sought treatment for a skin infection that may have been caused by anthrax. In 2008, however, the FBI identifies a suspect—Bruce E. Ivins—a microbiologist working in the Army's biodefense laboratory at Fort Dietrich, Maryland, and claims that Ivins acted alone. Ivins commits suicide before he is charged, and many doubts remain about the FBI's case against Ivins. To date, although the anthrax strain used in the attacks is thought to have originated in a U.S. military laboratory, the origins, motives, and authors of the anthrax attacks remain unknown.

September 20: President Bush addresses Congress and issues an ultimatum to the Taliban government of Afghanistan to close terrorist bases and turn over al Qaeda leaders residing in Afghanistan to the U.S.

October 7: The U.S. begins bombing Taliban and bin Laden strongholds in Afghanistan in the opening act of the war.

October 25: Congress passes the United and Strengthening America by Providing Appropriate Tools Required to Intercept and Obstruct Terrorism Act (aka the USA Patriot Act). President Bush signs it into law on October 26.

December 2: Al Qaeda member Richard Reid tries to blow up American Airlines Flight 62 using a shoe bomb. Passengers and crew members subdue him before he succeeds.

December 17: The last cave complex at Tora Bora in Afghanistan, where Osama bin Laden has been hiding, is taken by U.S. and coalition forces. Bin Laden is not found and is believed to have escaped to Pakistan.

Films in release—Fiction/Docudrama: *Collateral Damage, The Sum of All Fears, Swordfish*

Documentary: *WTC: The First 24 Hours*

2002

January 16: The first group of al Qaeda and Taliban captives arrives at the prison facility at Guantánamo Bay, Cuba.

January 23: Daniel Pearl, a reporter for the *Wall Street Journal*, is kidnapped in Karachi, Pakistan. He was investigating connections between al Qaeda and Pakistan's intelligence service, the ISI. Pearl is beheaded and his body found on May 16. Kalid Sheikh Mohammed claims to have killed Pearl.

May 8: José Padilla, a U.S. citizen, is arrested on terrorism charges, and President Bush declares that he is an illegal enemy combatant and therefore not subject to the authority of civilian courts. He is held in a military prison for more than three years on charges of plotting to detonate a radioactive "dirty bomb" inside the United States. The government eventually drops these charges and transfers his case to civilian courts. Padilla is convicted in 2007 of conspiring to commit murder in acts of jihad. His lawyers try to dismiss the case, alleging that he had been tortured while in prison.

August 1: Assistant Attorney General Jay S. Bybee submits a memo to Counsel for the President Alberto Gonzales stating that methods of interrogation that fall short of producing death, organ failure, or serious impairment of bodily functions are not torture. The memo also claims that Congress has no power to legislate procedures for the interrogation of enemy combatants. Any such laws regulating the President's ability to conduct interrogations of enemy combatants are unconstitutional. The memo becomes known as the "torture memo."

November 27: After months of refusing to authorize an investigation of 9/11, President Bush reverses course. The President and Congress authorize the National Commission on Terrorist Attacks Upon the United States (aka the 9/11 Commission).

October 10: Congress authorizes the use of military force by the President against Iraq.

Films in release—Fiction/Docudrama: *The Guys, Passenger 57, The President's Man: A Line in the Sand, 25th Hour*

Documentary: *In Memorium: New York City, 9/11*

2003

March 20: The Iraq War begins.

May 1: President Bush declares that major combat operations have ended in Iraq. He makes the declaration on board the USS *Abraham Lincoln* with a sign saying "Mission Accomplished" prominently displayed behind him.

August 25: Abu Ghraib prison opens as a U.S.-run facility in Iraq for housing prisoners and terrorist suspects taken during the Iraq War.

October-December: Prison abuse at Abu Ghraib is ongoing and is photographed by MPs.

Films in release—Fiction/Docudrama: *DC 9/11: Time of Crisis* (TV), *Saving Jessica Lynch* (TV)

Documentary: *Aftermath: Unanswered Questions from 9/11, Collateral Damages, Twin Towers, Uncovered: The War on Iraq*

2004

January 13: Joseph Darby, an MP at Abu Ghraib, reports prisoner abuse to military investigators and turns in copies of the photographs.

March 11: Four commuter trains are bombed in Madrid, Spain, killing 191 people and injuring more than 1,000. A Spanish inquiry concludes that a terrorist cell inspired by al Qaeda is responsible. The bombings are thought to have been an effort to topple the government of Prime Minister José Maria

Aznar, who had sent troops to support the U.S.-led war in Iraq. Three days after the bombings, the Spanish public voted Aznar out of office.

April 28: CBS's *60 Minutes II* airs the Abu Ghraib abuse photos. The story goes international.

June 7–8: The *Wall Street Journal* and the *Washington Post* obtain copies of the secret 2002 Bybee torture memo and publish stories stating that the Justice Department had advised the White House that torturing al Qaeda captives abroad may be legal.

June 28: In *Rasul v. Bush,* the U.S. Supreme Court rules that the prison at Guantánamo Bay is within United States territory, is therefore subject to U.S. laws, and that prisoners held there have the habeas corpus right to challenge their detention. In *Hamdi v. Rumsfeld,* the Court rules that American citizens held as enemy combatants are entitled to know the charges brought against them and to challenge those charges before an impartial judge. The Court rules that the military cannot detain an American citizen, held as an enemy combatant, for an indefinite period without due process proceedings.

July 22: The 9/11 Commission issues its final report, which provides a narrative history of the events of September 11 and the growth of al Qaeda and recommendations for reorganizing national intelligence gathering.

Films in release—Fiction/Docudrama: *The Terminal*

Documentary: *Buried in the Sand, Celsius 41.11, Fahrenheit 9/11, Fahrenhype 9/11, Inside Iraq: The Untold Stories, Last Letters Home, 911: In Plane Sight, Rush to War, 7 Days in September, Unconstitutional: The War on Our Civil Liberties, Voices of Iraq, WMD: Weapons of Mass Deception*

2005

July 7: Four Islamist suicide bombers attack a bus and three London Underground trains. Fifty-six people die, and more than 700 are injured. Two of the bombers leave videotaped messages condemning England's participation in the Iraq War.

July 21: A second wave of attempted suicide bombings of London transport systems fails when the detonators fire but the explosives do not go off. The bombers flee the scenes and are subsequently arrested by police.

Films in release—Fiction/Docudrama: *The Flight That Fought Back, Munich, V for Vendetta, War of the Worlds, The War Within, WTC View*

Documentary: *Baghdad ER, The Blood of My Brother, The Dreams of Sparrows, The Great Conspiracy, Occupation: Dreamland, Why We Fight*

2006

June 29: In *Hamdan v. Rumsfeld,* the U.S. Supreme Court strikes down the use of military commissions to try detainees held at Guantánamo Bay, Cuba. The court reasons that such commissions, established on executive order by President Bush, have no basis in federal or military law. The court rules that the proceedings must follow the rules of military courts-martial or that the President must request legislation to proceed differently.

October 17: President Bush signs the Military Commissions Act of 2006, authorizing trial by military commission for persons violating the laws of war. The act is intended to address the *Hamdan v. Rumsfeld* ruling.

Films in release—Fiction/Docudrama: *Day Night Day Night, Flight 93* (TV), *The Path to 9/11* (TV), *United 93, World Trade Center*

Documentary: *Combat Diary, The Ground Truth, Gunner Palace, Iraq for Sale, Iraq in Fragments, The Journalist and the Jihadi, My Country, My Country, 9/11 Mysteries, 9/11: Press for Truth, Off to War, On Native Soil, 638 Ways to Kill Castro, The War Tapes*

2007

January 11: The Director of National Intelligence announces that al Qaeda is reorganizing itself in Pakistan. He calls Pakistan a "safe haven" for al Qaeda.

February 19: American intelligence officials announce that Osama bin Laden and his deputy Ayman al-Zawahiri are building a base of operations in Pakistan's mountainous and remote tribal area known as North Waziristan. The chain of command inside al Qaeda has been reestablished, the officials conclude.

March 9–April 28: Combat Status Review hearings are held at Guantánamo Bay to determine whether fourteen high-value prisoners qualify for "illegal enemy combatant" status.

Summer: The National Intelligence Estimate, issued by the National Intelligence Council, concludes that al Qaeda has reconstituted itself and built a secure haven inside the mountainous tribal areas of Pakistan.

December 6: The CIA admits to destroying videotapes that it had compiled of detainee interrogations. The tapes depicted the waterboarding of Abu Zubaydah and other detainees. The agency had not disclosed the existence of these tapes to the 9/11 Commission during the period of its investigation.

December 27: Benazir Bhutto is assassinated in Pakistan while campaigning in upcoming elections. Bhutto had been prime minister twice before and was widely perceived as an ally of the United States. Although al Qaeda claimed responsibility for the killing, the parties responsible are not definitively known.

Films in release—Fiction/Docudrama: *Charlie Wilson's War, Déjà vu, Grace Is Gone, Home of the Brave, In the Valley of Elah, The Kingdom, The Kite Runner, Lions for Lambs, Live Free or Die Hard, A Mighty Heart, Redacted, Reign Over Me, Rendition, The Situation*

Documentary: *Alive Day Memories, America at a Crossroads, Ghosts of Abu Ghraib, Loose Change, Meeting Resistance, No End in Sight, Buying the War, Taxi to the Dark Side*

2008

February 5–6: CIA director Michael V. Hayden testifies that the agency used waterboarding on al Qaeda suspects in 2002 and 2003, and he identifies three prisoners on whom the torture technique was used. One was Kalid Sheikh Mohammed, one of the masterminds of the 9/11 attacks. The White House announces that waterboarding is a legal technique and that President Bush reserves the right to authorize its use according to future needs.

June 12: In *Boumediene v. Bush*, the Supreme Court rules that the Military Commissions Act of 2006 is an unconstitutional suspension of the right of habeas corpus and that detainees may challenge their detention in federal court.

August 12: The government's senior analyst at the National Intelligence Council states that al Qaeda's haven in the mountainous tribal areas of northwestern Pakistan has become increasingly secure, that al Qaeda is now more capable than in the past year of carrying out attacks inside the United States, and that it has trained dozens of agents capable of blending in to Western society in order to launch attacks.

September 3: American Special Operations forces conduct a ground assault inside Pakistan's mountainous tribal areas along the Afghanistan border, killing two dozen militants and civilians. In July, President Bush had approved commando raids against Islamist militants on the ground inside Pakistan.

September 20: Terrorists bomb the Marriott Hotel in Islamabad, Pakistan, killing more than 50 people. Officials view the attack as retaliation for U.S. attacks against militants on Pakistani soil.

October 9: A draft report released from an upcoming National Intelligence Estimate, scheduled to be concluded and made official after the November Presidential elections, concludes that Afghanistan is in a "downward spiral" and that the Taliban, which now control large parts of the country, cannot be defeated militarily by the Afghani government.

October 16: The U.S. and Iraq reach a draft agreement that calls for U.S. troops to leave Iraq no later than December 31, 2011. The pullout is contingent on the performance of Iraqi security forces at maintaining order in the country. The agreement also subjects private American security contractors to the provisions of Iraqi law in criminal cases.

October 20–22: Commentaries on al Qaeda Web sites celebrate the U.S. stock market's downward spiral as evidence that the wars in Iraq and Afghanistan are bankrupting the country. Al Qaeda and Taliban commentators also endorse Senator John McCain's candidacy for the Presidency, saying that he will be certain to continue "the failing march of his predecessor," President Bush.

October 26: The U.S. conducts its eighteenth airstrike inside Pakistan since August using CIA Predator drones deploying Hellfire missiles. American Black Hawk helicopters also strike inside Syria at militants conducting cross-border raids against American forces in Afghanistan.

October 31: Since July, militants opposed to Pakistan's alliance with the United States carry out more than 90 suicide attacks on civilian, military, and Western targets.

November 3: On the eve of election day, a poll by CBS News finds that President Bush's approval rating by the American public stands at 20 percent, the lowest Presidential rating since polling data has been compiled.

November 4: Democratic candidate Barack Obama is elected to become the forty-fourth President of the United States. He inherits wars in Iraq and Afghanistan and an al Qaeda that has reestablished a base of operations inside Pakistan.

Films in release—Fiction/Docudrama: *Body of Lies, Harold and Kumar Escape from Guantánamo Bay, Stop-Loss, Traitor, W., War, Inc.*

Documentary: *Baghdad High, Baghdad Hospital, 102 Minutes That Changed America, Standard Operating Procedure, Torturing Democracy*

APPENDIX 2
FILMOGRAPHY

FICTION/DOCUDRAMA

The Agency (TV, 2001–2003)

DIRECTORS: J. Miller Tobin, Peter Markle, Paul Michael Glaser, Nick Gomez

SCREENPLAY: Erik Oleson

CAST: Paige Turco, David Clennon, Will Patton

DVD: N/A

Air Force One (1997)

DIRECTOR: Wolfgang Petersen

SCREENPLAY: Andrew W. Marlowe

CAST: Harrison Ford, Gary Oldman, Glenn Close

DVD: Sony Pictures

Airport (1970)

DIRECTOR: George Seaton, Henry Hathaway

SCREENPLAY: George Seaton

CAST: Burt Lancaster, Dean Martin, Jean Seberg

DVD: Universal Studios, Goodtimes Home Video

Arlington Road (1999)

DIRECTOR: Mark Pellington

SCREENPLAY: Ehren Kruger

CAST: Jeff Bridges, Tim Robbins, Joan Cusack

DVD: Sony Pictures

Battle for Haditha (2007)

DIRECTOR: Nick Broomfield

SCREENPLAY: Nick Broomfield, Marc Hoeferlin, Anna Telford

CAST: Matthew Knoll, Eric Mehalacopoulos, Nathan De La Cruz

DVD: Image Entertainment

Betrayed (1988)

DIRECTOR: Costa-Gavras

SCREENPLAY: Joe Eszterhas

CAST: Debra Winger, Tom Berenger, John Heard

DVD: MGM/UA

Black Sunday (1977)

DIRECTOR: John Frankenheimer

SCREENPLAY: Ernest Lehman, Kenneth Ross, Ivan Moffat

CAST: Robert Shaw, Bruce Dern, Marthe Keller

DVD: Paramount

Blown Away (1994)

DIRECTOR: Stephen Hopkins

SCREENPLAY: Joe Batteer and John Rice

CAST: Jeff Bridges, Tommy Lee Jones, Suzy Amis

DVD: MGM Home Entertainment

Body of Lies (2008)

DIRECTOR: Ridley Scott

SCREENPLAY: William Monahan

CAST: Leonardo DiCaprio, Russell Crowe, Mark Strong.

DVD: Warner Home Video

Brave One, The (2007)

DIRECTOR: Neil Jordan

SCREENPLAY: Roderick Taylor, Bruce A. Taylor, and Cynthia Mort

CAST: Jodie Foster, Terrence Howard, Nicky Katt

DVD: Warner Home Video

Broken Arrow (1996)

DIRECTOR: John Woo

SCREENPLAY: Graham Yost

CAST: John Travolta, Christian Slater, Samatha Mathis

DVD: 20th Century Fox

Charlie Wilson's War (2007)

DIRECTOR: Mike Nichols

SCREENPLAY: Aaron Sorkin

CAST: Tom Hanks, Julia Roberts, Philip Seymour Hoffman

DVD: Universal Studios

Cloverfield (2008)

DIRECTOR: Matt Reeves

SCREENPLAY: Drew Godard

CAST: Lizzy Caplan, Jessica Lucas, T. J. Miller

DVD: Paramount

Collateral Damage (2002)

DIRECTOR: Andrew Davis

SCREENPLAY: David Griffiths and Peter Griffith

CAST: Arnold Schwarzenegger, Francesca Neri, Elias Koteas

DVD: Warner Home Video

Critical Assembly (MFT, 2003)

DIRECTOR: Eric Laneuville

SCREENPLAY: James Mills, Tom Vaughan, Carla Kettner

CAST: Katherine Heigl, Kerr Smith, J. August Richards

DVD: N/A

Dark Knight, The (2008)

DIRECTOR: Christopher Nolan

SCREENPLAY: Jonathan Nolan and Christopher Nolan

CAST: Christian Bale, Heath Ledger, Aaron Eckhart

DVD: Warner Home Video

Day Night Day Night (2006)

DIRECTOR: Julia Loktev

SCREENPLAY: Julia Loktev

CAST: Luisa Williams, Josh Phillip Weinstein, Gareth Saxe

DVD: IFC

DC 9/11: Time of Crisis (MFT, 2003)

DIRECTOR: Brian Trenchard-Smith

SCREENPLAY: Lionel Chetwynd

CAST: Timothy Bottoms, John Cunningham, David Wolos-Fonteno

DVD: Showtime Entertainment

Death of a President (2006)

DIRECTOR: Gabriel Range

SCREENPLAY: Simon Finch, Gabriel Range

CAST: Hend Ayoub, Becky Ann Baker, Brian Boland

DVD: Lions Gate

Déjà vu (2007)

DIRECTOR: Tony Scott

SCREENPLAY: Bill Marsilii and Terry Rossio

CAST: Denzel Washington, Paula Patton, Val Kilmer

DVD: Buena Vista Home Entertainment

Devil's Own, The (1997)

DIRECTOR: Alan J. Pakula

SCREENPLAY: David Aaron Cohen, Vincent Patrick, Kevin Jarre

CAST: Harrison Ford, Brad Pitt, Margaret Colin

DVD: Sony Pictures

Die Hard (1988)

DIRECTOR: John McTiernan

SCREENPLAY: Jeb Stuart and Steven E. de Souza

CAST: Bruce Willis, Bonnie Bedelia, Reginald VelJohnson

DVD: 20th Century Fox

Die Hard: With a Vengeance (1995)

DIRECTOR: John McTiernan

SCREENPLAY: Jonathan Hensley and Roderick Thorp

CAST: Bruce Willis, Jeremy Irons, Samuel L. Jackson

DVD: 20th Century Fox

Die Hard 2: Die Harder (1990)

DIRECTOR: Renny Harlin

SCREENPLAY: Steven E. de Souza and Doug Richardson

CAST: Bruce Willis, Bonnie Bedelia, William Atherton

DVD: 20th Century Fox

11'09"01–September 11 (2002)

DIRECTORS: Youssef Chahine, Amos Gitai, Alejandro Gonzalez Inarritu, Shohei Imamura, Claude Lelouch, Ken Loach, Samira Makhmalbaf, Mira Nair, Idrissa Ouedraogo, Sean Penn, Danis Tanovic

SCREENPLAY: Youssef Chahine, Sabrina Dhawan, Amos Gitai, Alejandro Gonzalez Inarritu, Paul Laverty, Claude Lelouch, Ken Loach, Samira Makhmalbaf, Idrissa Ouedraogo, Sean Penn, Marie-Jose Sanselme, Danis Tanovic, Daisuke Tengan, Pierre Uytterhoeven, Vladimir Vega

CAST: Maryam Karimi, Emmanuelle Laborit, Nour El-Sherif

DVD: First Run Features

Executive Decision (1995)

DIRECTOR: Stuart Baird

SCREENPLAY: Jim Thomas and John Thomas

CAST: Kurt Russell, Steven Seagal, Halle Berry

DVD: Warner Home Video

FBI Story, The (1959)

DIRECTOR: Mervyn LeRoy

SCREENPLAY: Richard L. Breen and John Twist

CAST: James Stewart, Vera Miles, Murray Hamilton

DVD: Warner Home Video

Fight Club (1999)

DIRECTOR: David Fincher

SCREENPLAY: Jim Uhls

CAST: Edward Norton, Brad Pitt, Helena Bonham Carter

DVD: 20th Century Fox

Flags of Our Fathers (2006)

DIRECTOR: Clint Eastwood

SCREENPLAY: William Broyles, Jr., and Paul Harris

CAST: Ryan Phillippe, Jesse Bradford, Adam Beach

DVD: Warner Home Video

Flight 93 (MFT, 2006)

DIRECTOR: Peter Markle

SCREENPLAY: Nevin Schreiner

CAST: Jeffrey Nordling, Brennan Elliott, Kendall Cross

DVD: UAV Corporation

Flight That Fought Back, The (MFT, 2005)

DIRECTOR: Bruce Goodison

SCREENPLAY: Phil Craig

CAST: Greg Benson, Jason LeGrande, Bryce Wagoner

DVD: Discovery Channel

Grace Is Gone (2007)

DIRECTOR: James C. Strouse

SCREENPLAY: James C. Strouse

CAST: John Cusack, Emily Churchill, Rebecca Spence

DVD: Weinstein Company

Grid, The (TV, 2004)

DIRECTOR: Mikael Salomon

SCREENPLAY: Tracey Alexander, Ken Friedman

CAST: Dylan McDermott, Julianna Margulies, Bernard Hill

DVD: 20th Century Fox

Guys, The (2002)

DIRECTOR: Jim Simpson

SCREENPLAY: Anne Nelson and Jim Simpson

CAST: Sigourney Weaver, Anthony LaPaglia, Irene Walsh

DVD: Universal Studios

The Happening (2008)

DIRECTOR: M. Night Shyamalan

SCREENPLAY: M. Night Shyamalan

CAST: Mark Wahlberg, Zooey Deschanel, John Leguizamo

DVD: 20th Century Fox

Harold and Kumar Escape from Guantánamo Bay (2008)

DIRECTOR: Jon Hurwitz and Hayden Schlossberg

SCREENPLAY: Jon Hurwitz and Hayden Schlossberg

CAST: Jon Cho, Kal Penn, Rob Corrdry

DVD: New Line

Home of the Brave (2007)

DIRECTOR: Irwin Winkler

SCREENPLAY: Mark Friedman

CAST: Samuel L. Jackson, Jessica Biel, Brian Presley

DVD: MGM

Homecoming (2005)

DIRECTOR: Joe Dante

SCREENPLAY: Sam Hamm

CAST: Jon Tenney, Thea Gill, Wanda Cannon

DVD: Starz/Anchor Bay

Hostel (2005)

DIRECTOR: Eli Roth

SCREENPLAY: Eli Roth

CAST: Jay Hernandez, Derek Richardson, Eythor Gudjonsson

DVD: Sony Pictures

I, Robot (2004)

DIRECTOR: Alex Proyas

SCREENPLAY: Jeff Vintar and Akiva Goldsmith

CAST: Will Smith, Bridget Moynahan, Alan Tudyk

DVD: 20th Century Fox

In the Valley of Elah (2007)

DIRECTOR: Paul Haggis

SCREENPLAY: Paul Haggis

CAST: Tommy Lee Jones, Charlize Theron, Jason Patric

DVD: Warner Home Video

Informer, The (1935)

DIRECTOR: John Ford

SCREENPLAY: Dudley Nicols

CAST: Victor McLaglen, Heather Angel, Preston Foster

DVD: Warner Home Video

Invasion U.S.A. (1985)

DIRECTOR: Joseph Zito

SCREENPLAY: James Bruner and Chuck Norris

CAST: Chuck Norris, Richard Lynch, Melissa Prophet

DVD: MGM

Juggernaut (1974)

DIRECTOR: Richard Lester

SCREENPLAY: Alan Plater and Richard Alan Simmons

CAST: Richard Harris, Omar Sharif, David Hemmings

DVD: MGM

King Kong (1977)

DIRECTOR: John Guillermin

SCREENPLAY: James Ashmore Creelman and Ruth Rose

CAST: Jeff Bridges, Charles Grodin, Jessica Lange

DVD: Paramount

Kingdom, The (2007)

DIRECTOR: Peter Berg

SCREENPLAY: Matthew Michael Carnahan

CAST: Jamie Foxx, Chris Cooper, Jennifer Garner

DVD: Universal Studios

Kingdom of Heaven (2005)

DIRECTOR: Ridley Scott

SCREENPLAY: William Monahan

CAST: Martin Hancock, Michael Sheen, Nathalie Cox

DVD: 20th Century Fox

Kite Runner, The (2007)

DIRECTOR: Marc Forster

SCREENPLAY: David Benioff

CAST: Khalid Abdalla, Atossa Leoni, Shaun Toub

DVD: Paramount

Lions for Lambs (2007)

DIRECTOR: Robert Redford

SCREENPLAY: Matthew Michael Carnahan

CAST: Robert Redford, Meryl Streep, Tom Cruise

DVD: United Artists

Little Drummer Girl, The (1984)

DIRECTOR: George Roy Hill

SCREENPLAY: Loring Mandel

CAST: Diane Keaton, Sami Frey, Klaus Kinski

DVD: Not Available in Region One

Live Free or Die Hard (2007)

DIRECTOR: Len Wiseman

SCREENPLAY: Mark Bomback

CAST: Bruce Willis, Timothy Olyphant, Justin Long

DVD: 20th Century Fox

Manchurian Candidate, The (1962)

DIRECTOR: John Frankenheimer

SCREENPLAY: George Axelrod

CAST: Frank Sinatra, Laurence Harvey, Janet Leigh

DVD: MGM/UA

Mighty Heart, A (2007)

DIRECTOR: Michael Winterbottom

SCREENPLAY: John Orloff

CAST: Dan Futterman, Angelina Jolie, Archie Panjabi

DVD: Paramount Vantage

Munich (2005)

DIRECTOR: Steven Spielberg

SCREENPLAY: Tony Kushner and Eric Roth

CAST: Eric Bana, Daniel Craig, Ciarán Hinds

DVD: Universal Studios

Nighthawks (1981)

DIRECTOR: Bruce Malmuth

SCREENPLAY: David Shaber

CAST: Sylvester Stallone, Billy Dee Williams, Lindsay Wagner

DVD: Universal Studios, Good Times Video

Panic in the Streets (1950)

DIRECTOR: Elia Kazan

SCREENPLAY: Richard Murphy

CAST: Richard Widmark, Paul Douglas, Barbara Bel Geddes

DVD: 20th Century Fox

Passenger 57 (1992)

DIRECTOR: Kevin Hooks

SCREENPLAY: David Loughery and Dan Gordon

CAST: Wesley Snipes, Bruce Payne, Tom Sizemore

DVD: Warner Home Video

Path to 9/11, The (MFT, 2006)

DIRECTOR: David L. Cunningham

SCREENPLAY: Cyrus Nowrasteh

CAST: Harvey Keitel, Michael Benyaer, Wendy Crewson

DVD: Not Available

Path to Paradise: The Untold Story of the World Trade Center Bombing (MFT, 1997)

DIRECTOR: Leslie Libman and Larry Williams

SCREENPLAY: Ned Curren

CAST: Peter Gallagher, Art Malik, Ned Eisenberg

DVD: HBO Home Video

Peacemaker, The (1997)

DIRECTOR: Mimi Leder

SCREENPLAY: Michael Schiffer

CAST: George Clooney, Nicole Kidman, Marcel Lures

DVD: Dreamworks

President's Man, The: A Line in the Sand (2002)

DIRECTOR: Eric Norris

SCREENPLAY: John Lansing and Bruce Cervi

CAST: Chuck Norris, Judson Mills, Jennifer Tung

DVD: Madacy

Redacted (2007)

DIRECTOR: Brian De Palma

SCREENPLAY: Brian De Palma

CAST: Sahar Alloul, Happy Anderson, Lara Atalla

DVD: Magnolia

Reign Over Me (2007)

DIRECTOR: Mike Binder

SCREENPLAY: Mike Binder

CAST: Adam Sandler, Don Cheadle, Jada Pinkett Smith

DVD: Sony Pictures

Rendition (2007)

DIRECTOR: Gavin Hood

SCREENPLAY: Kelley Sane

CAST: Omar Metwally, Reese Witherspoon, Aramis Knight

DVD: New Line Home Video

Rock, The (1996)

DIRECTOR: Michael Bay

SCREENPLAY: David Weisberg, Douglas Cook, Mark Rosner

CAST: Sean Connery, Nicolas Cage, Ed Harris

DVD: Walt Disney

Rollercoaster (1977)

DIRECTOR: James Goldstone

SCREENPLAY: Sanford Sheldon, Richard Levinson, William Link

CAST: George Segal, Richard Widmark, Timothy Bottoms

DVD: Universal Studios

Sabotage (1936)

DIRECTOR: Alfred Hitchcock

SCREENPLAY: Charles Bennett, Ian Hay, Helen Simpson, E. V. H. Emmett

CAST: Sylvia Sidney, Oskar Homolka, Desmond Tester

DVD: BCI/Sunset Home Video, Madacy

Satan Bug, The (1965)

DIRECTOR: John Sturges

SCREENPLAY: James Clavell and Edward Anhalt

CAST: George Maharis, Richard Basehart, Anne Francis

DVD: Not Available in Region One

Saving Jessica Lynch (MFT, 2003)

DIRECTOR: Peter Markle

SCREENPLAY: John Fasano

CAST: Nicholas Guilak, Laura Regan, Brent Sexton

DVD: NBC Home Entertainment

Saw (2004)

DIRECTOR: James Wan

SCREENPLAY: Leigh Whannell

CAST: Leigh Whannell, Cary Elwes, Danny Glover

DVD: Lions Gate

Siege, The (1998)

DIRECTOR: Edward Zwick

SCREENPLAY: Lawrence Wright, Menno Meyjes, Edward Zwick

CAST: Denzel Washington, Annette Bening, Bruce Willis

DVD: 20th Century Fox

Situation, The (2007)

DIRECTOR: Philip Haas

SCREENPLAY: Wendell Steavenson

CAST: Connie Nielsen, Damian Lewis, Mido Hamada

DVD: New Video Group

Skyjacked (1972)

DIRECTOR: John Guillermin

SCREENPLAY: Stanley R. Greenberg

CAST: Charlton Heston, Yvette Mimieux, James Brolin

DVD: Warner Home Video

Sleeper Cell (TV, 2005–2006)

DIRECTORS: Nick Gomez, Guy Ferland, Clark Johnson, Charles S. Duttoon, Leon Ichaso, Ziad Doueiri

SCREENPLAY: Ethan Reiff, Cyrus Voris, Kath Lingenfelter, Alexander Woo, Michael C. Martin

CAST: Michael Ealy, Oded Fehr, Henri Lubatti

DVD: Paramount and Showtime Entertainment

Speed (1994)

DIRECTOR: Jan de Bont

SCREENPLAY: Graham Yost

CAST: Keanu Reeves, Dennis Hopper, Sandra Bullock

DVD: 20th Century Fox

Stop-Loss (2008)

DIRECTOR: Kimberly Peirce

SCREENPLAY: Kimberly Peirce, Mark Richard

CAST: Ryan Phillippe, Joseph Gordon-Levitt, Laurie Metcalf

DVD: Paramount

Suddenly (1954)

DIRECTOR: Lewis Allen

SCREENPLAY: Richard Sale

CAST: Frank Sinatra, Sterling Hayden, James Gleason

DVD: Image Entertainment, Madacy

Sum of All Fears, The (2002)

DIRECTOR: Phil Alden Robinson

SCREENPLAY: Paul Attanasio and Daniel Pyne

CAST: Ben Affleck, Morgan Freeman, James Cromwell

DVD: Paramount Home Video

Swordfish (2001)

DIRECTOR: Dominic Sena

SCREENPLAY: Skip Woods

CAST: John Travolta, Hugh Jackman, Halle Berry

DVD: Warner Home Video

Targets (1968)

DIRECTOR: Peter Bogdanovich

SCREENPLAY: Peter Bogdanovich and Samuel Fuller

CAST: Tim O'Kelly, Boris Karloff, Athur Peterson

DVD: Paramount

Terminal, The (2004)

DIRECTOR: Steven Spielberg

SCREENPLAY: Sacha Gervasi and Jeff Nathanson

CAST: Tom Hanks, Catherine Zeta-Jones, Stanley Tucci

DVD: Dreamworks

Terminal Entry (1986)

DIRECTOR: John Kincade

SCREENPLAY: David M. Evans and Mark Sobel

CAST: Paul L. Smith, Yaphet Kotto, Heidi Helmer

DVD: Not Available

Terror in Beverly Hills (1991)

DIRECTOR: John Myhers

SCREENPLAY: Simon Bibiyan and John Myhers

CAST: Joe Davis, Lysa Hayland, Brian Leonard

DVD: Peacock Films

Terror Squad (1987)

DIRECTOR: Peter Maris

SCREENPLAY: Chuck Rose

CAST: Chuck Connors, Brodie Greer, Bill Calvert

DVD: Not Available

This Revolution (2005)

DIRECTOR: Stephen Marshall

SCREENPLAY: Stephen Marshall

CAST: Rosario Dawson, Nathan Crooker, Amy Redford

DVD: Screen Media Films

Threat Matrix (TV, 2003–2004)

DIRECTORS: Fred Gerber, Guy Norman Bee, Perry Lang

SCREENPLAY: Daniel Voll, John Shiban

CAST: James Denton, Kelly Rutherford, Will Lyman

DVD: N/A

300 (2007)

DIRECTOR: Zack Snyder

SCREENPLAY: Zack Snyder, Kurt Johnstad, Michael Gordon

CAST: Gerard Butler, Lena Headey, Dominic West

DVD: Warner Home Video

Towering Inferno, The (1977)

DIRECTOR: John Guillermin and Irwin Allen

SCREENPLAY: Stirling Silliphant

CAST: Steve McQueen, Paul Newman, William Holden

DVD: 20th Century Fox

Traitor (2008)

DIRECTOR: Jeffrey Nachmanoff

SCREENPLAY: Jeffrey Nachmanoff

CAST: Don Cheadle, Guy Pearce, Said Taghmaoui

DVD: Anchor Bay

Troy (2004)

DIRECTOR: Wolfgang Petersen

SCREENPLAY: David Benioff

CAST: Julian Glover, Brian Cox, Nathan Jones

DVD: Warner Home Video

True Lies (1994)

DIRECTOR: James Cameron

SCREENPLAY: Claude Zidi, Simon Michaël, Didier Kaminka, James Cameron

CAST: Arnold Schwarzenegger, Jamie Lee Curtis, Tom Arnold

DVD: 20th Century Fox

24 (TV, 2001)

DIRECTOR: Jon Cassar, Brad Turner, Bryan Spicer, Stephen Hopkins, Ian Toynton, Frederick King Keller, James Whitmore, Jr., Tim Iacofano, Kevin Hooks, Rodney Charters,

Winrich Kolbe, Davis Guggenheim, Paul Shapiro, Ken Girotti, Dwight H. Little, Milan Cheylov

SCREENPLAY: Robert Cochran, Joel Surnow, Howard Gordon, Michael Loceff, Evan Katz, Stephen Kronish, Manny Coto, David Fury, Duppy Demetrius, Matt Michnovetz, Virgil Williams, Gil Grant, Sam Montgomery, Peter M. Lenkov, Maurice Hurley, Michael S. Chernuchin, Andrea Newman, David Ehrman, Nicole Ranadive

CAST: Keifer Sutherland, Mary Lynn Rajskub, Carlos Bernard

DVD: 20th Century Fox

25th Hour (2002)

DIRECTOR: Spike Lee

SCREENPLAY: David Benioff

CAST: Edward Norton, Philip Seymour Hoffman, Barry Pepper

DVD: Walt Disney

28 Days Later (2002)

DIRECTOR: Danny Boyle

SCREENPLAY: Alex Garland

CAST: Brendan Gleeson, Megan Burns, David Schneider

DVD: 20th Century Fox

28 Weeks Later (2007)

DIRECTOR: Juan Carlos Fresnadillo

SCREENPLAY: Rowan Joffe, Juan Carlos Fresnadillo, Enrique López Lavigne, Jesús Olmo

CAST: Robert Carlyle, Catherine McCormack, Rose Byrne

DVD: 20th Century Fox

Two Minute Warning (1976)

DIRECTOR: Larry Peerce

SCREENPLAY: Edward Hume

CAST: Charlton Heston, John Cassavetes, Martin Balsam

DVD: Universal Studios

Under Siege (1992)

DIRECTOR: Andrew Davis

SCREENPLAY: J. F. Lawton

CAST: Steven Seagal, Tommy Lee Jones, Gary Busey

DVD: Warner Home Video

United 93 (2006)

DIRECTOR: Paul Greengrass

SCREENPLAY: Paul Greengrass

CAST: J. J. Johnson, Gary Commock, Polly Adams

DVD: Universal Studios

V for Vendetta (2005)

DIRECTOR: James McTeigue

SCREENPLAY: Andy Wachowski and Larry Wachowski

CAST: Natalie Portman, Hugo Weaving, Stephen Rea

DVD: Warner Home Video

W. (2008)

DIRECTOR: Oliver Stone

SCREENPLAY: Stanley Weiser

CAST: Josh Brolin, Richard Dreyfuss, Elizabeth Banks

DVD: Lions Gate

Wanted: Dead or Alive (1987)

DIRECTOR: Gary Sherman

SCREENPLAY: Michael Patrick Goodman, Gary Sherman, Brian Taggert

CAST: Rutger Hauer, Gene Simmons, Robert Guillaume

DVD: Bci/Eclipse

War, Inc. (2008)

DIRECTOR: Joshua Seftel

SCREENPLAY: Mark Leyner, Jeremy Pikser, John Cusack

CAST: John Cusack, Hillary Duff, Dan Aykroyd

DVD: First Look Pictures

War of the Worlds (2005)

DIRECTOR: Steven Spielberg

SCREENPLAY: Josh Friedman and David Koepp

CAST: Tom Cruise, Dakota Fanning, Miranda Otto

DVD: Dreamworks

War Within, The (2005)

DIRECTOR: Joseph Castelo

SCREENPLAY: Ayad Akhtar, Joseph Castelo, Tom Glynn

CAST: Ayad Akhtar, Firdous Barmji, Nandana Sen

DVD: Magnolia

World Trade Center (2006)

DIRECTOR: Oliver Stone

SCREENPLAY: Andrea Berloff, John McLoughlin, Donna McLoughlin, William Jimeno, Allison Jimeno

CAST: Nicolas Cage, Maria Bello, Michael Peña

DVD: Paramount

WTC View (2005)

DIRECTOR: Brian Sloan

SCREENPLAY: Brian Sloan

CAST: Michael Urie, Jeremy Beazlie, Jay Gillespie

DVD: Tia

DOCUMENTARIES

About Baghdad (2005)

DIRECTORS: Sinan Antoon, Bassam Haddad, Maya Mikdashi, Suzy Salamy, Adam Shapiro

DVD: AFD

Aftermath: Unanswered Questions from 9/11 (2003)

DIRECTOR: Stephen Marshall

SCREENPLAY: Stephen Marshall

DVD: Disinformation

Alive Day Memories: Home from Iraq (2007)

DIRECTOR: John Alpert and Ellen Goosenberg Kent

DVD: HBO Home Video

America: A Tribute to Heroes (2001)

DIRECTORS: Joel Gallen, Beth McCarthy-Miller

SCREENPLAY: Eli Attie, Bill Clark, Chris Connelly, Terry Edmonds, Tom Fontana, Marshall Herskovitz, David Leaf, Ann F. Lewis, Peggy Noonan, Eugene Pack, Philip Rosenthal, Robert Shrum, David Wild, Edward Zwick

CAST: Clint Eastwood, Robert DeNiro, Nicole Kidman

DVD: Warner Bros.

America at a Crossroads (MFT, 2007)

DIRECTORS: Martin Burke, Edward Gray

DVD: PBS Home Video

Baghdad ER (2005)

DIRECTOR: Jon Alpert and Matthew O'Neill

DVD: HBO Home Video

Baghdad High (aka The Boys from Baghdad High) (2008)

DIRECTOR: Ivan O'Mahoney and Laura Winter

DVD: HBO Films (expected release)

Baghdad Hospital (2008)

DIRECTOR: Omer Salih Mahdi

DVD: HBO Home Video

Battleground: 21 Days at the Edge of the Empire (2005)

DIRECTOR: Stephen Marshall

DVD: Homevision

Beyond Belief (2007)

DIRECTOR: Beth Murphy

DVD: N/A

Blood of My Brother, The: A Story of Death in Iraq (2005)

DIRECTOR: Andrew Berends

DVD: Lifesize Entertainment

Buried in the Sand: The Deception of America (2004)

DIRECTOR: David Wald

DVD: CYHL Pictures

Buying the War (Bill Moyers' Journal) (2007)

DIRECTOR: Ken Diego

DVD: PBS Home Video

Celsius 41.11: The Temperature at Which the Brain . . . Begins to Die (2004)

DIRECTOR: Kevin Knoblock

SCREENPLAY: Lionel Chetwynd and Ted Steinberg

DVD: BCD Music Group

Class of 83 (2004)

DIRECTOR: Kurt E. Soderling

SCREENPLAY: Kurt E. Soderling, Melinda Songer, Brigid Walsh

DVD: N/A

Collateral Damages (2003)

DIRECTOR: Étienne Sauret

DVD: Turn of the Century Pictures

Combat Diary: The Marines of Lima Company (2006)

DIRECTOR: Michael Epstein

DVD: A&E Home Video

Dreams of Sparrows, The (2005)

DIRECTOR: Haydar Daffar and Hayder Mousa Daffar

DVD: Go-Kart Records

Fahrenheit 9/11 (2004)

DIRECTOR: Michael Moore

SCREENPLAY: Michael Moore

DVD: Weinstein Company

Fahrenhype 9/11 (2004)

DIRECTOR: Alan Peterson

SCREENPLAY: Eileen McGann, Dick Morris, Lee Troxler

DVD: Trinity Home Entertainment

Ghosts of Abu Ghraib (2007)

DIRECTOR: Rory Kennedy

DVD: HBO Home Video

Great Conspiracy, The: The 9/11 News Special You Never Saw (2005)

DIRECTOR: Barrie Zwicker

DVD: 2450 Video Distribution

Ground Truth, The (2006)

DIRECTOR: Patricia Foulkrod

SCREENPLAY: Patricia Foulkrod

DVD: Universal Studios

Gunner Palace (2005)

DIRECTORS: Michael Tucker and Petra Epperlein

DVD: Sunset Home Visual Entertainment

Home Front (2006)

Director: Richard Hankin

DVD: Cinevolve Studios

Heroes of Ground Zero (2002)

DIRECTOR: Katharine English

SCREENPLAY: James McGrath Morris, John Uhl

DVD: N/A

In Memorium: New York City (2002)

Producer: Brad Grey

DVD: HBO Home Video

Inside Iraq: The Untold Stories (2004)

DIRECTOR: Mike Shiley

SCREENPLAY: Mike Shiley

DVD: Shidog Films

Iraq for Sale: The War Profiteers (2006)

DIRECTOR: Robert Greenwald

DVD: Brave New Films

Iraq in Fragments (2006)

DIRECTOR: James Longley

DVD: Typecast Releasing

Journalist and the Jihadi, The (2006)

DIRECTORS: Ahmed A. Jamal, Ramesh Sharma, Ramesh J. Sharma, Asad Qureshi

SCREENPLAY: Amit Roy

CAST: Christiane Amanpour—Narrator

DVD: HBO Home Video

Last Letters Home: Voices of American Troops from the Battlefields of Iraq (2004)

DIRECTOR: Bill Couturié

DVD: HBO Home Video

Loose Change (2006)

DIRECTOR: Dylan Avery

DVD: Louder Than Words Productions

Loose Change Final Cut (2007)

DIRECTOR: Dylan Avery

DVD: Louder Than Words Productions

Meeting Resistance (2007)

DIRECTORS: Molly Bingham and Steve Connors

SCREENPLAY: Molly Bingham and Steve Connors

DVD: First Run Features

My Country, My Country (2006)

DIRECTOR: Laura Poitras

SCREENPLAY: David Brancaccio

DVD: Zeitgeist Films

9/11 (2002)

DIRECTORS: James Hanlon, Rob Klug, Gédéon Naudet, Jules Naudet

SCREENPLAY: Tom Forman and Greg Kandra

DVD: Paramount Home Video

911: In Plane Sight (2004)

DIRECTOR: William Lewis

SCREENPLAY: Dave von Kleist

DVD: www.911inplanesight.com

911 Mysteries Part 1:Demolitions (2006)

DIRECTOR: Sofia Shafquat

DVD: www.911Mysteries.com

9/11: Press for Truth (2006)

DIRECTOR: Ray Nowosielski

SCREENPLAY: Kyle Hence, Ray Nowosielski, Paul Thompson

DVD: Disinformation

Occupation: Dreamland (2005)

DIRECTORS: Ian Olds and Garrett Scott

DVD: Rumor Releasing

Off to War (2006)

DIRECTORS: Brent Renaud and Craig Renaud

DVD: Kino Video

On Native Soil: The Documentary of the 9/11 Commission Report (2006)

DIRECTOR: Linda Ellman

CAST: Kevin Costner, Hillary Swank (narrators)

DVD: Lion's Gate

102 Minutes That Changed America (2008)

Producer: Nicole Rittenmeyer

DVD: The History Channel

Pentagon 911 (2007)

DIRECTOR: Joel Ratner

SCREENPLAY: Michael A. Dickerson, Joel Ratner, Al Shackelford, Rear Admiral William Thompson

DVD: N/A

Prisoner or: How I Planned to Kill Tony Blair, The (2006)

DIRECTORS: Petra Epperlein and Michael Tucker

SCREENPLAY: Petra Epperlein and Michael Tucker

DVD: Magnolia

The Road to Guantánamo (2006)

DIRECTORS: Mat Whitecross, Michael Winterbottom

CAST: Riz Ahmed, Farhad Harun, Wagar Siddiqui

DVD: Sony

Rush to War (2004)

DIRECTOR: Robert Taicher

SCREENPLAY: Robert Taicher

DVD: RTW Productions

7 Days in September (2004)

DIRECTOR: Steve Rosenbaum

DVD: Starz/Anchor Bay

The Short Life of José Antonio Gutierrez (2006)

DIRECTOR: Heidi Specogna

DVD: Atopia

Shut Up and Sing (2006)

DIRECTORS: Barbara Kopple and Cecilia Peck

DVD: The Weinstein Company

638 Ways to Kill Castro (2006)

DIRECTOR: Dollan Cannell

DVD: BCI/Eclipse

Soldiers Pay (2004)

DIRECTORS: Tricia Regan, David O'Russell, Juan Carlos Zaldivar

DVD: Cinema Libre

Standard Operating Procedure (2008)

DIRECTOR: Errol Morris

DVD: Sony Pictures

Taxi to the Dark Side (2007)

DIRECTOR: Alex Gibney

SCREENPLAY: Alex Gibney

DVD: Velocity / Thinkfilm

Torturing Democracy (2008)

DIRECTOR: Sherry Jones

DVD: www.torturingdemocracy.org

Twin Towers (2003)

DIRECTORS: Bill Guttentag and Robert David Port

DVD: Universal Home Entertainment

Unconstitutional: The War on Our Civil Liberties (2004)

DIRECTOR: Nonny de la Peña

SCREENPLAY: Nonny de la Peña

DVD: The Disinformation Company

Uncovered: The War on Iraq (2003)

DIRECTOR: Robert Greenwald

DVD: Cinema Libre

Voices of Iraq (2004)

DIRECTORS: The People of Iraq and Martin Kunert

DVD: Magnolia

War Tapes, The (2006)

DIRECTOR: Deborah Scranton

DVD: Docurama

Why the Towers Fell (2002)

DIRECTORS: Garfield Kennedy, Larry Klein

DVD: Nova

Why We Fight (2005)

DIRECTOR: Eugene Jarecki

SCREENPLAY: Eugene Jarecki

DVD: Sony Pictures

WMD: Weapons of Mass Deception (2004)

DIRECTOR: Danny Schechter

DVD: Cinema Libre

World Trade Center: Anatomy of the Collapse (2002)

DIRECTOR: Ben Bowie

DVD: Live/Artisan

WTC: The First 24 Hours (2001)

DIRECTOR: Étienne Sauret

DVD: New Video Group

NOTES

INTRODUCTION

1. See, for example, Wheeler Winston Dixon, "Introduction: Something Lost—Film After 9/11," in Wheeler Winston Dixon, ed., *Film and Television After 9/11* (Carbondale: Southern Illinois UP, 2004), 1. Dixon writes that media commentators "sense a definite shift in modes of perception, production, and audience reception for films" that offer stories about violent conflict.
2. Quoted in Dixon, ibid., 11.
3. See "In Focus: Teaching 9/11," *Cinema Journal* 43.2 (Winter 2004): 90–126.
4. Louise Spence, "Teaching 9/11 and Why I'm Not Doing It Anymore," *Cinema Journal* 43.2 (Winter 2004): 102.
5. Sarah Projansky, "Teaching Through Feelings and Personal Beliefs: 9/11 as Case Study," *Cinema Journal* 43.2 (Winter 2004): 105.
6. E. Ann Kaplan, "A Camera and a Catastrophe: Reflections on Trauma and the Twin Towers," in Judith Greenberg, ed., *Trauma at Home: After 9/11* (Lincoln: U of Nebraska P, 2003), 98.
7. E. Ann Kaplan, *Trauma Culture: The Politics of Terror and Loss in Media and Literature* (New Brunswick, N.J.: Rutgers UP, 2005), 2.
8. Irene Kacandes, "9/11/01 = 1/27/01: The Changed Posttraumatic Self," in Judith Greenberg, ed., *Trauma at Home: After 9/11*, 168–83 (Lincoln: U of Nebraska P, 2003).
9. Judith Herman, *Trauma and Recovery* (New York: Basic Books, 1997), 33.
10. Susan J. Brison, "The Uses of Narrative in the Aftermath of Violence" in Claudia Card, ed., *On Feminist Ethics and Politics* (Lawrence, Ks.: UP of Kansas, 1999), 200.
11. Herman, *Trauma and Recovery*, 38.
12. Ibid., 38–39.
13. Wulf Kansteiner, "Genealogy of a Category Mistake: A Critical Intellectual History of the Cultural Trauma Metaphor," *Rethinking History* 8.2 (June 2004): 207.
14. Ibid., 211.

15. Marita Sturken, *Tangled Memories: The Vietnam War, the AIDS Epidemic, and the Politics of Remembering* (Berkeley: U of California P, 1997), 11.
16. Alison Landsberg, *Prosthetic Memory: The Transformation of American Remembrance in the Age of Mass Culture* (New York: Columbia UP, 2004), 25–26.
17. Sturken, *Tangled Memories*, 2.

1. THEATER OF MASS DESTRUCTION

1. For a description of the campaign, excerpted from a column in *Irish World* published in 1880, see "O'Donovan Rossa's Dynamiters" in Walter Laqueur, ed., *The Terrorism Reader* (Philadelphia: Temple UP, 1978), 112–14.
2. Claire Kahane, "Uncanny Sights: The Anticipation of the Abomination," in Judith Greenberg, ed., *Trauma at Home: After 9/11* (Lincoln: U of Nebraska P, 2003), 107.
3. Most, quoted in Martin A. Miller, "The Intellectual Origins of Modern Terrorism in Europe," in Martha Crenshaw, ed., *Terrorism in Context* (University Park, Pa.: Pennsylvania State UP, 1995), 45.
4. Karl Heinzen, "Murder," in Laqueur, ed., *The Terrorism Reader*, 59.
5. Most details in this discussion of Galleanism derive from Paul Avrich's *Sacco and Vanzetti: The Anarchist Background* (Princeton: Princeton UP, 1991).
6. Beverly Gage, "The First Wall Street Bomb," History News Service (*see* www.h-net.org/~hns/articles/2001/091701a.html).
7. Quoted in Gage, "The First Wall Street Bomb."
8. Walter Laqueur, "Anarchism and Al Qaeda" (*see* liqueur.net/index2.php?r=2&rr=1&id=87).
9. Miller, "Intellectual Origins of Modern Terrorism in Europe," 31.
10. Walter Laqueur, *No End to War: Terrorism in the Twenty-first Century* (New York: Continuum, 2003), 9.
11. Walter Laqueur, *The Age of Terrorism* (Boston: Little, Brown, 1987), 202.
12. François Truffaut and Helen G. Scott, *Hitchcock*, rev. ed. (New York: Touchstone, 1983), 109.
13. Irving Howe, "Conrad: Order and Anarchy," in Ian Watt, ed., *Conrad: "The Secret Agent": A Casebook* (New York: Macmillan, 1973), 143.
14. Jack G. Shaheen, *Reel Bad Arabs: How Hollywood Vilifies a People* (New York: Olive Branch Press, 2001), 104.
15. See, for example, Laqueur's discussion in *The Age of Terrorism*, 220–21.
16. Chalmers Johnson, *The Sorrows of Empire: Militarism, Secrecy, and the End of the Republic* (New York: Henry Holt, 2004), 120–21.
17. Osama bin Laden, "The Towers of Lebanon," in Bruce Lawrence, ed., *Messages to the World: The Statements of Osama bin Laden* (New York: Verso, 2005), 239.
18. Osama bin Laden, "To the Americans," in Lawrence, ed., *Messages to the World*, 162, 163.

19. Steve Coll's *Ghost Wars: The Secret History of the CIA, Afghanistan, and Bin Laden, from the Soviet Invasion to September 10, 2001* (New York: Penguin, 2004) covers this background.
20. Laqueur uses the term "international brigade" to describe this development, in *The Age of Terrorism*, 220.
21. Quoted in Peter H. Merkl, "West German Left-Wing Terrorism" in Crenshaw, ed., *Terrorism in Context*, 192.
22. Richard Gillespie, "Political Violence in Argentina: Guerrillas, Terrorists, and Carapintadas," in Crenshaw, ed., *Terrorism in Context*, 212–13.
23. Eric Lichtblau and Mark Mazzetti, "Military Expands Intelligence Role in U.S.," *New York Times*, Jan. 14, 2007, 1, 18.
24. Shaheen, *Reel Bad Arabs*, 26–27.
25. Eric Lichtenfeld, *Action Speaks Louder: Violence, Spectacle, and the American Action Movie* (Middletown, Conn.: Wesleyan UP, 2007), 166.
26. Timothy McVeigh quoted in Gore Vidal, *Perpetual War for Perpetual Peace* (New York: Nation Books, 2002), 108.
27. Coll, *Ghost Wars*, 424.
28. Ibid., 426.
29. Ibid., 428.
30. Tim Weiner, *Legacy of Ashes: The History of the CIA* (New York: Anchor, 2008), 546.
31. Davis discusses this in his audio commentary appearing on the DVD release of the film.
32. For a discussion of the Hollywood films about these wars, see Stephen Prince, *Visions of Empire: Political Imagery in Contemporary American Film* (New York: Praeger, 1992), 81–113.
33. For a discussion, see the Human Rights Watch November 1996 report, "Colombia's Killer Networks" (*see* www.hrw.org/reports/1996/killertoc.htm).
34. Quoted in Coll, *Ghost Wars*, 380.
35. See Coll, *Ghost Wars*, 255.
36. On this point, see Jim Dwyer and Kevin Flynn, *102 Minutes: The Untold Story of the Fight to Survive Inside the Twin Towers* (New York: Times Books, 2005), 54–60.
37. Quote in Reihan Salam, "The Sum of All PC: Hollywood's Reverse Racial Profiling," *Slate*, May 28, 2002 (*see* www.slate.com/id/2066272/).
38. Jonah Goldberg, "Pfizer vs. al Qaeda: Give Me a Break," *National Review Online*, Aug. 31, 2005 (*see* www.nationalreview.com/goldberg/goldberg200508310810.asp).
39. See, for example, Barrie Zwicker, *Towers of Deception: The Media Cover-Up of 9/11* (Gabriola Island, B.C.: New Society, 2006).
40. "Ashcroft Flying High," CBS News, July 26, 2001 (*see* www.cbsnews.com/stories/2001/07/26/national/main303601.shtml).

41. Rather, quoted in Howard Kurtz, "Journalists See an Alarming Trend in Terror Warnings," *Washington Post*, May 27, 2002, C1.
42. Paul Hirsh, "'We've Hit the Targets,'" *Newsweek*, Sept. 13, 2001, 36.
43. Quoted in Coll, *Ghost Wars*, 278.
44. Ibid., 274.
45. Lawrence Wright, *The Looming Tower: Al-Qaeda and the Road to 9/11* (New York: Knopf, 2006), 235–36.
46. Quoted in Coll, *Ghost Wars*, 279.
47. Shaheen, *Reel Bad Arabs*, 189.
48. Daniel Mandel. "Muslims on the Silver Screen, *Middle East Quarterly* 8.2 (Spring 2001): 19.
49. Coll, *Ghost Wars*, 134.
50. Quoted in Wright, *The Looming Tower*, 219.
51. Malise Ruthven, *A Fury for God: The Islamist Attack on America* (London: Granta, 2002).
52. Ibid., 30.
53. Osama bin Laden, "Terror for Terror," in Lawrence, ed., *Messages to the World*, 129.
54. Quoted in James Glanz and Eric Lipton, *City in the Sky: The Rise and Fall of the World Trade Center* (New York: Times Books, 2003), 228.
55. Interview with Lawrence Wright, BookClubs.ca (*see* www.bookclubs.ca/catalog/display.pperl?isbn = 9781400030842&view = auqa).
56. Erik Lundegaard, "Saddam Hussein Is Bombing Us! How Hollywood Portrayed Terrorism Before 9/11" (*see* www.msnbc.msn.com/id/9230038).
57. David Cole and James X. Dempsey, *Terrorism and the Constitution: Sacrificing Civil Liberties in the Name of National Security* (New York: New Press, 2006), 191.
58. Ruthven, *A Fury for God*, 103.
59. Jordan Wagge, "A Captive Audience: The Portrayal of Terrorism and Terrorists in Large-Scale Fictional Hollywood Media" (*see* www1.appstate.edu/~stefanov/proceedings/wagge.htm).
60. Ross Douthat, "The Return of the Paranoid Style," *Atlantic Monthly*, April 2008.
61. Tracy McVeigh, "'Dear Tracy'—by Mass Killer Timothy McVeigh," *The Observer*, May 6, 2001 (*see* www.guardian.co.uk/world/2001/may/06/news.mcveigh).
62. Hasan al-Banna, *Five Tracts of Hasan Al-Banna*, trans. Charles Wendell, Near Eastern Studies Vol. 20 (Berkeley: U of California P, 1978), 61.
63. Ibid., 106.
64. Ruthven, *A Fury for God*, 76.
65. Sayyid Qutb, *This Religion of Islam*, trans. "Islamdust" (Palo Alto, Calif.: Almanar, 1967), 26.
66. Ibid., 25.

67. Miller, "Origins of Modern Terrorism in Europe," 58.
68. Ibid., 61.
69. Paul Berman, *Terror and Liberalism* (New York: Norton, 2004).
70. Murray Pomerance, "The Shadow of the World Trade Center," in Dixon, ed., *Film and Television After 9/11*, 59.
71. Susan Sontag, "The Imagination of Disaster" in Sontag, *Against Interpretation and Other Essays* (New York: Farrar, Straus, and Giroux, 1966), 216.
72. Quoted in Henry David, "Prelude to Haymarket," in Laqueur, ed., *The Terrorism Reader*, 111.
73. Lichtenfeld, *Action Speaks Louder*, 176.
74. James W. Hall, "A Fireball Too Far," *New York Times*, Nov. 19, 2001 (*see* http://query.nytimes.com/gst/fullpage.html?res=9B0CE4DF123BF93AA25752C1A9679C8B63).

2. SHADOWS ONCE REMOVED

1. "Altman Says Films Inspire Terrorism," Associated Press Wire Story, Oct. 17, 2001.
2. Wright, *The Looming Tower: Al-Qaeda and the Road to 9/11*, 303, 309.
3. In *Action Speaks Louder: Violence, Spectacle, and the American Action Movie*, Eric Lichtenfeld provides numerous descriptions of the assault on public landmarks that typified disaster movies of the 1980s and 1990s.
4. Max Page, *The City's End: Two Centuries of Fantasies, Fears, and Premonitions of New York's Destruction* (New Haven: Yale UP, 2008), 4.
5. Ibid., 190.
6. Wien, quoted in James Glanz and Eric Lipton, *City in the Sky: The Rise and Fall of the World Trade Center*, 135.
7. Ibid., 213–14.
8. Osama bin Laden, "Terror for Terror," 119.
9. For discussion, see Glanz and Lipton, *City in the Sky*, 118–44, and Jim Dwyer and Kevin Flynn, *102 Minutes: The Untold Story of the Fight to Survive Inside the Twin Towers*, 103–112.
10. Glanz and Lipton, *City in the Sky*, 200.
11. Gene Williams and Byron Hollander, "High-Rise Fire Safety/Human Response," in Donald J. Conway, ed., *Human Response to Tall Buildings* (Stroudsburg, Pa.: Dowden, Hutchinson, and Ross, 1977), 311–12.
12. David Von Drehle, *Triangle: The Fire That Changed America* (New York: Grove Press, 2003), 157.
13. Ibid., 126.
14. Ibid., 154, 155.
15. Illuminati Conspiracy Archive (*see* www.conspiracyarchive.com/NWO/Hollywood_911.htm).

16. McCarthy, quoted in Steven Jay Schneider, "Architectural Nostalgia and the New York City Skyline on Film," in Wheeler Winston Dixon, ed., *Film and Television After 9/11* (Carbondale: Southern Illinois UP, 2004), 38.
17. Sharon Waxman, "White House Looking to Enlist Hollywood in Terrorism War," *Washington Post*, Oct. 20, 2001, C1.
18. Paula J. Massood, "The Quintessential New Yorker and Global Citizen: An Interview with Spike Lee," *Cineaste* 28.3 (Summer 2003): 5.
19. Ibid., 6.
20. Anthony DePalma, "Ground Zero Illnesses Clouding Giuliani's Legacy," *New York Times*, May 14, 2007, A1, A19.
21. John Solomon and Barton Gellman, "Frequent Errors in FBI's Secret Records Requests," *Washington Post*, Mar. 9, 2007, A1, A6.
22. David Stout, "FBI Head Admits Mistakes in Use of Security Act," *Washington Post*, Mar. 10, 2007, A1, A10.
23. Jim Dwyer, "City Police Spied Broadly Before G.O.P. Convention," *New York Times*, Mar. 25, 2007, 1, 27.
24. Ibid., 27.
25. Lester Friedman, *Citizen Spielberg* (Chicago: U of Illinois P, 2006), 284.
26. Spielberg's remarks appear in a video interview contained on the film's DVD release.
27. Warren Buckland, *Directed by Steven Spielberg: Poetics of the Contemporary Hollywood Blockbuster* (New York: Continuum, 2006), 215.
28. Friedman, *Citizen Spielberg*, 160.
29. Koepp, quoted in Lichtenfeld, *Action Speaks Louder*, 236.
30. Simon Reeve, *One Day in September* (New York: Arcade, 2000, epilogue 2006), 260.
31. Ibid.
32. Rebecca Traister, Elisabeth Franck, and Ian Blecher, "Oliver Stone and Christopher Hitchens Spar Over Hollywood's Efforts to be Relevant," *New York Observer*, Oct. 14, 2001 (*see* www.observer.com/2001/oliver-stone-and-christopher-hitchens-spar-over-hollywoods-efforts-be-relevant).
33. Stephen Applebaum, "Oliver Stone: 'I didn't want to be the bad guy again,'" (*see* http://stephenapplebaum.blogspot.com/2006/12/oliver-stone-i-didnt-want-to-be-bad-guy.html).
34. Ibid.
35. Cal Thomas, "'World Trade Center' is a World Class Movie," July 20, 2006 (*see* www.townhall.com/Columnists/CalThomas/2006/07/20/world_trade_center_is_a_world_class_movie).
36. See the essays in Sayyid Qutb, *Milestones* (Cedar Rapids, Ia.: The Mother Mosque Foundation, n.d.).
37. Samuel P. Huntington, "The Clash of Civilizations?" in *Foreign Affairs* (Summer 1993): 22–49.

38. Osama bin Laden, "Terror for Terror," 121.
39. Ibid., 124.
40. Zachary Karabell provides a lengthy iteration of this history in *Peace Be Upon You: The Story of Muslim, Christian, and Jewish Coexistence* (New York: Knopf, 2007). Ismael Hossein-Zadeh makes this point in "The Muslim World and the West: the Roots of Conflict," *Arab Studies Quarterly* 27.3 (Summer 2005): 1–20.
41. John Podhoretz, "Stone Sinks—New Film Misses 9/11's Essence," *New York Post*, July 21, 2006, 35.
42. Greengrass' remarks about the film and its design can be found in his audio commentary on the film's DVD release.
43. *The 9/11 Commission Report: Final Report of the National Commission on Terrorist Attacks Upon the United States* (New York: Norton, 2004), 31.
44. Ibid., 532.
45. Ibid., 25.
46. Ibid., 16.
47. Ibid., 13.
48. Alan Moore and David Lloyd, *V for Vendetta* (New York: DC Comics, 1989), 6.
49. Zbigniew Brzezinski, "Terrorized by 'War on Terror,'" *Washington Post*, March 25, 2007, B1.
50. Osama bin Laden, "The Example of Vietnam," in Bruce Lawrence, ed., *Messages to the World*, 141, and bin Laden, "Terror for Terror," 120.
51. Brison, "The Uses of Narrative in the Aftermath of Violence," 200.

3. GROUND ZERO IN FOCUS

1. Carl Plantinga, *Rhetoric and Representation in Nonfiction Film* (New York: Cambridge UP, 1997), 220.
2. Lawrence L. Langer, *Preempting the Holocaust* (New Haven: Yale UP, 1998), 1.
3. Edward T. Linenthal, *The Unfinished Bombing: Oklahoma City in American Memory* (New York: Oxford UP, 2001), 46.
4. Ibid.
5. Dwyer and Flynn, *102 Minutes*, xxii.
6. Linenthal, *The Unfinished Bombing*, 56.
7. Susan Sontag, *Regarding the Pain of Others* (New York: Penguin, 2003), 24.
8. Jack C. Ellis and Betsy A. McLane, *A New History of Documentary Film* (New York: Continuum, 2005), 335.
9. Michael Wilson, "Among Firefighters in New York, Giuliani Is Both Hailed and Hated," *New York Times*, June 17, 2007, 1, 16.
10. Langer, *Preempting the Holocaust*, 21.
11. Barbie Zelizer, "Photography, Journalism, and Trauma," in Barbie Zelizer and Stuart Allan, eds., *Journalism After September 11* (New York: Routledge, 2003), 51.

12. Dennis Cauchon and Martha Moore, "Desperation Forced a Horrific Decision," *USA Today*, Sept. 2, 2002.
13. Ibid.
14. Joshua Hirsch, "Post-traumatic Cinema and the Holocaust Documentary," in E. Ann Kaplan and Ban Wang, eds., *Trauma and Cinema: Cross-Cultural Explorations* (Aberdeen, Hong Kong: Hong Kong UP, 2004), 98.
15. Cauchon and Moore, "Desperation Forced a Horrific Decision."
16. See Christopher Sweet, ed., *Above Hallowed Ground: A Photographic Record of September 11, 2001, by Photographers of the New York City Police Department* (New York: Viking Studio, 2002), 146.
17. Kaplan, *Trauma Culture*, 13.
18. R. Jeffrey Smith, "Hussein's Prewar Ties to Al-Qaeda Discounted," *Washington Post*, Apr. 6, 2007, A1, A4.
19. The blurb appears on the film's Web site (*see* www.911report.com).
20. James Ridgeway, *The 5 Unanswered Questions About 9/11* (New York: Seven Stories Press, 2005), 160.
21. Philip K. Zelikow and Condoleezza Rica, *Germany Unified and Europe Transformed: A Study in Statecraft* (Cambridge: Harvard UP, 1995).
22. For details, see Philip Shenon, *The Commission: The Uncensored History of the 9/11 Investigation* (New York: Twelve, 2008).
23. Richard A. Falkenrath, "The 911 Commission Report," *International Security* 29.3 (Winter 2004/05): 181.
24. Ernest May, "When Government Writes History," *The New Republic*, May 23, 2005, 34.
25. *The 9/11 Commission Report*, 172.
26. Ridgeway, *The 5 Unanswered Questions*, 160–61.
27. Falkenrath, "The 9/11 Commission Report," 190.
28. *U.S. News and World Report* wrote, "She charged that George W. Bush may have known about the September 11 attacks in advance and allowed them to happen in order to make profits for the Carlyle Group, an owner of defense contractors with which former President Bush has connections." Michael Barone, "Lessons fr om Rep. Cynthia McKinney's Defeat," *U.S. News and World Report*, Aug. 29, 2002 (*see* www.usnews.com/usnews/opinion/baroneweb/mb_020829.htm).
29. An unofficial transcript of her testimony appears on Nowpublic's Web site (*see* www.nowpublic.com/node/16472).
30. *See* www.cooperativeresearch.org/project.jsp?project=911_project).
31. See www.911independentcommission.org/bush2162004.html).
32. Thomas H. Kean and Lee H. Hamilton, "Stonewalled by the CIA," *New York Times*, Jan. 2, 2008 (*see* www.nytimes.com/2008/01/02/opinion/02kean.html?_r=1&oref=slogin).

33. Moore, quoted in Larissa Macfarquhar "THE POPULIST (Michael Moore)," *The New Yorker* 80.1 (Feb 16, 2004): 133.
34. See, for example, Dave Kopel, "Fifty-nine Deceits in *Fahrenheit 9/11*" (*see* www.davekopel.com/Terror/Fiftysix-Deceits-in-Fahrenheit-911.htm).
35. Stanley Kauffmann, "Accusation," *The New Republic*, July 19, 2004, 24.
36. The Complete 9/11 Timeline (*see* www.cooperativeresearch.org/timeline.jsp?timeline=complete_911_timeline&day_of_9/11=bush).
37. Osama bin Laden, "The Towers of Lebanon," 242.
38. Macfarquhar, "THE POPULIST (Michael Moore)," 133.
39. Craig Unger, *House of Bush, House of Saud* (New York: Scribner, 2004), 295–98.
40. Ken Nolley, "*Fahrenheit 9/11*: Documentary, Truth-telling, and Politics," *Film and History* 35.2 (2005): 15.
41. Christopher Hitchins, "Unfairenheit 9/11: The Lies of Michael Moore," *Slate*, June 21, 2004 (*see* www.slate.com/id/2102723).
42. Steve Coll, *The Bin Ladens: An Arabian Family in the American Century* (New York: Penguin, 2008).
43. Unger, *House of Bush*, 285.
44. Hitchins, "Unfairenheit 9/11."
45. Ibid.
46. Sabrina Tavernise, "Iraqi Death Toll Exceeded 34,000 in 2006, U.N. Says," *New York Times*, Jan. 17, 2007, A1, A8.
47. Iraq Body Count Project (*see* www.iraqbodycount.org).
48. Steven Lee Myers, "U.S. Considering Stepping Up Pace of Iraq Pullout," *New York Times*, July 13, 2008, A1, A10.
49. For a sympathetic discussion of these films, see Christopher Sharrett, "Without Restraint: 9/11 Videos and the Pursuit of Truth," *Jump Cut* 50 (Spring 2008).
50. Richard Hofstadter, "The Paranoid Style in American Politics," *Harper's Magazine*, Nov. 1964, 77.
51. James B. Meigs, "Afterward: The Conspiracy Industry," in David Dunbar and Brad Reagan, eds., *Debunking 9/11 Myths: Why Conspiracy Theories Can't Stand Up to the Facts* (New York: Hearst, 2006), 102.
52. *See* www.loosechange911.com/company.htm.
53. Nancy Jo Sales, "Click Here for Conspiracy," *Vanity Fair*, Aug. 2006 (*see* www.vanityfair.com/ontheweb/features/2006/08/loosechange200608).
54. The Web site www.loose-change-911.com offers the film as streaming video in a viewer's choice of seven languages.
55. Michael Schermer, quoted in Meigs, "Afterword," 95.
56. An abridged version of the NIST report appears in Dunbar and Reagan, eds., *Debunking 9/11 Myths*, 113–34.

57. Remarks by civil engineering professor Mete Sozen as paraphrased in Dunbar and Reagan, eds., *Debunking 9/11 Myths,* 69. The ASCE report on the Pentagon is excerpted on pages 135–53.
58. Dunbar and Reagan, eds., *Debunking 9/11 Myths,* xx–xxi.
59. National Institute of Standards and Technology, *Final Report on the Collapse of the World Trade Center Towers* (Washington, D.C.: U.S. Government Printing Office, 2005), xxxviii.
60. Ibid.
61. Loizeaux, quoted in Dunbar and Reagan, eds., *Debunking 9/11 Myths,* 42–43.
62. Paul Kane, "Senate Authorizes Broad Expansion of Surveillance Act," *Washington Post,* Feb. 13, 2008, A1; Eric Lichtblau, "Senate Approves Bill to Broaden Wiretap Powers," *New York Times,* July 10, 2008 (*see* www.nytimes.com/2008/07/10/washington/10fisa.html?pagewanted = all).
63. *See* www.publicintegrity.org/WarCard/Charts/PollInfo.aspx.

4. BATTLEGROUND IRAQ

1. These and other statements about Iraq and al Qaeda are in a database compiled by the Center for Public Integrity as part of a study entitled "The War Card: Orchestrated Deception on the Path to War" (*see* www.publicintegrity.org/WarCard).
2. Cole and Dempsey, *Terrorism and the Constitution,* 196.
3. Ibid., 215.
4. Michael Scheuer, *Through Our Enemies' Eyes: Osama bin Laden, Radical Islam, and the Future of America,* rev. ed. (Washington D.C.: Potomac Books, 2006), 296.
5. Benjamin Wittes, *Law and the Long War: The Future of Justice in the Age of Terror* (New York: Penguin, 2008), 227.
6. Ibid., 55.
7. Jane Mayer, *The Dark Side: The Inside Story of How the War on Terror Turned into a War on American Ideals* (New York: Doubleday, 2008), 80.
8. "Rebuilding America's Defenses: Strategy, Forces, and Resources for a New Century," Project for the New American Century, Sept. 2000, 75 (*see* www.newamericancentury.org/RebuildingAmericasDefenses.pdf).
9. Ibid., 51.
10. David Ray Griffin and Richard Falk, *The New Pearl Harbor: Disturbing Questions About the Bush Administration and 9/11* (Northampton, Mass.: Interlink, 2004).
11. Richard A. Clarke, *Against All Enemies: Inside America's War on Terror* (New York: Free Press, 2004), 32.
12. Ibid., 30.
13. Scott Shane and Mark Mazzetti, "Ex-C.I.A. Chief, in Book, Assails Cheney on Iraq," *New York Times,* Apr. 27, 2007, A1, A14.

14. George W. Bush, "President's State of the Union Address," Jan. 29, 2002 (*see* www.whitehouse.gov/news/releases/2002/01/20020129-11.html).
15. Remarks by the Vice President to the Veterans of Foreign Wars 103rd National Convention (*see* www.whitehouse.gov/news/releases/2002/08/20020826.html).
16. Jack Goldsmith, *The Terror Presidency: Law and Judgment Inside the Bush Administration* (New York: Norton, 2007), 209.
17. Steve Rendell and Tara Broughel, "Amplifying Officials, Squelching Dissent," Fairness and Accuracy in Reporting (*see* www.fair.org/index.php?page=1145).
18. David Barstow, "Behind TV Analysts, Pentagon's Hidden Hand," *New York Times*, Apr. 20, 2008, 1, 24–26.
19. The meaning of the term "Dixie Chicked" is explained in Barbara Kopple and Cecelia Peck's film *Shut Up and Sing* (2006), and the Bill O'Reilly remarks about "bad Americans" are excerpted in Bill Moyers' film *Buying the War* (2007).
20. Keith Mines memo, quoted in Thomas E. Ricks, *Fiasco: The American Military Adventure in Iraq* (New York: Penguin, 2006), 165.
21. Ibid., 238.
22. *Ex Partie Quirin*, 317 U.S. 1 (1942), quoted in Wittes, *Law and the Long War*, 38.
23. Jay S. Bybee, Memorandum for Alberto R.Gonzales, Counsel to the President, Aug. 1, 2002, in Karen J. Greenberg and Joshua L. Dratel, eds., *The Torture Papers: The Road to Abu Ghraib* (New York: Cambridge UP, 2005), 172–217.
24. Alberto R. Gonzales, Memorandum for the President, Jan. 25, 2002, in Mark Danner, ed., *Torture and Truth: America, Abu Ghraib, and the War on Terror* (New York: New York Review of Books, 2004), 83–87.
25. Wittes, *Law and the Long War*, 185.
26. Ibid., 187.
27. Dwight D. Eisenhower, "Farewell Address" (*see* www.eisenhower.archives.gov/farewell.htm).
28. See Scheuer, *Through Our Enemies' Eyes* and Anonymous [Michael Scheuer], *Imperial Hubris: Why the West Is Losing the War on Terror* (Washington, D.C.: Brassey's, 2004).
29. Jason Campbell, Michael O'Hanlon, and Amy Unikewicz, "The State of Iraq: An Update," *New York Times*, June 22, 2008, 11.
30. William J. Fallon, "Surge Protector," *New York Times*, July 20, 2008, 13.
31. Bill Nichols, *Representing Reality: Issues and Concepts in Documentary* (Bloomington: Indiana University Press, 1991), p. 40.
32. Tony Grajeda, "The Winning and Losing of Hearts and Minds: Vietnam, Iraq, and the Claims of the War Documentary," *Jump Cut* 49 (Spring 2007).
33. Nichols, *Representing Reality*, 41.
34. Osama bin Laden, in Scheuer, *Through Our Enemies' Eyes*, 21.

35. Steve Fainaru, "Shadow War in Iraq Escalates in Intensity," *Washington Post*, June 16, 2007, A12.
36. Jeremy Scahill, *Blackwater: The Rise of the World's Most Powerful Mercenary Army* (New York: Nation Books, 2007), 69.
37. Ibid., 326.
38. Fainaru, "Shadow War in Iraq," *Washington Post*, June 16, 2007, A12.
39. Trish Wood, *What Was Asked of Us: An Oral History of the Iraq War by the Soldiers Who Fought It* (Boston: Little, Brown, 2006), p. 121.
40. Michael Kamber and Tim Arango, "4,000 U.S. Deaths and a Handful of Images," *New York Times*, July 26, 2008 (*see* www.nytimes.com/2008/07/26/world/middleeast/26censor.html?pagewanted=all).
41. John Taylor, *Body Horror: Photojournalism, Catastrophe, and War* (New York: New York UP, 1998), 187.
42. Wood, *What Was Asked of Us*, 163.
43. Ibid., 175.
44. Philip Kennicott, "Images: Poles and Decades Apart, Two Silent Screams Issue Discomfiting Reverberations," *Washington Post*, Dec. 30, 2007, M6.
45. *See* www.defenselink.mil/news/newsarticle.aspx?id = 15745.
46. Wood, *What Was Asked of Us*, 196.
47. Paul von Zielbauer, "Lawyers on Haditha Panel Peer into Fog of War," *New York Times*, May 17, 2007, A12.
48. Carlotta Gall and David E. Sanger, "Civilian Deaths Undermine Allies' War on Taliban," *New York Times*, May 13, 2007, A1, A8.
49. Thom Shanker, "Civilian Risks Curbing Strikes in Afghan War," *New York Times*, July 23, 2008 (*see* www.nytimes.com/2008/07/23/world/asia/23military.html?hp).
50. Carlotta Gall, "Evidence Points to Civilian Toll in Afghan Raid," *New York Times*, Sept. 7, 2008 (*see* www.nytimes.com/2008/09/08/world/asia/08afghan.html?pagewanted=all).
51. Alfred W. McCoy, *A Question of Torture: CIA Interrogation, from the Cold War to the War on Terror* (New York: Metropolitan Books, 2006), 8.
52. Trish Wood, *What Was Asked of Us*, 193.
53. "Report of the International Committee of the Red Cross (ICRC) on the Treatment by the Coalition Forces of Prisoners of War and Other Protected Persons by the Geneva Conventions in Iraq During Arrest, Internment and Interrogation," in Karen J. Greenberg and Joshua L. Dratel, eds., *The Torture Papers: The Road to Abu Ghraib* (New York: Cambridge UP, 2005), 388.
54. Ibid.
55. "The Taguba Report" in Greenberg and Dratel, eds., *The Torture Papers*, 416.
56. David S. Cloud, "General Says Prison Inquiry Led to His Forced Retirement," *New York Times*, June 17, 2007, 10.

57. Seymour Hersh, "The General's Report: How Antonio Taguba, who Investigated the Abu Ghraib Scandal, Became One of Its Casualties," *The New Yorker*, June 25, 2007.
58. Ibid.
59. Philip Gourevitch and Errol Morris, *Standard Operating Procedure* (New York: Penguin, 2008), 142.
60. Ibid., 137.
61. Ibid., 149.
62. startworkIbid.
63. Errol Morris, "The Most Curious Thing," *New York Times*, May 19, 2008.
64. Gourevitch and Morris, *Standard Operating Procedure*, 200–201.
65. Morris, "The Most Curious Thing."
66. Charles Musser, "War, Documentary, and Iraq War Dossier: Film Truth in the Age of George W. Bush," *Framework* 48.2 (Fall, 2007): 9.
67. Gourevitch and Morris, *Standard Operating Procedure*, 148.
68. Dexter Filkins, *The Forever War* (New York: Knopf, 2008), 116.
69. *See* http://meetingresistance.com/faqs.html.
70. Anonymous [Scheuer], *Imperial Hubris*, 19.
71. The Iraq Foundation (*see* http://iraqfoundation.org).
72. Eartha Melzer, "A Dubious Doc," *In These Times*, Dec. 23, 2004 (*see* www.inthesetimes.com/article/1744).
73. Pat Aufderheide, "Your Country, My Country: How Films About the Iraq War Construct Publics," *Framework* 48.2 (Fall 2007): 63

5. TERRORISM ON THE SMALL SCREEN

1. Spencer Ackerman, "Battlestar Iraqtica: Does the Hit Television Show Support the Iraqi Insurgency?" *Slate*, Oct. 13, 2006 (*see* www.slate.com/id/2151425).
2. Surnow, quoted in Jane Mayer, "Whatever It Takes," *The New Yorker* 83.1 (Feb. 19, 2007): 66.
3. For a refutation of the thesis that a ticking bomb justifies torture, see Bob Brecher, *Torture and the Ticking Bomb* (Malden, Mass.: Blackwell, 2007).
4. Martha K. Huggins, Mika Haritos-Fatouros, and Philip G. Zimbardo, *Violence Workers: Police Torturers and Murderers Reconstruct Brazilian Atrocities* (Berkeley: U of California P, 2002), 195.
5. Mayer, *The Dark Side*, 270–79.
6. Ibid., 178.
7. Darius Rejali, *Torture and Democracy* (Princeton: Princeton UP, 2007), 465.
8. Mayer, *The Dark Side*, 104–108, 134–38.
9. For a discussion of these points, see Mayer, *The Dark Side*, 116–17.
10. Scott Shane, "China Inspired Interrogations at Guantánamo," *New York Times*, July 2, 2008, 1, 14.

11. Albert D. Biderman, "Communist Attempts to Elicit False Confessions from Air Force Prisoners of War," *Bulletin of the New York Academy of Medicine* 33.9 (Sept. 1957): 618, 620.
12. *Kubark Counterintelligence Interrogation Manual,* 94. The manual was a secret document obtained by the *Baltimore Sun* in 1997 under a Freedom of Information Act request. It can be found online at The National Security Achive (*see* www.gwu.edu/~nsarchiv/NSAEBB/NSAEBB122).
13. Mayer, *The Dark Side,* 134.
14. Wittes, *Law and the Long War,* 197.
15. Rejali, *Torture and Democracy,* 25.
16. Ibid., 478.
17. Ibid., 576.
18. Jane Mayer, "Whatever It Takes."
19. Huggins, Haritos-Fatouros, and Zimbardo, *Violence Workers,* 213.
20. Ginia Bellafante, "In the '24' World, Family Is the Main Casualty," *New York Times,* May 20, 2007, 30.
21. Joshua L. Dratel, "The Legal Narrative" in Karen J. Greenberg and Joshua L. Dratel, eds., *The Torture Papers: The Road to Abu Ghraib* (New York: Cambridge UP, 2005), xxi.
22. Philippe Sands, "The Green Light," *Vanity Fair,* May 2008 (*see* www.vanityfair.com/politics/features/2008/05/guantanamo200805?currentPage=8.)
23. Wittes, *Law and the Long War,* 206.
24. Ridgeway, *The 5 Unanswered Questions About 9/11,* 44.
25. Scot J. Paltrow, "Government Accounts of 9/11 Reveal Gaps, Inconsistencies," *Wall Street Journal,* Mar. 22, 2004 (*see* http://online.wsj.com/article_print/0,,SB107991342102561383,00.html).
26. *The 9/11 Commission Report,* 39.
27. Ibid., 36.
28. Ibid., 38.
29. Ibid., 43.
30. Ibid., 41.
31. James Ridgeway covers this in some detail in *The 5 Unanswered Questions About 9/11,* 61–88.
32. Mike Allen, "White House Drops Claim of Threat to Bush," *Washington Post,* Sept. 27, 2001, A8.
33. Adam Liptak, "Judges Say U.S. Can't Hold Man as 'Combatant,'" *New York Times,* June 12, 2007, A1.
34. Dana Priest, William Booth, and Susan Schmidt, "A Broken Body, A Broken Story, Pieced Together," *Washington Post,* June 17, 2003, A1.
35. "Saving Private Lynch 'film plan,'" BBC News (*see* http://news.bbc.co.uk/2/hi/entertainment/2938589.stm).

36. Letter from Arthur Schlesinger, in "Open Letter to ABC: Don't Airbrush 9/11" (*see* http://openlettertoabc.blogspot.com/2006/09/leading-historians-call-for.html).
37. Cyrus Nowrasteh, "The Path to Hysteria," *Wall Street Journal*, Sept. 18, 2006 (*see* www.opinionjournal.com/extra/?id=110008958).
38. Shenon, *The Commission*, 357–60.
39. Coll, *Ghost Wars*, 409.
40. Ibid., 412.
41. Shenon, *The Commission*, 359–60.
42. Letter from Sandy Berger, in "Open Letter to ABC."
43. Shenon, *The Commission*, 193.
44. Ibid., 357.
45. Coll, *Ghost Wars*, 395.
46. Mark Mazzetti, "U.S. Aborted Raid on Qaeda Chiefs in Pakistan in '05," *New York Times*, July 8, 2007, 1, 6.
47. Clarke, *Against All Enemies*, 225.
48. Ibid., 224.
49. *The 9/11 Commission Report*, 260.
50. Ibid., 262.
51. Elizabeth Jensen, "PBS Buys a Lot of Arguments for $20 Million," *New York Times*, Apr. 1, 2007, 28.
52. Gary Kamiya, "'America at a Crossroads' Veers to the Right" (*see* www.salon.com/opinion/kamiya/2007/04/17/crossroads).
53. Jensen, "PBS Buys a Lot of Arguments."
54. Wittes, *Law and the Long War*, 248.
55. John Solomon, "FBI Finds It Frequently Overstepped in Collecting Data," *Washington Post*, June 14, 2007, A1, A4.
56. A. J. Frutkin, "Peril Hits Prime Time," *MediaWeek* 16.28 (July 24, 2006): 7.

6. NO END IN SIGHT

1. Wittes, *Law and the Long War*, 257.
2. ". . . happily, for the busy lunatics who rule over us, we are permanently the United States of Amnesia. We learn nothing because we remember nothing." Gore Vidal, *Imperial America: Reflections on the United States of Amnesia* (New York: Nation Books, 2005), 7.
3. Joshua Clover, "Marx and Coca-Cola: All That Is Solid Melts into War," *Film Quarterly* 61 (Fall 2007): 6.
4. Rajiv Chandrasekaran, *Imperial Life in the Emerald City* (New York: Vintage, 2006), 168, 169.
5. See the filmmakers' remarks in Michael Cieply, "'The Kingdom' Gambles That Entertainment Can Trump Politics," *New York Times*, June 19, 2007, B1, B7.

6. A. O. Scott, "F.B.I. Agents Solve the Terrorist Problem," *New York Times*, Sept. 28, 2007, E17.
7. Asra Q. Nomani, "A Mighty Shame," *Washington Post*, June 24, 2007, B1.
8. Frederick A. O. Schwarz, Jr., and Aziz Z. Huq, *Unchecked and Unbalanced: Presidential Power in a Time of Terror* (New York: The New Press, 2007), 101–102.
9. "'Rendition' and Secret Detention: A Global System of Human Rights Violations," Amnesty International, Jan. 2006 (*see* http://web.amnesty.org/library/index/eng-pol300032006).
10. Ibid.
11. Filkins, *The Forever War*, 230, 231.
12. Fatemeh Keshavarz, "Banishing the Ghosts of Iran," *Chronicle of Higher Education*, July 17, 2007, B6.
13. David Ansen, "Charlie Wilson's War," *Newsweek*, Dec. 17, 2007 (*see* www.newsweek.com/id/74399).
14. De Palma, quoted in Jim Hemphill, "War and Truth," *American Cinematographer*, Dec. 2007, 22.
15. De Palma, quoted in Anne Thompson, "De Palma Defends Redacted from Venice" (*see* http://weblogs.variety.com/thompsononhollywood/2007/09/redacted-in-ven.html).
16. Zelizer, "Photography, Journalism, and Trauma," 49.
17. Barbie Zelizer, *Remembering to Forget: Holocaust Memory Through the Camera's Eye* (Chicago: U of Chicago P, 1998), 10.
18. Walter Laqueur, "The Terrorism to Come," *Policy Review* (Aug.-Sept. 2004): 53–54.
19. Goldsmith, *The Terror Presidency*, 189–90.
20. Ibid., 181.
21. Chalmers Johnson, *Nemesis: The Last Days of the American Republic* (New York: Metropolitan Books, 2006), 278, 279.
22. Naomi Klein, *The Shock Doctrine: The Rise of Disaster Capitalism* (New York: Metropolitan Books, 2007), 301.
23. Ibid., 307.
24. Goldsmith, *The Terror Presidency*, 216.

BIBLIOGRAPHY

Ackerman, Spencer. "Battlestar Iraqtica: Does the Hit Television Show Support the Iraqi Insurgency?" *Slate,* Oct. 13, 2006 (*see* www.slate.com/id/2151425).

Al-Banna, Hasan. *Five Tracts of Hasan Al-Banna.* Trans. Charles Wendell. Near Eastern Studies Vol. 20. Berkeley: U of California P, 1978.

Allen, Mike. "White House Drops Claim of Threat to Bush." *Washington Post,* Sept. 27, 2001, A8.

"Altman Says Films Inspire Terrorism." Associated Press Wire Story, Oct. 17, 2001.

Anonymous [Michael Scheuer]. *Imperial Hubris: Why the West Is Losing the War on Terror.* Washington, D.C.: Brassey's, 2004.

Ansen, David. "Charlie Wilson's War," *Newsweek,* Dec. 17, 2007 (*see* www.newsweek.com/id/74399).

Applebaum, Stephen. "Oliver Stone: 'I didn't want to be the bad guy again.'" (*see* http://stephenapplebaum.blogspot.com/2006/12/oliver-stone-i-didnt-want-to-be-bad-guy.html).

"Ashcroft Flying High." CBS News, July 26, 2001 (*see* www.cbsnews.com/stories/2001/07/26/national/main303601.shtml).

Aufderheide, Pat. "Your Country, My Country: How Films About the Iraq War Construct Publics." *Framework* 48.2 (Fall 2007): 56–65.

Avrich, Paul. *Sacco and Vanzetti: The Anarchist Background.* Princeton: Princeton UP, 1991.

Barone, Michael. "Lessons from Rep. Cynthia McKinney's Defeat." *U.S. News and World Report,* Aug. 29, 2002 (*see* www.usnews.com/usnews/opinion/baroneweb/mb_020829.htm).

Barstow,David. "Behind TV Analysts, Pentagon's Hidden Hand." *New York Times,* Apr. 20, 2008, 1, 24–26.

Bellafante, Ginia. "In the '24' World, Family Is the Main Casualty." *New York Times,* May 20, 2007, 30.

Berger, Sandy. Letter from Sandy Berger (*see* http://openlettertoabc.blogspot.com).

Berman, Paul. *Terror and Liberalism.* New York: Norton, 2004.

Biderman, Albert D. "Communist Attempts to Elicit False Confessions from Air Force Prisoners of War." *Bulletin of the New York Academy of Medicine* 33.9 (Sept. 1957):. 616–25.

Bin Laden, Osama. "The Example of Vietnam." In Bruce Lawrence, ed., *Messages to the World: The Statements of Osama bin Laden*, 139–44. New York: Verso, 2005.

—. "Terror for Terror." In Lawrence, ed., *Messages to the World*, 106–129.

—. "To the Americans." In Lawrence, ed., *Messages to the World*, 160–72.

—. "The Towers of Lebanon." In Lawrence, ed., *Messages to the World*, 237–44.

Brecher, Bob. *Torture and the Ticking Bomb*. Malden, Mass.: Blackwell, 2007.

Brison, Susan J. "The Uses of Narrative in the Aftermath of Violence." In Claudia Card, ed., *On Feminist Ethics and Politics*, 200–225. Lawrence: UP of Kansas, 1999.

Brzezinski, Zbigniew. "Terrorized by 'War on Terror.'" *Washington Post*, Mar. 25, 2007, B1.

Buckland, Warren. *Directed by Steven Spielberg: Poetics of the Contemporary Hollywood Blockbuster*. New York: Continuum, 2006.

Bush, George W. "President's State of the Union Address," Jan. 29, 2002 (*see* www.whitehouse.gov/news/releases/2002/01/20020129-11.html).

Campbell, Jason, Michael O'Hanlon, and Amy Unikewicz. "The State of Iraq: An Update." *New York Times*, June 22, 2008, 11.

Cauchon, Dennis and Martha Moore. "Desperation Forced a Horrific Decision." *USA Today*, Sept. 2, 2002 (*see* www.usatoday.com/news/sept11/2002-09-02-jumper_x.htm).

Chandrasekaran, Rajiv. *Imperial Life in the Emerald City*. New York: Vintage, 2006.

Cheney, Dick. Remarks by the Vice President to the Veterans of Foreign Wars 103rd National Convention (*see* www.whitehouse.gov/news/releases/2002/08/20020826.html).

Cieply, Michael. "'The Kingdom' Gambles That Entertainment Can Trump Politics." *New York Times*, June 19, 2007, B1, B7.

Clarke, Richard A. *Against All Enemies: Inside America's War on Terror*. New York: Free Press, 2004.

Cloud, David S. "General Says Prison Inquiry Led to His Forced Retirement." *New York Times*, June 17, 2007, 10.

Clover, Joshua. "Marx and Coca-Cola: All That Is Solid Melts into War." *Film Quarterly* 61 (Fall 2007): 6.

Cole, David and James X. Dempsey. *Terrorism and the Constitution: Sacrificing Civil Liberties in the Name of National Security*. New York: New Press, 2006.

Coll, Steve. *The Bin Ladens: An Arabian Family in the American Century*. New York: Penguin, 2008.

—. *Ghost Wars: The Secret History of the CIA, Afghanistan, and Bin Laden, from the Soviet Invasion to September 10, 2001*. New York: Penguin, 2004.

"Colombia's Killer Networks." *Human Rights Watch Report* (November 1996). *See* www.hrw.org/reports/1996/killertoc.htm.

Danner, Mark, ed. *Torture and Truth: America, Abu Ghraib, and the War on Terror*. New York: New York Review of Books, 2004.

David, Henry. "Prelude to Haymarket." In Walter Laqueur, ed., *The Terrorism Reader*, 109–112.. Philadelphia: Temple UP, 1978.

DePalma, Anthony. "Ground Zero Illnesses Clouding Giuliani's Legacy." *New York Times*, May 14, 2007, A1, A19.

Dixon, Wheeler Winston. "Introduction: Something Lost—Film After 9/11." In Wheeler Winston Dixon, ed., *Film and Television After 9/11*, 1–28. Carbondale: Southern Illinois UP, 2004.

Douthat, Ross. "The Return of the Paranoid Style." *Atlantic Monthly*, Apr. 2008 (*see* www.theatlantic.com/doc/200804/iraq-movies).

Dratel, Joshua L. "The Legal Narrative." In Karen J. Greenberg and Joshua L. Dratel, eds., *The Torture Papers: The Road to Abu Ghraib*, xxi–xxiii. New York: Cambridge UP, 2005.

Drehle, David Von. *Triangle: The Fire That Changed America*. New York: Grove Press, 2003.

Dwyer, Jim. "City Police Spied Broadly Before G.O.P. Convention." *New York Times*, Mar. 25, 2007, 1, 27.

Dwyer, Jim and Kevin Flynn. *102 Minutes: The Untold Story of the Fight to Survive Inside the Twin Towers*. New York: Times Books, 2005.

Eisenhower, Dwight D. "Farewell Address" (*see* www.eisenhower.archives.gov/farewell.htm).

Ellis, Jack C. and Betsy A. McLane. *A New History of Documentary Film*. New York: Continuum, 2005.

Fainaru, Steve. "Shadow War in Iraq Escalates in Intensity." *Washington Post*, June 16, 2007, A12.

Falkenrath, Richard A. "The 911 Commission Report." *International Security* 29.3 (Winter 2004/05): 170–90.

Fallon, William J. "Surge Protector." *New York Times*, July 20, 2008, 13.

Filkins, Dexter. *The Forever War*. New York: Knopf, 2008.

Friedman, Lester. *Citizen Spielberg*. Chicago: U of Illinois P, 2006.

Frutkin, A. J. "Peril Hits Prime Time." *MediaWeek* 16.28 (July 24, 2006): 7.

Gage, Beverly. "The First Wall Street Bomb." History News Service (*see* www.h-net.org/~hns/articles/2001/091701a.html).

Gall, Carlotta. "Evidence Points to Civilian Toll in Afghan Raid." *New York Times*, Sept. 7, 2008 (*see* www.nytimes.com/2008/09/08/world/asia/08afghan.html?pagewanted=all).

Gall, Carlotta and David E. Sanger. "Civilian Deaths Undermine Allies' War on Taliban." *New York Times*, May 13, 2007, A1, A8.

Gillespie, Richard. "Political Violence in Argentina: Guerrillas, Terrorists, and Carapintadas." In Martha Crenshaw, ed., *Terrorism in Context*, 211–48. University Park, Pa.: Pennsylvania State UP, 1995.

Glanz, James and Eric Lipton. *City in the Sky: The Rise and Fall of the World Trade Center*. New York: Times Books, 2003.

Goldberg, Jonah. "Pfizer vs. al Qaeda: Give Me a Break." *National Review Online*, Aug. 31, 2005 (*see* www.nationalreview.com/goldberg/goldberg200508310810.asp).

Goldsmith, Jack. *The Terror Presidency: Law and Judgment Inside the Bush Administration.* New York: Norton, 2007.

Gourevitch, Philip and Errol Morris. *Standard Operating Procedure* New York: Penguin, 2008.

Grajeda, Tony. "The Winning and Losing of Hearts and Minds: Vietnam, Iraq, and the Claims of the War Documentary." *Jump Cut* 49 (Spring 2007) (*see* www.ejumpcut.org/archive/jc49.2007/Grajeda/index.html).

Griffin, David Ray and Richard Falk. *The New Pearl Harbor: Disturbing Questions About the Bush Administration and 9/11.* Northampton, Mass.: Interlink, 2004.

Hall, James W. "A Fireball Too Far." *New York Times,* Nov. 19, 2001 (*see* http://query.nytimes.com/gst/fullpage.html?res = 9B0CE4DF123BF93AA25752C1A9679C8B63).

Heinzen, Karl. "Murder." In Walter Laqueur, ed., *The Terrorism Reader,* 53–64. Philadelphia: Temple UP, 1978.

Hemphill, Jim. "War and Truth." *American Cinematographer,* Dec. 2007, 22.

Herman, Judith. *Trauma and Recovery.* New York: Basic Books, 1997.

Hersh, Seymour. "The General's Report: How Antonio Taguba, who Investigated the Abu Ghraib Scandal, Became One of Its Casualties." *The New Yorker,* June 25, 2007 (*see* www.newyorker.com/reporting/2007/06/25/070625fa_fact_hersh).

Hirsch, Joshua. "Post-traumatic Cinema and the Holocaust Documentary." In E. Ann Kaplan and Ban Wang, eds., *Trauma and Cinema: Cross-Cultural Explorations,* 93–12. Aberdeen, Hong Kong: Hong Kong UP, 2004.

Hirsh, Paul. " 'We've Hit the Targets.' " *Newsweek,* Sept. 13, 2001, 36.

Hitchins, Christopher. "Unfairenheit 9/11: The Lies of Michael Moore." *Slate,* June 21, 2004 (*see* www.slate.com/id/2102723).

Hofstadter, Richard. "The Paranoid Style in American Politics." *Harper's Magazine,* Nov. 1964, 77–86.

Hossein-Zadeh, Ismael. "The Muslim World and the West: The Roots of Conflict." *Arab Studies Quarterly* 27.3 (Summer 2005): 1–20.

Howe, Irving. "Conrad: Order and Anarchy." In Ian Watt, ed., *Conrad: "The Secret Agent": A Casebook,* 140–49. New York: Macmillan, 1973.

Huggins, Martha K., Mika Haritos-Fatouros, and Philip G. Zimbardo. *Violence Workers: Police Torturers and Murderers Reconstruct Brazilian Atrocities.* Berkeley: U of California P, 2002.

Huntington, Samuel P. "The Clash of Civilizations?" *Foreign Affairs* (Summer 1993): 22–49.

Illuminati Conspiracy Archive (*see* www.conspiracyarchive.com/NWO/Hollywood_911.htm).

"In Focus: Teaching 9/11." *Cinema Journal* 43.2 (Winter 2004): 90–126.

Iraq Body Count Project (*see* www.iraqbodycount.org).

Jensen, Elizabeth. "PBS Buys a Lot of Arguments for $20 Million." *New York Times,* Apr. 1, 2007, 28.

Johnson, Chalmers. *Blowback: The Costs and Consequences of American Empire.* New York: Metropolitan Books, 2000.

——. *Nemesis: The Last Days of the American Republic*. New York: Metropolitan Books, 2006.

——. *The Sorrows of Empire: Militarism, Secrecy, and the End of the Republic*. New York: Henry Holt, 2004.

Kacandes, Irene. "9/11/01 = 1/27/01: The Changed Posttraumatic Self." In Judith Greenberg, ed., *Trauma at Home: After 9/11*, 168–83. Lincoln: U of Nebraska P, 2003.

Kahane, Claire. "Uncanny Sights: The Anticipation of the Abomination." In Judith Greenberg, ed., *Trauma at Home: After 9/11*, 107–116. Lincoln: U of Nebraska P, 2003.

Kamber, Michael and Tim Arango. "4,000 U.S. Deaths and a Handful of Images." *New York Times*, July 26, 2008 (*see* www.nytimes.com/2008/07/26/world/middleeast/26censor.html?pagewanted=all).

Kamiya, Gary. " 'America at a Crossroads' Veers to the Right" (*see* www.salon.com/opinion/kamiya/2007/04/17/crossroads).

Kane, Paul. "Senate Authorizes Broad Expansion of Surveillance Act." *Washington Post*, Feb. 13, 2008, A1.

Kansteiner, Wulf. "Genealogy of a Category Mistake: A Critical Intellectual History of the Cultural Trauma Metaphor." *Rethinking History* 8.2 (June 2004): 193–221.

Kaplan, E. Ann. "A Camera and a Catastrophe: Reflections on Trauma and the Twin Towers." In Judith Greenberg, ed., *Trauma at Home: After 9/11*, 95–103. Lincoln: U of Nebraska P, 2003.

——. *Trauma Culture: The Politics of Terror and Loss in Media and Literature*. New Brunswick, N.J.: Rutgers UP, 2005.

Karabell, Zachary. *Peace Be Upon You: The Story of Muslim, Christian and Jewish Coexistence*. New York: Knopf, 2007.

Kauffmann, Stanley. "Accusation." *The New Republic*, July 19, 2004, 24.

Kean, Thomas H. and Lee H. Hamilton. "Stonewalled by the CIA." *New York Times*, Jan. 2, 2008 (*see* www.nytimes.com/2008/01/02/opinion/02kean.html?_r = 1&oref = slogin).

Kennicott, Philip. "Images: Poles and Decades Apart, Two Silent Screams Issue Discomfiting Reverberations." *Washington Post*, Dec. 30, 2007, M6.

Keshavarz, Fatemeh. "Banishing the Ghosts of Iran." *The Chronicle of Higher Education*, July 17, 2007, B6.

Klein, Naomi. *The Shock Doctrine: The Rise of Disaster Capitalism*. New York: Metropolitan Books, 2007.

Kopel, Dave. "Fifty-nine Deceits in *Fahrenheit 9/11*" (*see* www.davekopel.com/Terror/Fiftysix-Deceits-in-Fahrenheit-911.htm).

Kubark Counterintelligence Interrogation Manual. Unpublished classified document (1963), The National Security Achive (*see* www.gwu.edu/~nsarchiv/NSAEBB/NSAEBB122).

Kurtz, Howard. "Journalists See an Alarming Trend in Terror Warnings." *Washington Post*, May 27, 2002, C1.

Landsberg, Alison. *Prosthetic Memory: The Transformation of American Remembrance in the Age of Mass Culture*. New York: Columbia UP, 2004.

Langer, Lawrence L. *Preempting the Holocaust.* New Haven: Yale UP, 1998.

Laqueur, Walter. *The Age of Terrorism.* Boston: Little, Brown, 1987.

—. "Anarchism and Al Qaeda" (*see* liqueur.net/index2.php?r=2&rr=1&id=87).

—. *No End to War: Terrorism in the Twenty-first Century.* New York: Continuum, 2003.

—. "The Terrorism to Come." *Policy Review* (Aug.-Sept. 2004): 49–64.

Lichtblau, Eric. "Senate Approves Bill to Broaden Wiretap Powers," *New York Times,* July 10, 2008 (*see* www.nytimes.com/2008/07/10/washington/10fisa.html?pagewanted = all).

Lichtblau, Eric and Mark Mazzetti. "Military Expands Intelligence Role in U.S." *New York Times,* Jan. 14, 2007, 1, 18.

Lichtenfeld, Eric. *Action Speaks Louder: Violence, Spectacle, and the American Action Movie.* Middletown, Conn.: Wesleyan UP, 2007.

Linenthal, Edward T. *The Unfinished Bombing: Oklahoma City in American Memory.* New York: Oxford UP, 2001.

Liptak, Adam. "Judges Say U.S. Can't Hold Man as 'Combatant.'" *New York Times,* June 12, 2007, 1, 19.

Lundegaard, Erik. "Saddam Hussein Is Bombing Us! How Hollywood Portrayed Terrorism Before 9/11" (*see* www.msnbc.msn.com/id/9230038).

Macfarquhar, Larissa. "THE POPULIST (Michael Moore)." *The New Yorker* 80.1 (Feb 16, 2004): 133.

Mandel, Daniel. "Muslims on the Silver Screen." *Middle East Quarterly* 8.2 (Spring 2001): 19(12). *Academic OneFile.* Thomson Gale. Virginia Tech. Feb. 8, 2007.

Massood, Paula J. "The Quintessential New Yorker and Global Citizen: An Interview with Spike Lee." *Cineaste* 28.3 (Summer 2003): 4–6.

May, Ernest. "When Government Writes History." *The New Republic,* May 23, 2005, 30–35.

Mayer, Jane. *The Dark Side: The Inside Story of How the War on Terror Turned into a War on American Ideals.* New York: Doubleday, 2008.

—. "Whatever It Takes." *The New Yorker* 83.1 (Feb. 19, 2007): 66.

Mazzetti, Mark. "U.S. Aborted Raid on Qaeda Chiefs in Pakistan in '05." *New York Times,* July 8, 2007, 1, 6.

McCoy, Alfred W. *A Question of Torture: CIA Interrogation, from the Cold War to the War on Terror.* New York: Metropolitan Books, 2006.

Tracy McVeigh, "'Dear Tracy'—by Mass Killer Timothy McVeigh," *The Observer,* May 6, 2001 (*see* www.guardian.co.uk/world/2001/may/06/news.mcveigh).

Meigs, James B. "Afterward: The Conspiracy Industry." In David Dunbar and Brad Reagan, eds., *Debunking 9/11 Myths: Why Conspiracy Theories Can't Stand Up to the Facts,* 91–107. New York: Hearst, 2006.

Melzer, Eartha. "A Dubious Doc." *In These Times,* Dec. 23, 2004 (*see* www.inthesetimes.com/article/1744).

Merkl, Peter H. "West German Left-Wing Terrorism." In Martha Crewnshaw, ed., *Terrorism in Context,* 160–210. University Park, Pa.: Pennsylvania State UP, 1995.

Miller, Martin A. "The Intellectual Origins of Modern Terrorism in Europe." In Martha Crenshaw, ed., *Terrorism in Context*, 27–62. University Park, Pa.: Pennsylvania State UP, 1995.

Moore, Alan and David Lloyd. *V for Vendetta.* New York: DC Comics, 1989.

Morris, Errol. "The Most Curious Thing," *New York Times*, May 19, 2008 (*see* http://morris.blogs.nytimes.com/2008/05/19/the-most-curious-thing/?scp = 5&sq = erroll%20 morris&st = cse).

Musser, Charles. "War, Documentary, and Iraq War Dossier: Film Truth in the Age of George W. Bush." *Framework* 48.2 (Fall 2007): 9–35.

Myers, Steven Lee. "U.S. Considering Stepping Up Pace of Iraq Pullout." *New York Times,* July 13, 2008, A1, A10.

National Institute of Standards and Technology. *Final Report on the Collapse of the World Trade Center Towers.* Washington, D.C.: U.S. Government Printing Office, 2005.

Nichols, Bill. *Representing Reality: Issues and Concepts in Documentary.* Bloomington: Indiana UP, 1991.

9/11 Commission Report, The: Final Report of the National Commission on Terrorist Attacks Upon the United States. New York: Norton, 2004.

Nolley, Ken. "*Fahrenheit 9/11*: Documentary, Truth-telling, and Politics." *Film and History* 35.2 (2005): 12–16.

Nomani, Asra Q. "A Mighty Shame." *Washington Post*, June 24, 2007, B1.

Nowrasteh, Cyrus. "The Path to Hysteria." *Wall Street Journal*, Sept. 18, 2006 (*see* www.opinionjournal.com/extra/?id = 110008958).

"O'Donovan Rossa's Dynamiters." In Walter Laqueur, ed., *The Terrorism Reader*, 112–14. Philadelphia: Temple UP, 1978.

"Open Letter to ABC: Don't Airbrush 9/11" (*see* http://openlettertoabc.blogspot.com/2006/09/leading-historians-call-for.html).

Page, Max. *The City's End: Two Centuries of Fantasies, Fears, and Premonitions of New York's Destruction.* New Haven: Yale UP, 2008.

Paltrow, Scot J. "Government Accounts of 9/11 Reveal Gaps, Inconsistencies." *Wall Street Journal*, Mar. 22, 2004 (*see* http://online.wsj.com/article_print/0,,SB107991342102561383,00.html).

Plantinga, Carl. *Rhetoric and Representation in Nonfiction Film.* New York: Cambridge UP, 1997.

Podhoretz, John. "Stone Sinks—New Film Misses 9/11's Essence." *New York Post*, July 21, 2006, 35.

Pomerance, Murray. "The Shadow of the World Trade Center." In Wheeler Winston Dixon, ed., *Film and Television After 9/11*, 42–62. Carbondale: Southern Illinois UP, 2004.

Priest, Dana, William Booth, and Susan Schmidt. "A Broken Body, A Broken Story, Pieced Together." *Washington Post*, June 17, 2003, A1.

Prince, Stephen. *Visions of Empire: Political Imagery in Contemporary American Film.* New York: Praeger, 1992.

Projansky, Sarah. "Teaching Through Feelings and Personal Beliefs: 9/11 as Case Study." *Cinema Journal* 43.2 (Winter 2004): 105–109.

Qutb, Sayyid. *Milestones.* Cedar Rapids, Ia.: The Mother Mosque Foundation, n.d.

——. *This Religion of Islam.* Trans. "Islamdust." Palo Alto, Calif.: Almanar, 1967.

"Rebuilding America's Defenses: Strategy, Forces, and Resources for a New Century." Project for the New American Century, Sept. 2000 (*see* www.newamericancentury.org/RebuildingAmericasDefenses.pdf).

Reeve, Simon. *One Day in September.* New York: Arcade, 2000, epilogue 2006.

Rejali, Darius. *Torture and Democracy.* Princeton: Princeton UP, 2007.

Rendell, Steve and Tara Broughel. "Amplifying Officials, Squelching Dissent." Fairness and Accuracy in Reporting (*see* www.fair.org/index.php?page = 1145).

"'Rendition' and Secret Detention: A Global System of Human Rights Violations." Amnesty International, Jan. 2006 (*see* http://web.amnesty.org/library/index/engpol300032006).

"Report of the International Committee of the Red Cross (ICRC) on the Treatment by the Coalition Forces of Prisoners of War and Other Protected Persons by the Geneva Conventions in Iraq During Arrest, Internment and Interrogation." In Karen J. Greenberg and Joshua L. Dratel, eds., *The Torture Papers: The Road to Abu Ghraib,* 383–404. New York: Cambridge UP, 2005.

Ricks, Thomas E. *Fiasco: The American Military Adventure in Iraq.* New York: Penguin, 2006.

Ridgeway, James. *The 5 Unanswered Questions About 9/11.* New York: Seven Stories Press, 2005.

Ruthven, Malise. *A Fury for God: The Islamist Attack on America.* London: Granta, 2002.

Salam, Reihan. "The Sum of All PC: Hollywood's Reverse Racial Profiling." *Slate,* May 28, 2002 (*see* www.slate.com/id/2066272/).

Sales, Nancy Jo. "Click Here for Conspiracy." *Vanity Fair,* Aug. 2006 (*see* www.vanityfair.com/ontheweb/features/2006/08/loosechange200608).

Sands, Philippe. "The Green Light." *Vanity Fair,* May 2008 (*see* www.vanityfair.com/politics/features/2008/05/guantanamo200805?currentPage=8).

"Saving Private Lynch 'film plan,'" BBC News (*see* http://news.bbc.co.uk/2/hi/entertainment/2938589.stm).

Scahill, Jeremy. *Blackwater: The Rise of the World's Most Powerful Mercenary Army.* New York: Nation Books, 2007.

Scheuer, Michael. *Through Our Enemies' Eyes: Osama bin Laden, Radical Islam, and the Future of America.* Rev. ed. Washington D.C.: Potomac Books, 2006.

Schneider, Steven Jay. "Architectural Nostalgia and the New York City Skyline on Film." In Wheeler Winston Dixon, ed., *Film and Television After 9/11,* 29–41. Carbondale: Southern Illinois UP, 2004.

Schwarz, Frederick A. O., Jr., and Aziz Z. Huq. *Unchecked and Unbalanced: Presidential Power in a Time of Terror.* New York: The New Press, 2007.

Scott, A. O. "F.B.I. Agents Solve the Terrorist Problem." *New York Times,* Sept. 28, 2007, E17.

Shaheen, Jack G. *Reel Bad Arabs: How Hollywood Vilifies a People.* New York: Olive Branch Press, 2001.

Shane, Scott. "China Inspired Interrogations at Guantánamo." *New York Times,* July 2, 2008, 1, 14.

——. "Inside the Interrogation of a 9/11 Mastermind." *New York Times,* June 22, 2008, 1, 8–9.

Shane, Scott and Mark Mazzetti. "Ex-C.I.A. Chief, in Book, Assails Cheney on Iraq." *New York Times,* Apr. 27, 2007, A1, A14.

Shanker, Thom. "Civilian Risks Curbing Strikes in Afghan War." *New York Times,* July 23, 2008 (*see* www.nytimes.com/2008/07/23/world/asia/23military.html?hp).

Sharrett, Christopher. "Without Restraint: 9/11 Videos and the Pursuit of Truth." *Jump Cut* 50 (Spring 2008) (*see* www.ejumpcut.org/currentissue/9-11Sharrett/index.html).

Shenon, Philip. *The Commission: The Uncensored History of the 9/11 Investigation.* New York: Twelve, 2008.

Smith, R. Jeffrey. "Hussein's Prewar Ties to Al-Qaeda Discounted." *Washington Post,* Apr. 6, 2007, A1, A4.

Solomon, John. "FBI Finds It Frequently Overstepped in Collecting Data." *Washington Post,* June 14, 2007, A1, A4.

Solomon, John and Barton Gellman. "Frequent Errors in FBI's Secret Records Requests." *Washington Post,* Mar. 9, 2007, A1, A6.

Sontag, Susan. "The Imagination of Disaster." In Sontag, *Against Interpretation and Other Essays,* 209–225. New York: Farrar, Straus, and Giroux, 1966.

——. *Regarding the Pain of Others.* New York: Penguin, 2003.

Spence, Louise. "Teaching 9/11 and Why I'm Not Doing It Anymore." *Cinema Journal* 43.2 (Winter 2004): 100–105.

Stout, David. "FBI Head Admits Mistakes in Use of Security Act." *Washington Post,* Mar. 10, 2007, A1, A10.

Sturken, Marita. *Tangled Memories: The Vietnam War, the AIDS Epidemic, and the Politics of Remembering.* Berkeley: U of California P, 1997.

Sweet, Christopher, ed. *Above Hallowed Ground: A Photographic Record of September 11, 2001, by Photographers of the New York City Police Department.* New York: Viking Studio, 2002.

Tavernise, Sabrina. "Iraqi Death Toll Exceeded 34,000 in 2006, U.N. Says." *New York Times,* Jan. 17, 2007, A1, A8.

Taylor, John. *Body Horror: Photojournalism, Catastrophe, and War.* New York: New York UP, 1998.

Thomas, Cal. "'World Trade Center' is a World Class Movie" (*see* www.townhall.com/Columnists/CalThomas/2006/07/20/world_trade_center_is_a_world_class_movie).

Thompson, Anne. "De Palma Defends Redacted from Venice" (*see* http://weblogs.variety.com/thompsononhollywood/2007/09/redacted-in-ven.html).

Traister, Rebecca, Elisabeth Franck, and Ian Blecher. "Oliver Stone and Christopher Hitchens Spar Over Hollywood's Efforts to be Relevant." *New York Observer,* Oct. 14, 2001 (*see* www.observer.com/2001/oliver-stone-and-christopher-hitchens-spar-over-hollywoods-efforts-be-relevant).

Truffaut, François and Helen G. Scott. *Hitchcock*. Rev. ed. New York: Touchstone, 1983.

Unger, Craig. *House of Bush, House of Saud.* New York: Scribner, 2004.

Vidal, Gore. *Imperial America: Reflections on the United States of Amnesia*. New York: Nation Books, 2005.

—. *Perpetual War for Perpetual Peace.* New York: Nation Books, 2002.

Von Zielbauer, Paul. "Lawyers on Haditha Panel Peer into Fog of War." *New York Times,* May 17, 2007, A12.

Wagge, Jordan. "A Captive Audience: The Portrayal of Terrorism and Terrorists in Large-Scale Fictional Hollywood Media" (*see* www1.appstate.edu/~stefanov/proceedings/wagge.htm).

Waxman, Sharon. "White House Looking to Enlist Hollywood in Terrorism War." *Washington Post,* Oct. 20, 2001, C1.

Weiner, Tim. *Legacy of Ashes: The History of the CIA*. New York: Anchor, 2008.

Williams, W. Gene and Byron Hollander. "High-Rise Fire Safety/Human Response." In Donald J. Conway, ed., *Human Response to Tall Buildings*, 310–15. Stroudsburg, Pa.: Dowden, Hutchinson, and Ross, 1977.

Wilson, Michael. "Among Firefighters in New York, Giuliani Is Both Hailed and Hated." *New York Times,* June 17, 2007, 1, 16.

Wittes, Benjamin. *Law and the Long War: The Future of Justice in the Age of Terror*. New York: Penguin, 2008.

Wood, Trish. *What Was Asked of Us: An Oral History of the Iraq War by the Soldiers Who Fought It*. Boston: Little, Brown, 2006.

Wright, Lawrence. *The Looming Tower: Al-Qaeda and the Road to 9/11*. New York: Knopf, 2006.

Zelikow, Philip K. and Condoleezza Rice. *Germany Unified and Europe Transformed: A Study in Statecraft.* Cambridge: Harvard UP, 1995.

Zelizer, Barbie. "Photography, Journalism, and Trauma." In Barbie Zelizer and Stuart Allan, eds., *Journalism After September 11*, 48–68. New York: Routledge, 2003.

—. *Remembering to Forget: Holocaust Memory Through the Camera's Eye*. Chicago: U of Chicago P, 1998.

Zwicker, Barrie. *Towers of Deception: The Media Cover-Up of 9/11.* Gabriola Island, B.C.: New Society, 2006.

INDEX